D1527683

The Birth of Western Economy

With a Foreword by
PHILIP GRIERSON
*Fellow of Gonville and Caius College,
Cambridge*

Translated by
E. M. WILKINSON

The Birth
of Western Economy

ECONOMIC ASPECTS OF THE DARK AGES

ROBERT LATOUCHE

*Doyen honoraire de la Faculté des Lettres
de l'Université de Grenoble*

METHUEN

LONDON AND NEW YORK

First published in Great Britain in 1961
Second edition 1967
This edition reprinted in 1981 by Methuen & Co. Ltd
11 New Fetter Lane, London EC4P 4EE

Published in the USA by
Methuen & Co.
in association with Methuen, Inc.
733 Third Avenue, New York, NY 10017
English translation © 1961 and 1967 Methuen & Co. Ltd
The original edition was first published in France, under the title
Les Origines de l'Economie Occidentale, by Editions Albin Michel,
Paris, in 1956

Printed in the United States of America

British Library Cataloguing in Publication Data

Latouche, Robert
The birth of western economy.
(Methuen library reprints)
1. Europe – Economic conditions
I. Title   II. Les origines de l'économie
occidentale. English
330.94'01   HC240

ISBN 0-416-32090-2

Contents

Contents

Illustrations

Foreword

THE CAROLINGIAN EMPIRE, short-lived as it was, is the central feature of those centuries of European history which are usefully if now somewhat unfashionably known as the Dark Ages. Pepin of Heristal and his three successors took over and ruled in turn the débris of the Merovingian kingdom, the greatest of the states which had been founded amid the ruins of the Roman Empire in the west. They restored its lost unity and expanded its frontiers until it included almost the whole of Latin Christendom. Pepin the Short exchanged the title of Mayor for that of King, and his son added the kingship of the Lombards to that of the Franks and finally the imperial title to both. Though the empire did not long survive the death of its founder, from it half the institutions of medieval Europe derived. Only the populations of the British Isles and Scandinavia and the surviving fragments of the Visigothic and Lombard states in northern Spain and southern Italy could claim to maintain direct contact with their Germanic, Celtic or Roman pasts independent of Carolingian influence.

This dominating rôle of the Carolingian Empire is less evident in the field of economic history than in those of institutional life and culture, and since the days when Gibbon commented sardonically on Charlemagne's preoccupation with 'the care of his poultry and even the sale of his eggs' scholars have been divided in their estimate of its economic importance. That it was heir to a past at once Roman and Germanic is evident, but of what precisely did this inheritance consist and how much had been lost before the Carolingians made good their title? What truth is there in the cherished belief of classical scholars from the Renaissance to the nineteenth century that the Roman Empire

ix

was not significantly different from the world of their own day, or were they deceived into thinking that different things were the same because they were called by the same names? When did the economic breakdown of the ancient world occur, in the third, the fifth, or the seventh century A.D.? Did the Empire founder because of internal stresses and defects – the prevalence of slavery, the parasitism of the towns, bureaucratic over-development and consequent high taxation, the neglect of scientific invention – or because of Germanic or Saracen attack? Was the rôle of the Germans purely destructive, or had they a positive contribution to make to the economic future of the west? How much of the trade and municipal structure of the Roman Empire survived into the eighth century? Were Carolingian standards of living and economic organization higher or lower than those of the Merovingian age? Can one ascribe a coherent economic policy to the sovereigns of the Carolingian house, or did they deal with each problem empirically as it arose? What rôle in the economic history of Europe is to be assigned to the Northmen and the Saracens of the Abbasid and post-Abbasid periods? Can the economic revival of the tenth and eleventh centuries be explained by internal causes, or was it stimulated by Arab or Byzantine influence from outside?

These are the problems with which Prof. Latouche's book is concerned. Although his story starts well before the genesis of the Carolingian Empire and carries on into the eleventh century, the economic structure and history of the kingdom of the Franks is the central theme of his book. He holds with truth that the economic history of the British Isles and of the Byzantine Empire are not germane to his tale, and he leaves them deliberately on one side. If he deals at unexpected length with the opening-up of the North Sea and the Baltic and the economic history of the Scandinavian peoples in the Viking age, this is not only because of their intrinsic interest but because they played a vital rôle in the economic rebirth of the west. Gaul and Germany, however, are throughout in the centre of the picture: when he speaks of Roman town life, the towns are those of Gaul and not of north Africa or Syria; when he speaks of the denier, it is that of the Carolingians and their successors in

France and Germany and not those of the West Saxons in England or the German emperors in Italy. One of the few criticisms that can fairly be brought against his book is that he is too reluctant to allow his gaze to wander across the Alps.

The greatest merit of the book arises from the author's appreciation of the complexity and diversity of economic conditions in the Dark Ages and his refusal to oversimplify or fit his conclusions into the framework of a rigid system. The liberal-romantic notion of the *Markgenossenschaft* naturally finds no favour with him, and Fustel de Coulanges plays the rôle that Frederic Seebohm would in an English work on economic life in Anglo-Saxon times. Prof. Latouche holds, and here he is surely right, that Pirenne was justified in ascribing to the Saracens a major part in bringing about the emergence of western Christendom, but wrong in believing that the ancient world had survived almost intact up to their day. He likewise refuses to accept Maurice Lombard's attractive picture of a renaissance in European economy brought about in the tenth and eleventh centuries by the stimulus of Arab gold: the evidence for the massive imports of bullion required by this theory is wholly lacking. He does justice to the real achievements of western economy in the Carolingian age, and his exploitation of such sources as the *Gesta episcoporum Cenomannensium* provides him with material to counterbalance the impression of 'manors, manors everywhere' one is apt to derive from the *Capitulare de villis* and the Polyptyque of Irminon.

This does not mean that Prof. Latouche is afraid of generalization. There are plenty of trenchant expressions of opinion and vivid and apposite details to lend force to his arguments. The towns of Roman times 'were centres not of production, but of expenditure; they constituted for the Empire sources not of wealth, but of impoverishment'. 'Great estates but small farms is the formula which best defines the régime of the *villa*.' The fact that *vague* is a word of Scandinavian origin is in itself 'additional and decisive proof of Frankish indifference to things of the sea'. Excellent pages are devoted to such subjects as the functions of money in the Merovingian era, the influence of pilgrimages on commerce, and the economic contrast between

France and Germany in the tenth century. New light is thrown on such varied topics as the importance of the salt trade in Frankish Gaul and the place of the *vicus* in the agrarian organization of the Carolingian age. English readers have been compelled in recent years to take their economic history of the Dark Ages in the form of translations from foreign tongues, and the English edition of Prof. Latouche's book will take its place worthily beside those of Dopsch and Pirenne on the shelves of the student of the middle ages.

PHILIP GRIERSON

Introduction

ANY ATTEMPT TO TRACE the origins of medieval economic
life in the West must inevitably raise in its most
material form the problem, often debated but never
solved, of the transition from the ancient world to the Middle
Ages, a problem which contemporary German historians, borrowing an expression from the French, like to call 'Kontinuität'.
It is indeed no easy task to make a contribution to the study
of so complex a subject after such giants as Henri Pirenne,
Ferdinand Lot and Alfons Dopsch. Whoever ventures to do so
may perhaps be content to achieve his aim by correlating the
findings of his predecessors, aware that he is but a faint, inadequate echo of eloquent voices, but his labours will be sadly
unproductive. The wiser and more sensible course is to offer the
reader the results of personal observation, even though these
may afford his curiosity only temporary satisfaction. The whole
conception of a middle age is gradually breaking down, or at
least is in process of changing. The idea of inserting this vast
period between the ancient world and modern times sprang
first from the imagination of seventeenth-century scholars, and
it was not until 1838 that its chronological limits were officially
laid down. Less than a century after they had been duly
enshrined in the public educational syllabus, a sensational, but
unhappily posthumous book by Henri Pirenne, *Mahomet et
Charlemagne*, reopened the whole question, if not exactly of a
middle age, at least of its chronological boundaries.

In view of the concerted efforts of destructive critics, which
may eventually shatter the very idea of a middle age, our aim
will be a modest one: to trace the gradual development of
economic life in Western Europe during the period ending with
the eleventh century – the great eleventh century, as Joseph

Bédier used to call it. It is harder to know where to begin than where to end. We shall choose that point of time which saw the break-up of the Mediterranean economy, known also by a more general term – the economy of the ancient world. This second designation is the more accurate, since the Mediterranean did not lose its attraction either after the Great Invasions, or even after the Saracen conquest, nor, on the other hand, did the people of the West wait for the Western Empire to fall before coming under the spell of the northern seas.

We shall find various idols along our way. We shall have to explain our attitude to the dangerous illusion fostered by those who differentiate sharply between a natural economy (*Natural-wirtschaft*), regarded as the typical economic system of the Early Middle Ages, and a money economy (*Geldwirtschaft*), believed to have prevailed in the ancient world and to have made a diffident reappearance at the end of the eleventh century. We shall also come up against other traditional ideas, which will have to be less rigidly interpreted, as for instance that of a closed economy, for many years the classical definition of the Carolingian economic system. Without wishing to anticipate a controversy which will be dealt with at some length later, need we also continue to accept as axiomatic the predominance of the great landed estate during Merovingian and Carolingian times? If for almost a century the great domain has been considered as the basic framework of rural life under the Carolingians, the unanimity with which scholars have accepted the idea must be attributed to Charlemagne, the author of a detailed Capitulary on the organization of his *villae*, and also to several wealthy abbots of the eighth and ninth centuries, to those of Saint-Remi of Rheims, of Prüm, and in particular of Saint-Germain-des-Prés, who have left us in the form of polyptyques minutely detailed inventories of the property owned by their monasteries. It is, however, all too readily forgotten that side by side with the great landowners whose numbers and whose power are not in question, there existed a host of small, illiterate landowners who kept no archives and of whose way of life we know little.

Then, too, the eclipse of town life in the West after the first barbarian invasions was not so complete as has been asserted. The third century did not in fact pronounce its death warrant any more than the eleventh marked its resurrection. These are hard and fast conceptions to which patient research, intent upon extracting the truth from faulty and inadequate documents, must supply the necessary correctives. The town continued to exist, despite the blows dealt it by successive invaders, and which sometimes came in new and unexpected forms. It underwent a gradual transformation, so that even in centuries seemingly hostile to urban life we can still speak of the town in terms not merely of growth but of increasing prosperity, and even discuss its actual creation in Germany, which was slowly opening up to western civilization.

We shall encounter those invaders from the North, the Vikings. That their forays disrupted the work of economic restoration undertaken by the early Carolingians cannot be denied, but the Scandinavian contribution, taken as a whole, was not purely negative. It may even be that those Danes, Norwegians and Swedes, bold seafarers that they were, did more than is generally supposed to bring about the economic revival of the Middle Ages which, as we shall see, was as much Nordic as Mediterranean – perhaps even more so. To them we owe the very idea of an Atlantic world.

We shall not go so far as to claim that they were the first medieval traders, the forerunners of the merchant class. The revival, or rather the birth, of trade as it was understood in the Middle Ages, was brought about by a multiplicity of factors which are not always easy to distinguish or to recognize. The same may be said of the development of industry, which remained under the aegis of the merchants. Capitalism makes its timid début in the ninth and tenth centuries, and we shall have to go back to the shores of the Mediterranean, to Venice, to witness its emergence, since the transactions in which the Northmen were at that time engaged were more in the nature of piracy. The contract of *commenda* which crops up from time to time in the ninth century is the first capitalist operation mentioned in medieval history.

The whole of this early medieval activity, less moribund than has often been supposed, is dominated by the problem of money, especially of gold, the minting of which slowed down, then stopped altogether, in the Frankish Empire from the seventh century onwards, though the metal itself did not entirely disappear, and continued to exert a powerful attraction. Contemporary scholarship is passionately interested in this question of gold, the currency of large-scale international trade, and which, absorbed and drained away by the Moslems after their conquest, led to the formation of new trade links in which the West eventually became integrated. These are new and astonishing points of view, and so disconcerting that all traditional ideas about an early medieval economy which was self-sufficient and based on the domain will have to be drastically revised.

For this reason we shall make it our particular aim to detect such evidence as will enable us to give a truly realistic picture of economic life during the Early Middle Ages. Yet the material cannot simply be presented as if it were a documentary film; it will have to be explained, in other words logically connected. If it is made clear that the medieval economy in its early stages did not break decisively with the past, that it contracted less than has been maintained and that it had to its credit bold ventures some of which, like the discovery of Greenland in the tenth century, amazingly foreshadowed the future, this connexion of ideas will be more easily achieved.

The present study is no textbook, which may perhaps disappoint some of its readers, since there is as yet no adequate guide through early medieval economics, but to have written such a book would have been out of keeping with the whole spirit of this series[1], and would have broken a promise made to Henri Berr. What it does offer is a collection of opinions on a subject which has long engaged our thoughts. Its plan has been inspired by individual research and personal preferences in the way of reading. Subjective factors too have determined its geographical framework. Great Britain has been almost completely by-passed, since its economic evolution from the fifth to

---

[1] 'L'Evolution de l'Humanite', founded by Henri Berr, of which in its French edition this book is volume 43.

the eleventh centuries differed considerably from that of the
Continent and would not have fitted comfortably into the
present synthesis. Gaul and Germany have attracted our
attention more readily than Italy, which deserves a separate
study.

It will be noted that Western France and Maine in particular
occupy an important place in this book. The history of that
region was the starting point of the author's medieval studies.
Rich in early medieval documents, it has provided a wealth of
valuable and little-known material, and in ranging through
seven centuries we have returned to it again and again, and
always with delight, as one who seeks to tread the safe and
familiar ground of home. The information gleaned from this
province has afforded a means of testing several of our hypotheses.

In concluding the introduction to this work dedicated to the
memory of Henri Berr, it is to be hoped that it contains nothing
of what he liked to call ironically 'l'histoire historisante'. At the
close of a career begun in the Ecole des Chartes and devoted to
the study of the past, a few marginal reflections may perhaps
not come too much amiss. A certain conception of history held
by our first and honoured masters has come under fire from an
eager and enthusiastic generation which is endeavouring to
reconcile history with life. Without any disloyalty to the teaching of those who guided our studies, who imbued us with a love
of sound criticism, trained us in rigorous methods of research
and taught us a scrupulous regard for accuracy and precision,
we have welcomed this breath of keen, fresh air. The devotees of
living history are doing most valuable work in regarding the
lay Benedictine as a man essentially of his own day. But mobility
is the very essence of life, and they should take care not to let
their ideas harden into formulae which, though fresh and
alluring, are over-authoritative; by so doing they may well
appear to assume an air of secrecy and mystification which
could antagonize the young and induce a kind of inferiority
complex in the uninitiated. A sympathetic and open-minded
approach to every sincere and successive attempt, past, present
or future, to turn history into a true science is perhaps the most

appropriate attitude for those who ask the past to yield up some of its secrets. The misfortune and at the same time the glory of history, as indeed of every branch of human knowledge, is that patient and Herculean labours are needed if it is to achieve self-definition; but thanks to the exertions of those who pursue it, it moves steadily forward, even whilst making every effort to see itself as it really is.

PART I

The Component Forces

1. Baptistry of St Jean, Poitiers, built between 356 - 368, and perhaps the oldest Christian building in France

CHAPTER I

The Roman World:
State Control in the Late Empire

HE ECONOMY OF THE ancient world deteriorated at a
comparatively early date. The first signs of approaching
decay appeared at the end of the second century A.D.,
and even before that time its inherent weakness had been
vigorously denounced by clear-sighted contemporaries. It is a
mere platitude to recall the anxiety felt by elderly Romans at
the neglect of agriculture. The Elder Pliny was no doubt being
rather absurd when he expressed regret that generals no longer
cultivated the land;[1] nevertheless he was voicing an opinion
common to every conservative Roman. Wistfully they looked
back to those far-off days, which seemed like a golden age,
when the State of Rome, confined within the narrow bounds of
Latium, was inhabited by small landowners who were at the
same time ploughmen and soldiers. The plot of ground possessed
by each of them was no bigger than 50 *ares*.[2] Certainly things
had changed since the close of the third century B.C.; the
patriarchal age had gone for ever; trade and banking had
already made their appearance. A *laudator temporis acti* like the
Elder Cato viewed with disapproval[3] the growing number of
merchants (*mercatores*) and moneylenders (*foenatores*), and held
stoutly to the opinion of his forebears that the good citizen was
essentially the good husbandman and the good farmer. He
himself, however, no longer tilled the ground with his own

---

[1] The Elder Pliny, *Hist. Natur.*, XVIII, 4: 'Quaenam ergo tantae ubertatis causa
erat? Ipsorum tunc manibus imperatorum colebantur agri.'
[2] 1 *are* = a square of ten metres.
[3] M. Porcius Cato, *De re rustica*, introd.

hands, though within easy reach of his town residence he had his country house, his *villa*, managed for him by a steward (*villicus*) upon whom this aged Roman, with meticulous attention to detail and considerable peevishness, kept a close and vigilant eye.

Corn had already ceased to be the staple crop; the vine was competing with it for first place, and when Cato's advice was asked as to what crops could most profitably be grown on the land, he went so far as to say that the most advantageous way of using it was to have good pasturage.[1] The time was not far distant when Italy would turn her back on farming and when the Romans would go for their corn to countries overseas, and for their grapes to the Cyclades, to Baetica and to Gaul, to the disgust of an expert agriculturist like Columella.[2] Those who looked back to a past to which they remained devoted felt that conquest was dazzling, changing and corrupting their fellow-countrymen. The Romans were not content with asking their conquered peoples to feed them, a demand which in itself was already causing uneasiness, but even more serious in its consequences was the fact that conquest brought them undreamed-of wealth, which they looked upon as inexhaustible. It secured for them a means of exchange, in the precious metals found in the East and in Spain, implements, and a plentiful supply of manual labour in the prisoners of war whom they turned into slaves.

The skilful exploitation of these riches, which the author of *L'économie antique*[3] has described with striking clarity, won for the West two centuries of prosperity symbolized in the two words: *pax romana*; but a prosperity so suddenly achieved was by its very nature too artificial to stand up to hard knocks. Life in Rome during the first century was undoubtedly attractive; there was bustle and movement, endless argument and discussion, entertainment in plenty, and even a certain amount of work. But the population of this Babel, which to use a modern historian's vivid simile drew in the produce of the whole world

[1] The remark is reported by Columella, *De re rustica*, Liber VI, *Praefatio*, and by the Elder Pliny, XVIII, 6.
[2] Columella, I, *Praefatio*.
[3] J. Toutain, *L'économie antique*, Paris, 1927 (L'Evolution de l'Humanité, 20).

like an octopus,[1] was being fed at the expense of the 'Public Assistance' by free distributions of every kind. Life in the provinces was apparently less turbulent. Nevertheless even there urbanization was pushed to its furthest limits. The Empire infused new life into old towns, created numerous colonies, turning both into religious and administrative centres as well as places of entertainment, well provided with theatres, arenas and circuses, and with suburbs full of luxurious houses. Unlike our modern towns, however, these cities so delightful to live in, and which have left behind unmistakable traces of opulence, lacked the stimulus of great industries, which were unknown to the ancient world. They were centres not of production, but of expenditure. They constituted for the Empire sources, not of wealth, but of impoverishment.

The dangers resulting from this economic transformation did not pass unnoticed. The writers of the first and second centuries emphatically pointed them out; but since in their eyes the land still remained the essential source of all wealth, they were particularly sensitive to the unbalanced economy which was evolving at the expense of the countryside: 'We, the heads of families, have abandoned the scythe and the plough,' wrote Columella[2] following in the wake of Varro, 'to creep inside city walls and instead of using our hands to dig up fallow fields and vineyards, we would rather use them to applaud with at the theatre and the circus.' Latin literature is full of such strictures which sound banal and rhetorical to modern ears; but they were not so at the time, and often have the ring of sincerity. The fact was that in spite of improvements in technique which produced remarkable results, notably in vine and fruit growing on the Continent and in the cultivation of olives in North Africa, the decline of agriculture was deeply disturbing. It had become the prey of speculators, of powerful opportunists (*praepotentes*), who acquired estates so vast that they could not even ride round them; on these they dumped flocks of sheep or had them

[1] F. Lot, *La fin du monde antique et le début du moyen âge*, revised ed., Paris, 1951 (L'Evolution de l'Humanité, 31), p. 81. (English ed.: *The End of the Ancient World*.)

[2] 'Omnes enim . . . patresfamiliae, falce et aratro relictis, intra murum correpsimus et in circis potius ac theatris quam in segetibus et vinetis manus movemus.' (*De re rustica*, I, *Praefatio*.)

farmed by slaves chained together. The Younger Pliny asserted
that the half of Africa was owned by six of these great landlords.[1] A day was to come when these ill-farmed estates would
revert to waste land, when through the depopulation of the
countryside and the dwindling supply of slave labour, agriculture would face a serious shortage of manpower, when imports which, thanks to a vigorous shipping system and an
excellent network of roads, had greatly increased during a long
period of peace, would be completely cut off by invasions from
without and anarchy within.

The threat was rendered all the more grave and imminent
by the fact that a people averse to working on the land found
the profession of soldiering equally distasteful. There was thus
no one to plough, and no one to fight. Gradually the burden
was lifted from them by foreigners and especially by Germans,
who have never been reluctant to assume this dual rôle.

These gloomy prophecies were fulfilled in the third century,
a sinister age, the least known in the whole history of Rome,
since the chief historical work devoted to it, the *Historia Augusta*,
is a later fabrication of the fourth century.[2] After the reign of the
Severi we seem to plunge into a long tunnel, to emerge only at
the beginning of the Late Empire under Diocletian, and when
we step out again into daylight, unfamiliar country lies all
about us. An illusion maybe, but it cannot be denied that the
Late Empire struck new ground, and that the entire economy
of the Early Middle Ages was conditioned by the grandiose and
often unduly maligned schemes of restoration achieved by the
fourth-century Emperors.

*

[1] V. Chapot, *Le monde romain*, p. 460.

[2] *Historia Augusta* is the name given to a series of imperial biographies in which
the so-called authors have continued the work of Suetonius up to Carus, the predecessor of Diocletian. Modern critics have let themselves go on the subject of this
valuable but untrustworthy composition. According to Henri Stern, the most recent
of these scholars (*Date et destinataire de 'l'Histoire Auguste'*, Paris, 1953, p. 98), the
work was probably written in the middle of the fourth century after the defeat of
the usurper Magnentius at Mursa (351) but before the disgrace of Constantius
Gallus had become known in Rome (autumn 354). M. Piganiol (*Hist. de Rome*,
coll. Clio, p. 302) believes several of the biographies to be pamphlets of the time
of Constantine.

The most spectacular transformation was in the outward appearance of the towns.[1] Since the defence of the Empire was based on the protective system of *limes* on the frontiers, many towns were open and the absence of fortifications allowed them to spread and grow unhindered. Spacious and airy, possessing many fine, handsome public buildings, they were often completed by residential suburbs much favoured by the wealthiest inhabitants, as for instance those of Trinquetaille at Arles and of Sainte-Colombe at Vienne, separated by the Rhône from the main block of town buildings. Even where encircling walls had been built immediately after the conquest of the first century B.C. they covered an area of 200 hectares as at Autun.

The appearance of these towns underwent a drastic change after the first barbarian invasions in the third century, the result perhaps of a wave of panic or a series of panics. The burying of hoards of coins dated the second half of this century lends support to this theory. Most of the cities in Italy and Gaul were fortified between the end of the third and the middle of the fourth century.[2] In many cases the ramparts were hastily thrown together, the masons using indiscriminately altars, inscriptions, columns, whatever material came to hand. An order may possibly have been sent out from Rome, where the second wall was started by Aurelian in 271 and hurried through without a break.[3] This cannot be affirmed with certainty, since in 238 Aquileia already had its walls, and Gallienus fortified Verona in 265. In Gaul the great invasion of 276, during which some sixty cities were destroyed, had proved to the native inhabitants that the *limes* was vulnerable. An irresistible impulse drove those who lived in the towns to barricade themselves behind walls.

[1] The towns did not disappear altogether, as Rostovtzef emphasizes (*Les classes rurales et les classes citadines dans le Haut empire romain, Mélanges H. Pirenne*, 1926, p. 15); but they ceased to be self-contained cities, Greco-Italian πόλεις; the bourgeoisie, no longer the class responsible for the organization of municipal life in co-operation with the Government, was now a group in subjection, a class of employees, a state of affairs which was to lead to its gradual disappearance. The first victim of the new régime was the civilization of the ancient world which had been a civilization of autonomous cities.

[2] A. Blanchet, *Les enceintes romaines de la Gaule*, Paris, 1907.

[3] L. Homo, *L'Empereur Aurélien*, Paris, 1904. Bibl. des Ec. françaises d'Athènes et de Rome, fasc. 89, p. 220 et seq.

At the same time the urban landscape was transformed. In order to meet the requirements of a hastily organized defence, the area squeezed into stone corsets was singularly reduced. An area of five to eleven hectares was usual for most Gallo-Roman cities. The perimeter of the first wall at Autun, that built in the Early Empire, was 5,922 metres; the second, erected during the Late Empire, was no more than 1,300.[1] At Nîmes a wall of 6,200 metres was reduced to 2,300. Fortification requirements meant that public buildings had to be left outside the walls, as with the arenas at Le Mans. The town took on the forbidding appearance of a stronghold. The luxurious houses scattered here and there around the city emptied; their well-to-do occupants began to drift away. Nevertheless, in spite of this severe blow, almost every one of the towns recovered, and we shall presently see how and why they did so.

It is tempting, moreover, to exaggerate this decline because we forget how great a gulf separated a Roman town from its modern counterpart. Most of the cities in the Empire, colonies founded as a result of conquest, were artificial creations, and although they contained workshops where craftsmen plied their trade they were never, at least in the West, industrial or commercial centres. Their citizens held only one branch of manual labour in respect – work on the land – and they themselves no longer engaged in it. The outlets open to their energies were forensic oratory, teaching, and above all the holding of magisterial office. If they wished to make money they went in for banking – usury in other words – or became publicans, that is to say farmers of the public taxes. Others indulged in trade, dealing in corn, wine, oil, consigning them to important centres and chiefly to Rome. The majority, however, like our own landed gentry, lived on the resources of their estates and occupied their leisure hours as pleasantly as possible. This way of life earned them no censure. On the contrary they would have lost dignity had they engaged in manual labour or industry. Such work was left to slaves or humble folk. In all the cities, the artisans whether freedmen or freeborn, joined together to form

[1] Blanchet, op. cit., pp. 14–20.

guilds which were both religious brotherhoods and mutual aid societies.

This long-standing prejudice against manual work had, however, disastrous consequences. The flight from the land, and contempt for work considered fit only for slaves, concentrated in the big cities and particularly in Rome, an idle plebs, a swollen proletariat, made up of freemen and freed slaves, which continued to grow in numbers under the Empire. This lower class existed on free, or nearly free, distributions provided by the state, distributions first of grain, or bread, then of oil and meat, to which were added from the third century onwards distributions of wine and salt and even of tunics and handkerchiefs. The stagnation resulting from the lack of balance between production and consumption reached even more tragic proportions with the onset of the first barbarian invasions. Fully alive to the danger, the Roman Emperors from Aurelian to Majorian applied a series of forceful remedies, so that the Late Empire figures in history as a decisive experiment in state socialism. Its results are open to question and have been widely and often harshly criticized; but the expediency and cohesion of the measures introduced cannot be disregarded.[1] This recovery, which began with the accession of the Illyrian Emperors (268), lasted until the middle of the fifth century, until such time as the Western Emperors, submerged beneath the barbarian infiltration, ceased to legislate.

It is unfortunate that the decrees of Aurelian and Diocletian were not codified along with those of their successors. Their preambles, could we but read them, would throw a clearer light on the reasons which inspired them; but there is no doubt that they inaugurated a social and economic policy which was to be carried on by the great Emperors of the fourth century. The aims and achievements of these men are revealed in the Theodosian Code, a valuable collection of imperial decrees compiled by Theodosius II, and an intensely interesting sourcebook, not only because it states clearly and precisely what the

---

[1] F. Lot, *La fin du monde antique*, p. 97: 'D'habitude on ne voit dans cette législation (du Bas empire) que le côté mesquin, despotique, chimérique; on n'en saisit pas le côté tragique, grandiose.'

reforms were, but also because in almost every case a detailed explanation of the motives which lay behind them discloses their origin. These explanations are of vital importance and put us on our guard against the ready temptation to attribute to the men of the Late Empire motives which are essentially those of our own day. Without these invaluable commentaries, we should be in grave danger of going astray.

In a study of Diocletian's financial reforms, the obscurities of which have given rise to almost insoluble arguments amongst modern scholars, the author of a recent work on Diocletian[1] has rightly pointed out that it was the army and its pressing needs which were at the root of these reforms and that they were empirical in character, inspired by his earnest desire to introduce regularity and order into a department which the military anarchy of the third century had thrown into confusion. Hence, in the fiscal system set up by Diocletian, certain inner contradictions which it is perhaps useless to attempt to resolve. It seems obvious that the defence of the threatened Empire was the mainspring of the body of reforms he introduced; but the contemporary school of history, with its bias towards aspects of the past too long neglected, is tempted to yield to the call of the siren's voice which urges: 'Economics first and foremost.' Whilst it may be true that underlying economic needs largely condition human evolution, it was comparatively rare for the reformers of the ancient world to be directly inspired by them. A certain delicacy led them to conceal them, and it was under cover of motives which appeared loftier and less materialistic, such as the defence of the Empire and the requirements of the army, that these needs formerly made themselves heard.

The effective force of the Roman armies defending all the frontiers numbered 300,000 men; it was raised by Diocletian to 400,000. The maintenance of this mass of human beings was a positive nightmare for those who governed the Empire. Every day they had to feed nearly half a million men spread out over the entire Roman world, in addition to an urban proletariat to whom distributions of food had to be made regularly. All these supplies, the army rations, as well as the food

[1] Seston, *Dioclétien et la Tétrarchie*, Paris, 1946, pp. 261–294.

distributed by the 'Public Assistance', were known officially as *annona*.[1]

This problem of food supplies was made increasingly difficult by the fact that agricultural output had been steadily diminishing from the second century onwards. The fertility of soil inadequately enriched by manuring progressively declined. In Italy and Greece its exhaustion did not pass unnoticed. As for the agricultural labour force, it was provided chiefly by slavery, but that source was drying up. Technical improvements did not compensate for these deficiencies. Up to the beginning of the second century, Rome had a number of excellent agriculturists, but true to the old Latin tradition, it was the technique of small-scale farming that they taught. Moreover, their methods and precepts had become fossilized, and the last of the Empire's agriculturists, Palladius,[2] writing in the fourth century, reels off school-boy fashion the maxims of the Elder Pliny and Columella, which is not altogether surprising, since the Romans of the Imperial Age, with a few notable exceptions, were rhetoricians and compilers; there were no longer any original thinkers or even technicians. No serious attempt seems to have been made to revive agriculture, to vary the old system of a two-yearly rotation of crops, to improve the wheel-less swing-plough used for tilling, to make work easier by inventing more efficient tools, or even, as the Merovingians did later, to take advantage of the water-mill, which was nevertheless known and the use of which would have effected a saving in manpower. This lack of initiative, intensified by the first barbarian invasions which increased the area of waste land, caused the threat of famine to weigh heavily and continuously upon the Empire and aggravated the difficulty experienced by the Emperors in feeding their soldiers.

The simplest solution was to demand more and more from taxation, from 'tributes' which were paid mostly in kind and

---

[1] For the *annona*, see Pauly-Wissowa, Vol. 1, 2 (1894), col. 2316–2321, art. *Annona*. This article is, however, somewhat out of date. F. Lot, *La fin du monde antique*, revised ed., p. 513, has an interesting and helpful note which gives a clear account of the much discussed and misunderstood nature of the *annona*.

[2] Schanz, *Geschichte der römischen Litteratur*, IV (1904), pp. 170–173, nevertheless has judged Palladius's work more leniently; he regards this author as 'ein praktischer Landwirt'. See also A. H. M. Jones, *The Later Roman Empire*, 1964, *passim*.

took the form of burdensome requisitions exacted from the provinces. This was the object of one of the financial reforms undertaken by Diocletian at the beginning of the fourth century. One of the Emperor's contemporaries, the Christian Lactantius, hating him for persecuting his co-religionists, has done his best to discredit it. In his lampoon on the *Death of Persecutors*[1] he has painted a deliberately sombre picture of the methods employed in the census taken when the land-tax and the poll-tax were assessed on a new basis. His pamphlet should not, however, be taken too literally. In justification of our scepticism, we have only to recall the violent recriminations and gloomy prophecies stirred up in France by the decision to impose income-tax, even though it was an unavoidable necessity. The truth is that Diocletian's financial reforms were both fair and expedient. They imposed uniformity on the tax paid by those living in the provinces and levied it also on the Romans who up to that time had enjoyed an exemption which had become a scandal.

This one measure of reform cannot be appreciated adequately in isolation from its wider context. It is an integral part of a programme of daring innovations, both administrative and economic, which gradually altered the very structure of the Roman world. To assess this achievement at its true worth, we have only to imagine the probable fate of Europe if the Roman Empire had collapsed once and for all at the end of the third century, and the anarchy which would have overtaken it. The Late Empire buttressed it about not only politically, but also economically and socially, with a strong supporting framework which made the birth of this same Europe possible. As we make our way through a world at once grown old and young again, we shall often find that the débris of the structure erected in the Late Empire provided the most substantial material for future reconstruction.

Initiated with the narrow aim of satisfying military requirements,[2] Diocletian's reforms, by a kind of inner determinism, rapidly expanded into a far-reaching and complex programme

---

[1] *De mortibus persecutorum*, 23.

[2] M. Seston has laid stress on Diocletian's essentially practical nature: 'Jamais', he writes (op. cit., p. 354), 'homme d'Etat ou administrateur n'a été plus attentif au réel, moins attaché à la théorie.'

of social and economic restoration with innumerable ramifications. Empirical at first, they were welded into a system not only by force of circumstances, but also by the stubborn willpower of his energetic successors. The monetary measures were perhaps the earliest of the steps towards rehabilitation taken by far-sighted Emperors. In every political and economic storm, the coinage is the most sensitive of all barometers. The monetary crisis began under the Severi. Since the ancient world had no knowledge of paper currency, the crisis showed itself in a depreciation in the weight and purity of the metal coins in current use. The Early Empire had minted gold pieces, *aurei*, as well as silver *denarii*, and had endeavoured to establish a steady relationship between the two metals, but stocks gradually dwindled. From the end of the second century the treasure flowing in from the loot of conquest was almost exhausted or had been hidden away; the loss of Dacia was soon to deprive the Empire of the Transylvanian mines. The growing scarcity of the yellow metal led to the almost total disappearance of minted gold. Once the *aureus* had become unstable currency it was no longer accepted except by weight. As for silver, a new piece with a nominal value of two *denarii* had become the current coin; it was known as the *antoninianus*, because it had been issued by the Emperor M. Aurelius Antoninus Caracalla. The percentage of precious metal it contained had been steadily whittled down during the course of the third century.

One of the first monetary reforms was undertaken by the Emperor Aurelian.[1] It affected not so much the coinage itself as those who manufactured it.[2] In the early years of the Empire, coining was in the hands of specialist slaves (*familia monetaria*), then in the third century, by a process of evolution common to almost every trade group, these slaves were replaced by guilds of freemen and freed slaves. But the scandalously high profits reaped by these moneyers, many of whom made immense fortunes, compelled the Emperor Aurelian to close their workshops, at least for the time being. A revolt fomented by them in

[1] Homo, *L'Empereur Aurélien*, p. 155 et seq.
[2] On the subject of moneyers in the Roman Empire and the Early Middle Ages, see Robert S. Lopez, 'An Aristocracy of Money in the Early Middle Ages', *Speculum*, January 1953, pp. 1–43.

Rome was suppressed with much bloodshed and the greatest possible cruelty (*ultima crudelitate*). At the same time, by a wiser move, the Emperor took vigorous steps to clean up the profession. The guilds were held responsible for the taxes owed by their members and for any forgeries committed by their employees. In addition they were gradually taken over by the state. During the fourth century the severest punishments, including the death penalty, were meted out to those who counterfeited coins and also to their accomplices, and rewards given to those who had denounced them. In the imperial decrees announcing these measures, and which have been preserved for us by the Theodosian Code, there is laid down for the first time the doctrine that money is minted for the service of the public[1] and is not in any sense a commodity but an instrument of exchange, official in character. So firmly did this conception take root that even after the fall of the Western Empire the Eastern Emperors claimed the right to keep the monopoly of minting gold throughout the length and breadth of the former Roman Empire. The declared intention of the Merovingian King Theodebert to mint gold coins bearing his own effigy (539) was considered, according to the historian Procopius, a shocking usurpation. The Merovingians, in whom any feeling for the public good was non-existent, lost sight of this conception, but the early Carolingians in their turn were imbued with this same sound idea and restored the task of minting money to the public authorities. Deprived yet again of this monopoly when, under the stress of feudal anarchy, the sovereign power had disintegrated, the French royal house from St Louis onwards insisted on the acceptance of the royal coinage rather than that of the seigneurs throughout the whole of their realm. Is it an extravagant claim to make that in this respect the Late Empire sowed a fertile and beneficial seed?

It was left for Diocletian and his successors to carry out a thorough-going reform of the actual coinage, a reform which consisted in bringing back into circulation coins of full weight

---

[1] *Theodosiani libri XVI*, IX, 21–23 (ed. Mommsen, pp. 471–476). See M. Piganiol's observations on the 'instruments of exchange' in *L'Empire chrétien*, Paris, 1947, pp. 294–300.

and purity. The gold which had vanished during the period of military anarchy now reappeared and Diocletian was able once more to issue coins of this metal. His mints struck a gold *solidus* weighing $\frac{1}{60}$ of a pound, or 5·45 grammes, and worth 18·90 francs at pre-1928 value. The *antoninianus* was a silver piece, very thinly plated, and widely discredited. Diocletian replaced it by the silver *denarius siliqua*, weighing 3·41 grammes and worth 0·90 francs pre-1928. To facilitate barter and especially to make things easier for the soldiers who made numerous small purchases, this same Emperor created copper money, in the form of a silvered copper coin.[1] His reforms were rounded off by those of Constantine who reduced the weight of the gold sou to $\frac{1}{72}$ of the Roman pound, bringing it down to 4·55 grammes.[2] The *solidus* of Constantine continued to be a fixed standard. The public, however, preferred a smaller gold coin, the third of a sou (*tremissis*), which was minted without a break throughout Merovingian times.[3]

It seems strange that the minting of gold was resumed at a time when the balance of trade was uneven and when the eastward drain of gold had exhausted the stock of precious metals available in the West. In actual fact, however surprising such an assertion may be, a certain amount of gold still remained in the West, not in circulation but in the hands of private individuals. During the fourth century there came into being a wealthy class of great landowners and high officials, of whom a modern historian has said[4] that they lived in a world of luxury poles apart from that inhabited by the plebs. These 'potentates', whom Constantine's successors were to strive in vain to bring within the common law, possessed much besides vast estates; they also held great fortunes in personal property, ingots of precious metal, many of which probably came from dismantled

[1] M. Besnier, *L'Empire romain de l'avènement des Sévères au Concile de Nicée*, Paris, 1937, pp. 312–314.

[2] A. Piganiol, *L'Empire chrétien*, p. 295.

[3] M. Prou, *La Gaule mérovingienne*, p. 175, notes that in the sixth and seventh centuries the current coin was the *triens*, which originally weighed 1·52 gr.

[4] A. Piganiol, 'Le problème de l'or au IVe siècle', *Ann. d'hist. soc.*, 1945, pp. 47–53. See also the description of 'La Gaule au temps d'Attila' given by this same historian in *Saint-Germain d'Auxerre et son temps*, Auxerre, 1950, pp. 119–133. This class of 'potentates' continued to live in real opulence in the fifth century.

pagan temples, and hoards of gold coins. We shall meet them again in the course of our survey, for entrenched behind their riches they survived the crisis of the Great Invasions to re-emerge under the Merovingians as the senatorial nobility. At the opposite end of the scale the rest of the population, the plebs, had to make do with what this same historian calls the currency of inflation, namely a small copper coin known as the *denarius communis* or *follis*, worth approximately $2\frac{1}{4}$ centimes at 1914 value.

The fourth-century Emperors must also be given credit for their tenacious, if not wholly successful, attempts to put the economy on a sounder footing. At the same time that they were setting the imperial finances in order by the imposition of taxes which, though exceptionally heavy, were fairly distributed, and were reforming the coinage by making coining a state industry, Diocletian and his colleagues were tackling the problem of the high cost of living. They decreed cheapness (*jusserunt vilitatem*) as a fourth-century chronicler so neatly expressed it.[1] The text of Diocletian's Edict on Prices (301) has come down to us almost in its entirety from numerous fragmentary inscriptions.[2] It is a detailed scale of prices for commodities sold in trading and also for workmen's wages. The preamble clearly states the intentions of the authors: 'They wished to put a stop to the dishonest practices of merchants who were forcing up unduly the price of provisions and other commodities thereby doing serious harm to the entire country, especially in places where troops were garrisoned and wherever soldiers were obliged to buy the necessities of life out of their army pay.' Once again can be seen the concern shown by the Emperors of the Tetrarchy for the army; but this Edict may also have been inspired by democratic considerations; these Emperors were thinking particularly of the plebs, since all the prices in the Edict are quoted in *denarii*, that is in the inflation currency, the only money available to these humble folk, and which, containing only a low percentage of precious metal, was extremely unstable, similar

[1] Pauly-Wissowa, V, 2, col. 1948.

[2] *Der Maximaltarif des Diocletian*, annotated by H. Blümner, 2nd ed., Berlin, 1958. On this Edict see Pauly-Wissowa, V, 2, col. 1948–1957, art. *Edictum Diocletiani*.

to our French paper money in that its intrinsic value was practically nil.

If the pamphleteer Lactantius is to be believed, Diocletian's Edict, which we know to have been circulated throughout all the provinces, was far from successful in its results. The only effect of its publication, he tells us, was to make the price controlled commodities vanish from the market, so that its authors were eventually compelled to repeal it.[1] Lactantius's assertion that price control did indeed produce such results may readily be believed in view of similar experiments tried out in our own day. Yet the example was infectious. The determination to clamp down on prices at all costs without shrinking from a fixed scale of wages, that is to say by regulating even cost prices as Diocletian attempted to do, was to persist throughout the whole of the Middle Ages. Under an energetic prince like Charlemagne was to be imposed a savage burden of taxation, the continuing sign of an economic system which could not bring itself to be liberal.

[1] Lactantius, *De mortibus persecutorum*, 7: 'Idem cum variis iniquitatibus immensam faceret caritatem, legem pretii rerum venalium statuere conatus est. Tunc ob exigua et vilia multus sanguis effusus, nec venale quicquam metu apparebat et caritas multo deterius exarsit donec ex necessitate ipsa post multorum exitium solveretur.'

CHAPTER II

The Roman World: Conditions of Rural Life

IT WAS IN THE ordering of rural life that the Late Empire introduced its most successful innovations; it was in this particular sphere that its achievements, for reasons which will have to be explained later, had the most far-reaching effects. The ancient Romans and the Gauls were familiar with the small estate, but it continued to exist, and we shall see that at the beginning of the Middle Ages there was still a large number of small landowners, many more than has often been supposed. It is nevertheless a fact that in Italy and in Gaul where very many colonies had been created and where town life exerted a strong attraction, many inhabitants of the Empire had deserted the countryside and ceased to work on the land. From the close of the Republican era there grew up a system of land-ownership on the grand scale, characterized by the creation of vast estates cultivated by gangs of slaves (*familia rustica*). This system, though easy to work, was a lamentable one, since the slave, treated as a mere thing (*res*) and totally devoid of interest in production, did little work and that badly. Moreover, as we have seen, he represented a source of labour which was becoming scarcer, since it was supplied chiefly from conquest, whilst by an opposite process the fairly general practice of freeing slaves was exhausting the available supply. For this reason the Emperors, who owned immense hereditary estates, soon adopted a different system for their management. For the administration of their *saltus* and their *villae*, they resorted to a different method of cultivation: the colonate. The *colonus* was a free man, but a small farmer tied to the land on which he worked. This particular method of cultivation was apparently first tried out in Africa, the country which became the granary of Italy, where they had vast lands to be cleared and where grain and olives were widely grown.[1] On these great domains was first evolved the organization of the *villa* with its two separate parts: the dwelling of the owner or of the steward – the reserve or demesne – and the holdings lived on and farmed by the *coloni*.

The obligations imposed on the latter were of two kinds: forced labour and dues paid in kind, the amount of which was fixed by a collective agreement, the law of the domain (*lex saltus*).[2] A certain amount of sympathy has been lavished on the fate of these free men transformed into *coloni*, or 'slaves to the soil', since the contract binding them to their master was for life, but realistic students of the period have come to see that this servitude, though a last resort, was very often also a godsend. This contract was, in fact, two-sided: even if the *colonus* was tied to the land, he could not on his side be removed from it, and all who know how deeply a peasant is attached to the land will realize that this prohibition was a precious guarantee.[3] Moreover the colonate seems to have had no lack of willing adherents. Into this condition there came together in the Late Empire a medley of men of widely different race, former slaves now freemen, small landowners weighed down with debts, barbarians too, and in Africa natives who exchanged an uncertain way of life for security under the protection of an imperial procurator. The merits of this domanial system were undeniable, and it was adopted by private individuals, the great landowners of the Late Empire, the *potentes* as they were called, and later also by the Germanic aristocracy and the Church. The Emperors, moreover, were not content merely to

[1] E. Beaudoin, 'Les grands domaines dans l'Empire romain d'après des travaux récents', *Nouv. revue hist. de Droit*, 1897, p. 554: 'La vraie patrie du *saltus*, ce sont les provinces et ce sont par excellence les provinces d'Afrique.'

[2] The inscription from Henchir-Mettich published by J. Toutain with a detailed commentary in the *Nouv. revue hist. de Droit*, 1947, pp. 373–415, is a typical example of *lex saltus*; it dates from the reign of Trajan.

[3] H. Pirenne, *Histoire de l'Europe*, Paris–Brussels, 1936, p. 64 et seq. (English ed.: *History of Europe*, London, 1939). The great Belgian historian remarks that it would be wrong to imagine that men tied to the land found this oppressive: 'Comment la liberté aurait-elle quelque prix pour des hommes dont l'existence n'est garantie que par la place qu'ils occupent sur la terre . . . et dont la sécurité est dès lors d'autant plus grande qu'ils sont plus intimement incorporés au domaine?'

establish the colonate in their great domains; those of the Late Empire laid down the most detailed rules for its administration and in a series of decrees imposed conditions of great severity on the *coloni*, whether they were in the service of the state or of individuals.[1] The binding of the *colonus* to the land, fore-shadowed first in contracts between private persons, became an act of public law. The Empire made it compulsory for financial reasons. Anxious to ensure regular collection of the *jugatio-capitatio* which was levied on land in cultivation, and to gather in the *annona* needed for its troops, it came to the help of the landowners who owed these taxes by taking the necessary steps to prevent farmers from leaving them in the lurch.

In actual fact, such servitude was not imposed on the *coloni* alone. This 'bondage to the soil' was an integral part of a much wider scheme, grandiose even in its scope, and characteristic of a general and systematic trend of the social and economic policy of the Late Empire which may be defined as immobiliza-tion within a profession. Haunted by the memory of the anarchy which had so nearly shattered the Empire in the third century, by renewed threats of disorder, by the stirring of barbarian hordes just beyond an ill-defended frontier, the great fourth-century Emperors proceeded to a thorough and lasting regi-mentation of those economic activities vital to the needs of the state and its inhabitants. At the same time as they tied the *colonus* to the land, they bound fast to his trade the shipper (*navicularius*), even though he owned his own boat, because he was in effect performing a public service, *onus naviculare*, and because it was necessary to ensure at all costs the safe transport from Sicily, Spain and Africa of the grain and oil so essential to the feeding of Italy; they tied down too the baker who also had his '*pistorium munus*', because it was his job to make bread, the staple food of the army and the common people; the pork-butcher (*suarius*) who slaughtered pigs and sold their meat because it was a main article of diet for soldiers and citizens alike; the lime-burners (*calcis coctores et vectores*)[2] who provided

---

[1] *Theodosiani libri XVI*, V, 17–19 (ed. Mommsen, pp. 238–241).

[2] See for instance *Theod.*, X, 20 (ed. Mommsen, p. 561 et seq.). The nationaliza-tion of industrial production has been brought to light by Piganiol, *L'Empire chrétien*, pp. 285–289.

the lime needed for building. This ruthless regimentation was extended to other trades also, and all the more easily since those engaged in them were banded together in guilds subject to imperial authority. Nationalization was still further strengthened by the creation of imperial factories, established in the first place to provide equipment for the army, but which were soon making woollen and silk materials and purple cloth for private individuals.

By a curious irony of circumstances, but by virtue of an implacable logic, the state, which bound the *colonus* to the land and forbade him to leave it, kept the imperial agent (*curialis*), on the contrary, in the town and prevented him from escaping into the country. During the heyday of the *pax romana*, the collection of taxes had been assured by groups of publicans to whom it brought in enormous profits. From the end of the second century, however, volunteers could no longer be found for the task, since the taxes were coming in only slowly or not at all, and tax-farming had ceased to be a source of gain; it had even become a crushing burden. From that time onwards it lay heavily upon the *curiales*, the municipal magistrates of cities, whom the Imperial Government made responsible for the collection of taxes, so that honorary public offices, once eagerly solicited by influential citizens, were now no longer sought after. They were even left vacant, and those on whom they devolved fled from the towns to seek refuge in the country. In the fourth century desertion had become a general stampede, and the sons of Theodosius grieved over those unfortunate cities which had lost their former splendour.[1] This concern was not in fact very sincere and their commiseration was dictated by underlying financial motives.

From the fourth century onwards rigorous measures, occupying several sections of the Theodosian Code,[2] were taken to slow down the exodus, to tie down the unfortunate *curiales* and prevent them from leaving the towns and moving their families and possessions into the country. They were continually being

[1] 'Destitutae ministeriis civitates splendorem quo pridem nituerant amiserunt.' 29th June 400. *Theod.*, XII, 19, 1 (ed. Mommsen, p. 733).

[2] See *Theod.*, XII, in which Section I is entitled 'De decurionibus' (ed. Mommsen, pp. 662–710). Cf. Piganiol, op. cit., pp. 356–359.

reprimanded and told again and again that, since their lot was
closely bound up with that of the public treasury, desertion
of their 'native land' was an act amounting to sacrilege. The
rebuke was reinforced by threats: the confiscation of the country
estate which they were unwise enough to prefer to the city of
their birth would be the price of their defection. By this
particular method of compulsion, as well as by others, both the
curiales and their descendants were forced to stay on in the cities
and to continue holding an office which not only ruined them
but at the same time lowered their prestige, bringing down upon
them as it did the hatred of the people. *Quot curiales tot tyranni*,
wrote the pamphleteer Salvian[1] echoing the grievances of his
contemporaries.

Modern historians have judged the Late Empire with a
harshness verging on injustice, and have even used the term
sclerosis[2] to describe the chief defect of the régime. It would be
more accurate to call it immobilization, for the Late Empire by
no means 'mortified' the West. The vigorous action taken by the
fourth-century Emperors prevented it from collapsing. It restored and shored up an edifice which was tottering to its fall,
thus contriving for the western peoples a temporary refuge
which stood them in good stead during the prolonged and difficult period of reconstruction, or more correctly of construction,
of medieval Europe.

The Late Empire had to battle not only against danger from
without; it also had subversive agents within its own frontiers
all the more insidious in that they were assiduous collaborators.
The fourth century saw a class of men known to historians as
the 'potentates' rise up to constitute something of a threat to the
solidarity of the state. The *potentes*,[3] first mentioned in documents about 360, were men of wealth, great landowners whose
position put them above the law. The class was drawn from
members of the senatorial order and from the high officials who

---

[1] Salvian, *De gubernatione Dei*, V, 4 (ed. Fr. Pauly, p. 107).
[2] F. Lot, op. cit., p. 115. Cf. William Carroll Bark, *Origins of the Medieval
World*, 1958, p. 30. In direct contrast, Piganiol ends his work on *L'Empire chrétien*
(p. 421) with the affirmation that 'il est faux de dire que Rome était en décadence'.
[3] See the description given by C. Jullian, *Hist. de la Gaule*, VIII, 1926, pp. 126–
146.

proliferated during the Late Empire, although it is uncertain whether the actual privileges they enjoyed were due to their personal fortunes or to their official position. In all probability they became magistrates in the first place because they were rich, then grew even richer in pursuance of their duties. The rise of this aristocracy was furthered by the dissensions of the third century; the experience of two successive wars helps us to understand the rise to power of men whom we are tempted to label the *nouveaux riches*. These individuals profited both from the military anarchy which wrought havoc amongst the bourgeoisie who had administered provincial towns, the class of *honestiores*, and from the rehabilitation measures of Diocletian and Constantine which greatly increased the number of high administrative posts. Taking full advantage of the new régime, they quickly gained the upper hand, and one of the most famous sections of the Theodosian Code, *De patrociniis vicorum*,[1] hints at the uneasiness caused by their activities.

Valentinian I, a harsh but far-sighted Emperor, was the first to denounce their shady dealings. A careful study of his decrees tells us the nature of the threat he sought to avert. They were, quite simply, defrauding the treasury. The small country land-owners living in villages (*vici*), unable to meet the demands of the fisc, sought refuge with powerful neighbours to escape from the unwelcome attentions of the *curiales* responsible for the collection of taxes, and even hoped by so doing to avoid payment of their poll-tax; but these potentates exacted a heavy price for their patronage. A vigorous controversialist[2] has described the actual working of the manœuvre adopted by these hunted farmers whom Valentinian calls variously *rusticus, vicanus, agricola*, in other words peasants who were free and owned a piece of land. Salvian shows us these unfortunates putting themselves into the hands of men more powerful than themselves in order to gain their guardianship and protection. 'The type of purchase contract they sign', adds the author of the *De gubernatione Dei*, 'is something quite new. The seller parts with

[1] *Theod.*, XI, 24 (ed. Mommsen, pp. 613–615). Cf. F. Martroye, 'Les patronages d'agriculteurs et de *vici* au IVe et au Ve siècle', *Rev. hist. de Droit*, 1928, pp. 201–248.
[2] Salvian, op. cit. (ed. Pauly, p. 115).

nothing at all and receives everything; the buyer receives nothing at all and loses everything he has. This kind of agreement is something unusual, since the resources of the sellers increase, whilst the buyers are left with nothing except beggary.'

Behind the author's repetitive paradoxes may be discerned a form of tenure known to classical Roman law as the *precarium*.[1] Under an almost identical name, *precaria*, this contract was to become infinitely more widespread. Thanks to Salvian, we can understand the reason for its return to favour in an altered form. The small landowner in desperate straits and badly in need of an influential patron, offered his land to the potentate and made it over to him. He received in exchange the use of the ceded land for a limited period, generally five years, but the concession could be renewed, and might be granted for life and even for the lifetime of the son of the contracting party. The saving clause which took the sting out of the agreement and contributed to its success was the fact that, perhaps from the very beginning and in any case later on, the 'precarist' obtained from the great landowner the use of a plot of land larger than the one he had handed over. This agreement remained in force even when those who had resorted to it had no longer any financial reason for doing so; but it may be assumed, and probably correctly, that a large number of farmers, short of money or even in debt, lacked the necessary resources to meet the expenses of cultivation. Practised collectively by a group of small landowners, living side by side and all in desperate straits, the *precaria* had the effect of incorporating whole villages of free farmers (*vici*) into great estates (*villae*).

Salvian alludes to yet another practice which he condemns even more severely: 'Here is something more serious and more revolting. When these men of whom we are speaking have lost their houses and lands as the result of a robbery or have been driven out by the tax-collectors, they take refuge on the estates of great landowners and become husbandmen (*coloni*) to the rich.' Yielding to a flight of fancy, the author goes on to describe the condition of these wretched men: 'Just as with that all-powerful and malevolent woman who was reputed to

[1] Fr. Girard, *Manuel élémentaire de Droit romain*, p. 584.

change men into animals, all who have settled on the estates of the rich undergo a transformation as complete as if they had drunk from Circe's cup, for the rich begin to regard as their own property those whom they welcomed in as strangers and on whom they had no claim whatever; these men actually born free are turned into slaves.'[1] This testimony is of great value, in spite of its over-emphasis and the exaggerations so characteristic of this writer. He lifts a corner of that veil drawn over the realities of country life by such complacent and smooth-tongued men of letters as Ausonius and Sidonius Apollinaris. Salvian's denunciation, written between 439 and 451, that is to say three-quarters of a century after the repressive measures taken by Valentinian I, reveals how ineffective these were. But its most outstanding disclosure is the rapid rate at which free peasants grouped in villages (*vici*) were handing over land to the powerful owners of large estates. The *precaria* contract for farmers who still owned a plot of land but had not the resources needed to cultivate it, the colonate for those who had no land or had lost that which they once possessed, both helped to extend the régime of the great estate and to multiply the number of *villae*.

In actual fact, notwithstanding the conflicts which arose between Valentinian I, a cantankerous ruler but devoted to the common people, and the potentates, the spread of patronage did not run counter to the agrarian policy of the Late Empire, the essentials of which consisted in preventing land from reverting to waste, in extending the area of cultivation, and consequently in keeping the peasants on the land by all possible means, even at the cost of their independence. Whilst recognizing the fact that the countryman's lot deteriorated rather than improved at the beginning of the fifth century, it has to be admitted that the institution of the *precarium* and the widespread extension of the colonate staved off disaster. As for the Emperors, who had been the first to introduce the *colonus* type of tenure into their *saltus*, they were probably neither surprised nor displeased to find themselves being copied by the great

[1] *De gub. Dei*, V, 9 (ed. Pauly p. 116): 'Exemplo quondam illius maleficae praepotentis, quae transferre homines in bestias dicebatur, ita et isti omnes qui intra fundos divitum recipiuntur, quasi circaei poculi transfiguratione mutantur . . .'

landowners. Moreover, the *potentes*, whom Valentinian accused
of defrauding the treasury, were for the most part high imperial
officials, since the social class which from the third century
onwards rapidly acquired honours, lands and money was
drawn almost entirely from the new men holding office under
the Late Empire which, state-controlled to an inordinate
degree, monopolized all forms of activity.

It would, however, be a serious mistake to assume that the
method of cultivating land was in any way changed as a result
of the incorporation of thousands of small estates into larger
groupings. Great estates but small farms is the formula which
best defines the régime of the *villa*. Though he had become a
'precarist' or a *colonus*, the former small landowner still kept to
his old routine. Nothing was changed in his way of life or his
method of work except that for the future he was obliged to
give up a proportion of his harvest to his new master and to
provide him with forced labour several days each week. The
'potentate', the great fifth-century landowner, cannot possibly
be compared to the American farmer of the twentieth. Nevertheless, though it brought no revolutionary change in farming
methods, the growing predominance and expansion of the great
villa stands out as a vital factor in the social and economic
evolution of the Early Middle Ages. It tied thousands of peasant
families to the land, and with that patience so peculiarly their
own they were to bide their time until a thousand years later
they took over, or more correctly took back, the real ownership
of their lands.

The new aristocracy too were attached to the land. They
lived in the country and certain of their number best qualified
to speak for them, Ausonius in the fourth century and Sidonius
Apollinaris in the fifth, have described with some complacency
their comfortable and even luxurious homes. Those potentates
who held high office in the Empire owned numerous and
extensive estates; but their wealth in land was more than
completed by fortunes in personal property; they also possessed
gold and silver. Their power enabled them to emerge triumphantly from the ordeal of inflation. The barbarians respected
them and left them alone. In the sixth century those men whom

Gregory of Tours calls the senators were still continuing to hold the highest rank, and in the Frankish kingdom the *leudes*, warriors in the royal following counted it an honour to amalgamate with them. Under the Merovingians there was to be only one single aristocracy based both on wealth and on the holding of public office.[1] It was to include Gallo-Romans as well as Franks, and barbarians from other nations.

In the world of the fifth century when town life suffered an eclipse, rural economy was all-important, but it would be wrong to speak of a return to a natural economy, since metal currency was still in circulation and in some hands there were still gold coins of good alloy. This gold, however, tended to drain away towards the East, which in increasing measure, especially after Constantinople became the second, then the chief capital of the Empire, dictated the trend of economic activity. Great commercial cities still flourished in the East, whilst in the West, and even in Rome,[2] activity had fallen off considerably. Industrial output was diminishing and the general insecurity made exporting almost impossible. On the other hand, Roman citizens who had taken advantage of the *pax romana* to get rich in big business gave it up for the same reason, and the profession of merchant fell into the hands of Orientals, chiefly Syrians, who for several centuries past had been well versed in the technique of commerce. These men engaged in trade fully alive to the risks it entailed in an unsettled age, and determined to reap enormous profits, drawing upon themselves universal execration in the process. Diocletian had already inveighed against them in his Edict on Prices, which was intended partly to curb their unreasonable demands. One tax affected them particularly, the chrysargyrum,[3] payable in precious metal, for it was

---

[1] F. Lot, *Les destinées* . . . , p. 311.

[2] The historian Gregorovius considers it impossible to estimate the population of Rome at the opening of the fifth century, owing to the lack of documentation. He believes that it had declined considerably since the time of Constantine because of emigration and general impoverishment. (*Rom im Mittelalter*, I, p. 29.) F. Lot is even more radical in his views; for he does not think that even when the city reached its maximum size, Rome could have numbered more than 300,000 inhabitants. (Op. cit., p. 79.) In order to justify his statement he has returned to this subject in *Ann. hist. et soc.*, VIII, 1945.

[3] Pauly-Wissowa, IV, I, col. 370, art. *Collatio lustralis.*

common knowledge that they were hoarding treasure and the
fisc went for its money to the place where it knew it could be
found.

It was probably at this time that the lack of merchants
resident in towns which were becoming ever more depopulated
gave rise to the practice of entrusting to specially commissioned
agents the task of buying articles and provisions unobtainable
in the local markets. When these agents were in the service of
the Emperors or of high officials, they enjoyed the privilege of
cursus publicus, or official means of transport, for their journeys.
This was the very last stage of interventionism, the ruler creating officials to purchase goods direct from the producers.[1]

To complete the picture and to bring to light one of the most
deep-seated reasons for this state control, it would be necessary
to search through the texts for reliable information about grave
social disorders. Contemporaries who have alluded to them
have often given them a strange name: the *Bagaudae*.[2] On the
fringe of society there was also a host of misfits, unemployed,
casual agricultural labourers, 'pub-crawlers', who on occasion
were rounded up into gangs in charge of a *conductor* when an
extra supply of manual labour was needed. The *circumcellions* of
North Africa are an example of one such group, whose existence
has been revealed to us by chance.[3] But above all there were
the barbarians. Their penetration into the Roman Empire
helped to transform the whole face of the western world. What
new ingredient did they contribute to the melting-pot?

[1] See below, p. 121. For the nature of the *tractoriae*, their content and form, cf.
Peter Classen, 'Kaiserreskript und Königsurkunde', *Archiv. für Diplomatik*, I, 1955,
Münster–Cologne, pp. 45–48.
[2] For the *Bagaudae*, cf. Pauly-Wissowa, II, 2, col. 2766, art. *Bagaudae*, and C.
Jullian, op. cit., VIII, pp. 174–176.
[3] Ch. Saumagne, 'Ouvriers agricoles ou rôdeurs de celliers. Les circoncellions
d'Afrique', *Ann. d'hist. éc. et soc.*, VI, 1934, pp. 351–364. Cf. Theodora Büttner and
Ernst Werner, *Circumcellionen und Adamiten*, Berlin, 1959.

CHAPTER III

The Germanic World: its Primitive Economy

THE MARK MADE BY the Germans on the economy of the West was deep and lasting. It was left to ethnologists to define the concept of a Germanic race and to determine the specific characteristics of those tall, fair-haired, dolichocephalics deficient in pigment cells.[1] Whether or not these traits have been fixed accurately enough to prove beyond doubt the essential unity of the race, we would not venture to assert. The fact which chiefly concerns the historian is that a human mass, the elements of which were already differentiated at the time of the Great Invasions, cannot be treated as one single block. The Roman Empire recognized two great Germanic families: the Western Germans who for long centuries had been settled in Continental Europe, and the Northern and Eastern Germans who had emerged in more recent times from Scandinavia. Each of these groups followed its own destiny and exerted a definite and distinctive influence on the economic life of Europe.

Living in the heart of Europe, the Western Germans were not nomadic, and from early times had been farmers; but the Germanic peasant bore no resemblance to the 'Romanic' peasant; he inhabited a cold country and cultivated a soil that was often hard and unrewarding. He had to wrest from virgin forest, from moorland and sometimes from bog, the land on which he settled, and the task of bringing Central Europe into cultivation was a slow and unremitting process of land clearance which went on until late into the Middle Ages. The German, though tenacious, is by nature restless and unsatisfied and his

[1] On the origins of the Germanic race, see H. Hubert, *Les Germains*, Paris, 1952 (L'Evolution de l'Humanité, 23).

gaze was turned towards the West, to Gaul, to Italy and to Spain. The so-called Great Invasions were really a penetration into the Roman Empire, achieved sometimes by war, but often and more effectively by peaceful means and by a slow infiltration which may be compared to that of the North Africans into Metropolitan France.[1] The analogy is all the more apt since the barbarian Germans in like manner brought with them to Rome a labour force and soldiers.

For over a hundred years German historians have been concentrating their attention on prehistoric Germany in a passionate endeavour to fathom its secret, but the scarcity of written documents makes the search singularly unprofitable. They have applied themselves to a detailed and meticulous interpretation of several brief passages from Caesar, the Elder Pliny and especially from Tacitus. By torturing these texts, and also – a method open to question – by appealing to other documents most of which date only from the later Middle Ages, sociologists have finally reached the conclusion that the rural régime of primitive Germany was one of agrarian collectivism.[2] From very remote times, according to this theory, there existed peasant communities known as *marcae*, consisting of several villages grouped together, and cultivating fields, meadows and forests in common. Unfortunately most of the documents on which this arbitrary assumption is based belong to the thirteenth, fourteenth and fifteenth centuries and are concerned with the common rights of village communities over forest land which had remained whole and undivided. In spite of the tenuous reasoning on which it is founded, this theory has had its enthusiastic supporters in France, amongst them the sociologist Laveleye[3] and the legal historians Glasson[4] and Paul Viollet.[5]

[1] See F. Lot, *Les Invasions germaniques. La pénétration mutuelle du monde barbare et du monde romain*, Paris, 1925.

[2] G. L. von Maurer, *Geschichte der Markenverfassung in Deutschland*, 2 vols., Erlangen, 1865–1866.

[3] E. de Laveleye, *De la propriété et de ses formes primitives*, Paris, 1874.

[4] E. Glasson, *Histoire du Droit et des institutions de la France*, Paris, III, 1889, pp. 68–82.

[5] Paul Viollet, *Précis de l'histoire du droit français*, Paris, 1886, pp. 471–474. This historian has modified the theory of collective ownership current in his day. He considers that 'depuis Tacite la propriété privée avait fait de nouveaux progrès'.

The historian Fustel de Coulanges set out to demolish this edifice built on sand. Relying confidently on his rigorous and discerning interpretation of the documents, he succeeded in proving from the very authorities themselves, and so conclusively as to defy all refutation, that the Franks and other Germanic peoples from very ancient times practised individual ownership, and that the *alodis* frequently referred to in barbarian laws is the equivalent of the Latin *hereditas*, and is none other than the hereditary estate.[1] His penetrating judgement has thus cleared from the field of research a crop of parasitic myths which had sprung up like so many weeds. Yet it must in fairness be added that contemporary German scholarship has reacted strongly against the sociological legend of *Markgenossenschaft*, which for several decades had been accepted as historical truth on the other side of the Rhine, and which still lingers on in an encyclopaedia of undoubted scientific worth such as the *Reallexikon der Germanischen Altertumskunde* of Hoops.[2] Taking the opposite point of view from their predecessors, contemporary German historians think it more likely that the Germans began with a system of family, rather than collective, ownership of the land. In the very beginning, they maintain, there were individual holdings (*Einzelhöfe*); often small groups (*Weiler*) came together to clear thickly forested areas. The villages (*Dörfer*) represent a more advanced stage of development and must have come into being when the improvement of agricultural implements had made a systematic organization of the cultivated zones essential.[3] As for the original existence of

[1] After criticizing the theory of the primitive agricultural community in his *Recherches sur quelques problèmes d'histoire*, Fustel de Coulanges continued and triumphantly completed his work of demolition by concentrating more particularly on a refutation of Glasson's train of reasoning in *L'Alleu et le domaine rural pendant l'époque mérovingienne*, Paris, 1889. Fustel concluded that the agrarian community was 'un roman qu'on a introduit depuis une trentaine d'années dans l'histoire' and which, he went on 'doit en être écarté, du moins si l'on croit que l'histoire est une science'. Ibid., p. 198.

[2] See for example the article 'Markgenossenschaft', by von Schwerin, III, 1915, pp. 192–194, where yet again the traditional theory has already undergone considerable modification. Similarly, the work of Auguste Meitzen, *Siedelung und Agrarwesen der Westgermanen und Ostgermanen*, Berlin, 1895, 3 vols., is conceived in a realistic rather than a dogmatic spirit.

[3] Note particularly the clear account given by Karl Wührer, *Beiträge zur ältesten Agrargeschichte des germanischen Nordens*, Jena, 1935, p. 35, and the solidly documented

agricultural communities, the legendary marks (*marcae*), they were a product of the imagination of sociologists who mistook for relics of protohistoric times certain associations evolved in the Middle Ages, often even in the later Middle Ages, for the purpose of exploiting intercommunal forests which had remained undivided. These were to be found almost everywhere in medieval times, especially in mountainous districts such as the Pyrenees and the Alps, and as a concrete example taken from a non-Germanic region, one need only cite La Terre de Cour, a vast wooded area which remained undivided between three of the communes in the former Comté of Nice and was split up only at the beginning of the twentieth century.

Once this inconsistent theory of *Markgenossenschaft*[1] had been cleared out of the way, a certain unanimity of views could be achieved as to what agricultural life was really like under the ancient Germans. Mention must be made of the provisional results of a research project which is still in progress, especially as it is being conducted methodically, with a skilful use of the most varied techniques: archaeological excavations, careful examination of the actual site, aerial photography, and the study of place names.

The hamlet appears to have been, in many instances, their primitive unit, for though the Germans had little liking for town life they seem from early times to have been loath to live in isolation. Families willingly joined together in small settlements (*Weiler*) consisting of several homesteads detached from each other, wooden huts covered with thatch, or even underground shelters roofed with turf, examples of which can still be seen in Iceland. Huts and shelters were dotted here and there without any preconceived plan and the same lack of order

chapter, full of shrewd observations, which Fr. Lütge has devoted to the *Markgenossenschaften* in his work entitled *Die Agrarverfassung des frühen Mittelalters*, Jena, 1937, p. 294 et seq.

[1] It is interesting to read what Rudolf Kötzschke has to say on the subject of *Markgenossenschaft* in the *Allgemeine Wirtschaftsgeschichte des Mittelalters*, pp. 213–220. Unaffected by the preconceived ideas held by his predecessors about an original so-called communal régime, he has reconstructed the agrarian organization existing in the various regions of Germany before the system of *Grundherrschaft* was instituted, and has stressed the part played by neighbourly relationships between farmers in the creation of communal institutions (*Allmende*).

was evident also in the villages, groups of dwellings believed to represent a more recent stage of settlement. To these villages which have no set plan, German scholars have given the name of *Haufendörfer* ('thrown-together villages'.)[1]

The originality of the Germanic system lies in the organization of the lands in cultivation. These formed vast zones adjacent to the dwellings, and on which each family had its own plots, which were long and narrow, real strips of land (*Streifen*). There is now no support for the legendary explanation of this field structure formerly advanced by the old school of sociologists who favoured the doctrine of *Markgenossenschaft*. They claimed that from the very beginning an identical share had been allotted, for his personal and exclusive use, to each member of the village collective in the zone set aside for cultivation, the clearance of which was due to the initiative of the *Genossenschaft*. A more realistic, and at the same time a more likely explanation has been put forward of this division of the land into narrow ribbon strips. The Germanic plough, a more effective instrument than the Roman swing-plough since it dug deep into the soil, had wheels and was drawn by several pairs of oxen. The turning of such a plough when it reached the end of a furrow was a difficult manœuvre, and it was the practical problems arising out of this operation which first brought about the division of arable land into long-drawn-out strips.[2] This choice had still further consequences. The Latin peasant who, with his light swing-plough, tilled an irregularly shaped field could plough it up in any way he pleased without fear of annoying his neighbour. With the Germanic farmer the situation was very different. The strip of land he ploughed in the same cultivated zone as his neighbour actually touched the belt farmed by the other man. Their close interdependence made it impossible to leave one strip lying fallow with cattle grazing on it whilst corn was being grown on the adjoining plot. Hence, by sheer force of circumstance, there evolved not perhaps a strictly regulated system, but a practice to which the Germans

[1] Aug. Meitzen, *Siedelung*, I, p. 47.
[2] M. Bloch, *Les caractères originaux de l'histoire rurale française*, p. 51 et seq. Cf. A. Homberg, *Die Entstehung der westdeutschen Flurformen*, Berlin, 1935.

have given the expressive name of *Flurzwang*. This was the necessity for all farmers in the same cultivated zone to submit to a uniform rhythm of cultivation and to observe the same rotation of crops.[1]

This condition imposed by nature had perforce to be accepted, and it may be to this that Tacitus was referring in a passage of the *Germania* which has given rise to frequent and heated controversy. The Latin version of this short but famous text is given below. In the opinion of the sociologist G. von Maurer[2] writing in 1854, it must be concluded from these few lines of Tacitus that the Germans had no knowledge of private ownership at the date when the Latin historian was writing, but that the land belonged to all the inhabitants of the community and was shared out afresh each year. This interpretation was criticized by Fustel de Coulanges, with whom it was a point of honour to interpret texts with scrupulous accuracy. His commentary, in which every word is explained and carefully assessed, is still of great value.[3]

Arable land is cultivated as well as it can be considering the small number of hands available to work it. It is farmed in sections and alternately. This is done for greater convenience by all the farmers together. Moreover each has his own lot proportionate to his rights. From time to time, periodically, they change the site of their ploughing and move on to a different part which has been manured by their herds. In this way there are always more plots of land than are being actually farmed, that is to say there is always some part of the land which is left uncultivated.[4]

Tacitus's description conveys the surprise of the Roman who,

[1] R. Kötzschke has shown how the *Flurzwang* became established as a material necessity, though without encroaching on the economic independence of the farmer-owner (doch nicht unter völliger Aufhebung der ökonomischen Selbstständigkeit). *Allg. Wirtschaftsgesch.*, p. 268.

[2] *Einleitung zur Geschichte der Mark.*

[3] *Recherches sur quelques problèmes d'histoire*, pp. 283–284. The chapter entitled 'Tacite signale-t-il chez les Germains l'absence de propriété?' should be read in full. Ibid., pp. 263–289.

[4] 'Agri pro numero cultorum ab universis in vices occupantur, quos mox inter se secundum dignationem partiuntur. . . . Arva per annos mutant et superest ager.' *Germ.*, 26.

visiting the site of a Germanic village, beheld on the one hand a cultivated zone, consisting of strips of land side by side, being ploughed by peasants who were helping each other, and on the other a second zone of the same size but lying fallow and given over to cattle who were grazing on it and manuring it at one and the same time. Is this not a picture of land on which the *Flurzwang* was being put into practice? However daring such an interpretation may seem, it is nevertheless probable. Can it also be assumed that the Germans of Tacitus's day already had some knowledge of a three-course rotation (winter cereals sown in autumn, spring cereals, fallow)? A remark by the Elder Pliny[1] perhaps gives ground for thinking so. In a chapter of his *Historia Naturalis* devoted to husbandry, the Latin writer mentions a recent incident which had occurred three years earlier in the territory of Trier. The corn crops having been spoilt by frost during a bitterly cold spell, the inhabitants sowed again during the month of March and reaped an abundant harvest. This experiment is noted as something quite exceptional by the Elder Pliny, accustomed to the two-course rotation practised by his compatriots, but if the inhabitants of Trier tried it out on their land, was it not because spring sowings were fairly customary with them, a fact which gives us good reason to suppose that they were already practising a different rotation of crops from the Romans? We should, however, be careful not to over-emphasize the rigidity of this system of crop rotation. The cultivated zones of those lands which were inadequately manured and fertilized must quickly have become exhausted; doubtless they had to be rested often and for long periods, thereby increasing the area of fallow.

Accustomed to a variety of crops, to fruit, vegetables and vines growing side by side with corn, the Romans were surprised to find none of these in Germany. They demand nothing of their land but corn, wrote Tacitus;[2] he could have gone on to say that the crops most widely grown were not wheat, nor even barley, but rye and oats, and he comments unfavourably upon the laziness and lack of initiative of the natives. The Latin

[1] *Hist. Natur.*, XVIII, 49.
[2] 'Sola terrae seges imperatur.' *Germ.*, 26.

author should, however, in all fairness have accounted for this uniformity by placing the German countryside in its true setting, which he certainly knew, since he has vividly described it for us, 'bristling with forests and disfigured with swamps'.[1] In this country the cultivated areas were little more than woodland clearings, and rural life can only be fully understood if seen against its grim background the forest, that primeval forest which separated one tribe from another, and which superstition long prevented from being felled with the axe.[2] Later it became an essential element in the rural economy, for it provided the peasant with the wood he needed for fuel and for building, and the acorns from its oak-trees were the favourite fodder of the herds of swine which were allowed to wander about in it. The woods and moors surrounding the areas which had been cleared were given up to the use of the community in general, and were only appropriated by an individual when a peasant from the village came forward to cultivate them. It is moreover believed, and with some probability, that the villages, larger groupings than the primitive *Weiler*, originated in the desire of certain farmers to reserve for their own use, and to farm in common, vast sections of forest land. Common rights were granted to each inhabitant of these villages; the communal nature of the forest and of the other areas not annexed by families is emphasized by the term *Allmende* applied especially to them,[3] whilst the cultivated zones are known as *Gewanne*, a symbolic word recalling the gain (*Gewinn*) accruing to those who had cleared them.[4]

In the absence of written documentation, this evocation of the rural past of Germany may seem pure conjecture. There is no known document dealing with a piece of Germanic land

---

[1] 'Aut silvis horrida aut paludibus foeda.' Ibid., 5.

[2] *The Cambridge Economic History*, I, 20.

[3] Georg von Below, *Geschichte der deutschen Landwirtschaft des Mittelalters*, Jena, 1937, p. 13: 'Wir benennen die nicht zur Beackerung an die Gemeindeglieder überwiesenen Stücke mit den historischen Bezeichnungen Allmende und gemeine Mark also die Weide-Wald-Heidegebiete, Flüsse und Moore.'

[4] 'Die Ackerflur besteht nicht aus einem zusammenhängenden Ackerstück, sondern aus einer Mehrzahl von Stücken, in denen dann wieder jedes Gemeindemitglied, jeder Bauer einen Streifen hat. Literarisch hat sich für diese Stücke der Ausdruck Gewann (von gewinnen = in Anbau nehmen) eingebürgert.' Ibid., p. 10.

earlier than 704; now, at the beginning of the eighth century, the drive for the creation of great estates, led by the aristocracy and the religious houses, had already begun to change the primitive structure of the Germanic village. The justifiable criticisms levelled against the exponents of the *Markgenossenschaft* theory for using documents of a later period might equally well be turned against those tempted to make use of Carolingian charters and polyptyques in order to reconstruct rural life as it was in Germany before the creation of the great ecclesiastical and secular estates. Nevertheless, in spite of the serious gaps in documentation, it was essential to attempt such a reconstruction, rash though the undertaking might be, since the agricultural traditions of the Germans spread across the Rhine in the wake of the Great Invasions, even whilst they were being perpetuated in the country of their origin. The bare plateaux of the nucleated villages of Eastern Gaul, with their narrow, rectilinear plots so characteristic of districts where the open field system was practised, have become what they still are today only because of the reshaping of the rural landscape carried out by occupants of Germanic origin.

It is not enough to stress the hypothetical nature of such a reconstruction: it is also important to avoid over-hasty generalization. The study of agrarian civilizations, or rather, to quote the definition given by a geographer who has specialized in this field of research,[1] the study of regions from the point of view of the lay-out and use of land, is still in its infancy; its exponents focus their attention on the actual ground itself, and their most useful aids are aerial photography, air surveys, and minute examination of the land-survey register, together with toponymic and even 'microtoponymic' research, since the names of plots of ground sometimes give far more valuable information than those of isolated habitations which are the only ones preserved in our topographical dictionaries. The results of their inquiry, which is still only in its early stages, are, however, somewhat disconcerting; they reveal, in fact, fundamental

---

[1] L. Champier, 'Qu'est-ce qu'une civilisation agraire?', *Annales Universitatis Saraviensis*, Philo-Lettres, 1952, p. 321. Cf. the same author's 'A propos de l'œuvre de Robert Gradmann. Méthodes de recherches en géographie agraire.' Ibid., pp. 190–202.

differences between territories which in many cases adjoin each other, as for instance Bresse and Mâconnais. They make it impossible to treat as one uniform region vast areas such as the whole of France. Marc Bloch had foreseen this difficulty when writing his great work on *Les Caractères originaux de l'histoire rurale française* in which, as elsewhere, he had already sketched out the threefold division he proposed to make of our territory: the open-field zone in the east, the irregular-field system in the south, the woodland region in the west.[1]

No greater degree of uniformity prevailed in primitive Germany, and certain corrections will have to be made to a picture which has been over-simplified. Evolution varied according to the region. In the mountainous parts of Southern Germany and of Switzerland, and in the Lower Rhineland and Westphalia, the population was for the most part widely scattered; these districts remained faithful to the *Einzelhof* system[2] and antagonistic to that of village settlement (*Haufendorf*) which tended to prevail elsewhere. We may therefore hazard the cautious conclusion that Germany, having achieved intensive cultivation at a comparatively late date, preserved over its entire area an agricultural structure more austere, more uniform, and less individualistic than Gaul, which was more easily accessible to Mediterranean influences.

It is impossible to make even a rough estimate of the population of Germany during the first centuries of the Christian era. It was thinly scattered, yet too dense for its farmers to feed it adequately, especially since farming methods were still rudimentary, and after a very few years the ill-manured soil was exhausted. Yet the inability of the land to feed its sons was not their only reason for leaving it. A second factor to be borne in mind was the temperament of the Germans themselves, delighting in war and adventure. Instability is not necessarily synonymous with nomadism. The Germans are not a pastoral

---

[1] In the concluding pages devoted to 'régimes agraires' in his work on *Les Caractères originaux de l'histoire rurale française*, p. 64, he wrote: 'Reconnaissons que pas plus que les faits de langage ne se groupent aisément en dialectes . . . les faits agraires ne se laissent enfermer dans des limites géographiques qui pour toutes les catégories de phénomènes apparentés seraient rigoureusement les mêmes.'

[2] G. von Below, op. cit., p. 19.

people. They are agriculturists, who for hundreds of years have been searching for their 'vital living-space', and the famous formula 'Volk ohne Raum', too sweeping perhaps in the twentieth century, applied perfectly to ancient Germany.

Emigration into the Roman Empire began at an early date and took various forms. Tacitus already mentions Germans who were cultivating the Decumate lands;[1] the occupation took place with the consent of the Imperial Government which levied on these barbarians a tithe amounting to one-tenth of their harvest. Penetration also took the form of a slow infiltration, since Rome needed soldiers and husbandmen. This need increased during the Late Empire. At what date did Germans begin to enlist in the Roman army? It may have been in the reign of Marcus Aurelius. The first to do so were isolated individuals or small groups of men, poor folk, slaves or men half-free, known as the *laeti*. They were stationed, together with their families, near the Rhine frontier and even inside the Empire on lands of which they were left in full possession. Their reputation was not entirely above reproach; Ammianus Marcellinus speaks of the barbarian *laeti* quick to seize opportunities for theft.[2] Reports of this nature should not, however, be taken too literally; rightly or wrongly foreigners settling in a strange country are almost always the object of suspicion.

The type of land tenure granted to the *laeti* persisted into the Carolingian era, for *mansi lidiles* are still to be found in the Polyptyque of Saint-Germain-des-Prés drawn up at the beginning of the ninth century.[3] These *laeti*, who settled in North-Eastern Gaul, were farmers as much as soldiers, perhaps even more so; in the regions in which they chose to live they gave an impetus to the formation of rural communities grouped together in villages and practising an enforced rotation of crops. Emboldened by their initial successes, the Germans then gradually and by progressive stages penetrated into the Empire along the entire length of the *limes* in ever-increasing numbers, until eventually whole nations (Burgundians, Visigoths, etc.) had

[1] 'Non numeraverim inter Germaniae populos . . . eos qui decumates agros exercent.' *Germania*, 29. Cf. Pauly-Wissowa, I, 1, col. 893, vº *Agri Decumates*.

[2] Ammianus Marcellinus, XVI, 11.

[3] *Polyptyque de Saint-Germain-des-Prés* (ed. Aug. Longnon), I, Introd., pp. 87–91.

settled not merely on the periphery, but actually within the
Empire, by virtue of treaties concluded with the Emperors
themselves, and which gained for them the title of federates.
This last stage was reached in the fifth century.[1]

It is important to bear in mind, for our particular purpose,
the economic consequences of this first barbarian infiltration.
It was marked by a retrogression. Tacitus had already noted
with astonishment that speculation on capital and the lending
of money at interest were practices unknown to the Germans.
The barbarian kings only began to mint coins when they
settled within the Empire, consequently not before the end of the
fifth century, and at first they imitated the imperial coinage.
Before that time, only those Germans nearest the frontier were
acquainted with its use, because they had been visited by
Roman traders. Marc Bloch has observed[2] that the German
word for merchant (*Kaufmann*) is derived from the Latin 'caupo',
meaning an innkeeper. From this he concluded that the
Germans learnt the art of trading by frequenting Roman
'mercantis' living near the frontier, who sold in their shops both
drink and small wares. A comment by Tacitus on the barbarians' preference for silver rather than gold confirms the
soundness of this observation, since silver coins are more convenient for making small purchases.[3]

The balance-sheet of this first intermingling of Germans and
natives of the Empire may perhaps seem meagre: the barbarians received an initiation, though as yet only a rough and
ready one, into retail trade and the handling of metal coinage,
and in return they spread over a restricted area of the Empire –
North-Eastern Gaul – the system of crop rotation habitually
practised by the Germans. There was, however, one further
consequence which had more lasting effects in the economic
field. Along the banks of the Rhine right down to its mouth,
and in the Moselle region, there was established a zone of

[1] F. Lot, 'Du régime de l'Hospitalité', *Revue belge de philologie et d'histoire*, VII,
1928, pp. 975–1011.
[2] 'Une mise au point. Les invasions. Deux structures économiques', *Ann. d'hist.
soc.*, 1945.
[3] 'Argentum quoque magis quam aurum sequuntur . . . quia numerus argen-
teorum facilior usui est promisca ac vilia mercantibus.' *Germ.*, 5.

contact between Gaul and Germany which was to be the scene of ever-increasing activity, and which later in the eleventh and twelfth centuries was to become one of the cradles of medieval capitalism.[1] It was military in origin, resulting from the construction of the *limes*, and the continual presence of troops on the frontier. The garrisons, from the Early Empire onwards, attracted numerous merchants to this area, but artisans' workshops – manufactories would be too ambitious a name for them – were also to be found there. A few examples will suffice. A flourishing pottery works, a branch of the one at Lezoux, is known to have been established at Heiligenberg in Alsace. Other centres for different types of manufactured goods were set up in the Rhineland; Cologne was the site of important glassworks. Side by side with workshops founded by private enterprise, the Roman State created others, in far greater numbers, to meet the needs of the army: shield factories at Alt-Ofen, and at Lorch, weapon factories at Trier and Strasburg, pottery works at Xanten, Neuss and Weisenau near Mainz. These numerous establishments can partly be accounted for by the difficulty of communications and the high cost of transport which in certain cases doubled the cost price. It was preferable to produce on the spot everything required for the clothing and arming of the troops. But they had also to be fed, and the intensification of cultivation along the *limes*, and the land concessions made to the barbarian *laeti*, were intended to meet these needs. If the banks of the Rhine and the Moselle were at an early date planted with vines, in spite of the unsuitability of the climate, it was for the same reason. Wine was needed for the Rhine garrisons. We also gather from Ammianus Marcellinus that in these same areas there were depots stocked with biscuits for troops on active service. A lively centre of industrial and agricultural life sprang up there, and thanks to a conjunction of favourable circumstances it survived.

The presence of the fourth-century Emperors, who made Trier one of their capitals, helped to stimulate economic activity in the north of Gaul.[2] The barbarian invasions and the

[1] See *L'art mosan*, Paris, 1953 (Bibl. de l'Ec. prat. des Hautes Etudes, 6th section).
[2] Cam. Jullian, *Hist. de la Gaule*, VII, p. 248. Cf. Piganiol, *L'Empire chrétien*, p. 176.

fall of the Western Empire did not bring it to an end. The large number of Frankish and Alemannic cemeteries discovered in Lorraine and Alsace is evidence of a dense population. The Salian Franks took over from the Empire. By settling in Toxandria, this nation, which was destined to dominate Gaul, prepared the way for the greatness of the future Netherlands.

*

Now let us turn to Eastern Germany. Tacitus and the Elder Pliny have described it somewhat cursorily, but their information was not gleaned exclusively from books. Pliny refers to a mission entrusted to a merchant of Carnuntum, a town in Pannonia; this merchant had been sent to the mouth of the Vistula to buy amber. We may therefore assume, without straining probability too far, that in addition to extracting information from the works of Greek geographers, the two Latin authors endeavoured to fill the gaps in their knowledge by questioning such of their venturesome contemporaries as had actually visited Eastern Germany; yet their knowledge remained sketchy; it was confined to proper names, to the names of peoples – sometimes given in a garbled form – and to several legendary traditions.

Jordanes, the historian of the Goths, writing in the sixth century, places the cradle of the race in Scandinavia, which he calls the Isle of Scanzia.[1] The entire ancient world believed the peninsula to be an island. The Elder Pliny speaks of a gulf called *Codanus*, full of islands of which the most famous is *Scandinavia*;[2] but he admits that he knows nothing about its size and adds that only one single part of it is known. The very word Scandinavia may be simply a wrong spelling, transmitted through the faulty manuscript of a Roman scribe,[3] and mistakenly sanctioned by general use. The correct form would be 'Scadinavia', a term meaning dangerous islands. What probably happened was that, from the first century A.D., sailors

---

[1] *Getica*, chap. IV.

[2] '. . . sinum qui Codanus vocatur, refertus insulis, quarum clarissima Scandinavia est, incompertae magnitudinis.' *Hist. Natur.*, IV, 27.

[3] Lucien Musset, *Les peuples scandinaves au moyen âge*, Paris, 1951, p. 18, note 3.

landed on the south coast of Scania, but did not penetrate into the interior. By a reverse process, Scandinavian navigators were early attracted by the enchanting mirage of Roman civilization; they imported into their own country weapons, glassware, ceramics, jewellery, and several Roman coins have been discovered in the neighbourhood of Bergen.[1]

There was a second and more serious reason for their emigration. Although the southern part of Scandinavia was brought into cultivation at an early date, and though the country had its ploughed fields as early as the Iron Age, the barrenness of a cold soil forced a section of the inhabitants to leave it, all the more since the density of its population was legendary in the ancient world.[2] Jordanes calls the Isle of Scandinavia a factory of peoples, a womb of nations. A prolonged phase of emigration, lasting until the ninth century, set in from the end of the second century with the exodus of the Cimbri and the Teutons, and the author of a recent *Histoire des peuples scandinaves au moyen âge* has stated[3] that for a thousand years this history consisted chiefly of vast pulsations which spilled masses of men over Europe. The first invaders of the continent were followed by Vandals, possibly by Burgundians, and by Rugians. After them came the Goths, though several modern scholars query their Scandinavian origin;[4] but there is no serious reason to challenge the evidence of Jordanes, who makes his ancestors come from the isle of Scanzia, in other words from the south-east of Sweden. The memory of these ancient settlers has surely been preserved in the country's old name: Götaland. The Goths had already crossed the Baltic in the time of Tacitus and the Elder Pliny, for these writers place the *Guttones* and the *Gothones* in Eastern Germany. Having settled on the banks of the Vistula, they did not remain there. An excess of population, attested by numerous cemeteries discovered in Eastern Germany, may perhaps explain

[1] L. Musset, op. cit., p. 12. On the contacts of Norway with Rome, see O. A. Johnsen, *Norwegische Wirtschaftsgeschichte*, Jena, 1939, p. 5.

[2] On the subject of the Gothic emigration and the settlement of the Goths in Eastern Europe, it is interesting to read a short synthesis by Ernst Schwarz, 'Die Urheimat der Goten und ihre Wanderungen in Weichland und nach Südrussland', *Saeculum, Jahrbuch für Universalgeschichte*, IV, 1953, pp. 13–26.

[3] L. Musset, op. cit., p. 18.

[4] Ibid., p. 20.

why they left that poverty-stricken region and continued their trek across the continent.

Folk traditions collected by Jordanes have preserved the more or less legendary memory of their march to the Black Sea. The crossing of the Pripet marshes slowed it down. One section of the emigrants remained behind, and it was perhaps at this point that those who had separated from the main body formed an independent group, that of the Visigoths. The Ostrogoths, more daring, continued on their way and about the end of the second century must have reached the shores of the Black Sea where they founded an Empire bounded by the Sea of Azov, the Crimea and the lower reaches of the Don. A second-century inscription found in a Buddhist temple in India, some sixty miles to the east of Bombay, has been claimed as evidence of their enterprising spirit, since it makes mention of two Gothic merchants. The Goths, however, were no more essentially nomadic than the Franks or the Alamans, they were simply unfortunate. Driven to wander hither and thither for more than two centuries, coming to rest now outside, now inside the Empire, they eked out a wretched existence, perpetually searching for lands to cultivate. One episode in their long wanderings, recorded by Ammianus Marcellinus, throws a sinister light on the sharp practices indulged in by the officials of the Eastern Emperor Valens, who had incorporated bands of Visigoths into his army with the promise of settlement in Thrace. These agents deliberately starved them, then turned their hunger to gain by selling them dogs, collected for the purpose, at a charge of one slave each. Even influential men amongst them were reduced to parting with their own children. This shameful trade was the prelude to the disaster of Adrianople.[1]

When considering the stormy career of the Goths up to the time when the Visigoths settled in Aquitaine and the Ostrogoths in Italy, and also the fitful light shed by a few rare historians[2] on the remote past of Central and Eastern Europe,

[1] Ammianus Marcellinus, XXXI, 4.

[2] In particular Eugippius, the author of the *Vita sancti Severini, Corp. script. eccl. latin.*, IX, 2nd part, Vienna, 1886.

the salient point to remember is the atmosphere of turmoil and unrest which prevailed there almost up to the year 1000 A.D. Exposed on the east to invading barbarians, Iranians (Sarmatians and Alans), Mongols (Huns and Avars), Slavs, and later, Hungarians, this part of the continent offered only a precarious shelter to those who sought refuge in it. There was to be a startling contrast between those countries condemned to long centuries of insecurity and those in Western Europe: the western part of the Roman Empire, the Rhineland, and even, once the Saxons had been subdued, Germany as far as the Elbe. Of these latter areas it could be said that some form of economic life, though very rudimentary in character, was taking shape. Nevertheless, the balance-sheet of Central Europe is not entirely negative. Certain techniques, as for instance cloisonné enamelling, and even certain artistic innovations, such as the stylization of the animal and plant motifs native to Scythian and Sarmatian art, may have reached the West through the Goths.[1] Merovingian craftsmanship and pre-Romanesque art were to make full use of them. The influence of the civilizations of the Eurasian steppe made itself felt in other spheres also: in food through the use of butter, which may have come down to us from the Scythians, and in agriculture through the cultivation of the hop, which is believed to be of Eastern origin.[2]

The Iranian and Mongol invasions, however, had a different effect, and one which was immensely significant. They were horsemen, whilst the Roman armies and also those of the continental Germans, and in particular of the Franks, consisted essentially of foot-soldiers. Under the influence of the invading Sarmatians, Huns and Avars, and later of the Saracens and Hungarians, the armies of those nations which had emerged from the Western Empire underwent a complete transformation, and modelling themselves on those of their adversaries,

[1] L. Bréhier, 'Les colonies d'Orientaux en Occident', *Byzantin. Zeitschrift*, XII, 1903. Cf. H. Hubert, *Les origines de l'art français*, p. 128. The latter describes this technique of soldering fillets of metal on to a surface and filling them with vitrified enamel.

[2] Marc Bloch, 'Les techniques, l'histoire et la vie. Note sur un grand problème d'influences,' *Ann. d'hist. éc. et soc.*, VIII, 1936, pp. 513–515.

became mounted troops.[1] The horseman supplanted the foot-soldier. The Franks had instituted universal military service, and all freemen, Gallo-Roman and Barbarian, were subject to it. But from the moment infantry was ousted by cavalry, the fighting strength decreased. A horse cannot be equipped or a horseman armed without money, and the men destined to serve in the king's host were expected to possess a certain fortune which Carolingian capitularies were to assess in *mansi*. One of the most lasting results of this revolution in the art of war was that whilst compulsory military service was not officially abolished, it no longer applied to everyone. Those on whom it was imposed came to form a kind of aristocracy. No longer were all free men soldiers, but only the richest of them, and the term *homo liber* was to lose its normal, etymological meaning and be used to denote the man serving in the host; its meaning was to become restricted and to be applied to a kind of caste which, though not yet closed, gradually tended to turn into the nobility. A second word also was to be deflected from its primitive meaning. The *miles* was originally the trooper, the 'military man'; in future he was to be the knight, the chevalier. This was a symbolic change. From the time when the army began to be recruited exclusively from the ranks of the rich, it became a profession for noblemen, and what was more serious, it excluded them from all other lucrative employment.

The ancient Romans also had, side by side with the senatorial nobility, an aristocracy of men who, enjoying a high property qualification, were wealthy enough to serve in the cavalry; they were the knights (*equites*); but the knights did not, on that account, renounce the exercise of civil and lucrative professions. On the contrary they experienced a kind of pride at making money in banking, large-scale commerce, tax-farming, with the result that the class of Roman knights became a class of

[1] F. Lot, *L'art militaire et les armées au moyen-âge*, Paris, 1946, I, p. 92: 'Un grand changement s'était opéré dans l'armement et la tactique des armées. Les Francs des Ve et VIe siècles furent, parmi les Barbares, avec les Anglo-Saxons, les derniers bons fantassins. Partout ailleurs l'arme décisive était la cavalerie lourde. . . . La puissance de choc de la cavalerie lourde s'avéra tellement irrésistible que, peu à peu les Francs eux-mêmes durent s'adapter à la tactique de l'arme nouvelle. La chose était faite dès le milieu du VIIIe siècle.'

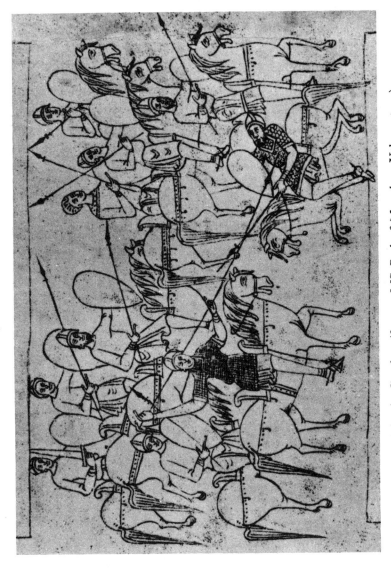

2. Knights in Combat (from a MS *Book of Maccabees*, Xth century)

businessmen. The psychology of the *milites* who during the Middle Ages became the military aristocracy was completely different. They were devoted wholly and exclusively to the profession of arms. For them to engage in trade, to undertake manual work, to cultivate the land, would have been degrading. It is true that the knights in the feudal armies did not always put their contempt for riches into practice; there were many amongst them who pillaged and plundered, and many amassed fortunes by brutal and illicit means, but they refused all productive employment, and the mechanism of economic life was to be thrown out of gear by the prejudice of a numerous aristocracy for whom a livelihood had to be found, and who consequently were to live on others. There were many reasons for the economic stagnation of the Early Middle Ages; some share of the responsibility falls squarely on the monied class of the Merovingian era, on the Gallo-Roman senators, and on the Frankish, Burgundian and Alemannic *leudes* who out of sheer heedlessness held aloof from every form of productive activity. But it is equally a cause for regret that their example was followed by the Carolingian nobility, that of the knights. For several centuries Western Europe was deprived of financiers, bankers, great merchants, contractors, in other words of specialists in production and exchange. It was not until the eleventh century that a new and wealthy, or at least well-to-do, class – the bourgeoisie – free from the prejudices of the military aristocracy, placed these despised activities once more on an honourable footing. Nevertheless it should be added that the neglect of them was, if not exactly encouraged, at least sanctioned by the Church, which even more thoroughly in the first centuries than in our own day, inculcated into its followers a contempt for worldly possessions.

CHAPTER IV

The Christian Church:
Its Economic Doctrine: The Result of
its Triumph

A THIRD FACTOR PLAYED its part in shaping the economic development of Europe: the fact of Christianity, the triumph of the Church. It is always difficult to measure with any precision the effect on an economic system of what one philosopher has called an 'idea-force'. The modern tendency is to under-estimate it, and a new discipline, the history of economic facts, is particularly inclined to bring back into prominence the material elements of human activity, too much neglected before our own day, and to stress their imperious determinism. The reaction, we hasten to add, was justified, since a century of financial stability, and the cushioned ease which for several generations prevailed in the circles in which history was written, made our predecessors insensitive to economic realities. The impact of two world wars has revived our awareness of them and has driven us to a salutary examination of conscience and a revision of outworn concepts; but certain of our contemporaries, dazzled by the essentially quantitative character of our industrial civilization, have perhaps been tempted to attach too little importance to certain factors which, though counting for much less than in the past, when their influence was considerable, are still to be reckoned with.

Christianity is one such factor, all the more so in that it originated in categorical imperatives. For this reason its rapid spread affected the economy of the Western world. Amongst the causes which brought about the decay of the economy of the ancient world, it is impossible to overlook the upheaval wrought in consciences by the adoption of a young, dynamic and demanding religion: it transformed the scale of values and gave a sense of direction and purpose to life. Once victorious, Christianity had probably no choice but to modify the rules of conduct laid down by its Founder, and to come to terms with economic requirements when it became the official religion; but the doctors of the Church did not relax their vigilance, and the adaptation was eventually achieved only because of certain changes which took place in the economic structure of the countries won over by Christianity. To explain the evolution which resulted in the medieval economic system and ignore the contribution made by Christianity would be like claiming to have solved a complicated problem by suppressing one of the data, and that not the least important, essential to its solution.

It is enough to recall, almost at random, some of the teachings of Jesus preserved in the Scriptures, to grasp the seriousness of the economic revolution they might well have brought about if followed literally. There is the curse on the rich in the Sermon on the Mount: 'But woe unto you that are rich, for ye have received your reward,' and the words gain an added harshness from that blessing on the poor which immediately precedes them: 'Blessed be ye poor, for yours is the kingdom of God.'[1] Then there is the answer given to the rich young man who had asked his Good Master what he should do to obtain eternal life: 'If thou wilt be perfect, go and sell that thou hast and give to the poor and thou shalt have treasure in Heaven.'[2] There is also the example of the birds of the air and the lilies of the field set before the disciples to induce them not to worry unduly about the material demands of life and to take no thought for the morrow.[3] It would be easy to multiply quotations and to extract from these examples a doctrine of austere simplicity which would seem to be a negation of capitalism,

[1] Luke vi. 20, 24.
[2] Matthew xix. 21.
[3] Matthew vi. 28.

but also and equally a repudiation of all attempts at planning the economy or organizing labour.

Christianity was fortunate in that, propagated in a troubled world undermined by a general crisis, it offered to thousands of disappointed and anxious beings the consolation and the *alibi* of which they dreamed. The Kingdom of Heaven was for them a reality, the advent of which, at first believed to be immediate, gradually receded into a more distant future, but without losing anything of its certainty.[1] It is outside our scope to follow step by step the evolution of this ideology and of this millenarianist hope. We shall note only their repercussions on the behaviour of Christians, and the attitude they induced towards the demands of social life and the economic set-up of their time.

The faithful of the first three centuries, whose zeal and convictions were continually being renewed in Christian communities, appear to have lived not so much apart from the world as on the fringe of it. Tertullian defended the Christians against the criticisms of those who reproached them with isolationism by declaring that they frequented the forum, the baths, the workshops, shops, markets and public squares exactly as did pagans, and also like them pursued the callings of sailor, soldier, farmer, merchant and artisan. His statement is no doubt true, but it must be admitted with a Catholic historian Jacques Zeiller,[2] that for these Christians worldly pursuits were of secondary importance, and that in varying degrees, according to individual temperament, they displayed a lack of interest in society and its activities which might possibly, in the long run, work out to its disadvantage.

The tendency to aloofness decreased as the number of Christians grew, but it did not disappear altogether. The stern teaching of the early Church, that earth was a place of exile and testing, was in no way modified. Adequate proof of this is to be found in the pronouncement made at the beginning of the fifth century – the beginning of the period under review in this book – by the most penetrating and widely read doctor of the Latin Church, St Augustine, on the economy of the temporal

---

[1] See Loisy, *L'Evangile et l'Eglise*, chap. II: 'Le royaume des cieux'.
[2] *Hist. de l'Eglise*, published under the direction of Fliche and Martin, II, p. 399.

world. In his work *De Civitate Dei*, which was to be the favourite reading of Charlemagne, he states that there exists an uncompromising opposition between the City of God, that of the elect, made up of men living according to the laws of God, and the City of the World, that of the impious and the wicked, made up of men living according to the laws of man. To this wicked city we must perforce belong, since we are living on earth; but we should take care not to attach ourselves to it by ties which are too close: 'When we have food and raiment,' declares St Augustine,[1] 'let us content ourselves therewith, for they that will be rich fall into temptation and snares, and into many foolish and hurtful desires, which drag men down to death and destruction, for covetousness is the root of all evil.' St Augustine reverts on several occasions to this same theme, condemning this transitory life which all good men should despise,[2] and reminding men that they brought nothing into this world nor can they carry anything out of it;[3] but that Divine Providence has 'prepared such goods in the world to come as the just only should enjoy and not the unjust'.[4]

These strictures were not isolated instances. Condemnation of worldly possessions, fear of the Last Judgement, the hope of eternal life, became commonplaces of Christian exhortations and the student of diplomatic still finds an echo of them in the dry-as-dust, stilted phraseology of a notary's formula in the preambles of innumerable charters where these themes are used to justify gifts made to churches. Also, though the curse pronounced against the riches of this world was not always effective, and though it did not prevent plenty of people, and even of Churchmen, from coveting them or even acquiring them, a certain stigma was nevertheless attached to the out-and-out pursuit of them. The fifth century, and perhaps even more the age of Charlemagne, would have thought twice before launching the famous slogan: 'Get rich.'

The most spectacular sign of this disapproval which clung

[1] *De Civitate Dei*, I, 10 (ed. de Labriolle, I, p. 32).
[2] 'Temporalem vitam quam boni contemnere debent.' Ibid., I, p. 31.
[3] 'Nihil enim intulimus in hunc mundum, sed ne auferre aliquid possumus.' Ibid., p. 32.
[4] Ibid., I, 8 (ed. de Labriolle, I, p. 23).

to the merchant, and more generally to all forms of economic activity, was the ban on lending money at interest, and consequently on credit. The Old Testament had already forbidden it. In the Book of Exodus we read: 'If thou lend money to any of my people that is poor by thee, thou shalt not be to him as an usurer, neither shalt thou lay upon him usury.'[1] This commandment was repeated in other books of the Bible, and was pressed home in ever more peremptory tones.[2] Enumerating the virtues which win access to the 'tabernacle of the Lord' David too, in one of his psalms,[3] recalls that the righteous man who walks uprightly does not put out his money to usury. The Book of Deuteronomy, however, makes one exception, for the writer empowers the Israelite to exact interest from a stranger,[4] but Christianity made the prohibition universal. Taking their authority from a verse of the Sermon on the Mount,[5] the doctors of the Church established it as a principle that lending should be free of interest, in other words an act of charity. Ecclesiastical law soon gave its sanction to this moral precept. From the beginning of the fourth century, the Fathers of the Council of Elvira decreed stern measures against those who lent at interest, whether clerics or laymen. The 20th Canon of this Synod runs as follows:[6] 'If a cleric is convicted of practising usury, he shall be disgraced and excommunicated. If, on the other hand, it is proved that a layman has indulged in usury, he shall be forgiven, but on condition that he promises to stop the practice and not to repeat the offence, for if he persists in this sin, he will be expelled from the Church.' The offensive against usury was carried on throughout that and the following centuries, ending finally in a general condemnation of lending at interest which was endorsed by the secular power in the time of Charlemagne.

It is important to stress this attitude of the Church to money

[1] xxii. 25.

[2] See Le Bras, art. 'Intérêt et usure' in the *Dictionnaire de droit canonique*, fasc. XXX, 1953, col. 1476.

[3] Psalm xv. 5.

[4] 'Unto a stranger thou mayest lend upon usury; but unto thy brother thou shalt not lend upon usury.' Deuteronomy xxiii. 20.

[5] 'Mutuum date, nihil inde sperantes.' Luke vi. 35.

[6] Bruns (H.-Th.), *Canones apostolorum et conciliorum saeculorum* IV, V, VI, VII, Pars altera, Berlin, 1839, p. 5.

and money transactions without at the same time over-emphasizing its significance. It has, in fact, been correctly noted that in the ancient world there was very little lending for production, and that it was almost exclusively for consumption.[1] The majority of borrowers were poor people in need of money to buy the basic necessities of life, and the lenders were usurers who exploited their creditors by demanding from them exorbitant rates of interest, 25 and even 50 per cent. The banning of such transactions was an act of sound morality and humanity; nevertheless, in making the prohibition general without drawing any distinction between a moderate interest, which is a fair remuneration for a service rendered, and usury, which is an abuse, the Church disclosed the very core of its economic doctrine. Anxious above all things to ensure for its followers the highest supernatural good – enjoyment of the Heavenly Kingdom – it never considered that the multiplication of worldly riches could be an objective worthy of human activity, since it feared that an excessive preoccupation with temporal things was an obstacle to the attainment of the only true good – the Kingdom of God.

Indifferent, or nearly so, to the stimulation of productivity, the Church concentrated rather on the fair distribution of temporal possessions so as to defend the interests of the poor in obedience to the teaching of Christ; but she did this throughout the early centuries without making the least move to reform the economic system of a world she held to be bad beyond redemption, and we may look in vain for any sign of planning, any organization of labour, any systematic redistribution or socialization of property in the teaching of the Early Fathers. This in itself throws light on the economic rôle of the Church during the Early Middle Ages, an active rôle which, to use a bold metaphor, was that of a brake rather than an accelerator.

On two points, however, which have a bearing upon economics, the action of the Church was positive and fruitful, although it made itself felt indirectly. The Church contributed in large measure to the rescue of town life by fitting her temporal government into the framework bequeathed her by

[1] Le Bras, art. quoted, col. 1475.

the Roman Empire, and it will soon become evident that the cities survived by what amounted to a process of substitution. On rural life too, though for quite different reasons, her influence made itself felt, and in a manner no less unexpected.

The early Christians, loyal to the teaching of their Master, paid as little heed as possible to their material needs and lived on alms; but in the third century, emerging from what a historian of ecclesiastical property[1] calls 'the inorganic phase', they began to acquire possessions, at first owning them jointly as *collegia*. The following century witnessed a radical change. The Church then became a great administrative body, with divisions based closely on those of the state. Its temporal needs increased as the number of its adherents grew, and a new concept was born. The Church became a moral entity endowed with juridical power. This fiction held out great advantages; it spared the clergy the reproach of excessive riches, since goods given to the Church, like those she bought for herself, were set apart for the service of God. Furthermore, it stimulated the generosity of the faithful, liberal giving to the Church being regarded as an act of piety. Equally numerous were the Christians who believed they could buy off their sins and earn divine forgiveness by giving up all or part of their wealth to a church, whether by deed of gift during their lifetime or by a bequest in their will. The archives of religious houses are full of such deeds; this practice was continued throughout the greater part of the Middle Ages, so that the Church's inherited wealth gradually increased.

The goods bequeathed consisted chiefly of country estates. The situation would have seemed paradoxical to a Christian of the third century, living at a time when there were still no churches except those in the capital of the *civitas*, for country parishes did not begin to exist in any number until near the end of the following century under the fruitful apostleship of St Martin. In actual fact it was the monks who were to be chiefly responsible for the wealth in land which accrued to the Church. The earliest monasteries in Gaul and Italy were still only

[1] Lesne, *La propriété ecclésiastique en France aux époques romaine et mérovingienne*, Paris, 1910, p. 1.

poverty-stricken establishments. The monks of the fourth and fifth centuries, abiding faithfully by the tradition of St Pachomius and the Egyptian desert fathers, sought out lonely and isolated retreats. St Honoratus found refuge in the island of Lérins, Romanus and Lupician in forests in the Jura. The end of the fifth century brought the monks nearer the towns, as we shall see later, and the outskirts of the cities were thick with monasteries. Later, under the influence of the Irish, and following a return to the earliest traditions of monasticism, wild and solitary places were again sought out by monastic founders, but without a fresh return to a general and complete isolation.

In this chapter, which attempts to assess the Church's share in shaping the economic structure of the medieval world, the chief points to bear in mind are first the attraction exerted by an original way of life, and the causes of which will have to be investigated, and second and more particularly, the prodigious wealth accumulated by the monasteries at the beginning of the Middle Ages. They had the unexpected good fortune to come into being and to expand at a time when the barbarian kings, heirs to the vast *latifundia* bequeathed by the Roman Emperors, had at their disposal a well-nigh inexhaustible store of wealth in the form of land which they were quite unable to manage themselves. With lavish generosity they gave away part of it to those monastic founders who approached them. The endowing of a monastery was for these superstitious men, troubled in conscience, an insurance against the threat of eternal punishment. Moreover, even if these kings distributed an even greater number of imperial fiscs to the feudal vassals in their entourage, all this wealth was not completely lost to the churches and to religious foundations. A great deal of it found its way back, since the consciences of these great men were no less uneasy than those of their sovereigns, and the most appropriate way of setting them at rest was obviously to heap gifts upon the servants of God.

Thus the institution of monasticism acquired in less than two centuries a vast number of estates which it accumulated without ever being able to shed, and which became mortmain property. It was from the sixth century onwards that the alienation of ecclesiastical property was strictly forbidden by the Councils. By the eighth century, when Charles Martel attempted a sensational process of blood-letting, the Church was the greatest landowner in Christendom. It is, however, only fair to point out that the lands given to monasteries, and generally speaking to churches, often consisted of waste lands and forests whose owners had used them only for hunting, and that the monks must be given credit for having brought them into cultivation. Much is heard of the widespread clearing of land in the eleventh century. In fact the clearance accomplished by these monks during the Merovingian period and the following century is equally remarkable. This was the credit side of the colossal fortune acquired by the churches from the fifth century onwards.

PART II
The Merovingian Age

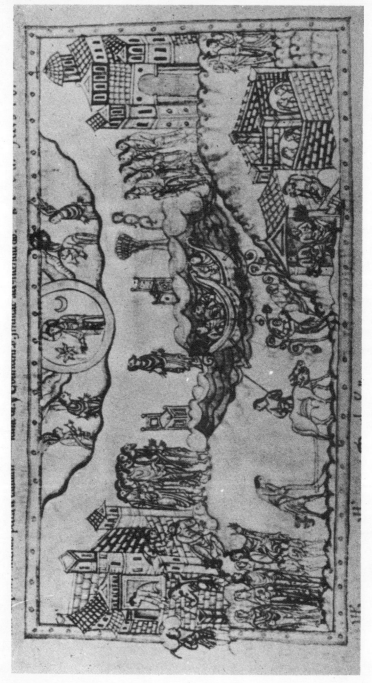

3. Illustration from *Canterbury Psalter* (folios 192) (Psalm CVII, verses 10, 23, 30, 36, 37)

CHAPTER I

Farming and Agriculture
in the Very Early Middle Ages:
Old Theories and New Horizons

AGRICULTURE WAS THE ALL-IMPORTANT factor in the economic activity of the Merovingian era. The flight from the towns, which set in at the end of the third century in the Western Empire, increased in pace during the fourth and fifth centuries. Moreover the Germanic peoples who penetrated into it, first by a process of slow infiltration, then in mass during the Great Invasions, were farmers, accustomed to a régime of individual ownership. The Merovingian civilization resulting from the fusion of the natives of Western Europe and these barbarians was a peasant culture.

It is difficult to say with certainty how far the arrival of these foreigners modified the rural economy of Western Europe, the more so since their influence was not uniformly felt. The first barbarian nations to settle as federates on Gallic soil, the Visigoths who installed themselves in Aquitaine, and the Burgundians in Savoy (*Sapaudia*), made little impression. They were treated as 'settlers' (*hospites*),[1] in other words they were given what amounted to 'billets de logement' on the lands in which those barbarians who offered their services to the Empire were required to live. The land was portioned out between them and the local landowners who gave them lodging; legal documents help to throw some light on the rules governing the allocation. Relatively few in number, these barbarians were quickly assimilated. There was no expropriation on a vast scale;

[1] On the 'régime de l'hospitalité' see the article by F. Lot already quoted.

59

only a few great Gallo-Roman landowners were compelled to share their estates with barbarian chieftains, who in turn settled their followers on the lands conceded to them.[1] The complaints of a fastidious aristocrat like Sidonius Apollinaris, who was considerably put out by the proximity of outlandish Visigoths, their hair greased with butter, are the only authentic accounts that have come down to us of these compulsory expropriations. Further to the north, however, in the regions occupied by the Franks and Alamans, the face of the countryside underwent a profound transformation, and it is certain that those open plains on which the plots of land form a strictly geometrical pattern of squares acquired their present shape because the Germanic invaders settled there, bringing with them and acclimatizing their methods of cultivation and their system of farming.

This barbarian impregnation was overlooked by Fustel de Coulanges whose book *L'Alleu et le domaine rural* contains a description of rural life in the Merovingian age which has remained a classic of its kind. The picture he paints is oversimplified. It is, in fact, an exaggeration to assert that the Germanic invasions brought about no change, and that the whole of Gaul except for the towns and a few *bourgs*, was covered with great estates (*villae*), all of which had remained exactly as they had been two hundred years earlier. It is impossible, without making numerous reservations, to accept the categorical conclusion which ends his book:[2] 'What the domain was in the fourth century it still continues to be in the ninth. It has the same area, the same boundaries. It often bears the same name, which is the one given it by a former Roman owner.'

Imposing, but too cut and dried, the theory conceived by the great French historian obscures the complex reality. It is based

---

[1] The word *fara* is often used to denote these bands of followers (Kötschke, *Allg. Wirtschaftsgesch. d. Mittel.*, p. 92). In its gallicized form 'Fère' it occurs in several place names in North-Eastern France, as for instance La Fère (Aisne), Fère-en-Tardenois (Aisne), Fère-Champenoise (Marne) (Longnon, *Les noms de lieu*, p. 214, no. 875). The learned historian has brought to light an article in an edict of the Lombard King Rothari (640) which confirms that this term referred to the retinue, the household, of a great man: 'Si quis liber homo potestatem habeat intra dominium regis *cum fara sua* migrare ubi voluerit.'

[2] p. 462.

entirely on the uniform and conventional meaning attributed by the author to certain Latin terms, and in particular to the word *villa*. Built up by a learned and cultured man, living surrounded by his books in the Rue d'Ulm in Paris, it is not founded on direct observation. Scholars of a younger generation, more concerned with concrete facts, less tied to documents and less anxious to arrive at simple formulae by way of abstract reasoning, have concentrated on the land itself, and have attempted to discover its secrets by using not only charters and historiography, but also the varied resources offered by examination of the ground on the actual site and from the air, as well as land-survey atlases and old plans, the interpretation of archaeological discoveries and place-names. They have made detailed local investigations, and the topographical limits set to their inquiries have not deterred them, by a certain irresistible contradiction between their passion for detailed observation and the eager promptings of their intuitive intelligence, from putting forward as the conclusions to be drawn from their researches, ingenious, even daring – not to say risky – hypotheses. This is the 'romantic' conception of historical research, as opposed to the analytical and 'classical' method of Fustel de Coulanges, or even of Henri Sée.[1] It has given us several thought-provoking and fascinating works, in which problems which seemed to have been exhausted have taken on new life and freshness; nevertheless they are inclined to leave the reader somewhat puzzled and bewildered.

Fustel de Coulanges and those who have accepted his views, also lay themselves open to criticism because their conclusions are so essentially static. Dynamism, on the contrary, is a marked characteristic of the researches embarked upon by the younger specialists in agrarian history. Their aim is to detect and 'film' the successive changes which a piece of land has undergone from prehistoric times to the great centuries of the Middle Ages, and even up to the modern era. Fitted into this film sequence, the Merovingian age as described by the 'classical' school, with its great *villae*, its vast *fundi*, is seen as a phase which, though reached by gradual stages, a fact by no

[1] *Les classes rurales et le régime domanial en France au moyen âge*, Paris, 1901.

means clearly established, was certainly soon outlived. It should not, however, escape notice that the *villa* described with such satisfaction by Fustel de Coulanges too closely resembles those model farms on show in contemporary exhibitions.

Anyone who wishes to find out exactly what farming is like in a particular district is not content simply to visit an exhibition, but makes enquiries on the spot. Information about rural life in the past must be obtained in the same way. The detailed reconstruction of a great estate, built up with the help of the *Capitulare de villis*, which is nothing more or less than the evocation of a model *villa* as seen through the eyes of the author of that document, cannot possibly take the place of a series of regional explorations. Such research has already been successfully attempted for Burgundy, Central Germany and several other provinces. We ourselves shall not hesitate to plunge into the debate with observations made over a small and restricted area – Maine – not with any thought of endowing them with a significance they do not possess, but because of the ideas to which they may give rise. The only outcome will be an invitation to carry on with regional research, and a warning of the dangers consequent upon premature theorizing in a subject – the cultivation of the land – in which reality can never be tied down to a formula.

Before embarking on a picture of rural life in Merovingian times, one important observation must be made. The clearing of the land was a slow business, and the soils most easily broken up and most fertile were naturally the first to be attacked. The successive stages of this gradual extension of cultivation have only rarely been the subject of specialized research. An able scholar has recently attempted such a study for one narrow sector, the district lying between Tarn and Garonne.[1] It has been undertaken on a wider scale in Burgundy which has many trained research workers.[2] These writers have indicated the

---

[1] Ch. Higounet, 'L'occupation du sol du pays entre Tarn et Garonne au moyen âge', *Annales du Midi*, 1953, pp. 302–330. See also for Viennois the thesis presented for the diploma of archiviste-paléographe by François Chevalier: *Etude sur le peuplement rural de la région de Vienne*, Nogent le Rotrou, 1940.

[2] It is enough to recall the works of Roupnel, Abbé Chaume, Déléage, de Saint-Jacob, Duby and Champier.

method to be followed. The pin-pointing of ancient *villae*, *oppida*, *tumuli*, a study of the ground itself, supplemented by information gleaned from place-names, help the investigator to fix the probable boundaries of those lands which have been longest in cultivation. From these studies, of which there are still too few, it has been discovered that for a long period the areas under cultivation were farmed only sporadically, and that for many centuries vast stretches of waste land separated the cultivated zones from each other.

The Gallo-Roman contribution to land clearance was considerable, and evidence of it is to be found in thousands of place-names ending in *-acus* and *-anus* and also in the remains of innumerable *villae*. We should not, however, be misled by their number. The Celtic and pre-Roman *vicus* continued to exist side by side with the great estate,[1] although the practice of taking villages under their patronage (*patrocinium vicorum*) enabled large numbers of influential fourth-century Gallo-Romans to annex for their own use old-established farming communities and to profit from the land clearance carried out by free peasants. Moreover, although the great estates were so ready to absorb them, not all the villages disappeared, and the problem of land distribution in the Late Empire and the Merovingian era does not call for the drastic solution adopted by Fustel de Coulanges, and after him by Henri Sée.

We should also beware of entertaining too rigid a conception of the *villa*. The *villae* so frequently mentioned in Merovingian and Carolingian documents were never as uniform in character as has all too often been supposed. Under one and the same name there often lie hidden widely differing realities. Nor were they permanent and unchanging. They too were subject to the processes of history. Their origin, unfortunately, is often difficult

---

[1] The juxtaposition of great country estates and *bourgs* inhabited by free peasants is a phenomenon to be found also in the Byzantine Empire and particularly in Egypt, for which the papyri furnish a wealth of documentation (Germaine Rouillard, *La vie rurale dans l'Empire byzantin*, Paris, 1953, pp. 13–65). In Byzantine Egypt also a 'decrease in the number of free peasants' is noticeable in the fifth century (p. 15). It is to be accounted for both by the 'anxiety to avoid the Treasury agents and by the Egyptian farmer's habit of borrowing not only money, but also provisions and grain. The peasant, heavily in debt and at the end of his resources, was obliged to turn *colonus* when he had pledged the whole of his patrimony.'

to detect, but their evolution, as we shall see, is easier to trace, especially from the ninth century onwards, as also are the stages of their disintegration.

In the course of this work one word continually recurs to denote the small holding designed to supply the needs of a single household, the word *mansus*, 'the basic unit of agrarian civilization in the Middle Ages', as it has been so aptly described by a scholar who has made a thorough study of the subject.[1] As with the *villa*, it will be necesssary to revise traditional ideas about the *mansus* if we are to avoid that worst of all obstacles to historical progress, an obstinate adherence to outworn concepts. Before proceeding further with this some-what vexed question, we should do well to study the documents closely; the lesson they teach is one of caution and humility. We shall base our inquiry on several Merovingian texts for the region of Maine.

*

The Chronicle of the Bishops of Le Mans (*Actus pontificum Cenomannis in urbe degentium*),[2] written in the middle of the ninth century in the household of Bishop Aldric, is a famous work familiar to every scholar who has specialized in the deciphering of Merovingian documents; but historians have not yet exploited it to the full, although the many charters with which it is crammed are so many mines rich in significant detail. At the outset of an inquiry into the rural economy of the Early Middle Ages, a close scrutiny of this work will prove rewarding, since several very clear and concise texts included in it encourage us to strike the first blow at certain traditional conceptions which have been too uncritically accepted. One chapter of Fustel de Coulanges's book on *L'Alleu et le domaine rural* is entitled: 'Le sol était-il distribué en domaines ou en villages?'[3] It contains this astonishing statement: 'Whilst the charters name and describe thousands of *villae*, I have come across the word *vicus* only seventeen times.' The *vicus* is the

[1] Déléage, *La vie rurale en Bourgogne jusqu'au début du XI⁰ siècle*, I, pp. 253–360.
[2] Ed. Busson-Ledru, Le Mans, 1901 (Arch. hist. du Maine, II).
[3] Pp. 198–220.

village, the *villa* the great estate. The conclusion to be drawn from these figures is surprising.[1] The *vicus* was in fact a type of settlement habitual to independent Gaul. Caesar makes frequent reference to it in the *De Bello Gallico*. He writes, for instance, that amongst the Helvetii alone there were four hundred of them.[2] What had become of these Gallic *vici*? The truth is that Fustel's statement was exaggerated. In the sixth century many villages were still in existence. According to Auguste Longnon, who went through the work of Gregory of Tours making a careful count,[3] the historian bishop applied the term *vicus* to something like seventy places, 'most of which belong to the provinces he knew best, Auvergne and Touraine'. All these *vici* are villages, groups of rustic dwellings, almost always possessing a 'basilica'; they are never great estates. Gregory of Tours does not confuse *vicus* and *villa*. Even in the ninth century the *vici* had not disappeared. The Chronicle of the Bishops of Le Mans offers explicit confirmation of their survival. In the biography of Julian, the first of the pontiffs, the author, a contemporary of Louis the Pious, tells how the holy Bishop Julian visited each of the *vici* in the diocese in order to dedicate churches and establish priests there.[4] The statement deserves particular mention, not that it is strictly historical, for the account is legendary in character, but because the biographer would not have alluded to *vici* if they had no longer existed in his day. Their number was still considerable, and we can form some idea of what a *vicus* was like in the region of Le Mans.

It was a group of dwellings already long-established. Artins, for example, referred to as *vicus Artini*, had possessed a temple of Jupiter.[5] The *vicus* of Jublains[6] was an old ruined city. It can also be proved that a *vicus* was not a large estate divided

[1] The distinction is equally clear in Byzantium, where it persisted up to the eleventh century. The *bourg* (γωρίον or χώμη) is distinct from the domain (γθῆαις). G. Rouillard, op. cit., p. 87.

[2] 'Vicos ad quadringentos', I, 5.

[3] *Géographie de la Gaule au VI* siècle*, p. 72.

[4] 'Per singulos vicos aecclesias dedicavit et sacerdotes instituit.' *Actus*, p. 36.

[5] Loir-et-Cher. 'Juxta Artinis situm, ubi et templum Jovis constructum atque ornatum erat.' *Actus*, p. 20.

[6] Cant. Bais (Mayenne). See E.· Laurain, *Les ruines gallo-romaines de Jublains*, Laval, 1928.

up into smallholdings, but a group of homesteads inhabited by farmers owning their own land. The *vicus Busiacus* was chosen in the eighth century by the monk Longis as a suitable spot for his cell because the place was inhabited; many peasants (*pagenses*),[1] the chronicler goes on to say, made him gifts of their inheritances and possessions. Moreover, the meaning of the term becomes even clearer when these allusions are taken in conjunction with a synodal decree contemporary with the composition of the *Actus*. An article of the Council of Meaux of 845 forbids priests to administer baptism in places other than *vici* and baptisteries, since the *vici* must be allowed to keep their ancient privileges.[2] This ban is directed against the claims of a large number of churches built by great landowners inside their *villae*. In drawing it up the Fathers of this Council were defending the rights of those churches founded at an earlier date and with canonical sanction in the *vici*, in other words in villages of freemen.[3] The Bishop of Le Mans most certainly knew of this prohibition and was all the more eager to enforce it since the churches in the *vici* of his diocese were obliged to pay an annual quota in silver, wax and oil to the mother-church, in other words to his cathedral. The official chronicler of the see has drawn up a careful list of these *vici*. Although not compiled until the ninth century, it throws light on an older state of things, since the monetary dues are calculated in triens (*treantes*), or thirds of a gold *solidus*, a coin which had been out of circulation since the beginning of the eighth century.[4] The number of *vici* in Le Mans is imposing; it amounts to ninety, scattered throughout the whole of the diocese, a far cry from

[1] 'Quadam die perveni ad Busiacum, vicum canonicum, ubi detentus sum a presbyteris et pagensis [*sic*] ejusdem loci. . . . Coeperunt me exhortare ut in eodem loco cellulam aedificarem, quia *popularis* locus est et elemosina multa ibidem venit.' *Actus*, p. 147. *Busiacus* is the modern Saint-Longis, cant. Mamers (Sarthe).

[2] Aug. Dumas, 'Quelques observations sur la grande et petite propriété à l'époque carolingienne', *Rev. hist. de droit*, 1926, p. 619. This article contains many new and relevant ideas.

[3] The note on the Bishops of Tours which Gregory of Tours placed at the end of the *Historia Francorum*, X, 31, shows that numerous churches were built by his predecessors in the *vici* of the diocese, and Aug. Longnon, *Pouillés de la province de Tours*, Introd., p. iv, note 2, concluded from this that the Frankish historian sometimes used *vicus* with the meaning of parish.

[4] Aug. Longnon, ibid., p. 15.

the seventeen *vici* listed by Fustel de Coulanges for the whole of Gaul. Many other indications also serve to put us on our guard, as for instance the host of *vici* inscribed on Merovingian coins, not to mention the seventy *vici* enumerated by Longnon in the work of Gregory of Tours.

What relationship existed between the settlements known as *vici* and the *villae*? The problem admits of no easy solution, because of the disconcertingly fluid vocabulary characteristic of Merovingian and Carolingian texts, but several of the Le Mans documents may help to resolve it. The will of St Bertrand, Bishop of Le Mans, includes a list of the numerous estates owned by this prelate, who was exceedingly wealthy. Some of these references are significant, in particular that of three *villae* which the testator locates by the name of the nearest *vicus*, exactly as we ourselves do in addressing letters when the recipient lives in a little-known spot which can be identified only through the proximity of a more important settlement.[1] Elsewhere the episcopal chronicler alludes to domains (*villulae*) lying round about a *vicus*, that of Bouessé.[2]

This subordination of the *villa* to the *vicus* is somewhat surprising, for we are accustomed to think of the early medieval *villa* as a vast estate, consisting of a demesne and innumerable tenant farms, and coinciding often in size and area with a modern commune which was its successor and continuation. The contradiction is only apparent and arises from our traditional and far too rigid conception of the *villa*. Not all *villae* resembled the model set before us by the *Capitulare de villis* or even those described in the *Polyptyque* of Irminon. In reality a wide diversity of types was concealed under one comprehensive term. It should also be noted that the organization of a *villa* was often, and undoubtedly, the result of a long and laborious process of land clearance. In the north-west most

[1] 'Villa Mareiliaco [*corr.* Marciliaco] seta decus Diablentas vico . . . Similiter villa secus Pocileno vico . . . Villam quam secus Berulfo esse dinoscitur.' Will of Bertrand, Bishop of Le Mans, A.D. 616, *Actus*, p. 126. *Marciliaco* is Marcillé (cant. Mayenne, Mayenne), which is situated a few kilometres from Jublains (Diablentas); *Pocileno* became Polin, which persists in the names of two communes in Sarthe: Parigné-le-Pôlin and Yvré-le-Pôlin; *Berulfo* is Bérus (cant. Saint-Paterne, Sarthe).

[2] 'Villulas in circuitu praefati vici Buxidi sitas.' *Actus*, p. 146. *Buxidum* is none other than Saint-Longis already referred to.

of the great estates must still have been, in part at least, waste
land; vast stretches were still covered with forests, like those still
to be seen in the sandy belt surrounding Le Mans. Merovingian
charters and hagiographic texts make it possible for us to
compare these still half-uncultivated estates with others more
highly developed with which we are familiar.

A charter of Domnole, Bishop of Le Mans, for the year 572
contains a description of the *villa* of Tresson, offered by this
prelate to the Abbey of Saint-Vincent of Le Mans. Its name is
perpetuated in that of a commune.[1] Judging by its boundaries
it was of great size, but still partially uncultivated, for there
were few hands to farm it. The document gives a list of the
slaves (*mancipia*) living on the land and who were handed over
with it: one married couple with a small child, four manservants,
two maidservants, one stable boy in charge of a string of horses,
in all ten persons living in the master's house and its out-
buildings. There is no mention of *mansi* or of farms worked by
coloni. Another estate which was part of the same bequest was
the *villa Fraxnetum*, previously owned by a priest named Aper:
it was run by ten slaves (*mancipia*). Its name is significant: La
Frênaie (*Fraxnetum*), the ash-grove. It was wooded ground, in
process of being cleared, and containing within its boundaries
a hunting reserve, the copse (*breuil*) of Marcillé. Further
examples taken from the same part of the country show that
other *villae* at that time were still only waste and woodland.
The *villa Doliacus*,[2] given to Bishop Hadoin (627–650) by a
wealthy landowner in memory of his son killed by a fall from
his horse when pursuing a hind, is also referred to as *brogilus*
(breuil), a term applied to a hunting reserve.[3] The domain of
L'Anille on which the hermit St Calais built his monastery was
similar in character. According to a legend discovered by the
Le Mans chronicler, Calais had begun by building a hut there
without asking permission and King Childebert, who had
arrived to hunt, made no attempt to conceal his displeasure;
his anger afterwards subsided, and he gave the holy man as

[1] Cant. Bouloire (Sarthe). The text of the deed is given us by the *Actus*, p. 84.
[2] Douillet, cant. Fresnay (Sarthe).
[3] *Actus*, p. 142. See 'Défrichement et peuplement rural dans le Maine du IXᵉ au
XIIIᵉ siècle', *Le Moyen âge*, 1948, pp. 78–79.

much land as he could ride round in one day on his little donkey,[1] a primitive method of fixing boundaries of which other examples are to be found in the Middle Ages. If the remainder of the story is to be believed, Calais set himself eagerly to the task of clearing the land, ploughing and planting vines. These examples will suffice. They show how innumerable *villae* often came into being.

Nevertheless certain great estates had a different origin, which a careful study of the Deeds of the Bishop of Le Mans has enabled us to detect. Certain localities mentioned therein – that of Ceaulcé[2] for example – are referred to indifferently as *vicus* or *villa*. This apparent confusion dates back to the Late Empire, since from the fourth century many villages of free peasants had been sacrificing their independence, as we have already seen,[3] by putting themselves under the patronage of powerful men (*potentes*), both secular and religious. This patronage took the form of an incorporation of the village (*vicus*) into the sphere of action of a great landowner or a great abbey, and resulted in the transformation of numerous *vici* into *villae*. The method of cultivation remained, in fact, the same, but the integration into great estates of plots of lands formerly under independent ownership came about, as has already been noted, because the farmer was compelled to pay dues in money and in kind to the master of the *villa*, and also to provide him with compulsory labour. This phenomenon of integration, brought about by the weakness of small farmers, continued through the following centuries, causing the gradual disappearance of numerous *vici* and their absorption by great estates.

Whilst this process of concentration was working out to the advantage of those who owned *villae*, who were expanding their

[1] *Actus*, p. 56. For this foundation deed and the Merovingian charters of St Calais which during the ninth century gave rise to a famous lawsuit between the Bishop of Le Mans and the monks from the abbey, see Julien Havet, *Questions mérovingiennes*, pp. 103–154.

[2] Orne. 'Vicum Celsiacum.' *Actus*, p. 33. 'Villas aliquas, id est . . . Celsiacum.' Ibid., p. 267. Elsewhere Ceaulcé is termed 'vicum canonicum', p. 279. This new designation gives us reason to conclude that the *vicus* had been incorporated into the revenues of the Canons of Le Mans.

[3] See above, p. 23.

estates, and to the disadvantage of independent farmers living in *vici*, a quite contrary evolution may also be observed. Quietly and unnoticed, it affected the method of farming the land, which underwent a slow and gradual change. Under the Roman Empire the ground had usually been cultivated by gangs of slaves under the supervision of the master himself or of a bailiff (*villicus*). In each *villa* there was a *familia rustica* or band of slaves responsible for the farm work. This supply of slave labour did not cease with the coming of the Merovingian era. There were still slaves in the sixth century, as also in the following centuries. The lands granted by Bishop Domnole to the Abbey of Saint-Vincent Le Mans were handed over with the slaves who farmed them (*cum mancipiis qui ibidem excolere videntur*) and over a long period this reference to *mancipia* was to appear as a stock phrase in formulae dealing with the transfer of property. Behind this façade, however, lay a serious problem, the recruiting of a labour force which for several centuries had been steadily diminishing. The derivation of names provides a partial solution and enables us to hazard a guess at the way in which this recruiting was carried out after the Great Invasions, since the names of slaves frequently crop up in charters. Those mentioned in charters from Maine are almost all Germanic and predominantly Frankish. Since these names had no doubt been in common use from Merovingian times, it may be assumed that the men who bore them were often Gallo-Romans; but we also know, thanks to several quite explicit texts, that barbarians worked for masters who were not. One such instance is provided by Bishop Bertrand who in his will refers to the slaves, barbarian as well as Roman[1] who are in his service. Moreover, no one now disputes the fact that most of the barbarians who penetrated into the Western Empire came not as conquerors, but exactly as, in our own day, North Africans, Italians, Poles cross into Metropolitan France to look for work. In the case of the Burgundians, the fact is expressly stated by the Greek historian Socrates, who describes them crossing the Rhine to carry on in Gaul their customary trade of carpenter

[1] 616. 'Famulos meos qui michi deservire videntur tam natione romana quam et barbara.' *Actus*, p. 135.

and to earn their living in that way.[1] A slave labour force, most of it barbarian in origin, continued to work on foreign soil.

This labour force, however, had no future, for side by side with the old tradition of entrusting the cultivation of the land and all forms of manual labour to gangs of slaves, the new system of the colonate, already flourishing in the Late Empire, was steadily gaining ground. Bishop Bertrand's will, to which reference has already been made, gives proof of this, and he was a shrewd administrator. It sets free a large number of slaves; but the Bishop adds that they are to keep their savings, and can increase them by hard work, and the word used to describe this work (*laborare*) makes it clear that, however sketchy our knowledge of seventh-century terminology may be, he is referring to work in the fields, to 'husbandry'. What was to be their subsequent position in life? Is it rash to surmise that a small plot of land intended for cultivation was made over to them? Perhaps not, for in a further passage of this lengthy will, the writer refers to a house he had built at his own expense at Jublains, with out-buildings, a cowshed, gardens and '*colonicas*',[2] that is to say smallholdings for *coloni*. Here then was one estate founded at the beginning of the seventh century and run, not by a band of slaves, a *familia rustica*, but by families of *coloni* settled on small farms. The system spread, smallholdings increased in number. They are to be found in many different forms, which we shall meet again in Carolingian times. Some were slave holdings; those who farmed them still bore the stigma which clung to the *mancipia*; but they led a family life, as for instance the slave called Gaudard (*Waldardum*) who at the end of the sixth century was living with his wife and children on the *colonica* of Chenon at Coulongé in Maine.[3] Others were known as freeborn holdings either because their lessees had reaped the benefit of a general manumission or because they were freemen who had put themselves under the

[1] Socrates, *Hist. ecclesiastica*, VII, 30 (*Patrol. graeca*, vol. 67, col. 805–806).

[2] 'Domum vero Diablentes quam meo opere aedificavi, cum curte et stabulum et ortus et colonicas.' *Actus*, p. 139.

[3] 581. 'Coloneca cognominante Cannono . . . et mancipiola dua: Waldardus cum uxore sua vel infantibus eorum qui ibidem commanere videntur.' Ibid., p. 313. Coloneca = Coulongé, cant. Mayet (Sarthe).

patronage of a great landowner. There were also holdings known as *lidiles*, a name which recalls that the first to take advantage of them were *laeti*, in other words barbarians, soldier-ploughmen who had come into the Empire to offer their services to it.[1] Nevertheless these holdings all have one feature in common: they are small farms intended to provide an adequate livelihood for a man and wife and their children.

This is the crux of the whole matter. Whether the term *villa* is actually used or not, and in spite of varieties of name which reveal the differing social status of the earliest tenants, the picture which emerges is one of peasant units, uniform in structure, and standing solid and four-square against the world. Although the men who farmed these holdings, known as 'colonges' (*colonicae*) in Maine and more often *mansi* elsewhere, were not all freeholders, and though many of them were still even in a condition of slavery, all in fact lived on the land they farmed, and without actually owning it thought of it as *their* land, and handed it down to their children. The episcopal chronicler of Le Mans, writing in the ninth century, gave a quaint example of the attachment felt by the peasants in his neighbourhood towards their land, when he told with a delightful touch of imagination the story of St Martin riding along on his donkey, looking for a suitable bishop for the diocese of Le Mans, and finding some distance away from this town, a clerk named Victor working in *his own* vineyard (*in vinea sua laborans*) with great zest and vigour, turning it over with his spade, and covered in dust from head to foot.[2] In this industrious vinegrower, the peasant proprietor of our own day will recognize his forebear.

[1] Caesarius, Abbot of Prum (prov. of Trier, Germany), who in 1222 made a copy of his abbey's rent-roll, originally drawn up in 893, attempted in the commentary attached to his copy to define the various types of *mansi* mentioned in this document: *de mansis servilibus, de mansis ledilibus, de mansis ingenualibus.* Wopfner, *Urkunden zur deutschen Agrargeschichte*, p. 61. His definitions are not without interest, since they reveal the meaning attached to these terms in the early thirteenth century, but they do not hold good for the Carolingian period and are even less valid for the Merovingian. For this rent-roll see Edm. Ch. Perrin, *Recherches sur la seigneurie rurale en Lorraine*, pp. 3 and 98.

[2] *Actus*, p. 46.

CHAPTER II

Farming in the
Very Early Middle Ages (cont.):
Mansus, Villa and Husbandry

WE MUST NOW TURN to a study of the *mansus*, although the word itself did not appear before the seventh century;[1] but the small country farm it denotes goes back much earlier than Merovingian times, for, to quote a shrewd observation made by a historian whose premature death robbed us of a fine scholar, the 'meix' (*mansus*) and its successors represent 'the many varied aspects and uses of a thousand-year-old institution closely bound up with the family group and the economy of the plough'.[2] The special contribution made by the Merovingian and Carolingian eras was the planting on the soil of Western Europe of innumerable peasant families who settled there permanently. The symbol of this settlement pattern is the *mansus*. The word came into common use in the ninth century. The polyptyques of religious houses adopted it to denote sub-divisions of the *villa*; but originally the word *mansus*, from the Latin *maneo*, meant the house, the dwelling-place, the home, and not the farm. The primitive meaning has moreover been preserved in French and Provençal in the words 'meix' and 'mas',[3] but naturally, in the

[1] M. Bloch, *Les caractères originaux* . . . , p. 155.

[2] Déléage, *La vie rurale en Bourgogne au moyen âge*, I, p. 357. See also G. Roupnel's observations on the *mansus*, *Histoire de la campagne française*, p. 263.

[3] Most modern historians have kept the word in its Latinized form, fully aware, as Marc Bloch points out (ibid., p. 155, note 1), that this is a neologism. Except for a few scholars like Déléage, they have not used the dialectal variants *mas* or *meix*, since in the south and in Burgundy these bore meanings different from that attached to the word *mansus* during the Early Middle Ages, and their use might possibly have

language of diplomatic, the connotation of the word was widened and it soon came to mean both the farmer's house and the lands he cultivated.

The structure of the *mansus* has already been the subject of innumerable studies. The author of one of the most skilful and competent analyses,[1] concentrating his researches on Burgundy, a region in which the rural population lives grouped together in villages, has observed that in those areas the peasant-holding is made up of three distinct parts: the actual building which is really the *mansus* or *meix*, a piece of land known as the 'aile', small in size but fertile and carefully tended, adjoining the 'meix' and set aside for growing vegetables, and finally the group of arable lands scattered about the confines of the village. These three features are to be found in every holding, even the smallest and meanest.

This scholar has made a special study of that part known as the 'aile', a curious name which might well give rise to a false impression, and which is perhaps merely a corruption of the word *alleu*, distorted at a time when its real meaning had been lost. This land adjacent to the house and more adequately protected from the encroachments of the seigneur than other plots further away from the *mansus*, often retained its freehold character. In other parts of the country, in Champagne for instance or in Maine, it is the 'ouche' (*osca* or *olca*) which corresponds to the Burgundian 'aile'; the word deserves mention because of its antiquity, since it was already being used by Gregory of Tours with the meaning to be given to it in the ninth century by the inhabitants of Le Mans. 'Not far from the basilica', says the Frankish historian, 'there was a field which had very fertile soil; fields of this kind are called "ouches" by the local people.'[2] The great antiquity of the 'ouche', like that of the 'aile', lends support to an ingenious theory according to

led to a certain tiresome confusion. Cf. Perrin, 'Observations sur le manse dans la région parisienne au début du IXe siècle', *Ann. d'hist. soc.*, VII, 1945, p. 39, note 1, and Dubled, 'Encore la question du manse', *Revue du moyen âge latin*, 1949, pp. 203–210.

[1] P. de Saint-Jacob, 'Etudes sur l'ancienne communauté rurale en Bourgogne', *Ann. de Bourg.*, XV, 1943, pp. 173–184.

[2] Gregory of Tours, *Liber in gloria confessorum*, 78. *SS. rerum merov.*, II, p. 795.

which this part of the holding corresponds to the *terra salica* of the Salic Law, that is to the land attached to the family house, and which could not be detached from the inheritance of which it had always been an integral part, whilst the fields spread over the *Gewanndorf* represented gradual later additions as waste land was cleared and brought into cultivation.

This view of the *mansus* opens up vast new horizons, since all the small farms which in Merovingian times sprang up in such numbers all over Western Europe follow an identical pattern, although in every part of the country the *mansus* or its equivalent had its own individual modifications. In the western, or so-called forest regions of France, where the population is scattered and the village is not a closely knit community, a cluster of cultivated plots may be seen round about the dwelling house, but the terseness and vagueness of the documents defeat any attempt to fix a date at which the countryside acquired the appearance it has today. Less permeated by Roman influence than other regions, inadequately defended against anarchy and the *Bagaudae*, sparsely populated, the west, for several hundred years, had only poor, spasmodically cultivated farms, interspersed with vast tracts of waste land, and it was only in the eleventh century that the peasant smallholding gained a firm footing. It is significant that the word *mansus* remained unknown in Maine, and its equivalent the 'bordage' does not appear before A.D. 1000. The word *factus*, 'fait',[1] which has not disappeared from popular speech, and which is the Angevin equivalent of 'bordage', is of earlier date; it occurs in the ninth century in diplomas of Charles the Bald. We know even less about the south, where there is an almost total dearth of Merovingian documents.

[1] Here are two examples: 845. Donation to the Abbey of Glanfeuil: 'In villa Bidisciaco casam dominicatam . . . et *factos* decem.' *Recueil des actes de Charles le Chauve*, I, p. 222, no. 79. – 850. Donation to Saint-Maur-sur-Loire: 'In pago Andecavo, in villa Solemniaco *factos* septem et medium cum corte dominicata.' Ibid., p. 354, no. 134. Marc Bloch believes this word to be 'hopelessly mysterious' (*Les caractères originaux* . . . , p. 156) since he cannot bring himself to accept it as a derivative of *facere*. Such a derivation, however, seems quite reasonable. The Sarthe peasant still speaks of 'mon fait' when referring to his land. In his *Glossaire du parler de Plechatel (Ille-et-Vilaine)*, Rennes-Paris, 1901, p. 64, Dottin gives the following definition of the word 'fé': '(fait), bien, avoir'.

In the east the predominant pattern was the group of
dwellings with fields dispersed in cultivated zones over the
arable portions of the territory outside the settlement. This
system, whilst not excluding individual ownership, imposed
certain communal obligations on the farmer. Was it perhaps
Germanic in origin, popularized in Eastern Gaul by the
barbarians who settled there, Burgundians, Alamans and
Franks? This seems a likely possibility. In Burgundy and
Lorraine the usual term was *mansus*, but here and there in the
latter province and even more frequently in Alsace, it was
already being replaced by the word *Hufe*,[1] in Low Latin *Hoba*.
It first appears in charters of the eighth century. The *Hufe* is a
type of rural holding found in Alemania, Thuringia, Bavaria
and Saxony. The word is related to the German *Hof*, meaning
a country estate. Attempts have been made to determine the
relationship between the *Hufe* and the *mansus*, since the two
figure side by side in certain Germanic texts, but the efforts of
German scholars to throw light on this point have been as fruit-
less as they are tortuous. Some, basing their conclusions on
documents of a comparatively late date, have taken the *Hufe*
to be a vast cultivated area of which the *mansus* was only a part.
Others believe the *mansus* to have been the centre of the holding,
whilst the term *Hufe* indicated the area of ploughland allotted
to the owner in the *Gewannland*, that is to say in the cultivated
zones belonging to the village. Finally one of the latest scholars
to tackle the problem has attributed to the *mansus* and the *Hufe*
two quite distinct functions: the *mansi*, he writes,[2] were those
parts of a great estate worked by day labourers, the *Hufen* were

---

[1] The problems raised by the *Hufe* are no different from those associated with the
mansus. The varied meanings attributed to the word have been enumerated by
Kötzschke, *Allg. Wirtschaftsgesch. d. Mittelalters*, p. 260.

[2] Lütge, 'Hufe und *mansus* in den mitteldeutschen Quellen der Karolingerzeit, im
besonderen in dem *Breviarum S. Lulli*', *VSWG*, 30, 1937, pp. 105–128. The author
soon afterwards returned to this question of the *Hufe* which he examined thoroughly
and systematically in *Die Agrarverfassung*, pp. 237–279. His conclusion confirms that
reached in the article previously quoted: 'Die Hufe in ihrem strengen Sinne ist eine
Schöpfung der Grundherrschaft . . . Es war die Ordnungsform, in die der Grund-
herr seinen abhängigen Besitz brachte und es war für den Bauern zugleich eine
feste Lebensbasis, ja der Unfreie wurde erst durch die Einführung der Hufen-
ordnung zum Bauern,' p. 275. See also the very thorough study of the Germanic
Hufe made by Déléage, op. cit., I, pp. 311–340.

lands owned by peasants. None of these interpretations is satisfactory, and their very complexity should have been enough to discredit them. *Hufe* and *mansus* are terms which, if not exactly interchangeable, are at least similar;[1] both denote a family smallholding, and the two words have undergone a parallel evolution. The *Hufe*, like the *mansus*, at first meant the central point of the peasant farm, though it cannot be stated with certainty that the word was originally applied to the peasant's dwelling. By degrees it came to mean a unit of cultivation, perhaps even, as one contemporary historian has ingeniously suggested, 'a customary area determined by the amount of land which could be worked by one plough in a year'.[2]

However that may be, one point must be emphasized: land clearance in Germany was a long, slow process and was achieved almost everywhere at the expense of the forest. Hence, in descriptions of recently created peasant farms, certain features which distinguish the old Germanic *Hufe* from the *mansus* of the Roman zone. The first point to note is that although it took place at a later date, no more is known about the initial clearing of Germany than about that of other regions. We need not linger over the legend of *Markgenossenschaft* which is now almost completely rejected. There was no such thing as agrarian communism in the early stages, and the land was cleared and brought into cultivation by the efforts of isolated individuals or groups of individuals, and not of anonymous collectives.[3]

[1] This opinion is held by Eberhard Schmieder, 'Hufe und *mansus*. Eine quellenkritische Untersuchung', *VSWG*, 31, 1938, pp. 348–356: 'Es scheint dass der eine Begriff (*Hufe*) der Volksmässige, der andere der Gelehrte sei.' This point of view is shared by Marc Bloch, 'La *Hufe*', *Ann. d'hist. éc. et soc.*, X, 1938, pp. 453–455. The Viennese historian Dopsch, however, refuses to attach an exact meaning to the term *Hufe*: 'Hufe ist also im allgemeinen ein mehr neutraler Begriff, etwa wie unser deutsches Wort Hof und Gut.' *Wirtschaftsentwicklung der Karolingerzeit*, p. 312.

[2] Déléage, op. cit., p. 339.

[3] K. Wührer, *Beiträge zur ältesten Agrargeschichte des Germanischen Nordens*, stresses the example of the Scandinavian peoples and in particular of the Icelanders to support his theory that from the very beginning there was in Germany individual and not collective appropriation of the land. Similarly, Fr. Lütge, editor of a posthumous work by Georg von Below already quoted, *Gesch. der deutschen Landwirtschaft*, emphasizes in an additional note of his own (p. 19), that in many contemporary studies the conclusion has been reached that 'in frühgermanischer Zeit das Einzelgehöft oder Weilersiedlung vorherrschend war'. This is, moreover, his own conclusion in the closing chapter of his *Die Agrarverfassung des frühen Mittelalters* which he entitled 'Zur Frage der Struktur der ältesten Siedlungen', pp. 333–351.

Unfortunately only a few transient gleams of light illuminate
the dark past, and even they shine only on the last century of
the Merovingian era. The truth is that we know hardly anything at all, since written documentation began in Germany
only with the spreading of Christianity at the beginning of the
eighth century, but that was also the time when the great landowners undertook their so-called civilizing mission which
obscured the work done by the early pioneers of land clearance.
Nevertheless, sporadic though they may be, these occasional
shafts of light may yield some information of value.

One example is given us by a certain Liudger[1] who, after
buying a plot of land covered with woods and pastures, broke
it up and ploughed it. He then exchanged this *Hufe* (hovam),
which he had brought back into cultivation, for a fallow plot
(rothum), but without surrendering all his rights over the plot
he had handed over to his neighbour, keeping for himself all
those rights of forest and of pasturage to which possession of the
original *Hufe* had entitled him. This document has not only the
merit of showing us how enterprising pioneers brought into
cultivation waste land reclaimed from the forest. Taken in conjunction with other early medieval charters, it helps to give us
some idea of what a small country farm was like in Germany.
The general lay-out was as follows. First came the peasant's
house, completed by a shed for storing grain, a stable, courtyard,
kitchen garden, the whole often surrounded by a fence; next
came the arable lands divided into quarters, and this part of the
farm increased as land clearance progressed. Finally the Germanic village group was completed and stamped with its own
peculiar character by a belt of forest and pasture, which could
not be annexed by any individual or family. This was the *marca
communis*; all who lived in the settlement had the right to use
it, the right to gather firewood and wood for building and
cooperage, the right to take their cattle and particularly their pigs
to graze in it. The words, defined in this way, are quite clear
in meaning, and it was only because sociologist historians were
obsessed with preconceived ideas about the communal nature

[1] 'Niederrhein. Tausch von Rotland zu Wynberg gegen eine Hufe zu Fischlaken'
(799), in H. Wöpfner, *Urkunden zur Agrargeschichte*, p. 36, no. 19.

of early Germanic society that they maintained that the *marca communis* denoted the sum total of land belonging to the village.

In support of their theory, these sociologists have also quoted Section 45 of the Salic Law: *De migrantibus*.[1] Its three clauses lay down what is to happen to the man who moves to a new place and who, made welcome by some of the inhabitants of the village (*villa*) in which he wishes to live, comes up against one or two others who accuse him of trying to settle on another man's land. Lengthy proceedings ensue, ending in the expulsion of the unwelcome stranger, the relinquishing of the land he had started to plough and his condemnation to a fine of 30 gold *sous* if the inhabitants hostile to the intruder persist in their refusal. If on the other hand the newcomer meets with no opposition during the first twelve months of his stay he can, the law adds, live in the village just like the other 'neighbours' (*vicini*). A kind of mystique has grown up around these 'neighbours' and as Fustel wittily remarked[2] it has been carried to the point where the Frankish village was envisaged as a closed circle which only those unanimously voted in by the inhabitants could join, just as members are elected to a select club. In an attempt to explain this procedure, one French historian has maintained that all the inhabitants possessed the right of common ownership over the 'march'.[3] The real explanation is, however, far simpler. Anyone who has ever lived in the country knows that the coming of an outsider to a village is an event of great importance, simply because of the close daily contacts which govern the lives of those who live in it. There is therefore no need at all to presuppose a régime of agrarian communism in order to explain the right of veto which the Salic Law allowed to each inhabitant. In an age when rural law and order were still rudimentary, villagers had to take matters into their own hands, and the arrival of a stranger was inevitably a source of anxiety. For further proof of this we have only to glance through the numerous clauses in barbarian laws devoted to the suppression of theft, assault and battery and homicide. The

---

[1] 'Pactus Legis salicae', ed. K. Aug. Eckhardt, *Die Gesetze des Merowingerreiches*, 1935, Weimar, pp. 66–68.   [2] *L'alleu et le domaine rural*, p. 187.
[3] Glasson, *Institutions de la France*, III, pp. 71–82.

law-makers thought it wise to give villagers some means of defence against the intrusion of suspicious strangers.

What a study of the Salic Law does bring out, on the contrary, is the strong preference of the Franks for individual ownership. Section 27, on diverse thefts (*de furtis diversis*),[1] is significant for the wide range of crimes it covers: turning cattle into another man's cornfield, breaking into *his* kitchen garden, stealing flax from *his* land, cutting hay in *his* meadow, gathering *his* grapes, ploughing *his* field. All these clauses, and others as well, in which offences are specified with a wealth of minute detail, prove with what jealous care the rights of ownership, and those of the small landowner, were defended by the Franks. One single word, which has had an extraordinary history, symbolizes the sacrosanctity of hereditary property – it is the word 'alleu' (*alodis*). In the very beginning this word stood for the ancestral home and its appendages. Subsequently it was extended to include the arable lands. The 'alleu' could be handed down only in the male line, not because women were without legal rights or were prevented from becoming landowners, but because it was believed that the male sex alone had the strength and ability to cultivate the land. It is important to stress the nature of the 'alleu' as it is revealed in the oldest known version of the Salic Law, dating from the end of the fifth century. This makes it clear that the Frankish occupation strengthened the small peasant and family holding in those areas in which the Franks settled, and the same may be said of those parts of the Western Empire where other Germanic races took root. If this type of tenure did not spread even more extensively, it was because it came up against the obstacle of an irresistible evolution which even before the Great Invasions had been taking place within the Empire to the advantage of the *potentes*, the great landowners. Small farms by no means disappeared, but they were often compelled to become part of the *villae*. Even those which stood out against such absorption gradually in their turn, but at a later date, ended by losing their complete autonomy, and under the pressure of feudal anarchy were brought within the

[1] Ed. Eckhardt, pp. 36–41. See P. Riché, *Les Invasions barbares* (coll. Que sais-je?), p. 78.

jurisdiction of a rural seigneurie, for we shall see that one consequence of this incorporation was a drastic curtailing of the rights of owners. The fact remains, however, that in spite of the encroachment of the great estates, the Merovingian age saw an increase in the number of small farms and smallholdings, and that these fulfilled, though still imperfectly it is true, the secret longing of every peasant – to have a plot of land big enough to support a family and which can be handed down to his descendants. The terms *mansus* and *Hufe* were used on the Continent to denote these family holdings; in Great Britain the usual word was *hide*, which in the seventh century Bede aptly defined in a phrase which can also be applied to its two counterparts: '*Portio unius familiae.*' [1]

In actual fact this small family unit, whether known as *mansus, colonge, Hufe* or hide, remained very much in the background until the Carolingian age; even then it was rarely mentioned in documents. It was only at the close of the eighth century that the *mansus* came into the limelight and appeared in numerous texts. Yet the meaning of the word was to remain fluid, like that of many others in an age when the careful and accurate use of vocabulary was almost non-existent. It is, however, very doubtful whether the *mansus*, as has been asserted, came to mean an agrarian unit of measurement, and the attempts made to calculate its area have yielded only vague and disappointing results. It appears to have varied from 12 to 70 acres according to the locality. [2] There would, moreover, have been no point in measuring a holding which often consisted not

---

[1] Déléage, op. cit., pp. 306–307.
[2] See Marc Bloch, *Les caractères originaux* . . . , pp. 158–159; Ch. Edm. Perrin, 'Observations sur le manse dans la région parisienne', *Ann. d'hist. soc.*, VIII, pp. 39–52; Déléage, op. cit., pp. 340–349; G. Roupnel, *Hist. de la camp. fr.*, p. 262. The latter states that all the calculations made regarding the area of the *mansus* end by assigning to it an average size of approximately 10 to 12 hectares (25 to 30 acres) and concludes: 'L'évidence s'impose: le manse est l'étendue normale de l'exploitation individuelle. Il correspond a une réalité de tous les temps et de tous les pays.' He then adds this very significant remark: 'Ce qui donne au manse sa réelle valeur, c'est moins son étendue que sa composition et sa stabilité. Il nous apparaît, en effet, constitué presque toujours de trois éléments agraires: champs arables, prés et bois.' See also the remarks of F. L. Ganshof, 'Manorial Organisation in the Seventh, Eighth and Ninth Centuries', *Transactions of the Royal Historical Society*, 4th Series, 31, 1949, p. 45.

of one compact block, but of several plots in different places. The *mansus*, in fact, expressed a reality which could not be translated into figures; it was the amount of land needed for one household to live on. It varied from one region, and even from one locality to another, according to their fertility. A further element also had to be taken into account – the manner of life adopted by those living on the *mansus*. There were, for example, ecclesiastical *mansi*; these were endowments meant to supply the needs of priests in charge of churches. Carolingian legislation laid down that these *mansi* should have a minimum area of 40 acres.[1] Insistence on such a substantial minimum was perhaps dictated not simply by solicitude for the clergy; the *mansus*, in fact, had to provide a living not only for the priest whose time was fully taken up with parish duties, but also for the serfs who cultivated it. This first picture of the *mansus* already gives us an important clue to the difference between two economic systems, that of the Early Middle Ages and our own. Money had not disappeared from circulation after the Great Invasions, and we shall see that even in the ninth century, that is to say when the closed economy was probably at its peak, there were still people in Gaul buying wheat, barley and oats; but it was more usual for a man to get enough for his own needs from his own land, and it was estimated that this result could be achieved by owning and farming a *mansus*. The *mansus* was the essential minimum for a peasant household, the equivalent of the monthly wage of 20,000 to 25,000 francs now thought of as the bare minimum for a family to live on, and the few silver deniers carefully hoarded in a chest were merely a reserve from which, if need be, he could make an outside purchase when his own land could not provide him with enough to satisfy his modest needs. No great stretch of imagination is needed to picture how a *colonus* or a free peasant family lived in the Early Middle Ages; we have only to think back to the way of life still prevalent half a century ago in certain of our remote mountain villages, which had no road leading to them, and could be reached only after a hard climb up a steep mule track.

*

[1] M. Bloch, op. cit., p. 159.

The great estates continued to spread during the Mero-vingian period. One word, *villa*, has been used to denote the great domain, but before this old word, used by the ancient Romans for a country house, acquired a hard and fast meaning, it was borrowed by the fifth-century Franks to describe a small settlement, a hamlet of several houses, the term *vicus* being re-served for older and more important villages. This meaning did not persist. As the various legal deeds, gifts, sales, wills in-volving great estates increased in number, the word *villa* was definitely applied to them in Merovingian times, although as we shall see it had not entirely gone out of use for other purposes.

What exactly was a *villa*? It has been ingeniously defined by Marc Bloch:[1] 'An area of land so organized that the greater part of the profits drawn from it accrue directly or indirectly to a single master.' The definition is simple enough to cover the many different types of *villa* revealed by a study of the docu-ments, but at the same time sufficiently accurate, since it stresses the basic characteristic of every *villa*, which was that it belonged to a master. The *villa* might be simply a hunting re-serve, a 'breuil' (*brolium*), as we have already seen, but more often it was a country estate given over entirely, or in part, to farming. The organization of the *villa* slowly and gradually took on a uniform pattern. Most great estates were divided into two sections: the first was reserved for the master (*dominus*); this was the *indominicatum*. It consisted of his own house with out-buildings which are referred to by names which are still vague and scanty in Merovingian charters. Descriptions of this part of the villa are not to be found earlier than the cartularies and polyptyques of the Carolingian era, but to gain some idea of what the *dominicum* (demesne) was like in the time of the Merovingian kings, we have only to imagine the buildings and outhouses of a large farm in Picardy or Beauce, since the luxury and amenities of the fine houses described by Ausonius and Sidonius Apollinaris no longer existed. Moreover, the grandees of the Merovingian age usually owned several estates in different parts of the kingdom, so that there was often only

[1] *Les caractères originaux . . .* , p. 67.

a steward (*villicus*), the manager of the *villa*, actually living in the *dominicum*.

Before a great estate could be properly run, it had to be staffed and equipped, and before all else a fairly large labour force had to be recruited to cultivate it. Up to the end of the ninth century the texts almost always refer to the slaves (*mancipia*) who were attached to the *villa*. These slaves worked on the reserve or demesne, that is the part of the domain which was farmed directly, but from the seventh century onwards the charters begin to mention what in the Carolingian era was to make up the second and largest part of the domain, the *mansi*[1] or 'colonges'. These were no new feature of rural life, since the colonate, as we have seen, was an institution dating back to the Late, perhaps even the Early Empire. It underwent in Merovingian times an expansion which sprang from a kind of inner necessity. In a period of economic stagnation, the most efficient method of running an estate, of preventing it from reverting to waste land and of getting the best out of it, was to plant peasant families on the various farms and to allow them free use of the land, exacting in return dues in kind, as for instance a share of their harvest and several days' work on the reserve. The benefit was mutual, since the system gave security to the small farmer who, in a world where metal currency was scarce, had little or no opportunity of earning money by the work of his hands, or of selling his farm produce, but who now found himself settled on a *mansus* which would provide a living for his family and which he had permission to hand on to his children.

*

A further original characteristic of the *mansus*, as of its counterparts, was that it became a recognized method of remuneration for a wide variety of services. The priest in charge of the church on the great estate would receive as payment a presbyterial *mansus*. The man who received a grant of land in reward for his services was known by the one word *casatus*, that is a man given a homestead of his own, a title which was applied to men of the

[1] See for example *Traditio Amalfridi de eadem cella*, of 8 February 685 (*Cart. de S. Bertin*, p. 29, no. XI), in which reference is made to *mansi* (*cum terris, mansis*).

most widely differing status. Side by side with the *servus casatus* was the mounted warrior for whom his grant of land was the equivalent of pay. At the court of the early Frankish kings lived a host of 'antrustions' who made up the royal following, pure parasites known as the king's guests and also as the 'kept men'. By degrees, and especially when cavalry took the place of infantry in the armies, the kings dropped the practice of feeding their followers and 'guests' at the royal table. The burden had become too heavy, especially as the horses had to be cared for at the same time. This reform was carried out in the reign of Charles Martel, who with considerable harshness and brutality had no hesitation in seizing Church property for distribution to his men.

Under an economic system in which metal currency tends to become scarcer, a man's wealth is assessed chiefly by the amount of land he owns. Great fortunes are principally fortunes in land. One such was that of Bertrand, Bishop of Le Mans, who owned a large number of *villae* in Maine, Bordelais and Northern Gaul, but who also, like his forebears, possessed metal currency, judging from the bequests contained in his will. This personal wealth, consisting of gold and silver coins, and doubtless ingots as well, was most highly prized. Gregory of Tours records that his contemporary Chilperic I one day showed him several gold medallions bearing the effigy of the Emperor which he was preserving as if they were museum pieces. Whenever a Frankish king won a victory his first care was to seize his adversary's treasure.

New fortunes were amassed during Merovingian times. Heirs to vast imperial revenues, the barbarian kings shared them out amongst their vassals, so that the upstart Frankish aristocracy soon rivalled in wealth the old Gallo-Roman senatorial nobility. This fact explains why so many places in the Ile-de-France, that is to say in districts adjacent to the two capitals of the kingdoms of Neustria and Austrasia, Paris and Metz, have Germanic personal names prefixed to the place-names *ville, villers, court*, as for instance Courville, Contrexeville, Rambertvillers, Gondrecourt.[1] These were lands rich in game, and sometimes also

[1] Aug. Longnon, *Les noms de lieu*, 2ᵉ fasc., *passim*, and especially F. Lot, 'De l'origine et de la signification des noms de lieu en *ville* et *court*', *Romania*, XIX, 1933, pp. 199–246.

good farm land, which the Merovingian kings distributed to their followers in order to win their adherence. Beauce was probably opened up to cultivation at this period; from this time too probably dates the great forest belt surrounding Paris, Marly, Saint-Germain, Fontainebleau and Orleans, for the noblemen of the age were passionately devoted to hunting.

The Church contributed extensively to the proliferation of the *villae*. The heroic age of poverty having worked itself out, the monks fitted themselves into the economic pattern of their time, a fact which is proved by the geographical distribution of monastic foundations in Merovingian times. More will be said later of the monasteries founded on the outskirts of towns and which were largely responsible for the increase in their numbers. Yet a more spectacular illustration of the effective work of the religious communities is to be seen in the results obtained by those monasteries founded far away from towns, in regions still sparsely cultivated, where they created not only centres of religious life, but also of economic and particularly of agricultural activity. On one point, however, there must be no misunderstanding. The chief aim of those who founded these establishments was predominantly spiritual. A study of the Rule drawn up by St Benedict for the guidance of his monks at Monte Cassino makes this abundantly clear. It made manual work (*opera manuum*) compulsory, not only for the sake of producing wealth, but in order to combat what St Benedict believed to be the soul's greatest enemy – idleness (*otiositas*).[1] It was a principle universally accepted that monks should work with their hands. Some broke up the ground with hoes; others cut wood with axes and shaped it with mattocks; some went considerable distances in search of water, wrote the author of the Life of St Guénolé, first Abbot of Landevenec.[2] Yet this division of labour, joyfully accepted, was only a means of allowing those

---

[1] *Histoire de l'Eglise* published under the direction of Fliche and Martin, IV, p. 595. Cf. *Inspiration religieuse et structures temporelles*, Lyons, 1948, pp. 214–217 (Coll. Bases de l'humanisme). The authors have endeavoured to outline the principles of monastic economy from a study of the Rule of St Benedict.
[2] Life of St Guénolé, chap. VI, *Cart. de Landevenec* (ed. A. de la Borderie, pp. 66–67).

who prayed to follow their spiritual calling without being harassed by material cares. Productivity and preoccupations of an economic nature remained in the background; nevertheless if we examine the map of the West, it is quite clear that in spite of the predominance of the spiritual element, so stubbornly upheld, and in the very nature of things, these monasteries were centres of land clearance and of agricultural progress, and so became as it were focal points of activity and contributed to the enrichment of the community.

A monastery like that of Fontenelle, founded in 645 by a pious personage named Wandrille on a site covered with brushwood and swamp on the banks of the Seine in the diocese of Rouen, became in three-quarters of a century a fabulously wealthy abbey,[1] enjoying an immense fortune in land as well as in personal property, since not only endowments of land, but gifts of precious metal flowed into its treasury. The monks set squads of men to clear these lands, and a whole district benefited from this stimulus given to the local economy. A similar phenomenon may be observed in many parts of the same region. Not far from Saint-Wandrille is the Abbey of Jumièges; further to the east is that group of vast monasteries Saint-Riquier, Saint-Bertin and Corbie. Austrasia has Stavelot, Prüm and Murbach. By settling at the foot of the Vosges, and particularly at Luxeuil, St Colombanus created centres of agricultural life in spite of the rigidity of the Irish Rule. Land clearance in Gaul and also in Italy was speeded up by the presence of these establishments, moral entities whose fate was not bound up with that of any single human life. Their permanence ensured the slow and steady progress of land clearance in the districts they dominated. It can be stated categorically that if in a vast area around Moissac or Saint-Benoît-sur-Loire cultivation went patiently and methodically forward, this was due to the guidance and advice issuing from the abbeys most interested in its progress. The polyptyque of Irminon, a supremely important Carolingian document, gives us invaluable information about the activity of a great abbey.

It would be easy to sneer at the contrasts existing between the

[1] F. Lot, *Etudes critiques sur l'abbaye de Saint-Wandrille*, p. xiii et seq.

detachment from worldly things ordained by the canonical and monastic Rules, and the prosperity of the religious houses. Yet the landed wealth which abbeys and sees owed to the generosity of the faithful, and the substantial income earned for them by skilful administration, were in fact balanced by the services these establishments rendered to the public: help given to the poor, the sick and travellers.[1] The problem raised by the increasing number and size of the great ecclesiastical and secular estates deserves a closer study. It is not merely a question of excusing monks apparently disloyal to their vow of poverty by finding a reason for their lapse. The real cause was to be found in the economic structure of the Merovingian age. Modern man, whether living in town or in the country, finds within easy reach, in small local shops or large department stores, in markets or in fairs, everything to satisfy his needs whether it be food, clothing, accommodation, light and fuel or articles in common use; his work, his income, his salary, his pay, even his retirement pension, bring in enough money to pay for what he has to buy. The public services come to his help; they keep the roads and streets in repair, organize means of transport by land, river or sea. Under the Roman Empire a state system, cumbersome it is true but efficient, dealt out free or cheap distributions which eased the living conditions of the common people in the towns. Under the Merovingians this manna no longer came down from Heaven; man was left henceforth to fend for himself and the problem of satisfying the most urgent demands of material existence presented almost insuperable difficulties. The simplest and perhaps the only effective way of meeting them was for a man to seek refuge on a great domain and ask its owner for a plot of land to cultivate. There at least he was sure of corn for his bread, acorns in the forest for fattening his pigs, a vineyard to provide him with wine, beehives to give him wax for candles, and on the 'ouche' he grew flax which the women, working in the workshop of the *villa* – the gynaeceum – wove into cloth for his garments; lastly in the *marca communis* he could gather wood for fuel and for building, repairing and furnishing his house. In the widespread upheaval caused not by the Moslem

[1] See *Inspiration religieuse et structures temporelles*, pp. 180–189.

invasion and the break-up of the Mediterranean economy, but more simply by the general 'barbarization' and the disintegration of the state, the *villa*, the great domain, became an attractive oasis.

The all-pervading wretchedness and poverty of a world in which the whole economic system had been put out of gear frequently compelled the bishops, who had become the real rulers of many cities, to take on a host of varied responsibilities which in normal times would be assumed by the public services of the state: the building of aqueducts and town ramparts, the distribution of public assistance to the poor who, entered on the church registers, were known as *matricularii*, the provision of hospitality to travellers and the sick in hostels named *xenodochia*. [1] The same urgent need forced the monks who in the early days of monasticism lived apart from the world in the forests of the Jura or on an island off the Mediterranean coast, to renounce their solitude and set up near towns or in less depopulated regions great abbeys surrounded by vast areas suitable for cultivation, and with workshops methodically planned to supply their needs and those of their dependants. These became havens of refuge which must have exerted an almost magnetic attraction, material as well as spiritual, to men of the sixth and seventh centuries. If the life they offered was austere and disciplined, it held also the promise of security. The Merovingian age was therefore the great period of monastic expansion. Most of the monasteries in Gaul which survived until the Revolution were founded at this time; kings and nobles lavishly endowed them with huge tracts of cultivable land in a passion of generosity which verged on the reckless; never again were they to show themselves so gracious. This expansion was to continue under the Carolingians, but times had changed. Public authority was no longer in eclipse, and under Pepin the Short, and still more under Charlemagne, there was to be a vigorous attempt at a planned economy. Consequently and

---

[1] On the subject of *xenodochia* see Dom Leclercq's article on Hospitals, *Dict. arch. chrétienne*, VI, 2, col. 2748–2770 and Lesne, *Histoire de la propriété ecclésiastique*, I, p. 146: 'Eglises et monastères prennent le rôle d'un dispensaire qui fournit aux besoins des infirmes et des indigents un abri qui recueille toutes les épaves d'une société bouleversée.'

inevitably, the monks no longer played the same rôle as before in economic life.

*

The predominance of agriculture was undoubtedly the out-standing feature of Merovingian life, and it received a fresh impetus from the Germanic invasion. The large number of clauses which the earliest compilers of the Salic Law devoted to rural law and order show how important it was in the life of the Frankish people; it was for a predominantly agricultural population that this law was drawn up.

This agriculture had evolved gradually; Mediterranean and Germanic influences intermingled in the process; it was already a polyculture. Compulsory rotation of crops, use of the com-munal forest by the villagers, and other customs brought in by the invaders penetrated into the interior of Gaul, whilst the cultivation of southern vines and fruit trees spread as far north as the banks of the Rhine and the Moselle. If this variety was made possible by a temperate climate, it was also one of the 'fruits' of history and it became apparent in the sixth century and not on the great estates alone. The *colonus* of Merovingian times expected his *mansus* to produce a variety of crops sufficient to satisfy all the needs of his existence.

Corn still continued to be the staple crop, since bread was already the basic article of diet. There was a hierarchy of grain. Rye and barley bread were held in low esteem. For reaping and threshing, which was done by horses treading out the sheaves on the threshing-floor, and for winnowing through a riddle, an ample labour-force was employed, and already, as in the countryside today, there was a system of mutual help between neighbours. Two picturesque descriptions by Gregory of Tours[1] show us farmers in Limagne assembling for these tasks as many as 70 workers[2] whom they supplied with food and drink. But this collaboration organized for the harvest does not imply any measure of agrarian communism. The rights of the owner[3] of

---

[1] *De gloria martyrum*, Book I, chap. 84 (ed. Bordier): *Les livres des miracles*, I, p. 234, and *De gloria confessorum* (same ed.), II, p. 342.

[2] 'Jam operariis in segete collocatis circa septuaginta.' Ibid.

[3] One account mentions the presence of the '*domnus fundi*'. Ibid.

the field and the harvest are stated quite categorically in numerous clauses of the Salic Law. From the moment the corn began to spring no one was allowed to walk through a ploughed field. One whole section[1] is devoted to the reparation for damage caused by animals to another man's harvest. Breach of close is strictly forbidden. Private ownership was absolute.

To the credit of Merovingian civilization should be attributed the popularization of the water-mill, known to the Romans. There were already several in Gaul in the time of Ausonius, but as Marc Bloch said, the water-mill was medieval in its expansion.[2] It was still rare enough in the sixth century for a rich Visigoth, a neighbour of the Abbot of Loches, to be jealous of him for installing one in his monastery on the Indre.[3] He constructed one on his own domain and tried to divert the water from the mill-race which turned the wheel of the abbey mill. It was the desire to economize in manpower which brought it into general use, since the grindstone or the stone roller had to be worked by men or animals and were extremely laborious. In Frankish villages the mill belonged to the miller and when a theft was committed there the culprit paid two fines, one to the miller, the other to the owner of the stolen corn.[4] Communal mills, material symbols of a village organization which failed to

[1] 'De damno in messe vel qualibet clausura inlatum' (ed. Eckhardt, p. 14).

[2] Marc Bloch, 'Avènement et conquêtes du moulin à eau', *Ann. d'hist. éc. et soc.*, VII, 1935, pp. 538–565. After enumerating the ancestors of the water-mill, the last of which was a grindstone turned by a man or animal, Bloch estimates that the oldest example dated probably from 120 to 63 B.C., but it was only after the Great Invasions that the need to develop this old invention made itself felt.

[3] 'Dum . . . fratres, molam manu vertentes, triticum ad victus necessaria comminuerent, pro labore fratrum visum est ei [to Ursus, Abbot of Loches]molendinum in ipso Angeris fluvii alveo stabilire . . . hoc opere laborem monachorum relevans.' Gregory of Tours, *Vitae patrum*, chap. 18 (ed. Bordier), *Livre des miracles*, III, p. 364. This text proves that the installing of a water-mill, described in minute detail, was meant to effect a saving in manpower. The following document, dating from the early tenth century, shows the amazement still being evoked by the water-mill even at that late date: 'Ibi etiam, quod mirabile nostris hactenus monstratur temporibus, molendinum fecit volvere aquis contra montem currentibus.' *Cart. S. Bertin* (ed. Guérard, p. 67, no. xlviii).

[4] See Section 22, 'De furtis in molino commissis', *Pactus Legis salicae* (ed. Eckhardt, p. 30).

keep itself intact, gradually disappeared, driven out by the mills on the great estates. These increased in number and in many descriptions of *villae* mention is made of one or more mills to be found on them. Something in the nature of a monopoly was building up to the advantage of the great landowners. The mill was becoming 'banal'.

Stock-rearing held a by no means negligible place in Merovingian agriculture. Plough oxen and cattle figure in the inventories. Bulls were reared for breeding. A stallion was referred to as *communis* by the Salian Franks, a further proof of village organization. There was one to every three villages, and the amount of the fine inflicted on anyone who stole it shows how highly this stud animal was prized.[1] They also reared sheep, ewes, goats and horses, which were tethered by one leg in the fields to prevent them from escaping. Cattle were grazed on *prata* and *pascua*. The *prata* were mowing fields in which the hay was cut then loaded on to carts and kept for fodder during the cold weather. The name *pascua* was applied to pastureland which was either arable land being rested or waste. In winter the cattle were shut up in byres and their dung collected for manure. In certain parts of the country flocks were moved for the summer (*ad aestivandum*) to Alpine pastures (*saltus montenses*).[2]

Vegetables were grown in the garden[3] or enclosure adjoining the house: turnips, beans, peas, lentils. In the 'ouches' and the fields, flax also was sown, as well as other textile plants which were spun in village workshops or in those of the *villa* to which the *mansus* was attached. The Franks were familiar with fruit trees, apple and pear,[4] but since these are mentioned only in the eighth-century appendices (*extravagantes*) of the Salic Law, it seems likely that they were introduced into the North comparatively late. Bee-keeping, on the other hand, was already

---

[1] Op. cit., Section 3, Clause 5, p. 8.

[2] Gregory of Tours, *De gloria martyrum*, I, 17 (ed. Bordier, *Livre des miracles*, I, p. 336).

[3] Gregory of Tours in the *Vitae patrum*, XII (ed. Bordier, III, p. 290), relates the life of the hermit Similian who had retired to Pionsat in Combraille and had contrived a patch of garden which provided him with the vegetables he needed for food.

[4] Extravagantes Legis Salicae, 27, 6a and 6c (ed. Eckhardt, p. 104).

well developed there when the oldest text of the Salic Law was drawn up. One old section is devoted to it,[1] a proof that there were large numbers of hives.' The lack of oil drove the people of the non-Mediterranean regions to an early and intensive production of wax.

Wood was cut in the communal forests where the villagers had common rights, though the exercise of these was controlled. The trees a man wished to reserve for his own use were marked with a sign, and this mark was an act of appropriation valid for one year. 'Affouage', the right to cut firewood, is perhaps no more than a survival of this ancient practice. During the Merovingian era the custom of taking pigs to feed in the communal forest became general. No single usage has been so persistent as this right to the acorn crop, the right of pannage. Germanic in origin, it spread throughout the greater part of Gaul. From Merovingian times the pig was of considerable importance as an article of food. Sixteen clauses of one of the first sections of the Salic Law[2] deal with thefts of pigs, and the wide range of contingencies covered proves the importance of pig-breeding. Sucking pigs, weaners, sows in pig, one- and two-year-olds are dealt with in turn, the amount of the wergeld varying with the sex and age of the animal concerned. Herds of swine, often of considerable size and sometimes numbering more than fifty, were driven into the forest in charge of a swineherd.

The Franks came to the vine as part of their Roman inheritance.[3] Already during the Late Empire vineyards had been planted in the valley of the Moselle and on the banks of the Rhine, but the cultivation of the vine gradually spread in the most amazing way. Religious observance, the sacrament of the Mass, the ritual of Holy Communion, formerly offered in two kinds – bread and wine – helped both to diffuse and to ennoble it. For every church in Christendom a daily provision of wine was essential and since difficulties of communication made transport

[1] Section 8: 'De furtis apium' (same ed., p. 12).
[2] Section 2, ibid., p. 4.
[3] See the excellent article by R. Dion, 'Viticulture ecclésiastique et viticulture princière au moyen âge', *Revue historique*, July–September 1954, pp. 1–22.

uncertain[1] vineyards were planted in ever-growing numbers even at the risk of producing only mediocre wine. The early medieval cultivation of the vine in countries which had a cold climate has led to a theory that they enjoyed a higher temperature at that time. Such was not the case. The only valid conclusion to be drawn is that they produced bad wine and made the best of it.

It is obvious that the drinking of wine became fairly widespread at an early date, and even in the monasteries, where food and drink were regulated with excessive strictness, wine was never completely banished from the monks' table. Moreover the place occupied by wine in the liturgy helped as much as did the Roman tradition to confer upon it a prestige it still enjoys today. The miracle of the marriage at Cana, the solemn homage paid to wine by Jesus himself and by his Mother, had the effect of increasing its popularity. This miracle, like all those performed by Christ, was echoed in the hagiography of the Early Middle Ages. The biographers of St Remi and St Airy, Merovingian Bishops of Rheims and Verdun, show them placed in situations as critical as that of their Divine Master in Cana and like him miraculously filling empty barrels with wine. Fortified by these examples, bishops did not scorn to take an interest in their cellars and their stocks of wine, and it has even been suggested, with some justification, that the desire for good vineyards near their residence made several prelates decide to move their episcopal seat. Saint-Quentin may thus have been abandoned in favour of Noyon which was more favourably placed for wine-growing, and the same reason may explain the transfer of the Bishopric of Tongres to Liège. In reading Gregory of Tours it is tempting to believe that his great-grandfather of the same name, who was Bishop of Langres, made his permanent home in Dijon which was only a simple

[1] Commenting on a further memoir on the vine by Dion, *Grands traits d'une géographie viticole de la France*, Lucien Febvre recalls that vineyard and transport were synonymous. A vinegrowing district must of necessity be an area served by navigable waterways or situated, like the vineyards of Champagne, near an ancient capital. *Annales E.S.C.*, 2, 1947, pp. 284–287. That explains why the vine was developed in certain regions such as Champagne, where natural conditions were not particularly favourable to its cultivation.

4. The baptism of Christ; and below, Christ blessing the water jars at Cana. About 1100 (from *Sacramentaire de St Etienne de Limoges*, présénté par Jean Porcher. Editions Nomis, pl. iii)

castrum because the town was surrounded by fertile hillsides covered with vines, from which the inhabitants obtained such a noble 'Falernian' that they preferred it to the wine of Ascalon. The information is of the greatest interest, since it is the earliest known reference to the excellence of the wines of Burgundy.[1] It is pleasant to speculate that the Merovingian bishops may not even have been ashamed to tend their vines themselves. Have we not already[2] seen St Martin raising to the episcopate of Le Mans a vinegrower-deacon who was digging in his vineyard? Legendary though it may be, the anecdote related by the official chronicler of the bishopric still opens up interesting possibilities.

Originating on the shores of the Mediterranean, vinegrowing spread with astonishing speed during the Late Empire and the following centuries, even reaching the shores of the North Sea. Nevertheless it was not acclimatized in Germany where they brewed beer, a beverage made from a 'decoction of cereals and barley'. More fastidious than our contemporaries, the men of the Early Middle Ages did not drink pure water;[3] those monks who were bound by the strictest rules mixed it with fruit juices or juices from tree-bark. St Radegunda, who practised a rigid asceticism, used to quench her thirst with water flavoured with pear juice.[4]

The astounding spread of viticulture had strange results. Since everyone who owned a plot of land had a vineyard, production very soon became excessive, but the seigneurs attempted to remedy this tiresome state of affairs by creating the right of 'banvin', by which their tenants as well as the other inhabitants of the seigneurie, were forbidden to sell their harvest so long as they themselves had not disposed of their own. By

[1] 'A parte autem occidente montes sunt uberrimi vineis repleti qui tam nobile incolis falernum porrigunt ut respuant Cabillonum.' *Hist. Franc.*, III, 19. According to G. Roupnel, however, there is an even older reference, a passage from the panegyric of Constantine, by the pseudo-Eumenius, written at the end of the third century. *Hist. de la camp. fr.*, p. 169. One fact emerges beyond dispute – the antiquity of the Burgundian vineyards.

[2] See page 72.

[3] Barley-beer was widely drunk throughout Gaul, England, Ireland and Germany. Salin, *Civilisation mérovingienne*, p. 444.

[4] Fortunatus, *Vita S. Radegundis* (ed. Br. Krusch, p. 44).

planting vines in such profusion from the fourth century onwards, without giving any thought to the balance between
production and consumption, our ancestors created a wine
problem which is not yet within sight of solution.

CHAPTER III

The Eclipse of Town Life
and the influence of the Church
on its Evolution

A FTER THE FIRST BARBARIAN invasions in the third
century, town life throughout Western Europe suffered
an eclipse from which it did not recover until the
eleventh century. This broad generalization has become something of a truism, a commonplace which has crept into every
textbook. Henri Pirenne, who took the view that the history of
the ancient world continued up to the Saracen conquest, conceded the towns a languishing survival during Merovingian
times. The reality was far more complex and subtle. The word
'town' is a general term which has still to be accurately defined.
It suggests a closely knit human settlement which, by reason of
its density and the way of life of its people as a whole, has
ceased to look like a village and at the same time has lost direct
contact with the land. This we believe to be the only valid
definition which will cover human communities as widely different from each other as a city of the ancient world, a medieval
and a modern town. Viewed in this light, the town represents a
permanent element in world civilization; it is the tangible
expression of man's need to live in groups. To speak of the
decay of town life is meaningless. At certain periods, however, it
does undergo a kind of temporary eclipse when economic conditions no longer allow the people crowded together in a community to find within its confines adequate provision for food
and lodging. In a country under enemy occupation, strict
rationing imposed on an entire population brings hardship to

97

those who live in towns and tempts them to seek refuge in the
country. For a variety of reasons the Early Middle Ages
experienced a centrifugal tendency of this nature. The towns
apparently ceased to spread and grow as they had done during
the golden age of the Roman Empire; but they did not vanish
altogether. The instinct which drives men to live in social
groups is indestructible and sometimes expresses itself in
strange ways. The great fascination of urban history during a
period of eclipse is that it stages the most unexpected come-
backs. Thanks to certain attractions, most of them religious –
one might even say superstitious – as for instance the presence
of deeply venerated relics, Roman cities threatened with decay
lingered on until such time as the revival of economic activity
gave them a new lease of life; the flame had never been completely extinguished.

It should be noted at the outset that the beautiful Gallo-
Roman towns of the first and second centuries, with their fine
public buildings and luxurious private villas, were themselves a
stage in the evolution of those ancient cities which the Romans
had taken over from their former Etruscan inhabitants. They
no longer resembled the early cities, built to a rigid plan,
centred on the *praetorium*, the seat of worship and government,
and divided into sectors by two great arteries, the *cardo maximus*
and the *decumanus maximus*, crossing each other at right angles.
These towns which had expanded under the *pax romana* in a
vast Empire which, though centralized, still left the provinces
their municipal autonomy, marked a passing phase of Roman
civilization.[1] The size of the public buildings, the astonishing
achievements in the realm of comfort and hygiene, the luxurious-
ness of the private houses, have aroused the enthusiasm of
modern town-planners. For almost two thousand years we
have been admiring the work of Rome, a little too forgetful of
the fact that this prosperity lasted barely two centuries, and
above all, as a contemporary historian has done well to remind
us,[2] that the miracle of the Roman Empire was achieved only
through the rape of kingdoms and the looting of peoples.

[1] Grenier, *Archéologie gallo-romaine*, Part 2, L'archéologie du sol, p. 580.
[2] Victor Chapot, *Le monde romain* (L'Evolution de l'humanité, no. 22), p. 483.

If the Emperors lavishly subsidized so many public works, roads, baths, forums, they did so with the immense wealth which they and their predecessors had accumulated by despoiling the temples and palaces of conquered peoples. These improvements were carried out at a speed which to us seems amazing in view of the limited mechanical means at their disposal at that time; here again admiration should be tempered with restraint. The results were achieved because there lay ready to hand an ample reserve of manpower – slavery, human plunder captured during and after the wars. At the end of the second century, these resources were in danger of becoming exhausted. Did the towns themselves contain sufficient wealth to maintain such a high level of prosperity? That would be a bold assertion to make. Their industrial activity was only moderate, and went no further than the artisan stage. The proverbial wealth of certain provincial cities such as Arles[1] came chiefly from the trading ventures of shrewd citizens who sold to the state on a vast scale basic provisions such as corn, oil, etc., for the use of the army and the common people of Rome. Part of their profits went in beautifying the towns to which they belonged, and in grants in money or in kind to help the poorest of their fellow-citizens; but if these generous gifts helped to raise the standard of living in certain cities of the Empire, the resources they represented were only temporary. The benefactors were not producers, but were more like the *nouveaux riches* of our own day in that their fortunes grew rapidly, yet had no solid foundation.

The ordeal of the first invasions in the third century proved just how precarious these fortunes were. Since the task of collecting taxes had become singularly difficult, tax-farming ceased to be financially worth-while and tax-collectors as a class disappeared. Tax-collecting had to be made compulsory for the municipal magistrates themselves, the *curiales*, who far from making money out of it, were completely ruined in the process. Nor did other practices in which opportunists had indulged in order to get rich quick survive the disorders of the third century.

[1] See particularly the rescript of the Emperor Honorius, 418, translated by G. Bloch, *La Gaule Romaine* (*Hist. de France* published under the direction of E. Lavisse, I, 2, p. 338).

As roads became less and less safe, and fell into even greater disrepair, the state becoming lax in payment, the profitable enterprises in which many provincials were engaged had to be given up. Almost simultaneously the urban aristocracy melted away, and the disappearance of these benefactors resulted in the impoverishment of the towns.

Their outward appearance changed also. The panic aroused by the first invasions, a feeling of insecurity which was everywhere abroad, led to the hasty erection of fortified ramparts, and the transformation of fine, spacious towns into cramped fortresses made them uncomfortable to live in. A new phase of urban history was about to begin. It took the form of an exodus of the rich. We hear no more of 'potentates' either inside the towns or on their outskirts towards the end of the fourth century. There was nothing to keep them there, and the towns were unpleasant. A certain Ausonius who had been a teacher in Bordeaux boasts in old age of the delights of his estate in Aquitaine as well as of the charms of the Moselle. The fashion, henceforth, was all for country *villae*, roomy, comfortable and even luxurious, but invariably remote from towns. The descriptions of such estates left by Sidonius Apollinaris in the middle of the fifth century are famous. This does not mean to say, however, that in the fifth century the towns were completely depopulated. Salvian, writing in that same century, speaks with his usual vehemence of cities as places of perdition whose inhabitants scorn the churches and flock instead to the theatre or the circus. Nevertheless, mentioning three cities he knows well, he is forced to admit that they no longer possess any places of entertainment:[1] Mainz because the building has been pulled down, Cologne because the town is full of enemies, Trier because the city has been looted four times and wiped out. His description of Carthage[2] is most unedifying; he makes it out to be one vast den of thieves and cut-throats. By piecing together a few old men's lingering recollections of certain derelict and disreputable quarters in several provincial towns, and also by remembering for ourselves what cities look like when they have

[1] *De gub. Dei*, VI, 8 and 15 (ed. Pauly, pp. 136, 149).
[2] 'Libidinum fornicationumque sentinam.' Op. cit., VII, 17 (ed. Pauly, p. 179).

been ruined in the course of two great wars, we may arrive at a fairly accurate picture of an imperial town at the time of the Great Invasions, and it is not difficult to see why families of means fought shy of them.

The barbarian occupation, notably that of the Franks, did not change the direction of their evolution. On the contrary it accentuated it. A tempting prima facie case can be made out for the opposite point of view. If Gregory of Tours is to be believed, Clovis established the seat of his kingdom in Paris.[1] The Frankish historian shows us the King of the Visigoths, Alaric II, storing his treasure at Toulouse.[2] Two Burgundian rulers, Gundobad and Godigisel, rival brothers, quarrelled for possession of the town of Vienne.[3] Chilperic I ordered circuses to be built in Paris and Soissons.[4] The Byzantine historian Procopius mentions the equestrian games over which the 'Germanic kings' presided in the amphitheatre at Arles.[5] We must not let ourselves be hoodwinked by such evidence, to which more could easily be added; it would be a mistake to interpret it as a sign of the rebirth of urban life. If the Frankish kings held on to cities, it was because they were strongholds. During the Great Invasions, the towns were centres of resistance. We should bear in mind the three sieges of Rome by Alaric (408–410), that of Orleans sustained by its bishop St Aignan against Attila (451), and the successful efforts of St Geneviève to put Paris and its population in a state of defence against the threat of the King of the Huns. The fratricidal struggles of the Merovingian kings are punctuated with sieges of towns, and the military rôle of the towns conferred on them in the eyes of these barbarian princes a considerable value, and one which was at the same time symbolical. Inheriting the palaces built by Roman governors in the capital cities of their provinces, they

---

[1] 'Parisius venit ibique cathedram regni constituit.' *Hist. Franc.*, II, 28 (38).
[2] 'Chlodovechus . . . cunctos thesauros Alarici a Tholosa auferens.' Op. cit., II, 27 (37).
[3] Op. cit., II, 23 (32) and 24 (33). The town of Vienne was still orderly and well-kept. A specialist was engaged to build the aqueduct which kept the town supplied with water. (Ibid.)
[4] 'Aput Suessionas atque Parisias circos aedificare praecipit eosque populis spectaculum praebens.' Ibid., V, 11 (17).
[5] *Les Grandes invasions et la crise de l'Occident*, p. 197.

used them as storehouses for their treasure. On their accession, they did not fail to proceed to the capital (*caput regni*) of their kingdom, there to be raised on a shield by their warriors. When they died, it was in the church of this same capital that they were buried. Yet these were mere gestures, and in no way implied a revival of urban life. There is no indication that these short-sighted kings attempted to make life in their towns less unpleasant. The example of Chilperic I, a fantastic character, who thought of restoring the circuses in two of his cities, is an isolated one. It proves chiefly that the love of games, still strong in the time of Salvian, had not died out a century later, though by that time he had little possibility of achieving his aim, since in the two capitals of the kingdom of Neustria there was no longer a single public building suitable for entertainments. Nor do any attempts appear to have been made to stimulate urban trade. The only fair known to have been instituted in the Merovingian era is that of Saint-Denis, founded by Dagobert I in 634 or 635, in the *vicus* of Saint-Denis and transferred to Paris shortly before 710 as the result of a fire.[1]

In fact the Merovingians, like the Gallo-Roman and barbarian aristocracy, remained true to the traditional Germanic love of country life and to the country ways adopted by the 'potentates' ever since the fourth century. Gregory of Tours and Pseudo-Fredegarius show us the kings and their entourage spending their days in their rustic *villae*, and pictorial art has familiarized us with their peregrinations, which Einhard, with a certain contempt for the predecessors of his hero Charlemagne, has also described; he shows us the last of the royal line, Childeric III, riding in a wagon drawn by oxen driven by herdsmen.[2] The estates were those of Chelles, Bonneuil, Berny, Rueil and Vitry. There these rough, uncouth kings, great eaters, great drinkers, great debauchees, felt perfectly at home; they had cellars and wine-vaults stocked to overflowing and which they and their comrades methodically emptied. A supply of peasant girls was also laid on, from whom they

---

[1] L. Levillain, *Etudes sur l'abbaye de Saint-Denis à l'époque mérovingienne*. Bibl. Ec. Chartes, XCI, 1930, p. 14.
[2] Einhard, *Vita Karoli Magni* (ed. L. Halphen, p. 10).

chose their concubines. A great part of their time was spent in hunting.

Abandoned by kings and nobles who paid them only rare, brief visits, often reduced to mere dilapidated fortresses, the Merovingian cities came near to foundering in neglect and squalor, especially since they were breeding-grounds for infection and again and again their populations were decimated by epidemics. Yet they were spared a lingering death. Towns are complex organisms, with varied functions, and can adapt themselves to changing needs and circumstances. A modern city almost wholly in ruins, rises from its ashes because it has an economic function to fulfil, and the post-war period can produce several apparently risen from the dead. A further deep-seated but different reason ensured the survival and permanence of most of the cities of Western Europe. Under the Early Empire they had been political and religious centres; to put it more aptly, they absorbed the whole public activity of the surrounding region. Endowed with administrative and ecclesiastical organisms, senates, municipal magistrates, priests of the imperial religion, they were, in imitation of Rome the city of cities (Urbs), veritable small states. This rôle did not lapse when the impoverished cities were abandoned by their officials, but deserted by those responsible for their administration, they continued to drag out an existence which was little more than stagnation. The end of paganism, the rejection of the imperial cult, speeded up this process of decay. There followed the slow, gradual break-up of municipal institutions, and what was equally disquieting, economic activity ebbed away from the cities in which the *nouveaux riches*, the 'potentates' of the Late Empire, did not step into the shoes of the vanished benefactors.

The future would have been black indeed had not the Christian Church, by fitting its administration into the framework of the imperial government and setting up its newly created bishoprics in the old cities, ensured their continued existence.

Striking examples of this process are to be found in Gaul. In all the *civitates* which became episcopal sees, town life continued without a break. The converse is no less conclusive.

Several Roman cities half-ruined during the Great Invasions were not willing to receive a bishop. Thus they signed their own death warrant and their decay became inevitable. The *civitas Boiorum*[1] situated in Novempopulania, never had a bishopric. The territory of the small tribe from which its name is derived is easily identified; it is the country round about Buch, whose seigneurs (*captaux*), won renown during the Hundred Years War, but for three hundred years Bordeaux scholars have been trying in vain to determine the exact site of its capital. Jublains, seat of the *civitas Diablintum*, met with a similar, though less drastic, fate. At an early date it was joined to the diocese of Le Mans, and never became an episcopal see.[2] Consequently this town which under the Roman Empire was an important fortified road post, as can be seen from its imposing ruins,[3] dwindled to little more than a modest village (*vicus*). Elsewhere the capital of the *civitas* was moved to another place. The bishop did not settle in the seat of the former municipal administration, and the consequences of such a removal were equally far-reaching. The population of the abandoned city declined and close at hand grew up a new urban centre which, having a bishopric, eventually supplanted it. Aps, the old capital of the *civitas Albensium*, is today nothing more than a small Ardèche township, whilst Viviers to which the Bishop had moved as early as the sixth century has become a busy little town.[4] The cases of Le Puy, successor to Saint-Paulien, and Mende, successor to Javols, are even more remarkable.[5] The prosperity of these two towns, which have become capitals of their respective departments, is due to the choice made by the first Bishops of Velay and Gévaudan of a residence other than that normally assigned to them. One last example is that of Tongres, pillaged by the Franks in the fourth century, and the

[1] F. Lot, *Recherches sur la population et la superficie des cités remontant à la période gallo-romaine*, 3rd part, Paris, 1953, pp. 195–200.

[2] See our *Histoire du Comté du Maine pendant le X*e* et le XI*e* siècle*, Paris, 1910, p. 8, and A. Ledru, *Répertoire des monuments et objets anciens existant ou trouvés dans le département de la Sarthe et de la Mayenne*, Le Mans, 1911, pp. 97–106.

[3] E. Laurain, *Les ruines gallo-romaines de Jublains*.

[4] Aug. Longnon, *Atlas historique de la France*, Paris, 1907, p. 140.

[5] Ibid., p. 146.

desertion of which by the episcopacy contributed to the prosperity of the two towns which became successively the seat of the bishopric of the *civitas Tungrorum,* Maastricht and, outstandingly, Liège.[1]

The list could easily be made longer, but it serves to bring out one important fact which needs to be stressed. Religious and ecclesiastical activity saved the lives of a host of Gallo-Roman cities, the existence of which was threatened by Merovingian apathy and the general stagnation of the economy. From this we shall venture to draw a conclusion which may perhaps seem self-evident. The life of a city is a sociological phenomenon and the conditions essential to the existence and working of that type of human settlement known as a town are not exclusively material. The presence of a religious element ensured the survival of old urban centres threatened with slow decay, and even brought others into existence. These centres were, it is true, comparatively poor and mean, since the most populous could barely rise to more than a few thousand inhabitants, but their continuity was assured. The spiritual, however, affects a social milieu only when translated into material terms. The establishing of a bishopric, the building of a cathedral, the exhibition of venerated relics in a sanctuary, were the sparks which rekindled the fire on the hearth, though the actual awakening of these moribund and sluggish towns was due to economic repercussions: the frequency of constructions, the upkeep of a large clerical population which, dedicated to religious duties, required a large body of domestic helpers, and the influx of pilgrims.

The cathedrals exerted a powerful attraction. During the first centuries after the introduction of Christianity, the mother-church was the only religious building in the diocese, and all Christians flocked to it. Later, churches were built in *vici* and even within *villae,* but the seat of the bishopric maintained its prestige and even increased it. In many towns, by a kind of tacit usurpation to which the inhabitants consented, the bishop became the first, and almost always the most influential, magistrate of the city, 'sometimes also by reason of his official

[1] Jean Lejeune, *La principauté de Liège,* Liège, 1948, pp. 17-27.

duties as *defensor civitatis*.[1] The most important religious
ceremonies, particularly baptism, continued to be celebrated
only in the capital of the diocese, which alone possessed a
baptistry. It was in that of Rheims that Clovis, and 3,000
warriors with him, were baptized. The description of the
ceremony by Gregory of Tours[2] gives us some impression of the
pomp and splendour of the festivals witnessed in these cities,
and of the great crowd of worshippers they attracted.

In the fascination they held for the crowds, one factor played
an amazing rôle: the cult of relics. Crowds flocked to cities
where the churches enshrined the bodies of holy men. The
fashion for pilgrimages began in the Merovingian age. Possession of the body of St Martin made the fortune of Tours;
possession of the remains of St Remi and St Julian that of
Rheims and Brioude. There are very many similar instances.
This crude form of devotion, which appealed to the starved
minds of an uncultured age, enjoyed an astounding success. One
unexpected result of this enthusiasm deserves particular mention. The yearning of the faithful to go and pay homage before
tombs enclosing holy bodies gave rise to a kind of pious 'tourist
traffic' which became fashionable not only amongst the rich,
but also with the common people, with quite ordinary folk who
were willing to face the greatest hardships in order to accomplish
a pilgrimage. In this way a love of travel grew up and spread
widely, and medieval society, too often thought of as being shut
in upon itself, indulged at an early date in journeys almost inconceivable in view of the difficulties of travel.

*

Journeys overland were made on foot, on horseback, by mule
or donkey, sometimes by carriage.[3] It has been estimated that

[1] There has been some dispute as to whether the dignity of *defensor civitatis* was
conferred on bishops. Chénon, for instance, whilst admitting that a few bishops
here and there may have been appointed defenders, believes that such an event
was always exceptional. *Etude historique sur le 'Defensor civitatis'*, Paris, 1889, p. 94.
This opinion will have to be revised. We shall see, for instance, that the title of
Defensor borne by the first known bishop of Angers is a clear indication that he held
this office. [2] *Hist. Franc.*, II, 22 (31).
[3] On the subject of journeys under the Late Empire during the Great Invasions,
see Gorce, *Les voyages, l'hospitalité et le port des lettres dans le monde chrétien des IV͏e et V͏e
siècles*, Paris, 1925.

5. Surface of Roman road (Vienne, France)

the travellers, whatever their mode of locomotion, did not cover more than 30 to 35 kilometres a day. The animals were not shod; the Roman roads, built on a concrete base and often paved, were massive constructions and excessively hard, deteriorating far more quickly than our modern roads, and there appears to have been no attempt to repair them after the fifth century. The halts and post-stages which existed under the Empire to serve the needs of the *cursus publicus*, or official transport system, had also fallen into disrepair. This degeneration of the roads did, however, give a certain fillip to sea transport.

Nice and Cimiez[1] afford significant proof of this. Nice had been a colony of Marseilles. When the Romans occupied the Narbonnais they set up a rival to it by founding along the *Via Julia*, built under Augustus, on the site of an old Ligurian *oppidum*, the city of Cimiez which became the capital of the province of the Alpes-Maritimes. The prosperity of this new city is attested by numerous inscriptions which reveal the generosity of its magistrates, of its flamens and of its priests dedicated to Augustus, as well as the activity of its corporate bodies; it is confirmed by impressive ruins of which the arenas are the most famous. The decadence, which probably coincided with the fall of the Western Empire, was doubtless caused by the abandoning of the land route, a fact of which Nice took advantage to annex the city's bishopric just at a time when its harbour was beginning to come back to life again. In the sixth century it was a port of call for boats sailing towards Italy from Narbonne and Marseilles.

Coastal navigation along the shores of the Mediterranean continued up to the Saracen conquest. Other ports were Narbonne, Agde, Marseilles, Toulon, Civita-Vecchia, Ostia. This coasting trade took ships as far as Greece and Egypt. Great vessels also crossed the width of the Mediterranean, sailing from Carthage and Caesarea to land at ports in Gaul, Marseilles or Narbonne. Mention of this sea traffic, however, becomes increasingly rare as we advance into Merovingian times, and it is only through the correspondence of several of the Church Fathers and monks who were contemporaries of St Jerome and

[1] See our *Histoire de Nice*, I, Nice, 1951, p. 4 et seq.

St Augustine that we have the slightest idea of the time taken to make the crossing. One monk who had embarked at Narbonne landed five days later on the coast of Africa, but his return voyage was less speedy. It took him thirty days to get from Alexandria to Marseilles, perhaps because there were many ports of call on the way. Both oars and sail were used.[1]

However, the all too rare descriptions left us by a few travellers show that the crossings were almost always dangerous. Fear of storms and fear of pirates were two threats which continually haunted the minds of passengers, and their hearts leapt for joy when, as the boat grounded on the sand, they realized they were once again on dry land. In the sixth century, the situation had deteriorated still further. When the King of the Franks, Chilperic I, sent ambassadors to the Eastern Emperor Tiberius, it was three years before they returned to their own country. They were unable to disembark at Marseilles because strife between the kings, who were quarrelling for possession of it, made it quite impossible to land there. They sailed on towards Agde, but were shipwrecked as they reached land, and the local inhabitants, who were subjects of the King of the Visigoths, stole part of their baggage.[2]

This chequered adventure, told in such a calm, matter-of-fact way by a contemporary, Gregory of Tours, is significant. It is a proof of the fecklessness of the barbarian governments; the indifference with which they tolerated acts of brigandage which they had not the will, perhaps not even the power, to suppress, increased the hardships to which passengers were exposed. Consequently a sea voyage came to be considered more and more as a dangerous enterprise. It no longer attracted any but 'dare-devils', men of unstable background like the Syrian merchants who during the Merovingian era kept an almost exclusive monopoly of what has been too ambitiously called the large-scale trade of the Western world. From the point of view of town life, it seems that in spite of the importance they

[1] Gorce, op. cit., *passim.* M. Salin also has collected some strange items of information about voyages to the East, particularly to Jerusalem, undertaken in the Merovingian period. *Civilisation mérovingienne*, I, pp. 479-485.

[2] Gregory of Tours, *Hist. Franc.*, VI, 2.

appeared to attach to possession of their ports, particularly of Marseilles and of Narbonne, neither the Frankish nor the Visigoth kings made any effort to improve them. On this point the documents are completely silent.

*

After the erection of city walls in the third and fourth centuries, town life did not immediately withdraw inside hastily built fortifications, as has sometimes been assumed. People went on living outside the ramparts and for many of them the town was a refuge to be sought when danger threatened, but which they left again when the peril was over. The existence of a population living outside the *pomoerium* of the city was, moreover, quite in the Roman tradition. An Italian scholar has reminded us that the area of a *civitas* included not only the town itself, the *urbs*, reserved for citizens, and the territory (*territorium*) in which lived the inhabitants of the *pagus*, the peasants (*pagani*), but that there existed also an intermediate zone, the *pagus suburbanus* or *suburbium*, and that between the *plebs urbana* and the *plebs rustica*, that is between the population living inside the walls and the peasant population, there existed the population outside the walls (*plebs extra muros posita*),[1] which had its own gods different from those of the city. This triple division was particularly characteristic of Rome and the Italian towns, but it existed also in Gaul and is the remote origin of a zone analogous to that found beyond the Alps, but based on different local measurements; this was the 'banlieue', extending to a radius of one Gallic league, and so named because in feudal times the legal authority of the seigneur of the town was valid there also.

The incorporation of suburbs in towns is a vitally important factor in urban history; that alone enabled the fortress-towns of the Late Empire, those skeleton towns which the disorders of the time reduced to 10, sometimes even to 7 or 6 hectares, to

---

[1] Mengozzi, *La città italiana nell'alto medio evo*, Florence, 1931, p. 29: 'La *plebs* è stata fino ad ora divisa in 2 grandi categorie: urbana, quella entro le mura . . .; rustica, l'altra. Questa bipartizione, secondo me, è errata e deve cedere il posto ad una tripartizione cosi formulata: plebs urbana, plebs extra muros posita, plebs rustica.'

spread out and begin to grow again from the early Merovingian period. Unfortunately the scarcity and vagueness of the documents give us hardly any idea of how this process came about or how far the suburban regions extended at that date. The historians of early medieval towns have concentrated on this problem, competing in condemnation of the inadequacy of the texts and reaching the judicious conclusion that the notion of a suburb was as yet not clearly defined. It has been noted that the word *suburbium* does not appear before the eighth century. Up to that time only the more general term, *loca suburbana*, was used to denote the areas surrounding the city, which were becoming more populated whilst preserving their rural character. According to statistics compiled by the author of a learned study of the *civitates* of *Belgica Secunda*, the term *suburbanus* occurs fifteen times in the work of Gregory of Tours.[1] One conclusion may easily be deduced from this. There was no longer any municipal administration in Merovingian times; the Count was in control of a wide area, the *pagus*, and was not a resident magistrate; the jurisdiction of the bishop extended over an entire diocese. There was therefore little point in fixing the topographical limits of a city which had ceased to be an administrative and religious entity, and it seems likely that the growth in population of the 'suburban' area came about without preconceived plan and in haphazard fashion. The line of demarcation between those known as *homines civitatis*, men of the city, and the 'suburbanites', *suburbani*, was probably not marked by any special privilege, nor was there a gulf between those two classes of inhabitants and the mass of the *pagani*.

Nevertheless a shrewd observer might perhaps have noticed that the suburban settlements were growing up around previously existing churches. A strict ban, rigidly observed under the Empire, soon contributed to the spread of the towns. It was forbidden to bury the dead within the *pomoerium*; cemeteries were always situated outside the walls. This order was scrupulously observed by the early Christians and since they formed the habit of founding their oratories on the site where their dead rested, their earliest communities grew up outside the towns.

[1] F. Vercauteren, *Etudes sur les 'civitates' de la Belgique seconde*, Brussels, 1934, p. 388.

We know for instance that the first church built at Rheims, that of Saint-Sixtus, was erected in the suburbs of the city, and that there existed nearby a cemetery chapel, that of Saint-Agricola, built a little before 367. The quarter in which these two edifices, together with several fourth-century chapels, were situated, was that in which the first Christian community had settled.[1] The oldest church in Paris was that of Saint-Marcel built inside the city's first Christian cemetery in the Avenue des Gobelins.[2] This was some distance from the 'town proper'. At Tours we know from Gregory of Tours, who was accurately informed about the past history of his diocese, that the first bishop, Gatien, had been buried in a cemetery outside the city, and that around this cemetery was grouped the first Christian community which the Frankish historian calls 'the Christian village'.[3] Similarly at Le Mans an oratory which later became the Church of le Pré, had been built on the bank of the Sarthe opposite the Gallo-Roman *oppidum* to house the remains of the man whom they regarded as their first bishop, St Julian; near this oratory the oldest Christian community must have settled.[4] It is tempting to adopt a similar hypothesis for the town of Grenoble: the tiny church of Saint-Laurent incorrectly known as the crypt of Saint-Laurent, one of the oldest Christian monuments in Gaul, was built on the right bank of the Isère whilst the Gallo-Roman city was on the left bank; it must have been used as a cemetery church by the early Christians.[5]

From all these examples, and from a host of others which could easily be discovered, and of which Rome itself, with its suburban cemeteries, is the most famous, the historian of towns will draw one important conclusion: the earliest centres of Christian life should be sought in the suburbs of towns, in the *loca suburbana*. A seed had been planted; settlements, *vici*, which were to spread and expand, had come into being near the

[1] Ibid., p. 46.

[2] Marcel Poète, *Une vie de cité*, Paris, I, pp. 37–38.

[3] 'In ipsius vici cimiterio qui erat christianorum.' *Hist. Franc.*, X, 31.

[4] A. Ledru, *Les premiers temps de l'église du Mans. Légende et histoire*, Le Mans, 1918, pp. 58–65.

[5] For this monument called the 'crypt of St Laurent', see David, *L'Eglise Saint-Laurent à Grenoble*, Grenoble, 1937.

towns and always outside their walls. Yet after the triumph of
the Church, the bishops did not tend this seed systematically.
On the contrary, to mark their victory, they settled inside the
civitates of which, profiting from the anarchy which prevailed in
the fifth century and moreover to the ultimate well-being of the
inhabitants, they often became masters. It was, in fact, almost
universal for the early cathedrals to be built on the ramparts of
towns.[1]

If the bishops shut themselves up in cities, the monks did not
follow their example, and to pursue the metaphor, it was they
who brought the seed to fruition. There was no room in cramped
towns for the vast buildings needed to house a large body of
monks. Furthermore it would have been pointless to put them
there, since the monastic rule forbade monks to take any part in
the life of the 'world'. Then too, monasteries frequently arose
around older cemetery churches which had been built outside
the walls. The rapid and amazing spread of monasticism in the
Merovingian period had unexpected repercussions on the
future of towns, near which a great number of abbeys were
founded. Springing up on the periphery, these establishments
became the nuclei of many of the districts of our modern towns.
The upkeep of a religious house required in fact the assistance
of many manual workers, domestics, gardeners, farm-labourers,
artisans. Lay settlements grew up around these religious centres,
which explains why so many of the streets and suburbs in our
modern towns bear the names of saints. These are the names of
the monasteries which once existed on that site.

A few examples will suffice, chosen at random but taken from
different parts of Roman Gaul. There was the Abbey of Saint-
Remi, founded half a mile to the south-west of the city of
Rheims, which several years later was to become an important
burg; the monastery of Saint-Médard outside the city wall of
Soissons; in Metz, Saint-Arnoul, which was to be the burial
place of the Carolingians; in Rouen the Abbey of Saint-Ouen;
in Paris the Abbey of Saint-Vincent founded by one of Clovis's
sons Childebert I, and which under the name of Saint-Germain-
des-Prés gave rise to a burg, then to a modern quarter on the

[1] F. Vercauteren, op. cit., p. 381.

left bank in Paris. Then too there were the Merovingian abbeys
of Saint-Vincent and Saint-Pierre de la Couture at Le Mans,
the monastery of Sainte-Radegonde at Poitiers, the Abbey of
Saint-Marcel at Chalon-sur-Saône, that of Saint-Baudille at
Nîmes and many others.

   Some historians have linked the growth of medieval towns too
closely with the revival of trade which accompanied the cessation
of the Viking invasions and the reopening of the Mediterranean
to shipping, and have made much of the creation of merchant
settlements first encountered in the ninth century. This conception of urban evolution seems altogether too cut and dried,
too incomplete. During the centuries which elapsed between the
fall of the Western Empire and this trade revival, towns were
continually and steadily expanding under the stimulus not of
trade but of monasticism. Richly endowed, enjoying valuable
privileges of immunity which benefited not only the monks,
but also those living on their lands, those abbeys which preferred the vicinity of towns to the solitude of the country were
focal points around which communities grew during the Merovingian era. Built for purposes of religion, they contributed to
the material development of the towns to which they had looked
only for spiritual shelter, and so involuntarily served the cause
of economic progress. Burgs came into being around most of
these abbeys. The word did not appear until the ninth century,
but it should be noted that, by a curious semantic evolution, it
was already devoid of any association suggesting a fortified
place when it was adopted to denote settlements of this kind.[1]
The idea it conjures up is a legal one, that of a human settlement under the jurisdiction, the *ban* of an ecclesiastical or secular
overlord. In dealing with an institution which became general
only in the eleventh century, let us at the outset avoid the mistaken belief that a medieval town consisted of a symmetrical
juxtaposition of two simple elements: an ancient Roman city
and a young medieval town. The reality is infinitely more
complex; in most cases the expansion of early medieval towns
came about through a series of human settlements growing up,
one after another, around a primitive core, sometimes near a

[1] See below, p. 257.

religious foundation – and these are generally the oldest – sometimes beside a feudal castle or a *portus*.

The slow decline of urban life from the time of the first Germanic invasions left its mark also on buildings and dwelling houses. The old cities, most of which were in ruins, were neither restored nor kept in repair. Already Sidonius Apollinaris, in one of those wordy poems in which the author's personal feelings and genuinely sincere sentiments are overlaid by the irritating pomposity of his style, was lamenting the fate of Narbonne. After waxing lyrical about the city walls, the shops, the theatre, the temples, the capitol, a eulogy which might give the uncritical reader a wrong impression of what life was really like in the fifth century, Sidonius ends his description on a note of sadness as he contemplates its fallen state: 'Proud amidst half-ruined ramparts, you flaunt the honoured scars of battles long ago and bear witness to the devastation caused by the blows that have been rained upon you; these splendid ruins make you even more precious in our sight.'[1] The same writer also alludes to Lyons, 'broken by terrible ordeals.'[2] Trier, the fourth-century capital of Gaul, also seems to have suffered terribly from its three sieges; it was still unrestored in the sixth century, for Fortunatus, visiting this town, speaks in one of his poems of the former Senate House, whose ruins bore witness to past glories.[3] Towns which, like Dijon, kept their walls intact, were few and far between. It should be noted also that the western cities, less exposed to invasion than those of the east, seem to have suffered less damage.

Living conditions became more crude. Stone houses of several storeys which, standing in groups like islands in the Roman towns, formed what were known as *insulae*, gradually disappeared through lack of repair. Gregory of Tours refers to one such house which must have crumbled into ruins.[4] As for the private mansions, the *domus*, they no longer existed. The old guilds of craftsmen – stonemasons – seem to have been dis-

[1] Sidonius Apollinaris, *Carm.*, XXIII (ed. Lvetjohann, p. 251).
[2] A. Loyen, *Recherches sur les panégyriques de Sidoine Apollinaire*, Paris, 1942. B.E.H.E., Sc. philol. et hist., fasc. 285, p. 79. (After the panegyric of Majorian.)
[3] Pauly-Wissowa, VI A2, col. 2301–2353, art. *Treveri*.
[4] *Hist. Franc.*, VIII, 42.

banded. Nevertheless, masons were still to be found in Gaul,[1] and the tradition of building in stone had not been lost, but the prevailing style for the private dwelling was the wooden house

North-East Gaul in the Merovingian Period •

with foundations, and sometimes the ground floor, of stone, whilst the upper storeys consisted of a wooden framework of which only the interstices were filled in with light masonry or with

---

[1] The use of stone being unknown in Britain, Benedict Biscop, Abbot of Wearmouth and Jarrow (675–680), had to send for masons from Gaul to build a church. See the Venerable Bede, quoted by Salin, *Civil merov.*, I, p. 490, no. 96.

rubble known as rough-walling (hourdage). A famous description by Fortunatus[1] shows how popular wooden houses already were in the sixth century, a fashion which can be accounted for by Germanic influence. This type of building persisted throughout the whole of the Middle Ages. Only the frequency of fires brought about the return to stone, at least for public buildings, but this reaction was barely perceptible before the eleventh century. One of the chroniclers of the bishops of Le Mans, author of the biography of Avesgaud who held the see in the early eleventh century, relates that this prelate had the episcopal residences rebuilt in stone, as well as the Hôpital des Ardents which had previously been of wood.[2] Not a single early medieval private house has survived, and it is only from the fifteenth-century houses to be found in many towns that we can form any idea of what their predecessors were like.[3]

With the Great Invasions and the Merovingian period, that comfort which had been such a feature of Gallo-Roman towns gradually disappeared. By quibbling over certain Merovingian texts such as the life of St Radegunda, it has been sought to prove that there were still thermae and public baths in the sixth century, but the evidence is only occasional and not sufficiently explicit. That such establishments were rare and few in number during the very early Middle Ages is obvious from the fact that people soon forgot the original purpose of those baths which, built under the Empire, were still left standing. The Palais des Thermes at Arles, part of which still exists and is known as the Palais de la Trouille, became the 'palace of Constantine', and the author of the old Life of St Pons mistook the ruins of the baths at Cimiez for a temple of Apollo. Such mistakes are not without significance.

---

[1] Reproduced by Ed. Salin, *Civil. mérov.*, p. 506, no. 124.

[2] *Actus*, p. 356: 'Fecit namque episcopales domos quae antea ligneae fuerant, petrinas; et hospitalem pauperum Christi, quae necdum et loco illo lignea erat, constituit petrinam.'

[3] The use of glass for windows was already known, and there were glassmakers (*vitri factores*) in Gaul. Benedict Biscop had some of them sent over with masons (*cementarios*) for the building of his abbey. Salin, *Civil. mérov.*, I, p. 490. Buildings were roofed with tiles or thatch. Ibid., 434–435.

6. Merovingian house construction, VIIth century (from the Pentateuque de Tours, Bib. Nat. n. acq. lat. 2334 for 56)

CHAPTER IV

The So-Called 'Grand Commerce' of the Merovingian Period

ENRI PIRENNE infused new life into the economic history of the Early Middle Ages by giving the Moslem conquest pride of place amongst the factors which transformed the structure of the ancient world. There is no need to summarize afresh a 'thesis' which was first presented to several historical congresses, which in 1922 and 1923 he condensed into two brilliant articles in the *Revue belge de philologie et d'histoire*, and which was fully and finally developed in a posthumously published work, *Mahomet et Charlemagne*.[1] In actual fact, however, as one of his disciples has written, it is perhaps doing Pirenne an injustice to apply the word 'thesis' to a vast body of original ideas on the whole evolution of Europe from the third to the tenth century. It would be more accurate to say that new horizons have been opened up to those who are attempting to find out just how the transition from the ancient world to the Middle Ages was effected. The main contention of Pirenne, whose natural bent led him to place particular emphasis on economics, is that the ancient civilization, the *ordo romanus*, lived on even after the Germanic invasions, that the real destroyer of this *ordo* was Mahomet, whilst the creator, or at least the symbolic representative of the new order of things, was Charlemagne. Hence the title of the first memoir in which Pirenne expounded his views, a title which has been revived by the editors of his great posthumous book. These two evocative words have caught the imagination to an extraordinary degree,

---

[1] *Mahomet and Charlemagne*, London, 1939.

and though for the past thirty-two years the original ideas put
forward by this great historian have been critically examined,
hotly disputed, carefully sifted, they were still fresh enough to
inspire in the *Revue historique* for November 1954 an article
entitled: 'Encore Mahomet et Charlemagne'.[1]

One of Pirenne's main theories is that in spite of the barbarian
invasions the movement of trade through the Mediterranean
continued throughout Merovingian times right up to the
Moslem conquest, and that the Mediterranean way of life which
was one of the characteristic features of the Late Empire persisted. Under the rule of the Ostrogoths Italy continued to get
supplies of grain and oil from the opposite shore of the Mediterranean, and trade relations with Byzantium were maintained,[2]
as may be seen from many references in the correspondence of
Theodoric edited by Cassiodorus. A first essential was the construction of light ships which Italy needed for the importation
of foodstuffs, particularly of corn. The ships bringing food
to Rome landed at the port of Ostia, where they were welcomed by the 'Count of the port of the city of Rome'. The
orders given by the King to this high-ranking official show
how anxious Theodoric was to maintain the volume of this
traffic:[3]

> It is a pleasant, rather than a heavy responsibility to hold
> the office of Count of the port of Rome. He supervises the
> arrival of innumerable ships. The sea, covered with sails,
> brings foreign peoples with merchandise from many different
> provinces. The task entrusted to you is therefore a privileged
> one; but it must be carried out with tact and good judgement.
> You are in a position to create prosperity by dealing fairly
> and justly with those who land there. An avaricious hand
> could close down the harbour altogether.

For a time, however, the occupation of North Africa by the

---

[1] The article is by E. Perroy.
[2] See *Les Grandes invasions et la crise de l'Occident*, p. 262. Sicily and Sardinia, however, had ceased, at least for the time being, to be the granaries of the *annona*:
'Eversis Sardinia ac Sicilia id est fiscalibus horreis atque abscissis velut vitalibus
venis,' writes Salvian, *De gub. Dei*, VI, 12.
[3] Cassiodorus, *Variae*, VII, 9 (ed. Mommsen, p. 208).

Vandals was a threat to Mediterranean sea traffic, and Sidonius Apollinaris, who shortly before the fall of the Western Empire had assumed the grave responsibility of ensuring Rome's food supplies, has told in one of his letters how difficult his task was and with what breathless joy he sighted the ships bringing the *annona*.[1]

This régime based on imports suited the indolent Romans to perfection, and Justinian's chief aim in reconquering North Africa from the Vandals was probably to regain for Italy a source of grain which had been partially lost to her for almost a century; yet in spite of the efficiency of the Byzantine merchant fleet, it is by no means certain that trade relations were fully restored. The Lombard invasion brought disorder, as well as poverty, to the peninsula. When Gregory the Great was elected Pope (590), an epidemic of the plague was raging in Rome, and when eventually it died down, famine threatened to descend upon the city. The letters written by the new Pontiff to the Praetor of Sicily urging him to speed up deliveries of corn seem to indicate that from the close of the sixth century Africa was no longer the great grain-provider.

Further concrete facts about the Mediterranean economy during the Merovingian period have also come to light, for instance the use of olive oil for food and lighting, replaced only at a later date by that of butter and wax, and the use of Egyptian papyrus for writing which persisted in Gaul until the middle of the eighth century. Coastal traffic along the shores of the Mediterranean was still relatively brisk in the sixth century in spite of the dangers involved. Pilgrims travelling from Central Gaul to Rome in the time of Gregory of Tours embarked at Marseilles and sailed along the coast of Provence and Italy. The island of Lérins was connected with the continent by a fairly regular service of boats. A hermit like St Hospice, who lived near Nice, fed on dates and herbs brought him by merchants from Egypt. The port of Marseilles was sufficiently busy for the Merovingian kings to quarrel for possession of it. At Fos, where the Rhône river-boats took over from seagoing ships, there was a warehouse belonging to the Treasury. A scholar who is also

[1] Sidonius Apollinaris, Letter to Campanianus (ed. Lvetjohann, p. 15).

a skilled chemist[1] has discovered that the glass factories in the Rhineland needed imports of Mediterranean natron, and that the garnet used in cloisonné enamelling up to the sixth century, but not later, came from markets in Asia Minor. Pirenne has listed other examples of this trade with the East which continued up to the Saracen invasion: ivory, silk, Syrian wines, spices such as pepper, cummin, cinnamon.

Such an accumulation of facts proves the existence of relations, uneasy perhaps but continuous, with the countries around the Mediterranean. We should not be deceived by their number. After the Germanic invasions the economy of Western Europe underwent a profound change, but without disputing the repercussions which followed the Moslem conquest it has to be admitted that it did not bring about the complete rupture, the clean-cut break, which has been attributed to it, since it was preceded by a long period of decay. The European economy was already in decline when the victorious Saracens closed, or tried to close, the Mediterranean to Christians. Pirenne never questioned, nor even minimized, the influence of the Germanic invasions, in describing which he coined the happy phrase 'barbarization'. Applied to economic life, it admirably epitomizes the muddled, spineless Merovingian world of the sixth century. There was, it was true, no definitive break between East and West, and Gregory of Tours in his History of the Franks, so rich in informative anecdote, gives facts which prove this, but the continuance of these relations simply means that the easy-going Merovingians left things as they were, the more willingly since it was in their own interests to maintain the *status quo*. The miserly Chilperic I found *laissez-faire* the best policy when the Emperor Tiberius made a point of presenting him with beautiful gold medallions each one lb. in weight. Childebert II was no less devoted to the Byzantine alliance, since it brought him 50,000 gold *solidi*, the price of his army's support for the Empire against the Lombards.[2] Yet no effort was made to revitalize trade with the East. The administration simply let things slide. The native nobility, the Gallo-Romans,

---

[1] Salin, op. cit., p. 136.
[2] Gregory of Tours, *Hist. Franc.*, VI, 2 and 28 (42).

who lived in the country, with certain very rare exceptions did not engage in trade, and the majority of Germans also seem to have been allergic to this calling, so that commerce passed almost wholly into the hands of foreigners.

It was chiefly the Syrians, whom St Jerome called the most avaricious of mortals, who seized upon it and acquired a monopoly. Large numbers made their way into Gaul, and in some cities such as Orleans they formed veritable colonies. They succeeded in infiltrating into the Rhineland, into Germany and even into Great Britain.[1] They had other eastern competitors: Greeks and Jews. One of the latter named Priscus had put himself at the service of King Chilperic I, who entrusted him with the purchase of goods.[2] At the beginning of the seventh century Dagobert also had his Jewish *negociator*, a certain Solomon.[3] They were commission agents, who filled the gap left by the lack or scarcity of merchants owning permanent shops. Shops were very rare, and the few allusions which might conceivably refer to them are not very convincing. When Gregory of Tours speaks of *domus negociatorum*, it is not certain that he means shops; they are more likely to be the merchants' actual homes.[4] This lack forced people of means to resort, as the Emperors and high officials of the Late Empire were already doing, to agents whom they sent to make purchases on the spot. The royal example was followed by the abbots of monasteries who, responsible for the food supplies of their communities, also had their abbey merchants, veritable quartermasters.[5] Thus the Abbot of Saint-Pierre de la Couture at Le Mans commissioned his agents to go periodically to buy fish in Bordeaux, where a house which had belonged

[1] L. Bréhier, 'Les colonies d'orientaux en Occident au commencement du moyen âge', *Byzantinische Zeitschrift*, XII, p. 1 et seq.

[2] 'Judaeus quidam Priscus nomine, qui ei ad species coemendas familiares erat.' Gregory of Tours, op. cit., VI, 5. It is tempting to translate 'species' by spices, but we believe that the word indicates a variety of merchandise. See the commentary by Henri Laurent, *Marchands du Palais*, p. 293.

[3] *Gesta Dagoberti* (ed. Krusch, Mon. Germ., SS. rer. merov., II, p. 413).

[4] It may, however, be assumed that these *negociatores* had storerooms for their wares. Gregory of Tours refers to the 'adpotecis ac promptuariis' which a wealthy inhabitant of Comminges owned in his town. *Hist. Franc.*, VII, 37. Cf. H. Pirenne, *Mahomet et Charlemagne*, p. 85.

[5] H. Laurent, *Marchands du Palais*, p. 293.

to Bishop Bertrand was put at their disposal during their stay.[1]

It would give quite a false impression of the merchants and their many-sided activities, which have been recorded for us in Merovingian documents, to equate them to merchants of our own day. These men were adventurers, whether they were Orientals come to the West to sell the produce of their native countries, or inversely, a few rare inhabitants of Gaul who were genuine pirates, like Samo of Senon, a contemporary of Dagobert. He had set out for Esclavonia, in other words Bohemia, to engage in trade, and imposing himself on the inhabitants of the country, had eventually become King of the Wends.[2] Amongst the Germanic barbarians one nation alone seems to have had a flair for trading – the Frisians. Inhabiting the strip of coast in the Low Countries between the mouth of the Scheldt and that of the Eider, they engaged in trade in the Merovingian period. The poverty of a country very little of which had been cleared for cultivation, and which was exposed to frequent inroads from the sea, doubtless impelled them to leave their own land to trade as hawkers abroad.[3] Their chief stock-in-trade was cloth (*pallia frisonica*) and it is tempting to think of them as ancestors of the Flemish cloth-merchants, but the connexion remains problematical.

Trading, carried on in these various ways, was frequently a dangerous undertaking and the men engaged in it banded themselves together for protection. In the sixth century the merchants of Verdun formed an association, and it was probably their influence which enabled the bishop to obtain from King

---

[1] *Actus*, pp. 122–123.

[2] M. Verlinden, 'Problèmes d'histoire économique franque, I. Le franc Samo', *Revue belge de philologie et d'histoire*, 1933, p. 1095, believes that the activities of this man Samo had nothing in common with those of a trading company. His trade was specialized and exclusive – the slave trade. According to Pirenne, Samo was an adventurer: 'On peut supposer', he writes in *Mahomet et Charlemagne*, p. 79, 'qu'il vendait lui-même aux barbares des armes, ainsi que le faisaient les marchands interlopes de la frontière contre lesquels les Capitulaires ont tant légiféré.' See below, p. 172.

[3] 'Durissima gens maritima.' Cf. Bechtel, *Wirtschaftsgeschichte Deutschlands*, pp. 168–169, and particularly Herbert Jankuhn, 'Der frankisch-friesische Handel zur Ostsee im frühen Mittelalter', *VSWG*, XL, pp. 193–243, and Dirk Jellema, 'Frisian Trade in the Dark Ages', *Speculum*, January 1955, pp. 15–36.

Theudebert a loan of 7,000 gold *solidi* for his town.[1] Samo himself did not set out for Esclavonia alone, but in the company of other merchants. It is recorded that one merchant armed six ships in order to undertake a certain expedition.

After a study of the various documents (most of which tell us very little, and which in any case are few in number) dealing with the Merovingian merchants, it is singularly difficult to define their activities. It is an exaggeration to speak in terms of big business, '*grand commerce*', international trade, import and export trade. Such phrases are far too grandiose to describe the modest activities in which most of these traders engaged. On the other hand we should not yield to the temptation, great though it may be, and not altogether wide of the mark, to compare them to the North Africans of our own day who hawk carpets and other native products, pester passers-by in the streets and haunt the cafés of our modern cities. They too form colonies in our cities, exactly as did the Syrians in Merovingian times, and who as we have seen did not live by themselves when they were in Gaul. Such a comparison would, however, rate the medieval merchants too low, since they did at least fill a gap in the contemporary economy by selling eastern products, such as spices, which were both useful and valued.

We cannot quite agree with those who have interpreted the presence in Gaul of foreign, and particularly of eastern merchants, as proof that large-scale trade continued to flourish in the West. We regard it, on the contrary, as evidence of the inertia of the western peoples and of the stagnation of their economic life. It was the deterioration of commercial activity resulting from the Great Invasions which spread over Gaul and Italy industrious eastern traders who hoped to make a substantial profit from the bundle of wares they had brought with them. Their advent in such large numbers was not the mark of a sound economy. Moreover, the goods in which they dealt were not always respectable. Slaves were the most profitable of their wares, and the money to be made from them attracted the Gallo-Romans also, who, following their example, went into business on their own account. The Frank Samo was a slave

[1] Gregory of Tours, *Hist. Franc.*, III, 34.

trader, of that there can be no doubt, since Esclavonia fed the slave-markets from the Early Middle Ages. The Great Invasions, by pushing the Germanic peoples westward, created east of the Elbe a vacuum which was filled by the Slavs. Certain of these peoples became human merchandise and traffic in them became so widespread that in the Romance languages the word slave, originally a man of Slav nationality, supplanted the Latin words *mancipium* and *servus*, which had been used to denote a human being in a state of slavery. But these dealers in human flesh sought their merchandise from many other countries as well. They made frequent expeditions to Great Britain whence many slaves were drawn, since, as Ferdinand Lot wrote:[1] 'The Anglo-Saxons used to sell their fellow-countrymen.' The Frisians, who traded on the other side of the Channel, certainly engaged in this traffic. Though it was so widespread and though slavery was not officially condemned by the Church, it shocked religious people, and the buying back of captives, wretched creatures who though endowed with a soul were herded about like cattle to be sold and dispersed, they regarded as a charitable duty. St Eloi, Dagobert's minister, who was very rich, practised this on a large scale, buying back in batches of fifty or even one hundred souls the very moment they set foot on Gallic soil the Britons and Saxons being brought in as slaves.[2] The slave trade increased in volume after the Saracen conquest; large numbers were imported into Spain which became an important market for the traders. It has even been asserted that this export trade brought in a little Moslem gold, that first dinars then Abbasid dirhams, flowed into the West, but its importance has probably been over-exaggerated.[3] A black market – and the slave trade was in fact a kind of black market – rarely benefits the community and brings its monetary gains into general circulation.

One serious defect in the Merovingian economy prevented

---

[1] *Les invasions germaniques*, Paris, 1935, p. 319. Lot adds: 'Au dire de Saint Boniface, Anglais cependant, il n'y avait pas de ville d'Italie, de Gaule ou de Germanie ou l'on ne rencontrât pas des prostituées et des entremetteuses anglaises.'

[2] *Vita Eligii*, SS. rer. merov., IV, p. 677.

[3] Maurice Lombard, 'L'or musulman du VII⁰ au XI⁰ siècle', *Annales E.S.C.*, 1947, pp. 143–160. See below, p. 168.

trade from establishing itself on solid foundations, namely the poor quality of the coinage, a subject which will be dealt with in the following pages. The points already discussed may perhaps serve to justify a sceptical approach to this so-called Merovingian economic activity which, so the theory runs, was inherited from the ancient world, continued to flourish until it was blocked by the Moslem conquest, went into rapid decline from the middle of the seventh century and finally petered out under the Carolingians. We believe the opposite to be the case, and shall endeavour to prove that the dawn of the Carolingian era marks a restoration or in any case a serious attempt to put the economy on a sound footing. The harm done to the western economy by the Saracen invasion was only moderate and localized, since this economy had been thrown out of gear and seriously crippled when the Moslems partially succeeded in closing the Mediterranean to Christians. We shall see that the havoc wrought by the invasions of the Northmen in the ninth century was far more serious, since it profoundly disturbed a healthy economy which had been well on the way to recovery.

CHAPTER V

Coinage and Currency.
The Seas and Shipping

MONEY BEGAN TO DEPRECIATE after the Great Invasions. The theory that the Merovingians kept to the gold standard and that the Carolingians replaced it by an exclusively silver coinage is incorrect and altogether too flattering to the Merovingians. The reality was less simple. When the barbarian monarchies took root in the West, they made no innovations, and were content to keep the Byzantine *solidus*.[1] Most of their kings were incapable of a monetary policy; the newcomers followed the example of the local inhabitants and used the imperial gold *solidus*, which was in circulation throughout the whole of Europe and was everywhere accepted. The Ostrogoth king of Italy, Theodoric, who died in 526 and who was devoted to the formalism of Roman administration, entrusted to the Count of the Sacred Largesse the minting of specie and of the gold *solidi* struck in the chief mints of his kingdom at Rome, Ravenna and Milan, and which continued to bear the Emperor's name. Only at the end of his reign did the king's monogram appear, but coining remained a public service under the Ostrogoths, and Theodoric made a point of energetically defending the monopoly: 'Moneyers', he declares in one of his letters, 'have been appointed in the general interest; they must not pass into the service of individuals.'[2] With the Burgundians and the Visigoths, who appear to have preserved the idea of the state more effectively than the Franks, coining, which had begun by being merely imitative, also kept

---

[1] Le Gentilhomme, *Mélanges de numismatique mérovingienne*, Paris, 1940, p. 132.
[2] Cassiodorus, *Variae*, V, 39, quoted by Blanchet, *Manuel de numis.* I, p. 235, n. 1.

its royal character when from the time of Gundobad, King of the Burgundians in the early sixth century, and Leovigild, King of the Visigoths from 573 to 586, the monogram, then the title, of the rulers began to figure on their *solidi* and their triens, worth 1/3 of a *solidus*.[1]

The monetary policy of the Merovingians was more haphazard and casual. At first the Salian Franks adopted the Roman coins with which, living as they did near the Rhine frontier, they had long been familiar. The inventory of treasure contained in the tomb of Childeric I, the father of Clovis, discovered at Tournai, affords proof of this: it included 90 imperial gold *solidi* and 200 Roman silver *denarii*. Once they had become masters of Gaul, the Franks continued to use these coins which they had no particular reason to abandon, thus following in the footsteps of other barbarian nations. They copied the imperial coinage. A grandson of Clovis, however, Theudebert, who reigned between 534 and 548, had the audacity to issue gold *solidi* bearing his own effigy and title followed by the word *victor*. He did this after a triumphant raid on Italy intended as a gesture of defiance against Justinian. We know from the Byzantine historian Procopius just how the Emperor reacted to this bold and impertinent stroke:

> The German kings [he wrote][2] are using gold from Gaul to mint *solidi* on which they have stamped, not the head of the Roman emperor, but their own effigy. Yet the king of Persia himself, who enjoys complete freedom with regard to his own silver coinage, would not dare to stamp his image on gold coins; that is a right which is denied both to him and to all the other barbarian kings, which is all the more remarkable since he has gold of his own and to spare, but he could not get such money accepted by the peoples with whom his subjects trade, even if they were barbarians. Only the Franks have succeeded in doing this.

Procopius was exaggerating; the Frankish kings did not command

[1] A. Blanchet, op. cit., I, pp. 184–188.
[2] See our *Grandes invasions*, pp. 196–197. The quotation from Procopius is a translation of the French text given by M. Prou in his *Catal. des monn. mérov. de la Bibl. Nat.*, p. xxx.

sufficient credit to be able to impose a coinage which com-
peted with that of the Emperors. We know from a letter of
Pope Gregory I to one of his agents, whom he had sent to
Gaul, that the gold *solidi* minted in the Frankish kingdom were
not accepted as currency in Italy.[1] Only a few of Theudebert's
successors followed his example; gold coins have come down
to us bearing the names of the kings Guntramn, Sigebert I,
Childebert II then Chlotar II, Dagobert I and several
others;[2] but unnamed imitations of imperial coins remained
the rule.

A more serious matter, and one which resulted in a speedy
deterioration of the Merovingian currency, was that at an
early date it escaped from the effective control of the public
authorities. Through the negligence of the kings, coining in the
Frankish kingdom became the monopoly of coiners. Holding
stocks of precious metal, they minted coins and signed them.
Incredible though it may seem, these mints which at that time
were exceedingly numerous not only in cities and *castra*, but
also in important villages (*vici*) and *villae*,[3] manufactured a
coinage over which the royal authority and its representatives
exercised a purely nominal supervision, though these coiners
were still often dignified with the name of *publici*. This was one
of the consequences, not the only one but actually one of the
most serious, of the privilege of immunity[4] which the early
kings handed out indiscriminately to influential laymen and
ecclesiastics. They surrendered their royal prerogative of minting money in the same way that they handed over to their
immunists the income from taxation, and forbade their officials,
the counts and their underlings, to dispense justice and carry

[1] 'Solidi Galliarum qui in terra nostra expendi non possunt.' *Gregorii I registrum
epistolarum* (ed. Ewald and Hartmann, I, p. 389).
[2] A. Blanchet, op. cit., pp. 201–205.
[3] The most comprehensive list of place-names and coiners' names stamped on
Merovingian coins is that given by A. Blanchet, op. cit., I, pp. 249–336. In an
attempt to explain the multitude of coiners' workshops in the Merovingian period,
Blanchet has assumed that, as in sixteenth-century Russia, goldsmiths had the right
to mint money for any individual who brought them gold and silver ingots. Ibid.,
p. 237.
[4] See L. Levillain's thorough study of immunity in *Rev. hist. de Droit*, 1927, pp.
38-67.

out the duties of their office on territories enjoying this privilege. These degrading concessions did not shock contemporaries; furthermore they were justified by the incapacity and dishonesty of the royal agents who, as we know from Gregory of Tours and Fredegarius, were often rogues. Never in our history has the conception of the state known so complete an eclipse. Numerous churches obtained privileges of immunity; many enjoyed that of minting money; most of their names are known, since specimens of the coins they issued are still preserved in public or private collections.[1] They were the churches at Angers, Bordeaux, Le Mans, Orleans, Rouen, Toulouse, etc. and the abbeys of Saint-Denis, Saint-Philibert de Jumièges, Saint-Médard de Noyon, Saint-Martin de Tours, Saint-Martial de Limoges, Saint-Julien de Brioude and Saint-Marcel de Chalon. Unfortunately the only royal charter granting coining rights to a church, that of Theuderic III in favour of Aiglibert, bishop of Le Mans (673–691), is not genuine;[2] but if a forger hit upon the idea of fabricating this particular document, authentic ones did exist. The right of coining was frequently regarded as arising naturally out of the privilege of immunity. There are, moreover, good grounds for thinking that the privilege was often usurped.

The result of this slackening of control was exactly what might be expected; it was in fact inevitable. Pierre le Gentilhomme[3] took the trouble to compare a triens found in the Bordeaux treasure, which he dates at 675, with a second discovered at Fontenay-le-Comte and minted at an earlier period. The latter weighed 1·42 gr. and was of fairly good alloy, whereas the coin from the Bordeaux hoard was mere silver gilt and weighed only 1·12 gr. The debasing of the coinage, the distortion of types, are adequately explained by the carelessness of the public authorities and the lack of conscience of coiners left to their own devices.

Did the stock of gold in the West diminish from the fourth

[1] See the chapter devoted to ecclesiastical coining by Blanchet in his *Manuel*, I, pp. 206–212. Cf. M. Prou, who in the introduction to his *Catalogue des monnaies mérovingiennes* has devoted one chapter to 'Les monnaies d'or des églises', pp. liv–lxi.
[2] It figures in the *Actus*, p. 208.
[3] Op. cit., p. 19.

century onwards? Its scarcity is mentioned by Symmachus in one of his letters;[1] the last emperors of the century, fearing lest it should drain away from the Empire, forbade barbarian merchandise to be paid for in gold. The stock of it was being steadily whittled away, since the westerners had no native products to barter for the exotic wares they bought from the Syrians and other eastern peoples. Yet the extent to which it was leaving the country has been exaggerated. A large quantity of gold was hidden away with individuals in the form of coins, ingots[2] and precious objects. It was even shut away in graves as may be seen from the inventory of King Childeric's tomb, so that Theodoric had no hesitation in requesting his agents to wrench it from the tombs and divert it into the public treasury.[3] This revolting measure shows that the precious metal was lying hidden rather than draining away. Yet one fact is certain: the state was growing poorer. Taxes were coming in badly or not at all; we know from the 'Life of St Eloi' that they were often collected in ingots. In the state of anarchy which prevailed in Gaul throughout the whole of the Merovingian period, it was often extremely difficult to keep the coiners supplied with gold, and it was easy to see how by slow degrees the *solidus* and the *triens* tended to become no more than token coins which were not accepted outside the realm.

It has been asserted that the Merovingians remained faithful to the one metal, gold, and that the breakdown of their monetary system was provoked by the Moslem invasion. The transition from gold to silver between 650 and 700 has even been taken to mark the collapse of civilization, but recent discoveries, and a more accurate interpretation of evidence relating to the coinage, lend support to different conclusions.[4] Under the Merovingians,

[1] See Marc Bloch, 'Le problème de l'or au moyen âge', *Ann. d'hist. éc. et soc.*, V, 1933, pp. 1–34.

[2] The large number of coiners' workshops to which the hoarders of precious metal brought their ingots proves that great quantities of it were held in private hands.

[3] Cassiodorus, *Variae*, IV, 34 (ed. Mommsen, p. 129).

[4] According to M. Prou, *Les monnaies mérov.*, p. cv, the gradual substitution of silver for gold was a revolution which had purely economic causes. It was connected with the fact that Gaul exported very little, and in return received from the East goods for which she paid in gold.

silver was minted earlier and on a larger scale than has been thought;[1] nor was it solely the shortage of gold which finally established its supremacy, but the preferences of the northern peoples and the requirements of internal trade. Tacitus had already noticed the Germans' love of silver, which is illustrated by the treasure contained in Childeric's tomb. It included silver deniers carefully stored beside gold *solidi*.[2] This same preference for minting in silver was shown by the Anglo-Saxons of Great Britain. They began by striking gold coins of a third of a *solidus* called thrymsas; but in the late seventh century they abandoned gold and replaced the thrymsas by silver pennies, sceattas,[3] for they had silver mines in their island. These coins enjoyed a great vogue, and the Frisian merchants who carried their packs to London and York came to know them well and spread them outside Great Britain. They even imitated them in their mints, notably in that of Duurstede, and circulated them around the continental markets, as for instance the St Denis fairs. The inventory of buried treasure in Gaul at the close of the Merovingian period proves how widely they had been spread abroad. Something like thirty were found in the treasure discovered at Bais in Brittany and eighty in that hidden at Cimiez near Nice in 737. This liking for a silver coinage marks an evolution which was taking place during the late seventh century. The gold *solidus* and even the *triens* were on the way out. They were being supplanted by a silver coin, the Merovingian denier, the history of which remains obscure. Imitated first from the Roman coinage, it was widely circulated at the end of the Merovingian era, whilst gold coins were becoming increasingly rare. The Salic Law proves how general its use had become.

[1] This fact has been convincingly proved by Pierre le Gentilhomme. He has shown (*Mél. de num. mérov.*, p. 18) that the silver denier ousted the gold coin in Gaul at the end of the seventh century. The German economist Kötzschke has made the same observation (*Allg. Wirtschaftsgesch. d. Mittelalt.*, p. 150). Blanchet also (*Manuel*, I, p. 244) acknowledges that the minting of silver was more widespread in late Merovingian times than was believed half a century ago. M. Prou had already noted (*Les monnaies mérov.*, p. xi) that in the eighth century gold coins had become a rarity in Gaul.

[2] Le Gentilhomme, op. cit., p. 138.

[3] This word, in Old Frisian *skat*, corresponds to the German *Schatz* = treasure. On the diffusion of the sceattas, 'real international currency', see Le Gentilhomme, ibid., pp. 71–81.

All the sections – and they are many – which involve a
monetary fine end by indicating the scale of compensation
reckoned in deniers and followed by the equivalent in *solidi*,
for example: *DC dinarios qui faciunt solidos XV*. The ratio is
always the same: the denier is 1/40 of the *solidus*. Many
historians have attempted to solve the enigma of the denier
in the Salic Law. Pierre le Gentilhomme has suggested a
solution which is as satisfactory as it is simple. In his expert
opinion this denier is none other than the denier struck in the
Frankish kingdom towards the close of the seventh century,
at a time when, because of the shortage of gold currency, this
silver denier had become legal tender.[1] It had to be given a
legal value in the scale of compensation, of which the fines
had originally been fixed in gold *solidi*. The equivalents would
in that case be later glosses. The silver denier, which had
the same weight as the gold *tiers de sou*, 1·30 gr., was valued in
these glosses at 1/40 of the gold *solidus*. This evaluation pre-
supposes an approximate ratio of silver to gold = 1/13, which
is feasible. On the other hand it is most unlikely that the
authors of the oldest version of the Law, who lived in the
late fifth century at a time when the Salian Franks still knew
no other coins but those circulating in the Roman Empire,
and probably did not know even those very well, should have
thought of noting in the provisions of their national Law, the
relationship existing between the *solidus* and the *denarius* of the
Romans.

*

The closing of the Mediterranean has always been regarded
as the least controversial, because the most obvious, result of
the Moslem conquest, yet this disaster may have been due, in
part at least, to the Merovingian policy of ignoring the sea
completely, and not only one sea, but every sea. The sole
ambition which the early Frankish kings pursued with any
degree of tenacity was that of reconquering Germany in its
entirety so as to annex it to their kingdom. The wars against
the Alamans and Thuringians were the first stages of that re-

[1] Op. cit., p. 139.

conquest, that reversal, which was completed when Charlemagne reunited to his empire Saxony and the lands dominated
and slavized by the Avars. For this conquest the Franks
possessed the necessary instrument, a land army for which recruiting was assured by the military service imposed on all
free men. But they had no fleet, and though masters of a kingdom bounded by several seas, they made no attempt to create
one. Charlemagne was aware of this serious lack, and Einhard[1]
shows him improvising two war fleets, one in the Northern
Ocean, that is to say the Channel and the North Sea, against
the Northmen who were laying waste the coast of Gaul and
Germany, the other against the Moors who were ravaging the
Mediterranean coast of Septimania as far as Rome, and these
measures taken against the Saracens prove that the Emperor
was not prepared to sit back and watch the Mediterranean
being turned into a Moslem lake.

The utter fecklessness of the Merovingians, and their indifference to the things of the sea, was all the more regrettable
since failure to keep the Roman roads in repair after the fall of
the Western Empire made it essential in many cases to travel
by water. We have seen that Mediterranean coastal shipping
was still fairly brisk in the sixth century, and that the inhabitants
of Gaul sailed along the coast on their way to Italy. The Atlantic
and Channel ports also were still fairly busy.[2] A list has been
compiled of products which were articles of barter, and which
were carried by boat along the Atlantic routes: salt from Saintonge and Noirmoutier; leather and raw wool exported from
Ireland which in turn imported wine from Gaul; tin was
brought from Cornwall and copper from England. A continuous
coastal traffic seems to have existed between Bordeaux and
Rouen in the Merovingian period. A Bordeaux *tiers de sou* has
been found in Rouen and conversely seven Rouen *triens* have

[1] *Vie de Charlemagne*, chap. xvii (ed. L. Halphen, pp. 52–53).
[2] A. Lewis, 'Commerce atlantique de la Gaule du Vᵉ au VIIIᵉ siècle', *Le Moyen
âge*, 1953, pp. 249–398. This trade was carried on particularly by the Cornish and
Irish. The author of the life of St Philibert, Abbot of Noirmoutier, refers to certain
'Brittones nautici' who had come to steal a young bull from his monastery. On
another occasion, however, a ship manned by Irishmen (*Scothorum*) and laden with
merchandise, came bringing shoes and clothing for the monks. *Vita S. Filiberti*, SS.
rer. merov., III, p. 603.

come to light in Bordeaux.[1] Again, at the end of the seventh
century, St Philibert, abbot of Jumièges, received a cargo of
oil from friends in Bordeaux. There is good reason to believe
that relations between the province of Rouen on the one hand,
and the southern Loire and Aquitaine on the other, were fairly
easy in Merovingian times, since the Abbey of Saint-Wandrille
was able to cultivate the estates it possessed near Nantes, in
Angoumois and in Saintonge.[2]

These economic necessities, and the legitimate demands of
shipping, which a statesman like Charlemagne felt impelled to
meet, never troubled the Merovingians. They gave no thought
at all to coastal defence. The occupation of Armorica, begun
in the fifth century but continued and carried through in their
time, is proof of their indifference. An early and copious hagiography has endeavoured to disarm its pious readers by making
the Bretons out to be luckless exiles who, pursued by cruel
invaders, Angles, Saxons and Scots, landed on the western tip
of Gaul in search of a refuge. Yet the violent struggles which the
Franks were compelled to wage against them show that these
refugees were not all peaceful exiles landing under the guidance
and direction of pious saints. The legend has softened the harshness of reality. The Saxon raids on the area around Boulogne,
their settling in the Bessin, are further signs that the Channel
was inadequately protected against these pirates, already
dreaded by the later Western Emperors who had organized
the defence of what they significantly called the Saxon shore
(*litus Saxonicum*). To whatever point on the coast we turn the
impression is exactly the same: the Frankish kings who preceded Charlemagne made no attempt at all to protect the
seaboard.

Further to the north were the Frisians.[3] Their zone of
occupation spread beyond Frisia proper and took in approximately a large part of the territory of Holland. The Frisians,
who had the sea in their blood, were sailors and traders. They

---

[1] Le Gentilhomme, op. cit., p. 16.

[2] F. Lot, *Etudes critiques sur l'abbaye de Saint-Wandrille*, pp. xxiv–xxv.

[3] Le Gentilhomme, op. cit., p. 71, shows the Frisians, at the end of the seventh
century, taking advantage of the scarcity of eastern merchants to monopolize the
western markets by bringing in Anglo-Saxon sceattas.

had both ports and mints. Quentovic,[1] which was in Frankish territory at the mouth of the Canche, made possible a brisk exchange trade between the continent and Great Britain. It was the starting point of a great highway leading to Rheims, Verdun and Strasbourg. When Charles the Bald, by the Edict of Pîtres (864), limited to nine the number of mints authorized to coin money, that of Quentovic was one of the privileged.[2] That, however, is the last known reference to the port, which was destroyed by the Northmen. In the eighth century, and for part of the ninth, thanks to the Frisians it played a rôle proportionate to that of Boulogne and Calais in modern times. Further to the east, on the banks of the Lek, one of the branches of the Lower Rhine, was situated the port of Duurstede;[3] that too was the site of a mint, and the reverse of a denier of Louis the Pious issued there shows a ship encircled by the name of the town (*Dorestatus*).[4] A third important mint in the same region was that of Maastricht, and the oldest coins struck there go back to the early seventh century. The activity of the Frisians was not limited to barter with Great Britain, where their merchants frequented the London markets. They acted as liaison between the Rhineland and Scandinavia,[5] having successfully occupied several islands off the west coast of Schleswig, Sylt Fohr, Pellworm and Nordstrand.[6] The goods they imported were ceramics from the workshops at Mayen and from their subsidiary branches in the Rhine Valley, as well as glassware made near Cologne in huts in the forest. Fragments of glass vases have been found on the west coast of Norway and in the Isle of Gotland. Trumpet-shaped goblets have even been found in Sweden, at Old Upsala as well as in the excavations at Lake Vendel. These goods were probably exchanged for furs, and perhaps also for slaves.

This seafaring existence remained quite outside the ex-

[1] For this port see Pierre Héliot, 'La question de Quentovic d'après les travaux récents', *Revue du Nord*, XXIII, 1937, pp. 260–265. Note that the port took its name from the River Canche: Quentovic = Quantia-Vicus.
[2] *Capitularia* (ed. Boretius, II, 1, p. 315).
[3] On this port see E. Ennen, *Frühgeschichte der europäischen Stadt*, pp. 56–58.
[4] Blanchet, *Manuel de Numismatique*, I, p. 344.
[5] H. Jankuhn, 'Der frankisch-friesische Handel', already quoted.
[6] *The Cambridge Economic History*, II, p. 176.

B.W.E.—F

perience of the Gallo-Roman and Frankish peoples, though
there is evidence of a fairly brisk river-transport system in
operation in Merovingian and early Carolingian times. Ships
laden with merchandise sailed up the Rhône, paying dues at
Marseilles, Fos,[1] Valence and Lyons, and these traffic dues
represented a considerable source of revenue for the kings.
Travellers sailed down the Rhône also, but if we are to believe
the author of the life of St Apollinaris, Bishop of Valence,[2]
who told the story of his hero's journey to Arles, the trip was
not without its dangers. The Loire too was navigable at least
as far as Tours,[3] as were its tributaries the Allier and the Cher.
The Abbot of Saint-Philibert de Noirmoutier, whose boats
sailed along these rivers, also had permission to sail freely on
the Garonne and the Dordogne. Similar exemption from all
dues was granted to the monks of Saint-Maixent as well as
to the Bishop of Nevers, who had asked for a *beneficium* for
transporting salt. His boats sailed up and down the Loire, the
Allier, the Cher, the Loir, the Sarthe and the Mayenne. Those
of Saint-Germain-des-Prés enjoyed a similar privilege for boats
along the entire course of the Seine and its tributaries the
Marne, the Yonne, the Oise and the Aisne. The granting of all
these privileges to the great abbeys of the realm by the early
Carolingians proves that at the beginning of the ninth century
river navigation had become the most widespread method of
transport for merchandise, and explains the inadequacy of the
roads from the time of the Great Invasions. The Austrasian
rivers also were used for navigation: the Rhine first and fore-

[1] Cant. Istres (Bouches-du-Rhône). At Fos there was a storehouse belonging to
the Treasury, a kind of goods warehouse for products most of which were exotic
and of eastern origin. This depot held the dues which the kings levied in kind on
eastern traders sailing up the Rhône with their merchandise. A list of the goods
deposited there was drawn up in a charter of Chilperic II dated 716 in favour of
the monks of Corbie, whom this king had authorized to receive a certain quantity
of them each year. The list mentions garum, pepper, cummin, cloves, cinnamon,
nard, *costum* (an aromatic plant), dates, figs, almonds, pistachio, rice, etc. Levillain,
Examen critique des chartes mérov. et carol. de l'abb. de Corbie, Paris, 1902, pp. 235–237.
Cf. H. Pirenne, *Mahomet et Charlemagne*, pp. 71–72.
[2] *Mon. Germ. Hist.*, SS. rer. merov., III, p. 200. The chronicle relates that the
saint 'cursum navigationis arripuit', but that his companions were terrified by the
dangers attending the voyage down the Rhône, 'quamvis ceteros pernicis Rodani
fluenta terrerent'.
[3] Gregory of Tours, *Hist. Franc.*, IV, 48.

most, the Scheldt, the Moselle, on which sailing was completely
safe. Gregory of Tours in fact tells us that a merchant from
Trier, who had brought from Metz a cargo of salt bought in
that town, was able to sleep throughout the whole of the
journey.[1] The pious historian attributes this happy state of
affairs to St Martin, into whose hands the traveller had
committed himself.

The transport operating along most of the rivers helped the
cities situated on their banks – Bordeaux, Nantes, Nevers, Paris,
Rouen and Amiens to mention only a few – to maintain a
certain liveliness and activity. A study of those places in which
Merovingian coins have been found has shown that a large
number of *solidi* and *triens* minted in Southern and Central
Gaul were imitated in the north of the kingdom, notably at
Troyes and Soissons. The tide of commerce followed not only
the old Roman roads, but also, we believe, the rivers.[2] This
development was checked only at the close of the ninth century
and was finally ended by the invasions of the Northmen. It
should, however, be borne in mind that the Merovingians were
in part and indirectly responsible for the destruction which was
to be wrought by the Northmen. They had not kept the fortifications of their towns in repair, and when in the second half
of the ninth century they began to think of restoring these
enclosing walls, it was to be too late. King Chilperic I, one of
the few Merovingians to have ideas which, though sometimes
odd, were original and intelligent, was the only one to give any
thought to their restoration,[3] but he did so for purely selfish
motives, as a defence against his brother Guntramn, who was
threatening to occupy his cities.

In contrast to the rest of Gaul, the south was devastated
early. The dramatic siege and destruction of the city of
Comminges in which the pretender Gundobald (585) had taken
refuge, is the only known event in the history of Novempopulania during Merovingian times.[4] From the sixth century

[1] Ibid.

[2] Vercauteren, op. cit., p. 448, and map p. 449.

[3] Gregory of Tours, *Hist. Franc.*, VI, 27 (41).

[4] F. Lot, *Recherches sur la population et la superficie des cités*, Part 3, p. 153. Cf. Ch.
Higounet, *Le comté de Comminges*, Toulouse–Paris, 1949, I, pp. 10–17.

onwards the Basque invasions began. The history of the south-west was to be a blank page until the tenth century. The most regrettable economic result of the cumulative devastation wrought not only by this occupation but also by the Saracen raids and the campaigns waged by the Franks in their attempts to reconquer the country was perhaps the final decay of the Aquitaine marble industry.[1]

In the south-east, Saracen piracy had consequences no less disastrous and more far-reaching.[2] One of the most prosperous regions in Gaul, the cradle of Gallo-Roman and Christian civilization, became from the seventh to the end of the tenth century if not a desert at least a country of silence. Gaps covering several centuries in the episcopal registers, a total lack of charters and of all written documents in an area which had been the home of the oldest monasteries in Gaul, Saint-Victor of Marseilles, Lérins, the complete stagnation of the port of Marseilles, all go to prove that the depopulated countryside remained for several hundred years defenceless against the pirates who were terrorizing the inhabitants. Most feared were the Spanish Moors who had settled at La Garde Freinet, near the small harbour of St Tropez, and who acquired a legendary fame.[3]

We shall deal purely with the repercussions which this collective panic, this powerlessness to react against the invader, had on the economy. One of the most marked was a general disruption of traffic. Armies and pilgrims alike were turned aside from their usual routes. Henceforth the inhabitants of Gaul and Germany had to make their way into Italy over the Alpine passes, and the people of that region were known as the Transalpines. The area of devastation cannot be determined with complete accuracy. At first it extended along the whole of the coast from which the population had fled, then spread over the

---

[1] Le Gentilhomme puts this in the latter half of the seventh century. Op. cit., p. 100.

[2] E. Duprat has devoted a chapter to the Saracens in Provence in his work on 'La Provence dans le haut moyen âge', Marseilles, 1923, pp. 47–63. Extr. from *L'Encyclopédie des Bouches-du-Rhône*, vol. II.

[3] See my article: 'Les idées actuelles sur les Sarrasins dans les Alpes', *Revue de Géographie alpine*, vol. 19, 1931, pp. 199–206.

entire Alpine region, Haute Provence, part of Dauphiné, Savoy, which were sparsely populated and became the targets for Saracen raids. The Rhône valley with its string of important cities was less attractive to them, and they left it alone.[1] The result of the Saracen infiltration and of that strange and widespread collective panic which lasted for several centuries was that the widely dispersed peoples living in the terrorized districts adopted – or perhaps preserved – a type of settlement which has survived to the present day. Afraid to stay in the plains and on the valley floors, they preferred to band together, or continued to live, crowded in *castra*, in villages perched on hilltops, and when at the end of the tenth century they brought their land back into cultivation, they evolved a type of agrarian life different from that prevailing elsewhere.

The balance-sheet of the Merovingian economy is singularly disappointing. The now fashionable, if unpleasant, word 'rot', describes it to perfection. Whether in the sphere of town life, commerce, barter, currency, public works, shipping, we find everywhere the same policy of neglect, the same selfish refusal to initiate reform. From this disastrous, drifting *laissez-faire* which left men and things as they had always been, pursuing unchanged their traditional way of life, there sprang the illusion that the ancient world still lingered on; it was, in fact, no more than a façade. The fact that Constantinian *solidi* continued to be minted up to the end of the seventh century is no reason for assuming that the Merovingians remained faithful to the monetary system of the Late Empire, for these so-called gold *solidi* no longer contained any yellow metal, and the minting of them was left to coiners who were often unprincipled. There have been some grounds for believing that the Merovingian kings had a Mediterranean policy because several of them quarrelled for possession of the port of Marseilles, but they did so from mean motives of self-interest, and the activity of the port diminished under their rule. The Frankish kings gave no thought at all to the possession of a fleet. So long as there was a Byzantine fleet to protect the sea routes, coastal shipping was possible

[1] 'La vallée du Rhône a-t-elle été une route d'invasion pendant le haut moyen âge?' *Mélanges Nicolas Jorga*, Paris, 1933, pp. 487–497.

along the Mediterranean, but from the moment the Near East, North Africa and Spain fell into Moslem hands, this traffic inevitably came to an end. The Merovingians made not the slightest effort to fill the gap left by Byzantium and to create a Frankish fleet. From their time dates that French indifference to things of the sea with which as a nation we have so often been reproached. In striking contrast, the Frisians, the ancestors of the Dutch, had as early as the seventh century clearly shown themselves to be both seafarers and merchants. Finally, under the Merovingians, town planning and development were sadly neglected. They neither sought to keep their city walls in repair nor to prevent them from crumbling into ruins. If most of the bishops built their cathedrals on the ramparts, they probably did so because that was where they could find material which could be used again; the kings allowed them a free hand.

From whatever point of view it is considered, the Merovingian period gives the impression of a vacuum. It was not, as is sometimes stated, the continuance of a Mediterranean economy; it was an economy hopelessly and helplessly adrift.

PART III

The Early Carolingians: A Temporary Restoration

The Emperor Maurice, struck
at Marseilles

The Frankish king Theudebert victorious
(Victor)

MEROVINGIAN TIERS DE SOUS

Bust of Clovis II
struck in the palace
by St Eloi (Eligi)

Triens struck by the
coiner Theodomaris at
Antre (Jura)

Triens struck by
the coiner Fragiulfus at
Verdun

CAROLINGIAN SILVER DENIERS

Denier of Pepin the Short
struck at
Troyes (Tricas)

Denier of the emperor
Charlemagne

 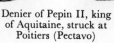

Denier of Pepin II, king
of Aquitaine, struck at
Poitiers (Pectavo)

Denier of Odo, king of
France, struck at the palace

7. Merovingian and Carolingian Money

CHAPTER I

Charlemagne and a Controlled Economy. Reform of the Currency

'A CONTRAST IN ECONOMIES: Merovingians and Carolingians',[1] is the title of a famous article by Henri
Pirenne, in which he sought to stress one of his favourite
theories – the contrast presented by two consecutive early
medieval periods viewed from the standpoint of economics:
one the Merovingian, still closely bound up with the economy
of the Mediterranean world, the other the Carolingian, the
dawn of a new age in which for several hundred years society
was to remain static within a localized framework and was tied
down to a purely agrarian and closed economy. There is no
need to reiterate the underlying cause of this cleavage – the
irruption of the Moslems into the western basin of the Mediterranean. It is the extent of the cleavage which has been exaggerated, but Pirenne had too keen a sense of reality to wish to see
his own ideas and even his most fruitful hypotheses interpreted
too rigidly. In order to throw his ideas into bolder relief, he
liked to strike hard and often, leaving to those who followed
him the more thankless task of refining and elaborating them.

The northward trend of political and economic activity, its
shift towards the Meuse and the Rhine basins, was in reality the
outstanding fact of the later seventh and the eighth centuries.
In Austrasia there were men who were energetic politicians,
and wealthy and influential families. One of the latter, that of
the Pepins, first monopolized the office of Mayor of the Palace,
then ousted the effete Merovingian dynasty.

[1] *Rev. belge de Philol. et d'Hist.*, 1923.

The early Carolingians did great and remarkable work, and Charlemagne was one of the privileged few of whom it is unanimously agreed that they made history.[1] Yet it must be admitted that agreement is far from general about his intentions and the significance of the work he accomplished. What exactly was his conception of the Empire? Did he actually seek and desire the imperial dignity or was he pushed into assuming it by his clerical entourage? Did he even weigh up the serious consequences of his revolutionary act? Was not the sharing out of his Estates between his sons in 806, which was in keeping with Germanic traditions, a disavowal of the work of unification symbolized by his coronation at Christmas in the year 800? This problem, and a host of others raised by modern historiography and not yet solved, indicate hidden motives, hesitancies, a certain fluidity in the intentions and conduct of a man who is generally and whole-heartedly admired for his straightforward thinking and his inflexible will-power. To admit this in no way detracts from Charlemagne's stature; it makes him, on the contrary, more human, more rewarding of study. We shall confine ourselves here to a careful review of his economic achievement, remembering that in a large number of cases the measures taken by this dictatorial Emperor were suggested by his counsellors; it was he, however, who had the ability, which many lack, to translate them into actual fact.

Pirenne's assessment of his work was fair and just. Severe in his strictures on an age which he regarded as the beginning of a period of retrogression and economic atrophy, he praised Charlemagne for having understood the times in which he lived and carried through a policy of adaptation which circumstances had made essential. After declaring that the picture which emerges from the end of the eighth century, and even during the great Emperor's most glorious years, is undoubtedly one of decadence, he adds: 'Charlemagne's originality consists in having broken new ground, in having abandoned the tradition of the ancient world and understood and acted on the

[1] Several interesting sidelights on the personality of Charlemagne are to be found in L. M. Hartmann's *Geschichte Italiens im Mittelalter*, III, 1, Gotha, 1908, p. 82 et seq.

realization that Western Europe could no longer live on the Mediterranean.' [1] To put it more bluntly, Charlemagne is to be congratulated on having been a skilful, even an inspired, liquidator. Historians are in a position to check this stern verdict which comes down so harshly on the age in which Charlemagne lived but is more lenient towards the man himself, since the Emperor, like his ninth-century successors, was a prolific law-giver, and Pirenne had good grounds for stating that 'the Capitularies still remain the finest monument left us by the Carolingian age'.

From a close study of this body of legislation, though unfortunately there is no good critical edition of the Capitularies, [2] many of which are still inadequately dated and are not presented in their true light, there emerges an impression of coherence and continuity from the mass of documents which for the most part are instructions addressed to *missi*. Charlemagne's Capitularies are often no more than hastily composed directives, rather like chapter headings, but always explicit enough for us to divine their author's intentions. Later, after the great Emperor's death, there may still be discerned the same determination to establish law and order and to put the economy on a moral basis, but the form becomes more turgid. The clerks who under Charlemagne were already acting as the sovereign's advisers assumed a more pompous air and imposed their own style. The voice we hear is no longer that of an imperious master, but the voice of preachers. From the latter half of the ninth century the driving will-power gradually weakens as feudal anarchy spreads and the invasions of the Northmen paralyse economic activity. At the close of the century, no more is heard from the authors of the Capitularies, and we have to wait until the twelfth century and the first ordinances of the Capetian kings for an awakening of legislative life.

*

[1] 'Un contraste économique', *Rev. belge de Philol. et d'Hist.*, 1923, p. 230.

[2] The edition of the Capitularies contributed by Boretius to the *Monumenta Germaniae* needs thorough revision. It has been severely criticized by Simon Stein in *Le Moyen âge*, 1940. The death of Louis Halphen prevented him from publishing a comprehensive study of the Carolingian Capitularies announced in *Charlemagne et l'Empire carolingien*, Paris, 1947, p. 511.

Pepin the Short, then Charlemagne, and their counsellors, must be given credit for their efforts to reform the economy at its roots by starting with a purification of the coinage. An expert numismatist has laid down a clear definition of the Carolingian monetary system:[1] it was monometallic, the silver denier, of good weight and alloy,[2] was universal throughout the Empire and minted gold was no longer anything but a rare exception. This reform was not empirical but systematic and the rulers imposed it on their peoples by a series of hard-hitting Capitularies. The oldest known example is that issued by Pepin the Short just before the Council of Vernon, 11 July 755. Section 5 deals with the relationship between the *solidus* and the *livre*, and fixes the remuneration granted to the coiner: 'We decree', said the king, 'that henceforth there shall be no more than 22 *solidi* in one *livre*. From these 22 *solidi* the coiner shall be allowed to take one and the others shall be handed over to their rightful owner.'[3] This was only a beginning; already the king's determination to assert the royal rights over the currency was becoming clear, but there was as yet no question of insisting on or regulating the minting and circulation of the silver denier.

The documents relating to this reform have not been preserved if they ever existed, but we possess numerous Capitularies designed to impose the new standard on the recalcitrant. Charlemagne's two most original innovations, introduced about 780, consisted in setting up a new division of the *livre* into 20 *solidi* and of the *solidus* into 12 deniers, and striking silver coins worth one denier for general circulation.[4] The only point on which there is some doubt is the official weight of this new

---

[1] A. Blanchet, *Manuel*, I, p. 359.

[2] Legally the Carolingian deniers were of pure silver; if this was not always so in practice, it was because of the lack of facilities for purifying metal at the disposal of the coiners, or was the result of deliberate fraud. M. Prou, *Les monnaies carol.*, p. xliii.

[3] *Capitul.* (ed. Boretius, I, p. 321).

[4] Since gold had already almost completely disappeared from circulation in the time of Charlemagne, we readily support the opinion expressed by a German scholar, Walter Hävernick, in a note published by the *VSWG*, LXI, 1954, pp. 146–147, under the title: *Die karolingischen Münzreformen: Ende der alten Zustände oder Beginn einer neuen Entwicklung*, in which he states that the monetary reforms of the early Carolingians were not in the least revolutionary in character and that their originators did not themselves consider them to be anything new.

denier, since modern numismatists disagree on the weight of Charlemagne's *livre*, their estimate varying between 367 and 491 gr.[1] The basic and most vital feature of these reforms was the generalization of the silver standard which was made compulsory. Evidence of its practical repercussions may be traced in several of the documents. In the seventh and eighth centuries payments were still being made in gold, then in gold and silver;[2] in the first half of the ninth century they were no longer paid in anything but silver, even when the amount owing was considerable.[3] Next came the creation of a money of account which, current in France throughout the whole of the Middle Ages and under the *ancien régime*, is still in use in Great Britain. The term 'money of account' is used deliberately. In fact the silver denier became for several centuries the only real currency, the only coin in circulation. No more *solidi* were issued, and if gold coins were minted in some Carolingian workshops, this was a rare occurrence; they may perhaps have been intended to pay for purchases made outside the Empire. The minting of silver money was made possible by an intensive exploitation of the Harz and Bohemian mines, and also of a mine situated in Poitou at Melle, a name which, derived from the Latin *Metalla*, recalls the industry carried on there.[4]

Charlemagne was determined to keep the monopoly of

[1] According to F. Lot, *Naissance de la France*, p. 713, the coinage had always been based on the Roman *libra* of 327 gr. It was probably only about the year 781 that Charlemagne increased the weight of the standard *livre* by 50 per cent. to bring it up to 491 gr. This he believes to have been the probable origin of the *livre du Roi* of 489½ gr. which lasted up to the French Revolution.

[2] Here are several examples:
Seventh century: 'Unde accepimus de vobis precium hoc est in *auro* valente soledos tantus.' Sale of goods from *Form. Andec.* in Thévenin, *Textes*, pp. 5–6, no. 4.

704: 'Unde accepimus a vobis in precio taxato . . . inter *aurum et argentum* solidos mille quingentos.' *Cart. S. Bertin*, p. 39, no. 18.

776: 'Unde accepi a vobis . . . inter *aurum et argentum* sol. CC tantum.' Ibid., p. 61, no. 41.

[3] 833: Sale of a *mansus*, *Cart. de Redon*, p. 35, no. xliii: 'Unde accepi pretio . . . aut in *argento* solidos CXX.'

846: Another sale in the same *Cart.*, p. 43, no. liii: 'Precium in quo nobis bene complacuit . . . hoc est in *argento* solidos xviii et ad poticulas quas simul bibimus denarios xviii.'

Eighth century: 'Accepi a predicto abbate precium *argenti* libram I'. *Formulae Augienses*, in Zeumer, p. 355.

[4] A. Blanchet, *Manuel*, I, p. 133.

coining exclusively for the Palace Mint and right up to his death persisted in this resolve, which is revealed in two Capitularies of 805 and 808.[1] He failed in his aim,[2] and his successors were too weak to follow up his plan successfully. Even so, for half a century a strict watch continued to be kept over the coining and circulation of money through the agency of counts, who were officially entrusted with this surveillance within their own cities,[3] and of *missi* who were in the nature of inspectors-general of administration. But there is one detail which shows that the coiners had lost the prestige and independence they had enjoyed under the Merovingians. Their names no longer figured on the inscriptions of the coins minted.[4] The reassertion of the royal right to coin money, in other words of a monopoly in favour of the sovereign, was successfully carried through by an energetic prince like Charlemagne. The weakening of the central power in the second half of the ninth century prevented its continuance. The Edict of Pîtres of 864 was the last measure of a general nature taken by a Carolingian ruler for the minting and circulation of money. The monetary concessions which had brought about the debasing of the coinage under the Merovingians began again with the close of the reign of Charles the Bald. Granted in the first place to bishops, these concessions were subsequently extended to laymen, and towards the end of the ninth century the ineffectiveness of the kings brought about the transition from royal to feudal coining. The counts who, as royal officials, were responsible for supervising and controlling the minting of money[5] began by appropriating, with or without the king's permission, the income from the mints in which it

---

[1] A. Blanchet, *Manuel*, I, p. 351. Section 7 of the Capitulary of 808 specifies 'ut in nullo loco moneta percutiatur nisi ad curtem'. *Capitul.*, I, p. 140.

[2] M. Lopez speaks ironically of Charlemagne 'se gargarisant avec l'idée de concentrer le monnayage à Aix-la-Chapelle dont il ferait une Constantinople en miniature', and adds: 'C'était trop ambitieux.' 'An aristocracy of money', *Speculum*, January 1953. Charlemagne's ambition seems to us, on the contrary, entirely legitimate.

[3] 820. Section I: 'Haec capitula in singulis locis observari debent . . . Ut civitatis illius moneta publice sub custodia comitis fiat.' Cap. de moneta, *Capitul.*, I, p. 299.

[4] The coiner's name disappeared to make way for that of the king. M. Prou has stressed the importance of this modification. *Les monnaies carolingiennes*, p. xlvi.

[5] 'The manufacture of coins took place under the direct control of the counts.' Prou, ibid., p. 1.

was coined, then later the growing weakness of the royal authority led them to usurp the actual right of coining.[1]

This lamentable reversion to the mistakes of the Merovingian era was all the easier since both Charlemagne, with all his prestige, and also his immediate successors, had great difficulty in getting these currency reforms accepted. The unpopularity of the measures showed itself in an obdurate suspicion and refusal to accept the new coins put into circulation. Capitularies spread over the years 794 to 864 had to reinforce with penalties the sovereign's injunction, binding upon all his subjects, to accept payment in what Charlemagne called his 'new deniers', and proof that offenders were numerous and persistent is furnished by the multitude of instructions it was found necessary to address to the *missi* and to the public in order to break down this silent and obstinate resistance. The penalties were nevertheless severe: a fine of 15 *solidi* if the offender was a free man, and corporal punishment, beating with rods, if he was a *colonus* or a serf. Moreover Charlemagne, who was determined to be obeyed at all costs, did not hesitate to strike in influential quarters by depriving of their offices the count, bishop or abbot who neglected to deal with anyone rejecting the royal deniers when the offence was committed within their jurisdiction.[2] On the other hand the authors of the Capitularies, who were not without a sense of what was fitting, saw no point in alienating public opinion by needless severities, and urged those responsible for suppressing currency offences to act with discretion and deal tactfully with old people who were naturally hostile to newfangled ideas, with invalids, and with 'the fair sex', it being in the nature of women to bargain (*barcaniare*) – in other words to haggle and argue.[3] These successive warnings show that the unification of the currency, the

[1] 'From the early years of the tenth century, money became in fact the property of the count. It was only in the second half of the tenth century that a few counts dared to inscribe their names first beside, then instead of that of the king.' Prou, ibid., p. lvii.

[2] 809. Capitulare missorum Aquisgranense alterum, clause 7, *Capitul.*, I, p. 152. – Cf. Synod of Frankfurt 794, clause 5, ibid., I, p. 74.

[3] 861. Constitutio Caroli Calvi de moneta: 'Considerent aetatem et infirmitatem et sexum personae, quia et feminae barcaniare solent.' *Capitul.*, II, 1, p. 301.

monopoly imposed by the sovereign, the introduction of new coins, came up against deep-rooted prejudices and doubtless also against private interests which, injured by the reforms, worked up against them an atmosphere of mistrust which was easily created in a society still crude and unsophisticated. Notwithstanding this opposition, one result was achieved through Charlemagne's vigorous efforts: a sound currency was established and a silver monometallism was imposed.

In actual fact things had been moving in that direction for more than a century past, for the percentage of gold in the *solidus* and the *triens* had become so insignificant that these coins were discredited and almost wholly supplanted in circulation by the Merovingian denier. Charlemagne's great merit lay in legalizing the existing situation and giving it his blessing, and putting into circulation a good silver denier with the fullest guarantees to those willing to accept it. The prejudice of certain liberal economists who link the fate of trade with that of the circulation of gold has led them to criticize the monetary system consolidated and regulated by Charlemagne. They have apparently forgotten that Western Europe in the ninth century was not that of the twentieth. A modern state like France or Belgium must have foreign exchange and gold to ensure the progress of its industries which buy their raw materials abroad, and to infuse new life into its trade. By isolating itself in autarky, it would stifle to death. But to seek to apply this concept to ninth-century Europe is to be the victim of a mirage, for we have seen just what was meant by the Merovingian '*grand commerce*', that Mediterranean trade in which Syrians, Greeks, Jews, acted as intermediaries between West and East. It consisted in procuring spices and silks for rich individuals, and bringing from North Africa and Egypt certain goods in everyday use such as oil, papyrus, indigo, though the demand for these was diminishing owing to the diffusion of native substitutes such as wax, parchment, woad. It is moreover quite possible that Charlemagne foresaw what effects the withdrawal of gold would have on economic relations with countries situated outside the frontiers of his vast domains, and the gold coinage minted in his workshops,[1] the amount of which was indeed very small, was perhaps intended for use in foreign trade. Moreover, and the fact cannot be too emphatically repeated, from the time of the Great Invasions, in spite of the efforts of the Byzantines – and in particular of Justinian – to maintain the close bonds between the West and their Empire, the western world was breaking away from the Mediterranean and its axis was shifting northward. This was an inexorable evolution which was only slightly speeded up by the Moslem conquest.

It was vitally important for the future, as Charlemagne seems to have realized perfectly, to ensure that the peoples of the vast Empire stretching from the Elbe to the Ebro had a sufficient quantity of metal currency to cover the requirements of internal circulation. His silver denier supplied this need. The Carolingians strove to maintain its legal weight and percentage of pure silver in order to prevent it from becoming a mere token money, a coinage of inflation, and took vigorous, even unpopular, steps to impose it on their subjects and encourage its circulation. It would be a serious error of judgement to forget that western economic life had already from the fourth century, taken on an essentially domanial character, and to claim that Charlemagne by his legislation hastened on the transition from a silver economy to a natural economy. The exact opposite is more likely to have been the case. A glance through the Capitularies – in other words the laws and administrative acts – of Pepin the Short, Charlemagne and their immediate successors, is enough to show how much thought they devoted to monetary problems. Unlike their Merovingian predecessors who had no general grasp of the problems of government, they were anxious

[1] Amongst the few mints coining gold in the Carolingian period, that of Uzès used to be considered the most important. However, an expert numismatist, P. Grierson, in a solidly documented article, 'Le sou d'or d'Uzès', *Le Moyen âge*, 1954, pp. 293–309, has recently queried the authenticity of the gold *solidi* attributed to Charlemagne. Only five specimens of this so-called gold coinage have been preserved. Their poor style and varying weights make it impossible to consider them as true currency. Grierson believes them to have been minted long after the reign of Charlemagne, to have come from a private mint and to have been meant as token payments on the occasion of some ceremony which took place at Uzès. The only gold coins issued under the early Carolingians were struck at Aix-la-Chapelle. Consequently the mint at Uzès which turned out gold coins is a myth.

to create a currency which answered their people's needs. Those needs were limited, not marginal but real though restricted, and could for the most part be satisfied in local markets. The great merit of the Carolingians, and in particular of Charlemagne, the most far-sighted of all the early medieval rulers, lies in the fact that they assigned to money its true place in the economy of the time, since it would have been absurd to put large quantities, or even quite a small amount, of gold into circulation to supply markets which were essentially agrarian and handled only modest transactions. Small silver deniers or half-deniers were all that was needed to enable people of moderate means to buy in these markets a piece of meat, a pound of bread, a setier (= 2 gallons) of wine or a little salt. Charlemagne's monetary reforms were inspired by sound realism. There is no indication that they were precipitated by an increasing shortage of gold. There was very little gold available at the close of the Merovingian period, but it is impossible to state with certainty that the stock of it diminished in Charlemagne's time. A glance through the inventories drawn up in his reign, and especially one of the most detailed, that in which the compiler of the *brevium exempla* listed the property of Saint-Michael of Staffelsee in the diocese of Augsburg,[1] is ample proof that churches, even quite unimportant ones, possessed numerous objects of gold and silver gilt. These were to be found also amongst the property of laymen, about which we know very little, but from the formularies of the Carolingian era and from several wills, it is obvious that gold objects were by no means rare. No effort was made to conceal them, and there was never any question of melting them down, for the simple reason that there was no particular demand for gold coins.

The unification of weights and measures was also one of Charlemagne's objectives, and sprang from his unwavering determination to clean up the markets. The principle is stated in the *Admonitio generalis* of 789:[2] 'Throughout the whole of the

---

[1] *Capitul.*, I, p. 250.

[2] Ibid., I, p. 60. Charlemagne claimed that the justification for this measure was to be found in the law of God: 'Et in lege Domini praeceptum habemus, etiam in Salomone [Prov. xx. 10], Domino dicente: Pondus et pondus, mensuram et mensuram dedit anima mea.'

realm', he wrote, 'weights and measures must be identical and accurate.' This aim was ambitious, too ambitious, and the widely differing standards prevailing in the various provinces of his vast states were an obstacle to its realization. Charlemagne's successors had to be content with establishing the unity of weights and measures within each separate province.[1] The Edict of Pîtres (864), that strange Capitulary containing, in a kind of unco-ordinated synthesis, everything that an effete administration had managed to salvage from the great Emperor's vast projects, returned to the attack and insisted that the counts should keep a careful watch on weights and measures, stating quite plainly the human reason which lay behind this decree: to prevent those who sold from cheating or robbing those who bought.[2]

The organizing ability which inspired not only the Capitularies on currency and weights and measures, but all those dealing with economic matters, deserves special emphasis. Those warrior princes, who still retained an underlying brutality and only gradually shed their uncouth ways, took their inspiration from the Church, the only source of spirituality available to men of their day. Whether in politics or in the organization of social life, the Church was their guide. They looked to her for a rule of conduct which their predecessors had failed to hand down to them for the simple reason that they had none to transmit. Charlemagne was undoubtedly sincere, anxious to educate himself and improve his mind, when he had read aloud to him during meals the works of St Augustine and particularly the *City of God*.[3] Yet one cannot help thinking that such readings must often have bored this pleasure-loving sportsman, and wondering what benefit he could possibly have derived from them. But he was a true believer, anxious to do his duty as a Christian to the best of his ability. Though his private life was not always exemplary, he saw himself as a second David, entrusted with the task of establishing the rule of justice throughout

[1] 829. 'Admonemus ut saltem nullus duplices mensuras in sua dominatione aut habeat aut haberi permittat'. *Capitul.*, II, 1, p. 44. Cf. a Capitulary addressed to the *missi* of Lothar, February 832. Ibid., p. 63.

[2] Ibid., II, 1, pp. 318–319.

[3] Einhard, *Vita Karoli Magni*, 24 (ed. L. Halphen, p. 72).

his far-flung Empire. In the sphere of economics, as in all others, his line of conduct was determined by the teachings of Holy Scripture and of the Church Fathers, and when he sought advice it was from men who were the guardians of Christian truth, from bishops and monks. It would therefore be pointless to look for an original economic or political programme in his Capitularies. They are really measures of expediency, inspired by godly counsellors and designed to cope with a famine or a war, or to redress abuses notified by conscientious *missi*, or by the Fathers of some Council; but Charlemagne's practical genius transformed them into clear, precise rules of public administration. His skill is all the more evident when his Capitularies are compared with those of his successor, the mediocre Louis the Pious. Promulgated at a time when harangues were the fashion, by a weak prince who was quite unable to stem the tide of pious exhortation, they turned into veritable homilies.

Side by side with the requirements of Christian morality went military necessities. The Carolingian economy was a war economy. Each year of Charlemagne's reign was marked by a campaign the preparations for which made heavy demands on the imperial economy. The victualling, fitting out and equipping of the army was a constant source of anxiety to the Emperor and his high officials. A large part of the produce from the imperial estates was, as we shall see, set aside for the army, and a watch kept on *negociatores* at the frontiers aimed at preventing trade with the enemy. It is interesting to note that many of the Capitularies were introduced in the spring, obviously with an eye to the summer campaign, and that they were intended partly to put the inhabitants of the Empire into a state of readiness. We have to think ourselves back into that restless, warlike atmosphere, to recall the crisp, militant directives which rang out year after year, if we are to see the Carolingian economy in its true light.

CHAPTER II

Trade and Barter under the Early Carolingians

HRISTIAN AND EVEN CLERICAL inspiration are plainly discernible in the rigorous measures taken by Charlemagne and his successors to forbid the lending of money at interest. It had been practised in the Merovingian period. Gregory of Tours tells how the Bishop of Verdun, having begged from Theudebert, King of Austrasia, a loan of 7,000 gold *solidi* on behalf of the inhabitants of his town, promised him, if he agreed, to repay the sum borrowed with the legal interest (*cum usuris legitimis*).[1] This bishop regarded the payment of interest as the natural accompaniment of the loan, and as an ordinary transaction which was obviously fair and aboveboard. This practice was, however, contrary to the doctrine of the Church, which forbade clerics to engage in it. Yielding to the admonitions of his clerical advisers, Charlemagne was the first ruler to extend the ban to laymen and to give to this prohibition, now made binding on all alike, the sanction of civil legislation.[2] Such a ban, the serious consequences of which he most certainly foresaw, could be imposed only by degrees. The *Admonitio Generalis* of 789 was the first Capitulary to contain provisions affecting lending at interest. In it Charlemagne refers to decisions of the Council of Nicea and of Pope Leo the Great in support of his ruling that the ban should apply to everyone (*omnibus*) and not only to the clergy.[3] No legal punishment was laid down for offenders.

[1] *Hist. Franc.*, III, 34.
[2] Inama-Sternegg, *Deutsche Wirtschaftsgeschichte*, 2nd ed., Leipzig, 1909, p. 670.
[3] *Capitul.*, I, p. 54.

The Capitulary of Nijmegen, March 806,[1] marks a new development. Published in a year when a great famine was raging in many parts of the Empire, it is a timely reminder of previous interdicts, made more dramatically real and urgent by the circumstances in which it was written. The Emperor begins by defining the crime of usury which he relates to the sin of avarice, and goes on to specify and condemn certain practices in which men were at that time engaging.

The clauses on usury in this directive intended for the *missi* are worth quoting, since they reveal the essential originality of Charlemagne's legislation, the enunciation of moral principles, scriptural and ecclesiastical in origin, followed by their appropriate application to concrete cases:

Clause 11. Usury consists in claiming back more than you give; for instance if you have given 10 *solidi* and ask for more back, or if you have given a hogshead of wheat and afterwards demand one extra.

Clause 14. Avarice consists in coveting other people's goods and in not giving them to others when one has obtained them. The Apostle declares this to be the root of all evil.

Clause 15. Those who by various manœuvres dishonestly plan to amass goods of all kinds with the express aim of making money are acquiring ill-gotten gains.

Clause 16. Lending (*foenus*) consists in providing something; the loan is fair and just when you claim back no more than you provided.

Clause 17. All persons who at harvest time or when the grapes are gathered acquire corn or wine which they do not need, but get simply through an underlying motive of greed, for instance buying a hogshead for two deniers and keeping it until they can sell it again for six deniers or even more, are guilty of what we call dishonest gain. If on the other hand they buy it because they need it, so as to keep it for themselves or give it away to others, that is a business transaction (*negocium*).

Charlemagne's severity, incidentally, is directed particularly

[1] *Capitul.*, I, p. 132.

against speculation, which at a time when capitalism did not exist could hardly be indulged in except at the expense of the poor.

The Emperor returned to the attack in 809, which was again a year of famine,[1] and forbade a moneylending transaction which must have been common practice in time of scarcity. It consisted in making an advance in money or in kind before the harvest, then demanding from the borrower when repayment was due double or treble the amount lent.[2]

There has been some question as to whether the civil law punished the offence of usury with a separate fine apart from that inflicted by the Church in the reign of Charlemagne. One of the Emperor's Capitularies, unfortunately undated, inflicts a heavy fine on usurers: 'We wish no one', he declares, 'to exact any further interest in any circumstance whatever. Anyone who does so will be made to pay the fine laid down for breaking this ban.' [3] This fine amounted to 60 *solidi*. It was quite unlike Charlemagne to issue a decree which he did not enforce. His successors hardened their attitude, and lending at interest continued to be very strictly forbidden until such time as the resumption of economic activity led to a return to a money economy.

The revelation of moneylending practices laid bare by Charlemagne throws light on the reasons underlying a ban as drastic as this veto on lending at interest. Its justification lay in the economic set-up of the Early Middle Ages, which had no large-scale trade or industrial activity maintained by contributions from capital, and in which as a result the only loans known were those connected with foodstuffs and agreed to at rates which were almost always exorbitant.

We have to get back into this same atmosphere of a non-capitalist economy if we are to understand other measures taken

[1] Clause 24. 'De famis inopia.' Ibid., I, p. 151.
[2] Clause 12. 'De illis qui vinum et annonam vendunt antequam colligantur et per hanc occasionem pauperes efficiantur.' Ibid., I, p. 152. Charlemagne returned several times to this subject of the avarice of the grandees, in order to defend those poor freemen who were obliged to sell their goods to pay their debts. Capitul. of Thionville, 805, clause 16, in *Capitul.*, I, p. 125. Cf. Inama-Sternegg, op. cit., p. 335.
[3] *Capitul.*, I, p. 219.

by the early Carolingians. Morality and charity alike required
stability of prices for the basic foodstuffs. That was why, at the
Synod of Frankfurt in 794, Charlemagne, who had just issued
his new deniers, fixed in agreement with the Fathers of the
Council the maximum retail price for the main corn crops.[1]
Oats were assessed at 1 denier a hogshead, barley at 2 deniers,
rye at 3 and wheat at 4. The king was determined to preach by
example, and grain from his own estates was sold at even lower
prices, whether it was oats at half a denier, or barley at 1 denier,
rye at 2 and wheat at 3.[2] The fixing of prices was extended to
baked bread which was bought retail. A scale of maximum
prices was fixed for its sale; these prices varied according to the
nature of the flour. To quote one example, the baker was
enjoined to give twelve 2-lb. wheaten loaves for one denier. No
variation in price was tolerated; this fixed scale of prices applied
not only to normal years, but also and most particularly to
years of scarcity.

It is almost impossible to say whether or not these measures
were effective. Their practical application was made easier by
the fact that food produce was sold in local markets. These
were numerous,[3] and were held not only in the cities but also
in *vici* and *villae*. In theory the sovereign's permission was
not necessary for the establishment of these markets, which
were often held weekly.[4] But the passion for interference which
characterized the early Carolingians led them to take an interest
in the conditions under which they were held, especially since
it was in the markets that forged money could most easily be
passed off and that opposition to the circulation of the 'good

[1] *Capitul.*, I, p. 74.
[2] In addition the sale of surplus produce from the royal benefices was controlled.
Since the produce of the land was intended primarily for feeding the farmers who
cultivated it, the king's vassals had to make quite sure that they were not dying of
hunger before deciding on the surplus. The king distrusted their greed.
[3] In the *Capitulare de villis* Charlemagne advises his bailiffs to see that the staff
work well and do not waste their time running about to *markets*. Clause 54, Bor., I,
p. 88. Certain criminals were punished by being taken to the market and whipped
in public. *Capitul.* of 820, clause 3, in Boretius, I, p. 298.
[4] The Capitulary of Aix-la-Chapelle, 809, decrees that markets must not be held
on Sundays 'nisi ubi antiquitus fuit et legitime esse debet'. Clause 8, Boretius, I,
p. 149. For the weekly character of these markets, see various examples in Inama-
Sternegg, p. 590, n. 1.

deniers' was most frequently in evidence.[1] In the Capitulary of
Pîtres, 864, the importance of which has already been pointed
out, Charles the Bald orders each of his counts to draw up a
list of the markets held within his district, his county (*de
comitatu suo*), distinguishing between those already existing in
his grandfather's day and those established under the rule of
his father or of himself.[2] It gives the impression that the
sovereign's permission was first sought under Louis the Pious.
Charles the Bald adds that markets which serve no useful
purpose are to be suppressed. A strange instance of increasing
authoritarianism at a time when the royal power was growing
weaker! This is one of those apparent contradictions of which
history affords innumerable examples.

The profusion of local markets and the fact that they were
held weekly suggest that the restricted nature of the Carolingian economy has been exaggerated. In the ninth century
there were many men and women who bought in the markets
articles essential for their sustenance and clothing. For these
people, whose numbers have been underestimated, the problem of the cost of living and of prices was as worrying as it is
for our contemporaries. A chapter in the Life of St Maurillus,
Bishop of Angers,[3] provides significant information on this
point. This bishop lived in the early fifth century, but his
biography was not written until the end of the ninth, consequently the sentiments expressed in the following lines are
those of a man living about the year 900:

How Maurillus, during the thirty years he administered
the See of Angers, contrived to keep wine, corn and other
foodstuffs at a stable price.

[1] 'Ut melius et commodius haec providentia de bonis denariis non reiciendis et
de monetae falsae denariis custodiri possit.' *Edictum Pistense*, 864, clause 19, Boretius,
I, p. 317. For markets in the Carolingian era see Kötzschke, *Allgem. Wirtschaftsgesch.*,
p. 289, in which the author is particularly concerned with royal markets founded
by the kings in the old cities. Religious establishments were also granted privileges
authorizing them to set up markets. Later in feudal times the founding of markets
was to be a source of ready money. The seigneurs were to take advantage of their
right of *ban* to increase the number of markets, the rights they exercised over the
goods sold bringing them in substantial profits.   [2] Ibid.
[3] *Les Livres . . . de Grégoire, évêque de Tours*, ed. Bordier, IV, pp. 149–150. Soc. Hist.
France.

We have thought it worth while to mention that from the beginning of the episcopacy of the Blessed Maurillus until the end of his life the town of Angers, thanks to his inestimable qualities, enjoyed such abundance that the public market was never without the produce of Ceres or Bacchus, and that these never deteriorated in quality, nor did their price increase, for that would have brought want upon the poorest of the people. The sum of money paid out for everyday expenditure remained the same. Each man's storehouse was filled with wine and wheat and, in trading, the prices of all goods remained constant.

Is it likely that the hagiographer would have written this page if in his own day there had not been in the cities and villages markets selling the basic necessities supplied by local producers, markets maintaining fixed prices? Side by side with local produce were sold goods from distant parts. One of the commodities most in demand was salt. In Gaul considerable use was made of sea-salt in particular; it was extracted from the sea along the Atlantic coasts, to the north and south of the Loire, at Batz, in the Guérande peninsula[1] and in the Bay of Bourgneuf as well as on the Ile de Noirmoutier.[2] The Mediterranean too provided its quota; as early as the ninth century salt-pits had been worked in the Narbonnais along the Lake of Sigean.[3] Those at Hyères were also exploited during the early Middle Ages.[4] A directive from Louis the Pious to the *missi*

---

[1] 'Vendidit Salun salinam . . . Factum est hoc in insula quae vocatur Baf.' Ninth-century *Cartulaire de Redon*, p. 48, no. lx. In the first half of the tenth century the 'île de Batz' (insulam quae nominatur Batz Uuenran) was given by Alain, Duke of Brittany, with 20 hogsheads of salt and exemption from all market dues on salt, to the monks of Landevenec. *Cartul. de Landevenec* (ed. A. de la Borderie, pp. 156–157). Cf. *Mélanges d'hist. de Cornouaille*, pp. 48–54. It was the presence of salt-marshes in the region of Batz and Guérande which impelled these monks to press for land which was some distance away from their monastery.

[2] W. Vogel, *Die Normannen und das Fränkische Reich*, p. 62.

[3] Jean Stocker, *Le sel*, Paris, 1949. Coll. Que sais-je?

[4] The oldest texts go back no further than the eleventh century, since there is a scarcity of old charters in Provence. We shall quote two: one dated 1075 granting to the monks of Saint-Victor de Marseille the salt they needed 'in territorio quod appellatur Eiras (Hyères)', *Cartul. de S. Victor*, no. 479, the other undated but also of the eleventh century cancelling the dues paid 'ad ripam' by the men sent by the monks of Lérins to Hyères to buy salt. *Cartul. de Lérins*, I, p. 287, no. 281; I, p. 301.

shows that the Frankish sovereigns were concerned about salt production: 'As for the lands along the sea shore where salt is made,' declares the Emperor, 'it is our wish that some of the producers come to our court of pleas and that we should hear their reports so that we may be in a position to proceed with them to a fair reckoning.' [1]

The terms of this clause are unfortunately too vague to allow any accurate definition of the conditions under which the production and marketing of salt were organized. In the east, in districts far from the sea coast, use was made of mineral salt. From Carolingian times it had been extracted at Reichenhall in the Bavarian Alps, in Styria, at Wich near Metz, where the salt-pit, owned by the Abbey of Prüm, was worked by an overseer (*magister*), and at Halle in Saxony on the banks of the Saale. [2] The salt was then sent to its destination by river. An inquiry made at the beginning of the tenth century at Raffelstellen by order of the Emperor Louis the Blind into the subject of market dues levied in Bavaria reveals the existence of 'salt-merchants' ' ships which, manned by three sailors, sailed down the Danube taking their cargo to Mautern (*Mutarum*) where the salt market was held; [3] some of them continued on to Moravia which also had its market. [4]

The multiplicity of traffic dues was a serious hindrance to trade. The Merovingians, who experienced the greatest difficulty in gathering in their direct taxes or tributes, to such an extent that they had often abandoned the attempt in face of the revolts of their subjects and the imprecations of the bishops, preferred to resort to indirect taxes and to multiply market dues such as tolls, octrois and customs duties. A great number of these are known to us thanks to the exemptions enjoyed by most of the abbeys, which are recorded in royal diplomas carefully

[1] *Capitula missorum*, 821 (ed. Boretius).

[2] Inama-Sternegg, op. cit., I, pp. 579-581, and Kötzschke, *Allgem. Wirtschafts-gesch.*, p. 277.

[3] 'Item de navibus salinariis, postquam silvam (Boemicam) transierint . . . De unaqueque nave legittima, id est quam tres homines navigant, pergant ad Mutarum vel ubicumque tunc temporis salinarium mercatum fuerit constitutum.' Inquisitio de theloneis Raffelstettensis, clause 7 in Boretius, II, p. 251.

[4] 'Si autem transire voluerint ad mercatum Marahorum . . . licenter transeant.' Clause 8, ibid.

preserved by the beneficiaries. The early Carolingians, well aware that these dues were open to abuse, regulated their collection and restrained the venality of agents who oppressed the common people. To take only two examples, they instructed them not to exact payment of market dues from boats passing in mid-stream under river bridges, or from those tied up by the river bank for a few days only without their occupants buying or selling anything.[1] Such instructions reveal the care with which Charlemagne and his immediate successors endeavoured to facilitate internal trade by doing away with useless obstacles.

It is important also to note their obvious desire to put it on a sound moral basis by preventing shady transactions and insisting that witnesses should be present when bargains were concluded. A Capitulary of 803[2] forbids the sale of gold vases, silver, slaves, pearls, horses and other animals at night-time and insists on such purchases being made in public. The only sales permitted at night were those of food and fodder when the requirements of a hurried journey made this imperative. Charlemagne had no faith in horse-dealers and another of this same Emperor's Capitularies[3] imposes a series of conditions on anyone wishing to buy a horse, ox, or other beast of burden: he must be acquainted with the man selling it, know which district he comes from, where he lives and the name of his seigneur – requirements which sprang from Charlemagne's robust and cautious good sense.

The slave trade affords a typical example of the docility with which the early Carolingians put ecclesiastical precepts into practice. In spite of its immorality, this trade was not forbidden by the Church, though she required due regard to be paid to the personality of the slaves and to the faith of such as were Christians. In a letter written to St Boniface, Pope Greory III went no further than to forbid the sale of Christian slaves to pagan purchasers. Pepin the Short merely repeated this prohibition in his Capitulary of Lestinnes.[4] The trade was more

---

[1] *Capitul.* (ed. Boretius, I, pp. 284 and 294). Cf. Inama-Sternegg. op. cit., p. 613.
[2] Inama-Sternegg, p. 590, n. 4.
[3] Ibid., p. 591, n. 1.
[4] Clause 3. *Capitul.* (ed. Boretius, I, p. 28).

carefully controlled by Charlemagne who in 779[1] decreed that
sales of slaves should take place before the count or bishop of the
place, and failing them their accredited representatives, and
forbade such sales beyond the frontiers (*foris marca*). After his
death, however, the trade in pagan slaves became much more
widespread during the ninth century. It was carried on particularly by Jews, and the trade was permitted, and even protected on condition that these slaves were not sold outside the
Empire.[2] The Jewish merchants, several of whom were in the
service of Louis the Pious, won their way into his favour because
he needed them. They even succeeded in making him take steps
against persons who incited slaves owned by Jews to defy their
masters and persuaded them to be baptized in order to gain
their freedom.[3] Agobard, Bishop of Lyons, bitterly reproached
this Emperor for his friendliness towards Jews. In the pamphlet
he wrote attacking them[4] he made out that he had taken up the
cudgels solely to forbid his co-religionists to sell slaves to Jews,
and Jews to sell Christians in Spain, doubtless in Saracen
markets. In spite of this writer's exaggeration, the restrictions
imposed by the Frankish sovereigns on the sale of slaves probably did not prevent the commission of abuses, since the trade
was the most prosperous of the time and a source of enormous
profits. Most of the slaves sold in the chief markets of the Empire,
particularly at Mainz and Verdun,[5] were Slavs. The fate of

[1] Ibid., p. 51, clause 19. He returned to this prohibition in the Capitulary of
Mantua, 781, applying it to all slaves (ut nullus mancipia christiana vel pagana . . .
foris nostro vendat). Ibid., I, p. 190.
[2] Diploma of Louis the Pious granting his patronage to the Jew Abraham, living
in Saragossa. He is allowed to buy and sell slaves but only within the Empire:
'Liceat etiam ei mancipia emere et non aliubi nisi infra imperium nostrum vendere.'
Formulae imperiales (ed. Zeumer, p. 325). This was to become the stock formula.
[3] See 'praeceptum Judeorum'. Ibid., p. 309.
[4] 'Haec passi sumus a fautoribus Judaeorum non ob aliud nisi quia praedicavi-
mus Christianis ut mancipia eis christiana non venderent, ut ipsos Judaeos Chris-
tianos vendere ad Hispanias non permitterent.' Agobard, *De insolentia Judaeorum*,
in *Patr. lat.*, 104, col. 72. Agobard's works contain other strange observations, some
of which have been brought to light by H. Pirenne, *Mahomet et Charlemagne*, p. 140:
'Les Juifs', he says, 'fournissent du vin aux conseillers de l'Empereur; les parents
des princes, les femmes des palatins envoient des cadeaux et des vêtements à des
femmes juives; de nouvelles synagogues s'élèvent. On croirait entendre un anti-
sémite parlant de "barons" juifs.'
[5] For Mainz, see Dopsch, *Die Wirtschaftsentwicklung der Karolingerzeit*, II, p. 191,
no. 3, and for Verdun, *Les destinées de l'Empire d'Occident*, p. 601.

these men deeply moved the Fathers of the Council held at Meaux in 845; they urged their pious princes to stop Christian and Jewish merchants in their realms from handing over to unbelievers poor wretches who might be saved if they were bought by Christians, but this was mere exhortation, and the wrath of God was the only punishment with which delinquents were threatened. The gradual development of Carolingian legislation relating to the slave trade follows a pattern with which we are already familiar. It began with an ecclesiastical precept scrupulously copied by the God-fearing Pepin the Short. Then came Charlemagne to give clear and authoritative form to the decrees. Later the abuses reappeared and in face of the scandals of a traffic practised by Jews, but doubtless with the complicity of Christians and perhaps even of the entourage of the Emperor Louis the Pious, churchmen registered their protest, but in vain.

The general impression left by a study of the whole body of measures taken by the early Carolingians to regulate economic life is one of sustained, though not always effective, endeavour to infuse it with Christian morality. The legislators had their feet firmly planted in their own age, which had no great industries, when craftsmen worked in villages and even more frequently, as we shall see, in workshops on the great estates, when buying and selling were done chiefly in local markets. Their efforts consisted in increasing these markets, in encouraging also the holding of annual fairs, in freeing the movement of goods from costly and irritating obstacles, in providing salesmen and customers with a sound money exchange adapted to the needs of the home market, in taxing several products which were basic necessities, in applying to all alike the ban on lending at interest, and in preventing the poor from being exploited by unscrupulous 'potentates'.

These were fundamentally authoritarian measures, but it would be a mistake to talk of planning. Charlemagne himself, a prolific law-giver, had no more intention of reforming the social organization of his day than he had of changing its political institutions. He accepted slavery as unquestioningly as he did lordship; he was content to establish the economy on a moral basis and to translate into clear directives the teachings of his clerical entourage.

His legislation and administration have been criticized for their lack of initiative and foresight: they were the outward expression of an economy which was not concerned with finding wider outlets, but it is rather too easily overlooked that the Empire, 'expanded' by Charlemagne's conquests, itself covered the equivalent of half a continent and that it represented western Christian Europe. We should note too that a close study of Charlemagne's Capitularies shows him to have been not uninterested in the economic relations maintained by his subjects with countries situated outside his dominions. It is important to realize that these relations were henceforth to be no longer essentially Mediterranean, a fact which justifies, or rather explains, the criticisms levelled against the Carolingian economy. Henri Pirenne has brilliantly outlined the economic transformation which coincided with the beginning of the early Carolingian Empire, a passage it will be helpful to quote in full:[1]

'In the West the coast along the Gulf of Lions and the Riviera as far as the mouth of the Tiber, laid waste by war and by pirates at a time when the Christians, having no fleet, were powerless to resist, was now merely a wilderness and fair game for plunder and pillage. Ports and towns were deserted. The connexion with the East was broken and no new link was being forged with the Saracen coasts. The torpor of death lay over the land. The Carolingian Empire presents the most striking contrast with that of Byzantium. It was purely a land Empire, closed in upon itself. The Mediterranean territories which had once been the busiest in the realm and had infused new life into the whole structure were now the most poverty-stricken, the most desolate, the most seriously threatened. The tradition of the ancient world was broken, since Islam had destroyed the old Mediterranean unity.'

The reality is more complex. Charlemagne was not borne helplessly along by the current which was sweeping the western world northwards. He was not so completely disinterested in Mediterranean affairs. Against the inroads of the Moorish

[1] *Mahomet et Charlemagne*, p. 163.

pirates he took measures which were by no means ineffective. In 809 he even attempted to conquer Venetia by sending his son Pepin to the Dalmatian coast with an improvised fleet. The peace concluded in 812 retained for the Frankish Empire the conquests won in Croatia and Istria; nevertheless, Venice and the outlet to the Adriatic eluded him because he had not the necessary weight of arms to maintain his position. The authority of Byzantium was re-established, though somewhat deceptively, since it became a purely nominal sovereignty. From the early ninth century, behind a façade which concealed the real position and at the same time favoured Venetian plans,[1] Venice was beginning her slow rise to power and her future as a seafaring nation was gradually taking shape. Did this abortive conquest of Venice by Charlemagne, who had just improvised a fleet in the Mediterranean, represent a bold bid to share the mastery of this sea with the other coastal powers? Probably not. We believe his conduct to have been dictated not by underlying economic motives but by a political aim, his longing to be revenged on the Byzantines who regarded him as an upstart. It is, in fact, unlikely that Charlemagne, with his genius for realism, planned to compete for Mediterranean trade against rivals better placed, and far better equipped, than himself, and to champion a cause which was lost even before it was begun. The Mediterranean was never for him the *Mare Nostrum*: his flair for realizing what was possible was too strong for him to become entangled in visionary ambitions. Yet his refusal to embark on the venture did not imply a complete renunciation. Relations were not broken off either with the East or with the Moslem world. The Royal Annals[2] deliberately emphasize Charlemagne's friendly relations with the Abbasid ruler Haroun al Raschid, and make much of the presents which this king heaped upon him, an elephant, rich materials, perfumes, a clock, etc. Not all Oriental markets were closed. It has been

[1] What these plans were has been clearly revealed by the historian Hartmann, *Gesch. Italiens im Mittelalter*, III, 1, p. 56.

[2] All the details concerning these relations have been grouped together by Louis Halphen in a note in his edition of Einhard's *Vita Karoli Magni*, p. 48, n. 2. It was in the reign of this Emperor that the question of the protection of the Holy Places was raised for the first time. Ibid., n. 1.

8. A storm at sea (photo from *Miniatures des premiers siècles du moyen âge.* Preface by Jean Porcher. Plon, Collection Iris, pl. iv)

rightly noted[1] that the trade in spices, though disrupted, still went on as did that in silk, which even increased in volume through the requirements of fashion, and the supplying of ivory to Carolingian workshops also implied a continuance of economic relations with the East. Louis Bréhier[2] has observed that Syrians and Greeks were still to be found at Charlemagne's court, and that it was with their collaboration that the Emperor brought out a corrected version of the text of the Four Gospels. If they were fewer in number, less closely grouped and above all less active, it was because Jews had become, if not under Charlemagne at least under Louis the Pious, the official palace merchants,[3] enjoying extensive credit.[4] Their position was maintained until the tenth century; their chief trade was, as we have seen, the traffic in slaves. It is therefore permissible to assume that the closing of the Mediterranean was less complete[5] and the cessation of trade less final, than the author of *Mahomet et Charlemagne* has asserted, and that the devastation was confined to certain areas which, like the coast of Provence, were particularly vulnerable.[6]

Should one go even further and adopt a point of view directly

[1] Jean Devisse, *La France carolingienne. Un nouvel essor*. In *Histoire de France*, libr. Larousse, I, 1954, p. 154.

[2] 'Les colonies d'Orientaux en Occident', *Byzantinische Zeitschrift*, 12 (1903), p. 18.

[3] Henri Laurent, 'Marchands du Palais et marchands d'abbayes', *Revue hist.*, CLXXXIII, 1938, p. 283. A protective formula granted by this prince to Christian merchants states that 'they are to be allowed, *like the Jews*, to serve our Palace'.

[4] The reign of Louis the Pious has been called a golden era for the Jews. J. Allen Cabaniss, 'Agobard of Lyons', in *Speculum*, 26, 1951, p. 59. We have seen above (p. 163, n. 4) that Agobard made himself the mouthpiece of those who disliked the 'fautoribus Judaeorum', as he called them. He chided Louis the Pious for his concessions in favour of Jews, even asserting that they had been extracted from him by violence and because he was weak. *Patr. lat.*, 104, col. 70–71.

[5] F. L. Ganshof, 'Notes sur les ports de Provence du VIIIe au Xe siècle', *Revue hist.*, CLXXXIII, 1938, pp. 28–37.

[6] In a thoughtful article 'Mohammed and Charlemagne, a Revision', in *Speculum*, 1943, pp. 14–38, R. S. Lopez has endeavoured to show that the decline of trade was not caused by the Saracen invasion and was not simultaneous with it. His thesis rests on three main points: the disappearance of minted gold, of papyrus and of eastern clothes worn by laymen. Merovingian mismanagement, by bringing the gold coins minted in the Frankish kingdom into disrepute, led to reform of the coinage based on a silver monometallism. Papyrus went out of use because of the practical advantages of parchment, and a whim of fashion accounted for the layman's loss of interest in eastern clothes.

contrary to that of Pirenne, declaring that the Moslem conquest, far from laying a dead hand on the economy of the
western world, brought it back to life? This thesis was
recently put forward. Its originator, with equal skill and brilliance,[1] began by paying tribute to that great historian who, he
said, was the first to consider the 'East–West' question in its
economic aspect and to realize that the rise of the Moslem world,
like the birth of the Hellenistic world after the conquests of
Alexander centuries before and that of the Roman world after
the triumphs of Rome, could not have failed to exert some influence on the economic evolution of neighbouring countries.
He believes, however, that Pirenne misinterpreted the signs.
This influence was exerted not in a negative, but in a positive
sense. The West did not lapse into slumber; on the contrary it
was jolted wide awake. This attractive paradox, which an un-
charitable but superficial reader might think was inspired by a
desire to 'score off' the Belgian historian, nevertheless has a
certain appeal and contains a core of truth. It cannot in fact be
denied that far from sealing up the West, Islam opened out new
trade routes and that the wealthy cities of the Moslem world
represented a challenge which was to infuse new vigour into the
West. The author was, however, in too much of a hurry.[2] The
influence exerted by Islam on the West was a delayed action;
it was not until a century or two later that it showed itself in a
manner at once positive and effectual. At the close of the eighth
century and throughout the ninth the still unsettled western
world stiffened its attitude as though in self-defence. Relations
between the Moslem and Christian worlds, which Lombard likes
to stress, were limited to contraband trade and an exchange of
courtesies between sovereigns. Venice, at the spearhead of the
trade drive, was still feeling her way and only just beginning to

---

[1] M. Lombard, 'Mahomet et Charlemagne. Le problème économique', *Ann. Ec.
Soc. Civ.*, 1948, pp. 188–199, and 'La route de la Meuse et les relations lointaines
des pays mosans entre le VIIIe et XIe siècle', in *L'art mosan*.

[2] It is most interesting to read the pertinent remarks of M. R. Boutruche on the
'rôle d'excitant universel' attributed to the Moslem world by reason of its 'injec-
tions d'or'. Bulletin d'histoire de France au moyen âge, *Revue hist.*, January–March
1955, pp. 61–62. Specially noteworthy is his plea for greater emphasis on the international rôle of silver, 'ce grand méconnu'.

move forward. Genoa was not even in the picture. Large-scale trade was being carried on in the Frankish Empire by middlemen – the Jews. The greatest ruler in Europe, Charlemagne, remained suspicious. He kept a sharp watch on his eastern frontiers. If he turned a blind eye to the transfer of slaves and the sale of furs, he forbade the sale of arms and of hauberks, so as not to play into his enemy's hands. The organization of the Empire as he conceived it excluded all collaboration with the Moslem world. If there were any commercial exchanges, they were confined to the 'black market'.

The only sphere in which the Saracen expansion achieved an immediate and direct influence, though a mainly negative one, was the coinage. At the end of the eighth century Moslem gold began to flow into the West; it appeared in the form of the *dinar*, which ousted the *nomisma*,[1] the gold coin of Byzantium; the gold pieces struck in Gaul, the traditional *solidi* or *triens*, were closely linked with this latter coin. Dislike of the *nomisma* and the influx of still unfamiliar coins in yellow metal may have contributed to the adoption of a silver monometallism, in other words to the total disappearance of the discredited *solidi* and *triens* and to the setting up of a new coinage, a silver currency unrelated to foreign and current monetary systems.[2] The fact remains that Charlemagne maintained an attitude of cautious reserve towards the Moslem world and that his example was followed throughout the whole of the ninth century.

His circumspection showed itself in the way in which traffic was organized within the Frankish Empire. Although he endeavoured to reconstitute a Mediterranean fleet, people were no longer prepared to risk sailing along the coast to Rome. The

[1] The recession was not complete. The Byzantine coinage still retained its prestige in mid-tenth-century Germany. Otto the Great having in 947 authorized the monks of St Gall to set up a mint at Rorschach renounced in their favour his rights over the minting of money which he referred to as 'percussura nomismatis', *Dipl. reg. et imp. Germ.*, I, 2, p. 172, no. 90, as if the Byzantine *nomisma* were still the coin *par excellence*.

[2] It may on the other hand have been that Charlemagne, as Mme Doehaerd assumes in an article on the Carolingian monetary reforms, *Annales E.S.C.*, 1952, pp. 13–20, wished to establish a relationship between the weight of his new denier and that of the Moslem *dirham*. The theory advanced by this Belgian scholar is ingenious but risky. Such is the opinion of M. Boutruche loc. cit., p. 63, who confesses his inability to share what he wittily calls her 'pan-Islamic euphoria'.

Carolingians revealed their preference for land travel by setting up customs posts for the collection of tolls at Les Cluses, in other words near the Alpine passes which had become the recognized routes for merchandise as well as for armies and pilgrims passing from Gaul into Italy. The routes into Italy, to which the pilgrimage to Rome brought a continuous stream of travellers, were covered from the ninth century onwards with pilgrim hostelries run by hospitallers (*scholae peregrinorum*).[1] The busiest route was that of the Mont Cenis,[2] along which lay the monastery of Novalesa founded in 726, the endowment of which was confirmed by Charlemagne in 789, and a hospice built at the instance of Louis the Pious. Unfortunately the Alpine routes, which seemed safer than the sea route, were in turn harried by Saracen pirates. From the end of the ninth century law and order were less efficiently maintained, and the brigands took to stationing themselves along the roads in order to rob pilgrims. The adventure which befell Maiolus, Abbot of Cluny, and his company in 972 or 983 just as he had crossed the Great St Bernard pass was the most notorious of these attacks.[3]

The economic policy pursued by Charlemagne was in fact a policy of realism, of direct and personal rule. The Emperor sent ambassadors alike to Cordova and Baghdad. He took an interest in trade relations between his dominions and Great Britain. There was a customs post at Quentovic on the Channel, another at Duurstede near the mouth of the Lower Rhine, where government agents collected dues. The lot of merchants who were Frankish subjects was his constant concern.[4] In 796 writing to Offa, the powerful King of Mercia, who was the real ruler of Southern England, he suggested that he might extend his

---

[1] J. Bédier, *Les légendes épiques*, II, p. 141 et seq.

[2] From the Merovingian period the most frequented Alpine passes were no longer the Mont Genèvre and the Little St Bernard, but the Great St Bernard and the Mont Cenis. Dept, *Le mot 'Clusas' dans les diplômes carolingiens. Mélanges Henri Pirenne*, Brussels, 1926, p. 93.

[3] 'Un Abbé de Cluny prisonnier des Sarrasins', in our *Le Film de l'Histoire Médiévale en France*, 1959, p. 85.

[4] Diploma of Charlemagne, 775, quoted by Inama-Sternegg, p. 616, n. 3; Ganshof, *Histoire des relations internationales, Le moyen âge*, p. 51. W. Vogel notes, *Geschichte der deutschen Seeschiffahrt*, I, p. 77, that in the ninth century Duurstede (Dorstad) was a well-known trading centre (*emporium, vicum nominatissimum, vicum famosum*).

protection to Anglo-Saxons trading in the Frankish kingdom, but claimed equal consideration for his own subjects in Great Britain.[1] The same letter makes it clear that Charlemagne was as much concerned about the merchandise as about the merchants. He complains about the length of the military cloaks (*saga*) exported from Great Britain to Gaul, and asks King Offa to see that the next batch were shorter and of the same cut as those previously sent. There was obviously a regular trade between the two countries, and the somewhat improbable theory has been put forward that the Frisian cloth so often mentioned in Frankish documents was actually Anglo-Saxon cloth sold on the continent through the agency of Frisian merchants.[2]

The connexions with the East opened up under the Merovingians were regularized and developed by the Carolingians. Trade increased by leaps and bounds in ninth-century Germany, which was becoming more civilized and was growing to be an integral part of the Frankish Empire. Traders from Mainz travelled to Upper Germany for corn to feed their city and took it back down the Main.[3] Maastricht (*Trajectus*),[4] which was still only a *vicus*, is described by Eginhard as thronged with merchants. The Danube was crowded with boats, many of them carrying salt. The Frankish armies fighting the Avars were kept supplied by the shipping along this river. Frankfurt, Worms, Cologne in the Rhineland, Regensburg, Passau, and Lorch in the Danube basin, were already commercial centres.[5] The *negociatores* were also attracted by the countries further to the east,

---

[1] L. Halphen, *Etudes critiques sur l'histoire de Charlemagne*, p. 295. Cf. Ganshof, *Hist. des rel. inter.*, p. 48.

[2] *The Cambridge Economic History*, II, p. 234. On the subject of Frisian cloth, see below, p. 245.

[3] 'Mercatores quidam de civitate Moguntiaca qui frumentum in superioribus partibus emere ac per fluvium Moenum ad urbem devehere solebant.' Eginhard, *Hist. translationis bb. Marcellini et Petri*, ch. 39 in *Patr. lat.*, 104, col. 560.

[4] 'In vico qui hodieque Trajectus vocatur et distat ab Aquensi palatio octo circiter leugas estque habitantium et praecipue negociatorum multitudine frequentissimus.' Ibid., ch. 81 in *Patr. lat.*, 104, col. 586. The proximity of the palace at Aix-la-Chapelle contributed greatly to the commercial activity of the city. Cf. H. Ammann, 'Maastricht in der mittelalterlichen Wertschaft', in *Mélanges Felix Rousseau*, Bruxelles, 1958, p. 25.

[5] Inama-Sternegg, op. cit., pp. 610–611.

those inhabited by Slavs and Avars, since there was 'good business' to be done there, but Charlemagne was determined to keep a watchful eye on a trade he suspected of being under-hand, since it might conceivably degenerate into trading with the enemy. The Capitulary of Thionville, 805, which is a directive for the *missi*, contains a series of regulations concerning merchants going to those areas. The author forbids them to sell arms or hauberks, that is to say military clothing. He then lays down what amounts to a customs frontier, which he forbids them to cross. Along this line which extended from the mouth of the Elbe in the north to the Danube in the south, was a chain of posts guarded by the Emperor's confidential agents: they were at Bardowick, Schesel near Celle, Magdeburg, Erfurt in Thuringia, Hallstadt where there were important salt-pits, Forcheim, Bremburg, Regensburg and Lorch at the junction of the Danube and the Enns.[1] Slaves were not the only merchandise sought in these border countries. The traders also procured furs (marten, otter, sable), as well as clothing, short military cloaks (*sagella*). These articles, which were very costly, were taxed by Charlemagne[2] like basic necessities, but for a different reason; they were bought principally for the army, a consideration which carried great weight with him. The measures outlined above offer positive proof of the vigilance with which Charlemagne controlled trading on the periphery of his dominions, but in this case his decrees were dictated by military motives.

In the general survey which economic historians devote to the early medieval period, the reforms attempted by Charlemagne are generally sketched in very rapidly. They were indeed ephemeral, and the invasions of the Northmen, followed by a period of feudal anarchy, pushed the West back into the old rut. The improvement achieved, and which was partially abortive, has received scant attention.[3] It is apparently forgotten, quite overshadowed by the domanial economy which is

---

[1] *Capitul.* (ed. Boretius, I, p. 123).

[2] 808. 'Capitula cum primis constituta.' Clause 5, ibid., I, p. 140.

[3] It has, however, been noted by a few historians, in particular Inama-Sternegg, and Dopsch, but they have been accused of exaggerating its importance. Halphen, *Etudes . . . sur le règne de Charlemagne*, pp. 277–306.

seen as the symbol of a long period beginning with the seventh century and lasting until the eleventh. This neglect is unfortunate. Charlemagne's political achievements, grandiose and spectacular, have always attracted notice. Everyone knows that he 'expanded' the Frankish kingdom and founded the Western Empire. It has long been customary to linger over this aspect of his work, although the Empire broke up less than half a century after its creation, and Charlemagne did nothing to prevent, and did not even attempt to delay, the development of feudal institutions, so heavy with menace for the future. The intellectual and religious renaissance of the Carolingian age is also the object of serious study, but the efforts made to tidy up the economic situation have aroused less interest because they had not time to produce their full effects. This is definitely a cause for regret. The experiment was in fact an interesting one, different from that attempted by the Byzantine Emperors, a reorganization based on sound Christian morals and not altogether divorced from military considerations, an economy which was clerical in inspiration, a war economy from which capitalism was quite deliberately banished by the general veto on lending at interest. It is indeed doubtful whether the word capitalism can be used at all in connexion with a world in which there were no great business concerns, no industries, and in which agricultural activity was predominant. The most effective measure in this process of rehabilitation was the reform of the currency replacing the gold monometallism which, though traditional, had had its day and was on the way out, by a silver monometallism which in the denier provided a coinage handy for use in local markets, the only organisms which showed any sign of activity at that time. The originality of this experiment lay in the fact that it was made in a vast Empire which could be entirely self-sufficient, and that it rejected all thought of profit; external trade was, however, permitted subject to certain controls, and gold was not abandoned altogether.

It is perhaps unfortunate that the pursuit of this policy was thwarted by fresh invasions, those of the Northmen and the Hungarians, since the efforts of Charlemagne and of his immediate successors were well on the way to bringing about the economic revival of Western Europe. If the task undertaken by the great Emperor had been carried through, the Frankish Empire might never have found itself bogged down in a purely agricultural economy and condemned to a state of chronic immobility which lasted until the eleventh century. The renaissance of town life would have begun as early as the ninth century. Already in the time of Charlemagne towns were being more frequented. He himself liked living at Aix-la-Chapelle; his wife Fastrada used to spend the winters in Frankfurt. The reform of ecclesiastical chapters gave the ninth century an incentive to build by creating a need for new and vast episcopal palaces, and for the restoration and enlargement of cathedrals which had become too small for their numerous ecclesiastics. Several ninth-century bishops were town-dwellers, as for instance Archbishop Ebbo (817–841), who undertook the rebuilding of the time-worn churches and buildings of the city of Rheims and went to the trouble of finding lodgings for the men he had brought in to do his work.[1] Leidrad, Bishop of Lyons, restored the churches in his city and the poet Theodulph has described the work of reconstruction he carried out in his episcopal city of Orleans.[2] The example of Aldric, a native of Metz, whom the Emperor Louis the Pious raised to the see of Le Mans in 832, is worth quoting.[3] No sooner had the new bishop reached this city than he had an aqueduct built to bring water to the citizens, since it had not previously been available inside the city. Until his arrival it had had to be fetched from the river Sarthe and cost one denier a barrel. At Auxerre too, in the same reign, an aqueduct was built at the instance of Dieudonné (*Deusdedit*), Abbot of St Germain d'Auxerre, but for the use of the monastery.[4] Such examples are proof enough that in several cities trouble was being taken to initiate important improvements in urban life. The towns were not losing their populations. They were less unpleasant to live in than has sometimes been imagined. Paris, for instance, is described by Abbo, author

---

[1] F. Vercauteren, *Les civitates de la Belg. Sec.*, pp. 63 and 75. Cf. Ed. Ennen, *Frühgesch. d. Eur. Stadt*, p. 109.

[2] Kleinclausz, *Charlemagne*, p. 258.

[3] *Actus*, p. 300. Aldric has left behind a great reputation as a builder.

[4] Zeumer, *Formulae imperiales*, p. 322.

of the *Siege of Paris by the Northmen*, as a very beautiful city (*praepulchra polis*).[1]

The rebuilt churches, larger than their predecessors, demanded new techniques from their architects. The basilica with marble columns and timber framework had to be replaced by a church with stone pillars including a vaulted apse with radiating chapels. Teams of stone-dressers, squads of masons were needed. This is only one aspect of the economic revival which was beginning to make itself felt when it was set back by the invasions of the Northmen. There were many others.[2] The initiative, beyond all shadow of doubt, came from Charlemagne himself. Einhard praises him for having been a great builder and quotes as an example the basilica at Aix-la-Chapelle, the palace built in that same city, those at Ingelheim and Nijmegen, and the bridge at Mainz.[3] These efforts to restore the towns deserve special mention, yet the fact remains that the Carolingian economy, from the very poverty of the means at its disposal, continued to be predominantly agricultural. We shall next turn to a study of the country estate.

[1] Ed. Waquet, p. 15. Another monk, Abbot of Saint-Denis in the first half of the ninth century, boasted of the commercial importance of Paris, which represented the wealth of kings and the mart (*emporium*) of peoples. M. Poète, *Une vie de cité*, Paris, 1924, I, p. 66.

[2] We might note, for instance, the progress made in the use of lead, which had been familiar to the ancient world, for the roofing of buildings and for conduits. Its use was developed under the Carolingians. It was imported from England, particularly from Wales and Cornwall. Van Werveke, *Note sur le commerce du plomb au moyen âge. Mélanges Pirenne*, pp. 653–662.

[3] *Vita Karoli Magni*, ch. XVII (ed. Halphen, pp. 50–51). Note that, as Marc Bloch has pointed out in 'Le maçon médiéval: problèmes de salariat', *Ann. d'hist. éc. et soc.*, VII, 1935, pp. 216–217, building in the Middle Ages was not a great urban industry. The mason, essentially mobile, was more often than not a countryman, and the 'perriers' who supplied the stone-yards with freestone recruited their carters from amongst the peasants. Cf. Marc Bloch, 'Une matière première au moyen âge: la pierre de taille', ibid., VI, 1934, p. 190.

CHAPTER III

The 'Villa' of Charlemagne's Time: Farming and Manufacture

THE *Admonitio generalis* published by Charlemagne in 789 contains in Section 81 a clause which calls for comment.[1] It concerns the sabbath rest and gives a list of menial tasks forbidden on Sundays: men are not to engage in work on the land; they are not to tend their vines, plough the fields, gather in the harvest, make hay, plant hedges, clear forests, cut down trees, hew stones, build houses, work in the garden, attend courts or go hunting. Only three kinds of transport are allowed on feast-days: carting for the army, the carrying of food supplies and if absolutely necessary the conveying of a body to the grave. Nor arc women to do any work connected with cloth: they are forbidden to cut out garments, sew them together, embroider, comb wool, crush flax, wash clothes in public, or shear sheep. The list is significant. Except for the reference to women's work, it makes no mention of artisan or industrial activities. Yet these were menial tasks, manual work which ecclesiastical law had always banned on Sundays, but the number of hands engaged in them was very small, and the authors of the Capitulary have concentrated their attention on the *villa*, the real 'factory' of the Carolingian age, in which men devoted themselves for the most part to agricultural work, whilst the women spun and sewed in the women's quarters.

The régime of land ownership and the organization of the great domain in Carolingian times have been the subject of innumerable studies both in France and abroad. There has been almost complete unanimity as to the predominance of the great

[1] *Capitul.* (ed. Boretius, I, p. 61).

estate. The Austrian historian Dopsch[1] is one of the few who have disputed this conception. Yet the choice does not necessarily lie between two exclusive alternatives. The reality is too complex to allow of so rigid an option. Our knowledge of rural life under the Carolingians is both facilitated and falsified by a wealth of clear and detailed documentation very different from the brief and scanty texts of the preceding period. Charlemagne's legislation, and especially his *Capitulare de villis*, the polyptyques of several religious houses and that of Irminon in particular, the abundance of charters, throw light on the organization and set-up of those great estates owned by the sovereign and a number of wealthy abbeys. These documents are a mine of valuable information, and we shall naturally make full use of them as many have done before us, but a preliminary word of warning is essential. In assessing at several million hectares the area of the great secular and ecclesiastical estates existing in the time of Charlemagne it must be recognized that they represented only a small part of the territory of the Frankish Empire, which may be estimated at approximately a million and a half square kilometres. The remainder consisted of waste lands, and uncultivated ground but also of independent *mansi* and isolated plots. The fact is that we know almost nothing about the history of these lands until the eleventh century. We know that there were still a great number of *vici*, and consequently of villages inhabited by small farmers, in the mid-ninth century. About their manner of life we are almost completely ignorant. The agreements they concluded with each other, those arising from problems connected with their lands, were often settled by word of mouth, and when they were drawn up in writing the scripts have been lost, since at that time only religious foundations preserved their documents and kept archives. Nevertheless several abbey cartularies contain chance and fleeting references to these transactions, in cases where the lands in question were subsequently sold or given to churches, and the old title-deeds relating to them were handed over to the purchasers or the donors at the same time as the property. Such instances are rare but not exceptional and go to prove the

[1] *Die Wirtschaftsentwicklung der Karolingerzeit*, Weimar, 1912–1913.

persistence in the ninth century of small freeholders who managed somehow to go on existing. Later their fortunes deteriorated; most of them, forced to become part of rural seigneuries, lost their full freehold status, but this debasement, this degradation, could not obliterate their past, their original freehold standing. Various examples – and many more could be quoted – taken from the *Formulae Augienses*, a formulary drawn up in the Abbey of Reichenau, from the *Formulae Salicae*, a collection compiled in a country under Salic Law,[1] from the *Cartulaire de Redon*, Breton in origin, and from the *Cartulaire de Saint-André-le-Bas* of Vienne in Dauphiné,[2] consequently from widely differing areas, show us sales, gifts, the division of *mansi*, fields and meadows being concluded between individuals without any reservation to suggest that they were not in full ownership of the property being given up. On the contrary some of the deals were even accompanied by clauses emphasizing that the property was completely freehold and stressing the absence of all encumbrances. The historian should never forget the existence of this silent reality, and when studying the organization of Charlemagne's 'fiscs' described in the *Capitulare de villis*, or with the help of their polyptyques enumerating the possessions of great abbeys, he should think of these as islets appearing above the surface of an uncharted, perhaps unchartable, sea.[3]

With this one reservation, which seems to us both wise and imperative,[4] the existence of great estates, of numerous vast

[1] Zeumer, *Formulae*, p. 348.

[2] *Passim.* A systematic scrutiny of all pre-eleventh-century deeds contained in the cartularies would be a useful piece of research.

[3] L. Halphen was aware of this when in one chapter of his *Etudes critiques sur l'histoire de Charlemagne* devoted to rural land ownership he referred to the lands cultivated by small owners whose importance we shall probably never be able to assess owing to the scarcity of documents. p. 266.

[4] Other shrewd scholars have realized the complexity of the problem. In reality, side by side with great landowners possessing numerous *villae* and small freeholders cultivating their single *mansus*, there existed the category of medium landowners at whom several of Charlemagne's Capitularies were directed, who owned several *mansi* and made quite a success of them. R. Kötzschke has stressed their importance; *Allgem. Wirtschaftsgesch.*, p. 226: 'Eine erhebliche Bedeutung kam den Kleingrundherrschaften der sozial höher stehenden Freien und der geringeren Vassallen zu.' There were, he states, thousands of them who, living on their own lands, oppressed their underlings more tyrannically than the greatest of the great landowners.

villae owned by the sovereigns and the secular and ecclesiastical aristocracy, is a fact which cannot be denied. Already in the Merovingian period the churches had succeeded in acquiring immense estates scattered all over Western Europe and the regular clergy possessed a vast fortune in land. The secular aristocracy also, and especially the Austrasians, vied with the ecclesiastical world in accumulating extensive lands. The great estate therefore, as Louis Halphen has[1] wisely reminded us, was no novelty in Charlemagne's day, but that dictatorial prince exerted considerable influence on the organization of rural life. It took the form, as in the case of the coinage, of written instructions which, when applied methodically, proved effective. Charlemagne understood the elementary truth that in a still crude and undeveloped economy the land is man's great foster-mother. He concentrated his attention on his own property, on the royal 'fiscs', and regulated in minute detail those aspects of their cultivation which seemed to him defective. He was not content merely to set a good example. On every hand he saw property owned by influential laymen and clerics. On several occasions he ordered an inventory to be made of these estates, and the Capitulary known as the *Brevium exempla*, only a fragment of which has been preserved,[2] shows us how personal property and real estate were to be inventoried.

What prompted Charlemagne to take such a step? Perhaps in the first place a taste for statistics, though it is more likely that this eminently practical administrator had immediate aims in view. With some of these we are familiar. In ordering an inventory of the privileges distributed to his vassals, he wished to detect certain sharp practices in which some of them were indulging. A number were running their own freeholds with the staff and resources properly belonging to lands granted to them as benefices. The benefices were being neglected and were reverting to waste land, whilst the freeholds were well-cultivated and prosperous.[3] Others were guilty of actual theft. They made

---

[1] Op. cit., p. 266.   [2] Published in the Boretius Edition, I, pp. 250–256.

[3] 'Auditum habemus quod homines illorum beneficia habent deserta et alodes eorum restauratos.' *Capitul. de causis diversis*, 807, clause 4, Boretius, I, p. 136. This order makes it clear that under Charlemagne there were large numbers of men owning medium or small freehold properties.

their benefices over to men of straw who sold them back again as if they were freehold. By means of these fictitious sales they thus acquired complete ownership of their benefices.[1] The inventory of church property was also designed to correct abuses. People would give to the Church property which was liable for quit-rent payable to the sovereign, who, however, had no intention of being cheated out of so much income to which he was entitled.[2] There was a further abuse which had sprung from the practice of the *precarium*, and which was denounced by the Fathers at the Council of Tours in 813.[3] Many small land-owners continued to make gifts to churches in accordance with a time-honoured tradition, no longer out of piety but out of self-interest, in order to receive in exchange for what they relinquished double and even threefold the amount in ecclesiastical property. In principle this was simply the granting of usufruct, the enjoyment of which was extended to the 'pre-carist's' descendants. The landed wealth of the Church was thus in some danger of fragmentation, and the practice was leading indirectly to a dissolution of the great estates, the 'precarists' to a man being anxious to loosen the ties binding them to the lords of the *villa*.

It is conceivable that Charlemagne foresaw the danger threatening the cohesion of the great estates and the Capitulary *de villis vel curtis Imperii*[4] proves that he was anxious to preserve the unity of his own. This famous document, consisting of seventy sections, deals with the administration of the imperial domains. It is undated, but as it contains four references to the Queen (*Regina*), most commentators – and their name is legion – have assumed that it was drawn up before the Emperor's coronation in the year 800. In any case we have only to read it carefully to discover, if not the hand, at least the inspiration of Charlemagne, and to support unhesitatingly the conclusion

---

[1] *Capitul. of Nijmegen*, 806, clause 7, in Boretius, I, p. 131. Cf. L. Halphen, op. cit., p. 269.

[2] *Capitul.* 'de terra tributaria' of Louis the Pious. Boretius, I, p. 287.

[3] L. Halphen, op. cit., ibid.

[4] Its title has been reproduced exactly by Winkler in his new edition of the Capitulary. 'Die Lokalisierung des sog. *Capitulare de villis*', in *Zeitschrift für romanische Philologie*, 37, 1913, p. 517.

reached by Marc Bloch,[1] and far less 'agnostic' than its author imagined, that it was inspired by the prince's entourage. We shall regard it as one of the many directives dictated or suggested by Charlemagne for the purpose of introducing order into the administration. The *Capitulare de villis*[2] was intended to reform abuses which had crept into the administration of the domains of the royal 'fiscs'. It is important to bear this point in mind, lest anyone hoping to find in it a comprehensive and systematic set of rules should be disappointed, and also in order to explain a certain lack of order evident in its composition and noticeable in many of the Capitularies. It is probable that Charlemagne, a man of lively and impulsive mind, paid little heed to the order and plan of his instructions; the various directions which make up the text follow each other in haphazard fashion as the spirit moved him.

The main supervision of the royal fiscs was entrusted to agents to whom in the Capitulary is given the title *judex*.[3] This title should not be allowed to mislead us as to the actual functions of the official who bore it. He was a bailiff with extensive powers, appointed often to manage a number of estates and required on occasion to arbitrate in disputes arising between farmers and sub-agents. Charlemagne was too shrewd an administrator not to foresee the abuses of authority which agents would be tempted to commit for their own profit if left to themselves. Those religious houses which entrusted the management of their property to lay stewards (*advocati*) were to have frequent and bitter experience of this. In the first two sections of his Capitulary, Charlemagne lays it down in principle that his lands are intended for his own use and that the staff living on them and running them are to be well treated and not

---

[1] 'L'origine et la date du Capitulaire *de villis*', *Rev. hist.*, 143 (1923), p. 55. Cf. Walther von Warburg, 'The Localization of the *Capitulare de villis*', *Speculum*, 15, 1940, pp. 87-91. The author shares Bloch's scepticism with regard to the attempts made to localize this document.

[2] The quotations are taken from the Boretius edition which is more accessible than that of Winkler. It is worth recalling that the older edition by B. Guérard contains also a valuable commentary and is followed by a good translation. 'Explication du Capitulaire *de villis*', in *Bibl. Ec. Chartes*, 1853. It was reprinted in the *Mém. de l'Institut. de France, Ac. des I. et B.-L.*, XXI, Ier p., 1857, pp. 165-309.

[3] Clause 3, Boretius, p. 83.

reduced to poverty.[1] The staff of the *villa* were known collectively by a traditional word (*familia*), applied by the Romans to the whole body of slaves cultivating the domain and living a communal life. Slaves still existed. In the Merovingian period they were called *mancipia* and were still to be found in the ninth and even in the tenth century on the estates of abbeys, although their number had been steadily diminishing during the Early Middle Ages.[2] The term does not appear in the *Capitulare de villis*. Not that all those cultivating royal domains were freemen. Large numbers of people of servile condition were to be found on them (*servi fiscalini*), but their way of life had changed. These non-free had become tenants; *mansi* were granted to them; they farmed them in order to get a living; but at the same time they were obliged to provide several days' work on their master's demesne. In this lay the fundamental difference between the treatment meted out to these 'serfs' and that of the freemen referred to in the Capitulary as *franci*.[3] Three whole days a week were exacted on principle from the *servi*;[4] the others, the *franci* or *coloni*, had to undertake on their master's reserve tasks fixed in advance and 'accurately specified', in other words they did task work for their master. This difference in treatment is not laid down in so many words in the Capitulary, but it follows from clearly defined provisos in the laws of the Alamans and Bavarians[5] which were revised in the reign of Charlemagne. There is no doubt that these regulations constituted in his day a common law applicable to all domanial estates, to those of the sovereign as to others. Nevertheless the difference between the two states gradually diminished, and it was inevitable that they should eventually draw closer together and finally even merge into each other, serfs and *coloni* being settled on the same estates and carrying out similar tasks.

---

[1] Clause 3, Boretius, p. 83.

[2] Perrin, *Rech. sur la seign. rur. en Lorraine*, p. 632.

[3] 'Franci autem qui in fiscis aut villis nostris commanent.' Clause 4, ibid.

[4] Perrin, *Rech. sur la seign. rur.*, p. 632.

[5] The obligations of *servi* are clearly specified in the *Lex Alammanorum*, clause 22, 3. *Germanenrechte*, Weimar, II, 1934, p. 14, and are followed by those of *coloni* (clause 23), but they are stated in greater detail in the *Lex Baiuvariorum*, I, 13, same ed., p. 88.

In the centre of the estate was the lord's house (*casae nostrae*) where the sovereign lodged with his retinue when visiting his *villa*. There were a great many out-buildings; each *villa* had its furniture repository,[1] kitchens, bakeries, wine-presses, several cowsheds, stables, byres, sheepfolds, pigsties, a hayloft, and one or more water-mills. This group of buildings, completed by a courtyard and a fishpond, with a church close at hand, was surrounded by an enclosure. In a separate quarter, surrounded by hedges and shut in by solid gates, were the women's lodgings,[2] where they busied themselves with weaving and making clothes; their quarters were really a weaving and sewing workshop. Since they actually lived there too, rooms with fireplaces were installed for their comfort.

The work done in the king's service was organized by a steward (*judex*) and supervised by sub-agents, the mayors (*majores*). They were most carefully selected by the king, who preferred to choose them from men of modest origin, but whom he felt he could trust. Working with them were numerous other officials: deans, foresters, stud grooms, cellarers, collectors of market dues, craftsmen expert in metal work (in iron, silver and gold), turners, carpenters, shield-makers, cobblers, fowlers, makers of fishing and hunting tackle, soap-makers, joiners, fishermen, bakers, brewers, etc.[3] Minor officials and specialist workmen were all known as *ministeriales* because each practised a trade (*ministerium*). They were recruited chiefly from the non-free class but by reason of the services they rendered, which brought them into frequent contact with the lord of the domain, and also because of the supervisory powers entrusted to some of their number, these *ministeriales* eventually became a kind of aristocracy of the servile class,[4] and all the more overbearing for being self-made.

The number and variety of trades carried on within the *villa*

---

[1] A list of furniture contained in the *casae* figures in clause 42 of the *Capitul.*, Boretius, p. 87.

[2] Clause 49: 'Ut genitia nostra bene sint ordinata.' Boretius, p. 87. The women's quarters also included huts in which the women spent the winter evenings. They were known as 'escrènes' (tuguriis id est screonis). Ibid.

[3] A list of these workmen (*artifices*) is to be found in clause 45 (Boretius, p. 87).

[4] Perrin, *Rech. sur la seign. rur.*, p. 678.

suggest a more fluid conception of this organism than that traditionally held. Marc Bloch has aptly described the great estate as 'a vast concern, farm and factory all in one'.[1] In fact, at a time when there were no factories, no great independent workshops and no capital with which to start them, the *villae* were the only existing centres of productive activity. In his domains the sovereign stored produce of every kind, particularly agricultural produce, and also manufactured goods made on the spot. He drew on these according to his personal requirements and those of the army, and was thus saved the trouble of looking for them elsewhere and borrowing them from outside.[2] The estates also took the place of shops, since unconsumed goods were disposed of to the king's profit, and every year on Palm Sunday, after the accounts had been audited, the bailiffs handed over to Charlemagne the money from the sale of farm produce (*argentum de nostro laboratu*).[3] The attention of scholars has centred mainly on agricultural problems, but any picture of domanial organization would be incomplete if it did not include the crafts and trades, one might almost say the industries, of the *villa*; and above all the brilliance of Carolingian civilization and Charlemagne's military successes would be difficult to explain in terms of an exclusively agricultural economy. The produce of the land was undoubtedly the most important and the greatest in volume, but clothing had to be provided, the army had to be fitted out and equipped with weapons, provided with horses and wagons for its annual and often far-distant campaigns, there were houses and churches to be built, furnished and decorated; ploughing implements had to be made for the farmers, barrels for storing drink, tackle for fishermen and huntsmen, parchment for the scribes; raw materials, leather, iron, lead, were needed for manufactured goods. Almost all the industries designed to fulfil these needs were carried on within the *villa*, where a staff of manual workers were trained to these crafts.[4] The *Capitulare de villis* has listed most of them, but in

[1] *Caractères originaux* . . . , 1st ed., p. 77.
[2] Clause 42: 'Ita ut non sit necesse aliubi hoc quaerere aut commodare.' Boretius, p. 87.
[3] Clause 28, ibid., p. 85.
[4] Cf. R. Kötzschke, op. cit., p. 230.

addition to these *ministeriales* living permanently on the *villa* where they held their *mansi*, it was sometimes necessary to call in specialists, masters of their trade (*magistri*), who were brought to the palace to make certain products such as barley beer. They were known as victuallers (*provendarii*). They were fed and doubtless paid whilst doing their job. These were already skilled workers, whom it is tempting to regard as the ancestors, the humble prototypes, of the modern workman.[1]

The *Capitulare de villis*, so rich in concrete facts, enables us to lift a corner of the veil which concealed those hives of trade and industry which the great domains presented. We have already seen something of the women's quarters where they wove linen, combed wool, dyed cloth, as may be gleaned from the dyes provided for them, woad, madder, vermilion.[2] They cut out and made clothes,[3] so that everything connected with clothing was made within the *villa*. From the presence of cobblers it may safely be assumed that the same applied to footwear. Shields were made there for the army, but there were also turners, joiners, cabinet-makers.[4] Carts for use in war, and litters, were built in the *villa*,[5] which also had its own forge for making weapons. There were in addition workshops for metal-workers, even for goldsmiths.[6] The working of iron and lead mines when these were to be found near the surface of the estate came within the province of the steward (*villicus*) who had to answer to the king for the minerals extracted.[7]

If the 'manufacturing' aspect of the royal fiscs cannot be disputed, it was nevertheless subsidiary, and to quote Marc

---

[1] See Clauses 31 and 61. Clause 50 mentions certain stud managers who, having neither benefices nor *mansi*, are to receive their keep (*provenda*) in the *villa* reserve (*de dominica*).

[2] Clause 43, Boretius, p. 87.

[3] These tasks were forbidden on Sundays. 'Item feminae . . . nec capulent vestitos nec consuent.' *Adm. generalis* of 789, clause 81, ibid., p. 61.

[4] See the list of 'ministeriales' already quoted.

[5] Clause 64, Boretius, p. 89.

[6] The compiler of the inventory for the fisc of Annapes mentions that there were neither gold nor silversmiths there: 'Ministeriales non invenimus aurifices neque argentarios.' Ibid., I, p. 255.

[7] 'Ut unusquisque judex per singulos annos . . . de ferraris et scrobis id est fossis ferrariciis vel aliis fossis plumbariciis . . . nobis notum faciant.' Clause 62, ibid., pp. 88–89.

Bloch's definition, the *villa* was first and foremost a farm for the growing of corn crops. All the tenants, free or otherwise, *franci* or *fiscalini*, including the *ministeriales*, had to do compulsory ploughing on the demesne, work which they did themselves or delegated to a substitute (*vicarium*). Sowing, ploughing, harvesting, all such tasks were supervised by the mayors under the direction of the *judex*, who was responsible for planning it out in advance. The author of the Capitulary insists in even greater detail on the dressing of vines and the making of wine, which in Charlemagne's day was drunk in great quantities.[1] He makes suggestions about cleanliness in connexion with the vintage, and pressing with the feet is forbidden.[2] Other instructions deal with the storing of wine. Several recommendations are made as to the use of sound barrels with iron hoops[3] and leather bottles are not advised for consignment to the palace or the army. The use of wine was not, however, general, and since water was not drunk at all other beverages were brewed also: mulberry wine; cider; mead, and above all *cervisia*, a beer made from sprouting barley (*bracium*), or malt. This beverage was much favoured by Charlemagne, who like all his fellow Austrasians was a hearty beer-drinker and insisted on being served with good quality liquor.[4]

The rearing of stock, oxen, sheep and goats, is given great prominence in this document. Horses were the objects of particular care. Charlemagne's *villae* figure as so many studs in which, according to the usual definition of such establishments, stallions and mares were kept for the propagation and improvement of the breed.[5] Young colts were brought to the Palace when the cold weather set in round about the Feast of St Martin on 11 November. This breeding was designed to cater for the needs of the army. Oxen and cows are draught animals, but provide butcher's meat as well. Charlemagne, with his practical turn of

---

[1] See above, pp. 93–96.

[2] 'Ut vendemia nostra nullus pedibus praemere praesumat, sed omnia nitida et honesta sint.' Clause 48, Boretius, p. 87.

[3] 'Bonos barriclos ferro ligatos.' Clause 68, ibid., p. 89.

[4] The inclusion in the *Capitulare de villis* of several clauses relating to the brewing of barley beer could be used to refute the theory of its Aquitanian origin.

[5] Clauses 13, 14, 15, Boretius, p. 84, and 50, p. 87.

mind, endeavoured to maintain a careful balance between their two functions. He ordered his bailiffs to see that the ploughs were kept well supplied with the animals which at that time were the only means of pulling them; he urged them not to slaughter too many beasts and to keep for meat lame animals no longer fit for work, taking every care to see that the meat set before him was wholesome and that the animals were not infected. This same section contains one sly touch characteristic of the author. In order to spare his own cattle, he advised his bailiffs to use cows belonging to his serfs for ploughing. At the same time he exacted from each of his domains a tribute of at least two fat oxen which were to be brought to him at the palace.[1] Fat was used in the preparation of food, and bacon, smoked meat and sausages were also eaten.[2] They made butter, but appear to have kept it for use on fast days instead of animal fat. The other articles of fast diet, cheese, fish, vegetables, were used in the same way,[3] and were reserved for the three weekly fast days as well as for Lent, when the eating of meat was forbidden by the Church.

Charlemagne's passion for economy and for detail is revealed in many of the provisos laid down in the Capitularies concerning sheep, goats, geese and chickens,[4] eggs, fish from the stews, bees, distributions of wax and soap.[5] His vigilance is most in evidence in his relations with his bailiffs; every year, at Christmas, he made them produce separate, clear and accurate accounts of all the goods in kind and all the income in money collected on his domains, in order, as he said,[6] to know the various things he had and what quantity of each. Yet this attention to detail did not exclude a love of the luxurious inessential. It did not prevent Charlemagne from breeding fancy birds, turtle-doves, pheasants, peacocks and other birds on his

[1] Clause 35, ibid., p. 86.
[2] 'Lardum, siccamen, sulcia.' Clause 34, ibid.
[3] Clause 44, ibid., p. 87.
[4] Clauses 18, 19, ibid., p. 84; 38, 39, p. 86. Charlemagne had fowls reared in the vicinity of flour mills (*ad farinarias*) where they found plenty of corn to peck. Hens and chickens were specially fattened for him.
[5] Clauses 17, 39, 59, 65, ibid., pp. 84–89.
[6] Clause 62, ibid., p. 89.

domains for purely ornamental purposes.[1] The same love of display, which went hand in hand with a strong strain of thrift,[2] prompted the long Section 70, the last in the Capitulary. This is a list of plants and fruit trees which the prince meant to plant in every garden and orchard on his estates.[3] The lengthy enumeration, which seems to have been tacked on as an afterthought, might easily be mistaken for a mere academic exercise, written by a learned clerk in Charlemagne's entourage, if we did not know that that prince was particularly fond of fruit trees and aromatic plants.[4]

The edicts about forests, scattered through the Capitulary, are of even greater interest: 'Let the bailiffs make it known on September 1st whether there is to be any pasturing or not.' This injunction, laid down in paragraph 25,[5] reminds us that village settlements in Germany and Austrasia included, alongside the cultivated areas, a marginal forest zone, the *marca communis*, of which the farmers had communal use. In places where the village had been turned into a great estate under the régime of the *villicatio*, the forest zone underwent a fresh transformation. The owners of *mansi* or *hobae* (Hufen) were not deprived of all their users' rights, but the new master of the *villa* annexed huge tracts for his own benefit and turned them into hunting reserves, marking out 'forests' (*forestes*), or protected hunting and game reserves. The forest[6] became the exact opposite of the *silva*, which was the wooded zone left free for common use. Administrative language also made use of a popular word 'breuil' (*brolium*) as a synonym for forest, but more

---

[1] Clause 40, ibid., p. 86.

[2] Chickens and eggs not required on the domain had to be sold. Clause 38.

[3] This list has frequently been annotated, notably by Guérard, *Mém. de l'Ac. des I. et B.-L.*, XXI, 1, p. 279; A. Dopsch, op. cit., I, p. 42; Baist, 'Zur Interpretation der *brevium exempla* und der *Capitulare de villis*', in *VSWG*, XII, 1914, pp. 64-70.

[4] See for example the inventory of the fisc of Annapes, Boretius, I, p. 256, which shows how Charlemagne cherished his fruit trees.

[5] 'De pastione autem, Kal. septembr. indicare faciant, si fuerit aut non.'

[6] The etymology of the word *forestis* is controversial. The root is probably the same as that of the German: Forst (forest). If so, it would be Germanic, but when transcribed into Latin as *forestis*, it was apparently contaminated with the adverb *foris*, indicating that the forest, incorporated into the domain proper, was in future outside (*foris*) or beyond common use. Petit-Dutaillis, 'De la signification du mot "forêt" à l'époque franque', in *Bibl. Ec. Chartes*, LXXXVI; 1915, p. 45 et seq.

often than not this word means a park enclosed by walls or hedges and containing game.[1] The wooded area unclaimed by the domain continued to be available for common use. Pigs were driven there to forage, but in the Emperor's *villae* the right of pasture, known in many districts as 'pasnage' (*pasnagium*), had to be specifically authorized every year. A public proclamation on September 1st announced the granting of pannage beginning in the month of October.[2]

The forest system characteristic of the Germanic countries was introduced gradually into Gaul, where it was unknown to the Gallo-Romans. The connecting link was the great forest of the Ardennes, which had lain uncultivated for long aeons and which was cleared and colonized by Austrasian kings and noblemen in the seventh century. This vast area was their special home, their land (*terra nostra*).[3] The system was next adopted by Neustria and became acclimatized in the west, a wooded region, spasmodically cultivated.[4] By slow stages the enjoyment of users' rights in the *silva* or the nearby *boscus* became an essential feature of rural settlement.

[1] *Cap de villis*, clause 46. For the word 'breuil' or 'breil' which is probably Celtic in origin, see *Défrichement et peuplement rural*, p. 78 et seq.

[2] B. Guérard, *Mém. de l'Ac. des I. et B.-L.*, XXI, 1, p. 215.

[3] Petit-Dutaillis, ibid., p. 113.

[4] This applied particularly to Maine, where the dual right of pannage and forestage is almost always mentioned in eleventh-century deeds laying down the status of the inhabitants of the small country towns created at that date. 'Un aspect de la vie rurale dans le Maine au XIe et au XIIo siècle: l'établissement des bourgs', *Le Moyen âge*, 1937, p. 15.

CHAPTER IV

The Structure of the Great Estate
and the origin of
the rural 'Seigneurie'

THE *Capitulare de villis* tells us nothing about the actual
structure of the great estate. The information has to be
gleaned from the abbots of several important monasteries
who have left on record the extent of their possessions and the
secrets of their administration. In fact, as we have seen, the
early Carolingians were probably responsible for the preservation of these details. First Pepin the Short,[1] then Charlemagne[2]
ordered their lay vassals and religious foundations to draw up
inventories of their property, though the heads of wealthy
abbeys most probably did not wait for a royal command
before compiling polyptyques of their landed possessions. The
word polyptyque, which during the Late Empire signified a
register of land survey,[3] was adopted in the early Middle Ages
to describe inventories compiled by churches, whilst in Merovingian times official documents relating to land survey were
known as *descriptiones*.[4]

The most famous and least incomplete of these documents is

---

[1] 'Res ecclesiarum descriptas atque divisas.' *Ann. Alam.*, a. 751, text quoted by
Inama-Sternegg, op. cit., p. 459, n. 1.   [2] See above, p. 179.

[3] Perrin, *Rech. sur la seign. rur.*, p. 765. Cf. Inama-Sternegg, op. cit., pp. 466–467.

[4] Perrin, ibid., p. 605. The *Cartul. de Saint-Victor de Marseille* (no. 31) contains a
valuable text of the late eighth century in which the Latin word *descriptio* replaces
polyptycum, the word traditionally used to describe a land survey document: 'Et sic
dixerunt quod ipsi Ansemundo, vicedomino Massiliense, ibidem *descriptionem* ad
partes S. Victoris Massiliensis facere viderunt. Et ipsum *poleticum* ipse episcopus . . .
ibidem ostendit ad relegendum.' The two words *descriptionem* and *poleticum* are here
synonymous and probably refer to a survey document.

9. An inventory of possessions and revenues: Polyptyque of Irminon. (Extract from the Bib. Nat. MS Latin 12832, fol. 3 vo.) This page refers to the *villa* of Palaiseau, one of the properties of the Abbey of St Germain-des-Prés

that of the abbey of Saint-Germain-des-Prés in Paris, and generally known as the Polyptychon of Irminon, from the name of the abbot who composed it.[1]

Irminon ruled over this monastery possibly from the late eighth and certainly during the first quarter of the ninth century.[2] This famous polyptyque is the only document of its kind dating back to the time of Charlemagne; all the others are later. It had also the supreme advantage of being not only the oldest, but the most detailed and the most accurate, and even in the Middle Ages Abbot Irminon was renowned for the scrupulous care with which he had amassed within the compass of one single document the particulars of every domain belonging to his monastery, down to the last egg, the ultimate chicken and even a piece of roofing timber.[3] The inventories of twenty-four of these domains have been preserved; all except five of these *villae* were situated in the great suburban belt surrounding Paris, between Mantes in the west and Château-Thierry in the east.[4]

One 'brief' (*breve*) or chapter is devoted to each *villa*, and each *breve* is modelled on one uniform plan. They begin with a short paragraph dealing with the reserve of the great estate (*mansus dominicatus, terra dominicata*), that part of the *villa* from which the produce went direct to the abbot, and which was cultivated chiefly by means of forced labour which the tenants of the *mansi* were compelled to provide. It consisted of several 'coutures' (*culturae*), great expanses of land which had been brought into cultivation and the area of which was reckoned in 'bonniers'.[5] The number of 'coutures' in each *villa* was far from uniform, and varied between 3 and 21. The domain of Verrières, for instance, possessed 4 'coutures' amounting in all to 355 hectares 94 centiares (about 850 acres). Included in each

---

[1] First published by B. Guérard, it was re-edited by Aug. Longnon, Paris, 1895, 2 vols., in-8°, in the *Publications de la Société de l'Histoire de Paris*. In vol. I, Longnon summarized his predecessor's learned introduction and made several additions, notably a most valuable study of personal names. This is the text referred to here.

[2] His predecessor died between 790 and 811 and Irminon, who was still alive in 823, lived on possibly until 828. *Polyptyque*, I, pp. 2–4.

[3] *Ibid.*, I, p. 6, n. 3.

[4] E. Perrin, *Observations sur le manse*, p. 41, n. 14.

[5] 1 hectare 28 ares (about 3 acres).

reserve were also vineyards and meadows, both measured in acres,[1] and woods measured in Gallic leagues.[2] Abbot Irminon, however, was not content with a mere calculation of surface areas, since his main concern was to assess the average income from his lands. Hence in each *breve* he indicated the number of hogsheads,[3] that is to say the quantity of grain to be sown in the fields, the number of hogsheads of wine to be produced in the vineyards, and of cartloads of hay to be expected from the meadows of the demesne. The picture is completed by an indication of the number of pigs to be led out to fatten in the wood (*silva*). Their number varies, and it is noticeable that the figure is generally in indirect ratio to the area of cultivable land, a connexion easily accounted for, since the bringing of land into cultivation was generally achieved at the expense of waste land and forest. On the domain of Nogent l'Artaud[4] there were 1,000 pigs but only 76 hectares (about 190 acres) of plough-land; at Palaiseau[5] on the other hand the forest maintained no more than 50 pigs, whilst the fields sown with seed covered 398 hectares (about 1,000 acres).

The description of the reserve or demesne is followed by that of the *mansi* occupied by tenants, whose names are listed, accompanied by the enumeration of the dues and forced labour incumbent upon each of them, and this information makes up the greater part of each brief. The details supplied are meticulously accurate and have already been turned to good account by the demographers, since they include a census of households with the number of children in each.[6] A document so coherent, 'such an admirable source of information',[7] has attracted and held the attention of scholars for over a century, and with the

---

[1] The field acre measured 12 ares 42 centiares (about 1,500 sq. yards), according to calculations made by Guérard, who adopts the same figure, though with certain reservations, for the vineyard. *Polyptyque*, I, pp. 19–20.

[2] One and a half Roman miles, or 2,222 metres (2,400 yards).

[3] Guérard reckons this hogshead mentioned in the Polyptychon to be approximately 52 litres 20 centilitres (about 12 gallons, or 1½ bushels), liquids and solids alike. *Polyptyque*, pp. 26–27.

[4] Cant. Charly (Aisne).

[5] County town (Seine-et-Oise).

[6] The tenants are almost always referred to by the name: *coloni*.

[7] Perrin, *Obs. sur le manse*, p. 42.

Capitulare de villis has become the historians' main source-book and one to which they still turn for a description of a great domain during the Early Middle Ages. In Fustel de Coulanges's *L'alleu et le domaine rural*,[1] to quote only one example, every page of the chapter devoted to a description of a great domain bears a reference to this polyptyque. The most important and revealing disclosure made by this document is the triumphs of organization achieved by churchmen with an outstanding gift for administration, and who in Carolingian times played a rôle comparable to that of the great chiefs of industry in our own day. They developed agricultural production, the only production of any real consequence in their day, by using to the best possible advantage the labour force which lay to hand.

Each of their *villae* became a kind of factory, in which the majority of the workmen were church *coloni* settled on *mansi* of which they had the use, and possession of which was their only remuneration. The duties exacted from them were almost the same as those enumerated in the Law of the Bavarians previously quoted.[2] It could hardly be otherwise, since every religious establishment had perforce not only to produce, with marginal resources, corn, wine, hay, textiles, honey, wax, fowls, eggs, for the needs of a vast community, but had also to rear cattle, keep large numbers of buildings in repair, and make every conceivable kind of cart and wagon. The monks seem to have been determined to get the best possible returns, which led them at an early stage to do away with team work and slave labour and substitute that of *coloni* entrusted with individual tasks. It became customary to allot to each tenant living on a *mansus* a plot of ground in the reserve; this plot was called an 'ansange' and it was his duty not only to plough it, but also to sow and harvest the crop, so that full responsibility for it rested on him alone.[3] It is an interesting fact that, of the fields which the abbey *coloni* were responsible for cultivating, some produced winter and others spring corn,[4] which suggests that a

---

[1] pp. 360–374.

[2] p. 182.

[3] Perrin, 'De la condition des terres dites "ancingae" '. *Mélanges F. Lot*, p. 627.

[4] 'Arat ad hibernaticum perticas IIII, ad tramisum (trémois) perticas II'. Breve de Vedrariis in *Polyptyque*, II, p. 48.

three-yearly system of crop rotation was already being practised on the lands belonging to the Abbey of Saint-Germain-des-Prés, as well as in many other parts of Northern Gaul, a year of fallow succeeding one year of winter wheat and one of spring corn or other crops.[1] This type of crop rotation, apparently Germanic in origin, came gradually to be adopted in Neustria, whilst the rest of the south remained more attached to the two-year system.

It may well be that the undoubted value of this polyptyque and its particular significance have been somewhat exaggerated. Abbot Irminon's *villae* were model farms, but the feats of organization they reveal were probably quite exceptional. We have already pointed out how risky it is for scholars to regard them as characteristic examples of ninth-century farming. Moreover Irminon's *Polyptyque* itself should be enough to put us on our guard against rash generalizations. Some of its briefs deal with abbey lands at a considerable distance from the Parisian centre. One of them refers to the hundred of Corbon, in the canton of Mortagne, Orne.[2] Its plan differs from that of the other briefs. It consists, in effect, of a series of résumés of gifts made to the abbey, their only common feature being that they refer to lands situated within this hundred. They no longer contain the solid core of instruction characteristic of the other briefs. The properties donated are never complete *villae*, but *mansi*. More often than not the reference is to a single, isolated *mansus*, which the author of the brief identifies by indicating the *pagus*, the hundred and the *villa* in which it is situated.[3] A study of this brief leads us to revise our traditional ideas of the *villa*, as did the Le Mans texts, the comparison with which acquires added point in that Corbonnais adjoins Maine.

[1] In the same paragraph there is also mention of a due owing 'ad tercium annum', which suggests a three-yearly cycle of cultivation, and the author adds the two words 'propter herbaticum'. Guérard had already noted (ibid., I, p. 28) that the *herbaticum* which figures in several paragraphs was exacted only every three years. This three-yearly cycle is quite naturally explained if this due is regarded as the counterpart of the tenant's right to graze his animals on the fallow land during the third year of the cycle.

[2] Breve de centena Corbonensi. Ibid., II, pp. 162–172.

[3] For example: 'Donationem quam fecit Johannes in pago Oximense, in centena Corbonense, in villa quae dicitur Gamarziacas.' Ibid., p. 164.

The brief mentions 19 *villae* within which were situated *mansi* given to the Abbot of Saint-Germain-des-Prés. What kind of *villae* were they?

It should be noted at the outset that the word *villa* is sometimes replaced by the word *locus* in the brief dealing with the hundred of Corbon, and that on several occasions a single place is called alternately *villa* and *locus*.[1] The term *locus*, which may quite suitably be applied to an inhabited spot or village, is hardly appropriate to an entire domain. In the second place it is noticeable that on several occasions a *mansus indominicatus*, which according to the traditional conception was a 'demesne' situated within the *villa*, is given to the monks without the *villa* itself appearing any the worse for the amputation; it seems in fact to have an existence independent of this *indominicatum*.[2] A reading of the text reveals no vital connexion between the *villa* and this so-called demesne, and we are forced to the conclusion that it was not a demesne in the accepted sense of the word. In fact the distinguishing feature of the *mansi indominicati* mentioned in the Corbon brief, and that which set them apart from other *mansi*, was that they were cultivated by slaves (*mancipia*) and not by *coloni*. The master farmed them directly, controlled and collected the income, but did not make use of forced labour provided by tenants living on other *mansi*. The *indominicatum* was self-sufficient. This represented a striking departure from the classical *villa* system, or rather it was a different system altogether.

Another fact which emerges not only from the brief describing the hundred of Corbon but also from most of the other briefs in Irminon's *Polyptyque*, is the break-up of the *mansus*. In many cases it is obvious that several families of *coloni* with their children were settled on one and the same *mansus*, which reinforces our previous conclusion that in the early ninth century the *mansus* had ceased to be a family farm and had completely lost its original status of a residence for a single

---

[1] Examples include *Curtis Ansgili* (p. 165), *Mons Acbodi* (p. 165), *Villaris* (pp. 168–169).

[2] 'Donationem Waltcarii . . . in villa quae dicitur Mons Aldulfi. Dedit ibi mansum indominicatum.' *Polyptyque*, p. 164.

family.[1] During the next few centuries other names were to take its place – *quartier* in Lorraine, *borderie* in Limousin, *cabannerie* in Dauphiné. Having lost its primitive meaning, the *mansus* was henceforth merely an agrarian unit, a unit of assessment, though never a uniform measure. Finally it disappeared from use in Latin charters, to linger on in Romance, and dialect forms in such words as *mas* and *meix*.

This brief survey of the *mansus*[2] is not merely a digression, since it goes to prove that in the official, administrative language of the Middle Ages a word rarely had a stable meaning. This holds good for the *villa* as well as for the *mansus*; it will help to resolve difficulties which would be insoluble if we did not know that many apparent contradictions, inherent in medieval history, spring from fluidity of vocabulary and from the fact that words have no precise connotation. The preceding observations therefore give us grounds for concluding that in the ninth century the nineteen *villae* in the hundred of Corbon were not – or were no longer[3] – great domains and that in Hiémois where they were situated the word *villa* was used from that time onwards to denote villages with a scattered population. By this fresh detour we arrive once again at the same conclusions as those suggested by a close examination of the Le Mans documents. The fragmentation of the plots of land given to Saint-Germain-des-Prés in this district coinciding with the diocese of Sées is one more proof that in North-Western Gaul, land was not concentrated in the hands of rich and powerful men. What did exist there was the *Streubesitz* so beloved of the Viennese historian Dopsch.[4]

Do we have to rest content with so timid a conclusion? When

---

[1] On half the *mansi* of the *villa* of Verrières we find two families of tenants in possession, and one-third of the *mansi* in this same *villa* are owned by three farmers. Perrin, *Obs. sur le manse*, p. 47. This is the most typical example, but the abbey's other domains were also suffering from over population.

[2] We shall have occasion later to examine in detail the causes of this transformation: intensification of forest clearance and increase in population.

[3] The alternative is appropriate, since some of the *villae* in question (*Curtis Saonis, Curtis Ansgili, Curtis Dotleni*) owed their name to the former existence of a great domain.

[4] 'Eindrucksvoll trat uns überall ein weithin verbreiter Streubesitz aller Grundherrschaften in der Karolingerzeit entgegen.' Op. cit., I, p. 364.

we bear in mind that the régime of the *villicatio* is known to us
chiefly through the *Polyptyque* of Irminon, and that the Abbey
of Saint-Germain-des-Prés obviously succeeded in imposing it
only on those of its estates which were in the vicinity of Paris –
in other words on those which the abbots could supervise at
close quarters – we feel called on to re-examine the whole conception of a general and widespread domanial system which, if
it was to function smoothly, required perfect organization, an
ever-watchful administration and continual careful supervision.
We have already expressed doubts about the claim that the
great estates were spread over a wide area and covered the
greater part of the soil of Gaul. We believe them to have been
more in the nature of islands.[1] Criticism will have to go deeper
and concentrate on the actual structure of the *villae*. In actual
fact, most of these so-called great domains about which Carolingian documents, less reticent than those of the preceding period,
give us more detailed information, only remotely resembled the
villae Imperii or even those described in the *Polyptyque* of Irminon.
They generally consisted of one main part known as the *casa
dominicaria*,[2] or sometimes simply as 'my *mansus*',[3] and several
holdings (*mansi*) and plots of land farmed by *coloni*. In certain
areas such as Limousin the word *curtis* was the one most frequently used to denote these domains,[4] perhaps through a
desire to prevent misunderstandings, the word *villa* gradually
tending to assume the meaning of village and to shed its
association with the domain; similarly in the Vienne region of
Dauphiné where the *villa*, a synonym of *ager*, was split up into
small independent holdings.[5] The word *villa*, however, underwent still further changes. In a district like Breton Cornouaille

---

[1] See above, p. 178.

[2] 856. *Cartul. de Beaulieu en Limousin*, p. 37, no. 16. – 943: 'Casam meam indominicatum, cum ipso superposito ubi ego visus sum manere, cum ipsa vinea indomini-
cata, cum ipso prato indominicato et cum ipso farinario.' Ibid., p. 104, no. 58.

[3] 833: 'Manso meo'. *Cartul. de Redon*, p. 5, no. 5. In order to distinguish between
them the *mansi* held by tenants are sometimes called 'little *mansi*' (*mansiunculi*): 'Cum
mansiunculis ubi ipsi manentes commanent.' Note in passing the use of the Latin
'manentes', from which came quite naturally the French word 'manants'.

[4] René Fage, *La propriété rurale en Bas Limousin pendant le moyen âge*, p. 41.

[5] Fr. Chevalier, *Etude sur le peuplement rural dans la région de Vienne*, p. 40. The
identity of meaning between *villa* and *ager* had already been noted by the editor of
the *Cartul. de Saint-André-le-Bas*, Lyons, 1869.

which had never experienced the *villicatio* system – and such areas are more numerous than is generally supposed – the word was adopted as an equivalent to *mansus*, unknown in those parts, and in the Cartulary of Landevenec it is surprising to come across parishes (*plebes*) divided into 'trèves' (*tribus*), which in turn are sub-divided into *villae*, one single 'trève' consisting of 22 or even 30 *villae*.[1] We shall also see that in Provence, by a curious semantic evolution, the *villa* became synonymous with the *castrum*, a fortified settlement, and in the tenth and eleventh centuries denoted a hilltop village.[2] These observations should, we feel, provide ample proof of the fluid and changing nature of this word *villa* on which a whole system has been erected, and should at the same time draw attention to the frailty of this system.[3] The excessive rigidity of the traditional conception of the *villa* did not escape the attention of Marc Bloch, and his statement that the supporters of the domanial theory forget the village showed him to be aware of the need to revise it.[4]

Let us leave the world of words for that of things and return to the ninth century in order to trace the general features of the countryside at that time. Contrary to the oft-stated belief, it was the small estate which predominated, and small-scale farming was then practised almost exclusively. It is true that in glancing through charters and turning over cartularies we come across domains of vast extent, *curtes* or *villae*. One qualifying word: *indominicatus*[5] often identifies for the reader that portion which the owner kept for himself; the rest were *mansi* in

---

[1] 'Tribum [trève] Petrani XXX villas.' *Cartul. de Landevenec*, ed. A. de la Borderie, p. 147, no. 6. – 'De tribu Lantrefharthoc . . . XXII villas', p. 149, no. 13. For the identification of these places see our *Mélanges d'histoire de Cornouaille*, pp. 84–85.

[2] *Quelques aperçus sur le manse en Provence*, in *Mélanges Clovis Brunel*, Paris, 1955, p. 103.

[3] It must be acknowledged that in certain regions such as Lorraine the *villa* apparently preserved its cohesion and consistency for a longer period, at least when it was in the hands of vigilant abbots.

[4] *Ann. d'hist. éc. et soc.*, I, 1929, p. 589.

[5] The word 'condamine' was sometimes used: 'Similiter in ipso pago cundaminam nostram indominicatam.' *Cartul. de Beaulieu*, p. 82, no. 45. It was the translation into the common speech of the Latin *indominicatum*, as is proved by a charter, unfortunately undated, brought to light by Chifflet: 'Tribui itaque campum unum indominicatum quem vulgari lingua condaminam vocant.' *Hist. de l'abbaye de Tournus*, 1664, p. 354.

varying numbers or plots of land often widely scattered. Sometimes we are told how the cultivation of these lands was supervised. In each of their *curtes* the abbots of Beaulieu placed a serf
known as the *servus judex* or *servus vicarius*, to keep order and see
that the services to which the monks were entitled were
properly carried out,[1] but the general deterioration of the
domanial system turned these agents into formidable figures; it
was feared that they might abuse their authority, and they
were forbidden to carry arms.[2] This is one instance of the state of
decay into which the domanial system soon fell.[3] For the rest,
more numerous than the great domains were the small independent farms consisting of only one, or several, *mansi*. The
owner did not always cultivate them himself, but had them
farmed by a family of *coloni* or by slaves (*mancipia*). Henri Sée,
in the course of his study of the rural classes in Brittany, was
surprised not to discover, during the Early Middle Ages, the
great Gallo-Roman estate which he had regarded as the normal
feature of the Carolingian age. He believed it to have been
affected by the Celtic invasions.[4] This worthy historian would
most probably have experienced similar surprises if he had
made the same careful survey of other parts of the country.

From whence, then, springs the *illusion* of large-scale land
ownership in the Carolingian age? Without claiming to re-
write history, we believe that a system of small estates similar
to that prevailing in contemporary France would gradually
have established itself in Western Europe from the ninth
century onwards, had not the growing feudal anarchy of the
middle years of that century changed its institutions as well as
its economic structure. The word anarchy is here used in its
strict etymological sense: absence of authority and the bank-
ruptcy of the sovereign state. It was an evil which had been

[1] *Cartul. de Beaulieu*, p. 92, no. 50.
[2] 'Et sic per omnes curtes sive villas imponimus judices servos in tali convenientia
ut nullus ex illis neque de posteris eorum efficiatur miles neque ullus portet scutum,
neque spadam neque ulla arma.' Ibid. In Lorraine also the domanial agents were
to become petty tyrants who could not be brought to reason.
[3] For the break-up of the domanial system see a thoughtful memoir by F. L.
Ganshof, *Une étape de la décomposition de l'organisation domaniale classique à l'abbaye de
Saint-Trond*. This evolution will be discussed later.
[4] *Etude sur les classes rurales en Bretagne au moyen âge*, Paris–Rennes, 1896, p. 17.

undermining Gaul and Western Europe ever since the Great
Invasions, and which Charlemagne and the early Carolingians
did not succeed in curing. The responsibility for it must be
placed fairly and squarely on the Merovingian rulers. Ferdinand
Lot has drawn up a strictly fair balance-sheet of that pernicious
government which exacted services from its subjects and gave
them nothing in return.[1] He has pointed out that a machine
which worked so inefficiently and which, it may be added, was
functioning in a vacuum, soon went off the rails.[2] Once that
conception of the general good, which still persisted during the
Late Empire, had disappeared, the grandees and churches who
owned vast estates naturally sought to contract out of a system
from which they gained nothing at all, since there was no
longer any expenditure of money for the public benefit. The
practice of immunity, the essential aim of which was exemption
from taxation,[3] became widespread and this serious abdication
of responsibility reached such vast proportions that it soon went
far beyond the realm of finance.[4] Vast tracts of the kingdom
were completely outside the jurisdiction of the central authority,
since the king expressly forbade his officials to enter the immunists' domains for the purpose of carrying out their administrative duties. This abandonment conferred on the abbeys,
bishops and laymen enjoying the privilege of immunity excessive
powers which we may be sure they exercised not only over their
own property but also over that of others in cases where lands
adjoined their own. Anarchy was temporarily and partially
checked under the early Carolingians and especially under
Charlemagne, who had a strong sense of authority and of the
general good. But the rot set in even more devastatingly in the
second half of the ninth century, and went from bad to worse,
since royal officials, including the highest in rank like dukes and
counts, as well as a host of minor agents, lords of the manor and
vicarious agents, annexed to themselves those royal rights they
were exercising in the name of the sovereign. An inextricable

[1] *La fin du monde antique*, 1st ed., p. 402.
[2] The Merovingian palace was 'a vast, ill-kept house', as we stated in *Les Grandes Invasions et la crise de l'Occident au V⁰ siècle*, p. 251.
[3] Levillain, *L'immunité*, pp. 38–67.
[4] The subject has been dealt with in detail in *Les Grandes Invasions*, p. 246.

muddle, which is one of the basic features of feudalism, resulted from this general usurpation.

One single aspect of the problem will serve to illustrate our point: the setting up, within a framework wider than and generally different from that of the *villa*,[1] of rural seigneuries which under cover of the ban (*bannum*) eventually spread over most of the realm. The right of *bannum*, of which the usurpers took full advantage, defies exhaustive and accurate analysis, as do most early medieval, institutional words. It has been defined in the following terms by one modern historian:[2] 'The right to command, to constrain, and to punish, a right which could be exercised within very variable limits.' The deliberately vague and general nature of this definition is significant and suggestive. It is the symbol of a double disintegration, that of the great domain and simultaneously of sovereignty.[3] The rural seigneurie inherited not only those residual rights which the owner, or perhaps simply the administrator, of great dismembered domains continued to exercise, but also and most particularly those royal rights which a king's official, representing the sovereign in a province great or small, had usurped from him, a motley collection varying from place to place and embodied for the inhabitants in a host of servile tasks: the obligation to grind corn in the common mill, the ban on the sale of wine before a fixed date after the vintage, payment of various traffic tolls, dues from sales concluded in markets, rights of succession, rights of pasturage and forestage, obligations of a military nature, and a variety of quit-rents which were either former public taxes or domanial dues. It would be impossible to draw up a complete and systematic list of these 'duties' and dues, since disorder and muddle are the hallmarks of feudal institutions, but they are often referred to by a word which has a

[1] In Dauphiné for example the framework was that of the castellany or mandate (bishop's ward), in other words the province within which a lord of the manor exercised his functions. G. Letonnelier, *Essai sur les origines des châtelains et des mandements en Dauphiné*, Grenoble, 1925.

[2] Perrin, *Rech. sur la seign. rur.*, p. 744.

[3] The reader should refer to J. Calmette's subtle analyses in his short work on *La société féodale*, Paris, 1923, coll. A. Colin. See also Aug. Dumas's shrewd observations in a memoir quoted above: *Quelques observations sur la grande et petite propriété à l'époque carolingienne, passim*.

strong symbolical value: customs (*consuetudines*). This evocative word reminds us that it was their traditional character alone which lent sanction to these impositions; men performed these duties and paid these dues because they had always done so. Their only justification lay in their extreme antiquity.

Thus the complete liberation of the small landowner was delayed for a thousand years, since most of the territories included in the rural seigneuries which shared out the land between them, except for certain rare allodial lands which remained intact, were left burdened for centuries to come with a heavy load of servitude. These seigniorial rights were in the main the equivalents of the many taxes which afflict the taxpayer in the twentieth century, but because they were not levied for the public good they were regarded as personal and oppressive. A man of the tenth century paid less to his overlord than we do today to the state; his military obligations were less heavy than those of a modern French citizen; but harshly exacted, on a local scale, by the neighbouring seigneur, and for his own good pleasure, these customs appeared as an unwarranted limitation of man's just rights over his own land, and not as the payment of dues owing to the community. Often arbitrary, they contributed to the deterioration of the condition of the freeman and the small country landowner. Yet at the same time the institution of rural seigneuries, which were established and multiplied under cover of feudal anarchy and the weakening of the central power, created the illusion of a régime of land ownership on the grand scale, since it was tempting to regard all these feudal seigneurs, great and small alike, as great landowners, though they were really no more than farmers and usurpers. The history of land ownership from the ninth to the eleventh centuries will, in fact, have to be rewritten. The task will be fraught with difficulty and may prove deceptive, since it will be necessary to impose order on anarchy.

*

It would, however, be a mistake to write off every aspect of the Carolingian age as negative. Forest clearance went steadily on. Germany was the scene of an agricultural activity which the documents, unfortunately, do not allow us to reconstruct as accurately as we could wish. The Great Invasions had spilled over the Western world, over Gaul and Italy, surplus Germanic populations which did not possess in their own country sufficient means of existence to ensure them a livelihood. The following centuries witnessed a reverse movement, when agricultural production was gradually being organized on Germanic soil, so that the native people, once they had settled down, could lead a stable existence. The romanticism of German historians, and their genius for the abstract reconstruction of social and economic developments of which written texts have left little if any trace, have led them to delineate the past in ways which are venturesome, but none the less ingenious and thought-provoking. One of the most recent of these studies was that attempted by Heinrich Bechtel.[1] German scholarship as we have seen, has abandoned the theory, so popular in the nineteenth century, of a primitive agrarian communism, and it is now agreed beyond the Rhine that at a relatively early date the Germans were familiar with individual ownership. The formation of *Markgenossenschaften,* the definition of which has given rise to such impassioned argument, is now no longer attributed to protohistory. They are no longer regarded as manifestations of an old collectivist régime, but as the general body of rights and privileges enjoyed by all the inhabitants of a village over pastures and communal woods, an interpretation which may be less impressive but which is much more likely. This institution developed comparatively late, for far from preceding forest clearance, it was a consequence of it. Since the areas which were uncultivated, unclaimed and available to all alike, diminished in extent as more and more land was cleared by peasants, village organizations were formed to stake out and fix the boundaries of pasture and woodland necessary to the group as a whole. Bechtel has retraced the early beginnings of the *Markgenossenschaften* in a lively synthesis which deserves to be quoted, affording as it does an interesting example of the

---

[1] *Wirtschaftsgeschichte Deutschlands*, 2nd ed., Munich, 1951, and particularly pp. 182–197. Cf. G. von Below, *Geschichte der deutschen Landwirtschaft des Mittelalters*, pub. von Lütge, Jena, 1937.

imaginative effort which German scholarship brings to the reconstruction of an historical evolution about which the documents are silent:

> The formation of *Markgenossenschaften* [he says][1] was no doubt helped on by a general feeling that the unoccupied area (*Niemandsland*), which up to then had appeared to be unlimited and quite inexhaustible, was beginning to contract and would have to be the object of systematic cultivation if they wished to safeguard it and to preserve their communal property. They were probably alarmed by the increase in population and the progress of forest clearance. The first steps taken towards the formation of *Markgenossenschaften* are obscure; there was certainly no actual founding in the true sense of the word; they probably came into being discreetly and unnoticed.

The economist concludes:

> The *Markgenossenschaften* did not play the rôle formerly assigned to them. They did not further the growth of villages united in a vast communal group; on the contrary it was the villages themselves which organized the communal lands and decided what common rights their inhabitants should have in the *Allmende* or common lands.

This new conception of the *Markgenossenschaft* has not been universally accepted. As early as 1912 it met with biting criticism from Alfons Dopsch, who denounced its mythical character.[2] He believed that the rights over common land, the explanation of which gave rise to this idea, were quite simply users' rights which had not been divided up amongst neighbours, the absence of division resulting from the fact that old inheritances had not been completely shared out. Subtle and skilful this argument may be, but it cannot be accepted in its entirety, since from the ninth century onwards we find the peasants (*pagenses*) of a district determined to band together to resist the claims of a religious house and make sure that the

---

[1] *Wirtschaftsgeschichte Deutschlands*, 2nd ed., p. 185.
[2] *Die Wirtschaftsentwicklung der Karolingerzeit*, I, p. 333 et seq.

portion of the forest in which they exercised their common rights should be accurately defined.[1] Actually there is no reason whatever why agrarian communities should not have existed from the Carolingian era.

One further factor played a part in the evolution: the seigneurie (*Grundherrschaft*).[2] It first appeared in Germany at the close of the Merovingian epoch when the rise of the Austrasian aristocracy and their territorial aggrandisement were just beginning. The German historian Georg von Below[3] has attempted to discover the causes of a social and economic transformation which brought about the eclipse of the small freeman landholder and the development of the great estate. He lays the blame on the revolution which had taken place in the army since the time of Charles Martel, and the substitution of restricted military service binding only on feudal vassals (*Lehndienst*) for compulsory service binding on all alike; this service was a heavy burden, since those called up had to have a horse, but it carried one compensation, the gift of land made by the king to those serving in the army as cavalrymen. The benefice granted was not always a large tract of land, often consisting of a single peasant holding, but von Below none the less declares, and probably with good reason, that the fact of giving men land as a reward for military service helped in the long run to increase the inequalities existing between landed proprietors, particularly as the fief was often added on as an extra to an already existing patrimonial fortune. The balance began to be disturbed, which was inevitable, if it is true, as the author maintains, that a force which has been the initial cause of a lack of balance always tends to make it worse. The great estate continued to gain ground in Germany, where the sovereigns seized

[1] Wopfner, *Urkunden*, p. 96, no. 55. This is a set formula, indicating that this was a common type of deed.

[2] The concept of the 'Grundherrschaft', the German equivalent of the rural seigneurie, has been thoroughly analysed by R. Kötzschke, *Allgem. Wirtschaftsgesch.*, p. 220 et seq. He believes that the institution evolved differently in the former territory of the Roman Empire and in Germany where it developed later.

[3] *Gesch. d. Deutschen Landwirtschaft*, p. 51. Cf. Inama-Sternegg, op. cit., I, p. 321 et seq. A. Dopsch, on the other hand, believes the rôle played in Germany by the great seigneuries to have been exaggerated: 'Man sah nur die grossen Grundherrschaften.' Op. cit., I, p. 249.

upon lands which were still unoccupied and wrested them from
their enemies and from those they looked upon as traitors,
heaping property upon their loyal adherents and founding
monasteries. The early part of the Carolingian era was marked
in the Eastern Frankish Empire by the creation of numerous
royal abbeys.[1] Since it was evangelized comparatively late, its
monastic foundations belong mostly to the eighth and ninth
centuries, and not to the sixth and seventh as in Gaul. Moreover, a vast and massive movement of controlled colonization
coincided with the reign of Charlemagne. The areas chiefly
affected were the lands recently conquered,[2] and the sovereign,
in order to achieve his aims, did not shrink from dictatorial,
even violent methods,[3] such as the transference of Saxon and
Slav populations. A longing for peace, a pious desire to multiply
the number of conversions to Christianity, a determination to
increase agricultural production by extending the acreage of land
sown with cereal crops, these three motives led this energetic
Emperor to direct his policy towards an eastward expansion of
his frontiers (*dilatatio imperii*) and a systematic exploitation of
conquered countries. The fact of most interest to the economist
is the speeding up of land cultivation in Germany. It was no
longer being carried out through *Weiler* and those small farms
which figured so largely in the early stages of forest clearance. In
this new phase it was the seigneurie which took the lead; it
eclipsed the small estate, but did not eliminate it altogether.
There is even evidence to suggest that at that time agricultural
peasant communities were beginning to take shape in order to
resist the new invaders and to defend themselves against the
encroachments of neighbouring lords who were seeking to
deprive them of their woods and pasture lands, which they
wished to annex for their own use, and in many cases to turn
into hunting reserves. The documents, which become less rare
from the ninth century onwards, hint at the patient efforts
being made to establish in that part of Western Germany which
belonged to the Carolingian Empire an agrarian system similar
to, if not identical with, that of Gaul.

---

[1] Inama-Sternegg, op. cit., pp. 283–4.   [2] Ibid., p. 275.
[3] L. Halphen, *Charlemagne et l'Empire Carolingien*, p. 71.

The work of forest clearance in the ninth century was not confined solely to Germany. Many other parts of the Empire came in for careful attention from the Carolingian sovereigns. The Spanish Marches captured from the Saracens, and in which there had taken refuge a host of Visigoths referred to as 'Spaniards' in documents in the Carolingian Chancellery, were brought back into cultivation. These Christians received from the sovereigns lands which were *res nullius*, and which were handed over to them by a deed of concession known as aprision.[1] A decree of Charlemagne of 8 April 812[2] shows us forty-one of these Spaniards coming to Aix-la-Chapelle to complain to the Emperor in person about the counts and other imperial officials in the Spanish Marches who were seeking to expel them. Actually, as they went on to say in justification of their claim, it was more than thirty years since these lands had been given them, waste and derelict; it was they who had brought them under the plough. Their request was favourably received by Charlemagne.

However great might be the number of plaintiffs with whom he had to deal, the great Emperor's decisions never lost their own individual touch. In contrast, Louis the Pious soon after his accession issued two declarations[3] generalizing the measures taken by his father, and the preambles of these two solemn acts, the first of which was drafted to allow three copies to each city,[4] and the second seven copies,[5] bring out with complete clarity the double objective which the Emperor set before himself. The first essential was to protect Christians who, wishing to shake off the Saracen yoke, had left their homes and hereditary lands to take refuge in Septimania and in the reconquered Spanish Marches, but it was also important to repopulate and bring back into cultivation lands which had been left derelict

---

[1] Brutails, *Etude sur la condition des populations rurales du Roussillon au moyen âge*, Paris, 1891, p. 99.

[2] *Capitul.*, Boretius, I, p. 169.

[3] One of 1 January 815, ibid., I, p. 261, the second of 10 February 816, p. 263.

[4] 'Cuius constitutionis in unaquaque civitate ubi praedicti Hispani habitare noscuntur tres descriptiones esse volumus.' p. 262.

[5] These seven examples were intended for the cities of Narbonne, Carcassonne, Roussillon, Ampurias, Barcelona, Gerona and Béziers. p. 264.

ever since the expulsion of the Saracens, and to rebuild on them.[1]

The good work was carried on in a remarkable spirit of continuity. In 844 the declarations of Louis the Pious were confirmed by Charles the Bald[2] when he was campaigning in Gothia, and numerous individual favours were granted by the king to the inhabitants of Septimania and the Spanish Marches, especially to those who continued to be known as Spaniards.[3] By degrees the settlers' rights conferred on the fugitives by aprision were consolidated and transformed into rights of ownership. To this policy of colonization was due the opening up and development of Roussillon and Catalonia, today one of the richest parts of Spain.

[1] The two declarations refer to the work done by the refugees who 'in desertis atque in incultis locis . . . aedificia fecerunt et agros incoluerunt'.

[2] 'Praeceptum pro Hispania', 11 June 844. Boretius, II, p. 258 et seq. Clause 6 is the most interesting: 'Placuit etiam nobis illis concedere ut quicquid de heremi squalore in quolibet comitatu ad cultum frugum traxerunt aut deinceps infra eorum aprisiones excolere potuerunt integerrime teneant atque possideant.'

[3] Lot and Halphen, *Le règne de Charles le Chauve*, pp. 99–112.

PART IV

The Laborious Birth of a Western Civilization

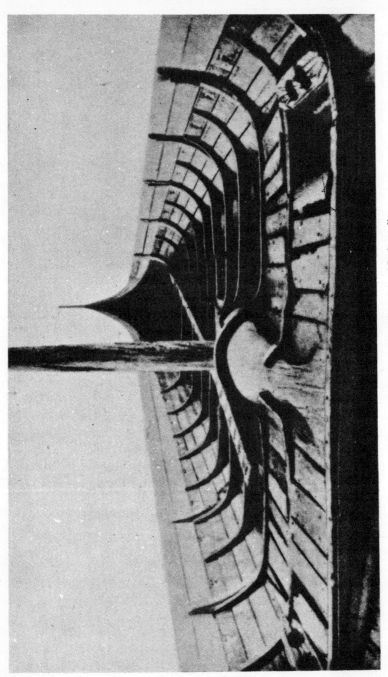

10. Inboard view of Viking ship (Gokstad)

CHAPTER I

The Vikings
and Scandinavian Expansion

THE TASK OF SHOWING how the heroic achievements of
the Scandinavian peoples, in agriculture and trade as
well as in warfare, enlarged the horizon of civilization,
could best be dealt with in a work devoted to the origins of
western economy – or so Marc Bloch declared.[1] We shall do
well to bear this challenge in mind as we approach that
century during which Western Europe was ravaged by the invasions of the Northmen. The economy of Gaul, of Northern
Germany and of Great Britain was seriously impaired by them,
but it would be a mistake to pay too much attention to the
accounts of chroniclers and hagiographers who have exaggerated
the destructive rôle of the invaders, and above all to forget the
decisive contribution made to the European economy by those
known by the general name of Northmen. They initiated their
contemporaries into the art of navigation on the high seas, and
as a historian has aptly put it, their essential rôle consisted in
welding the entire Atlantic front of Europe, from the Neva to
Gibraltar, into a single navigational bloc.[2]

This was not the first time that Scandinavian peoples had
surged over Western Europe in search of a new home, but it
was with the Viking expeditions that Scandinavia made her
real entry on to the stage of world history.[3] Unfortunately the
actual history of these Vikings is as elusive as it is fascinating.
It has come down to us chiefly in the form of numerous prose

[1] *La société féodale*, p. 30.
[2] W. Vogel, *Geschichte der deutschen Seeschiffahrt*, I, p. 98.
[3] The words are those of L. Musset, *Les peuples scandinaves au moyen âge*, p. 45.

stories, the sagas,[1] written in Icelandic – that is in Old Norse – which by their unaffected simplicity and rugged outlines inspire a confidence which they frequently deserve. Yet we should beware of excessive credulity, since the oldest of them are no earlier than the twelfth century and are hardly ever based on anything more than oral traditions.

These Scandinavians to whom continental Europeans have generally applied the collective name of Northmen, split up at an early date into separate groups which the future was to perpetuate since their names are still borne today by the inhabitants of the three largest Scandinavian countries, Norwegians, Danes and Swedes.[2] Each of these peoples seems to have played a distinctive part in the great Scandinavian expansion of early medieval times, a part chiefly determined by its geographical situation. The underlying causes of this migration have long been sought. To the pious ninth-century chroniclers, watching the onward sweep of the invaders, it seemed like a punishment inflicted by a wrathful God.[3] The historian can only speculate on the various theories put forward: excess of population, which a poverty-stricken land could not adequately feed, a longing for the sun, which found its dramatic expression in the nineteenth century in Ibsen's *Ghosts*, perhaps most of all a passion for loot and adventure, justifiable in an exceptionally skilful people remarkably well provided with ships capable of making long expeditions.

Funeral objects discovered in royal tombs in Norway have shown us what a Viking ship was like. One of the most famous is that unearthed during excavations at Oseberg, in the Vestfold district, in 1914. The ship was used as a grave for a queen, who

---

[1] There is a vast literature on the sagas. Most of them have been translated into German in the collection *Thule. Altnordische Dichtung und Prosa*, published in Jena. The work by L. Musset quoted above includes several substantial pages on their historical value. Op. cit., pp. 46–49.

[2] The Swedes absorbed the Götar, that is the inhabitants of Götaland, the southern part of the Scandinavian peninsula. L. Musset, op. cit., p. 24. In his picture of the Scandinavian peoples at the end of the eighth century, W. Vogel, *Die Normannen*, pp. 16–17, still distinguishes four peoples: the Swedes, the Götar (Goten), Danes and Norwegians. The problem of the relationship between the Götar and the Goths is still far from being solved.

[3] W. Vogel, *Die Normannen*, p. 25.

was buried in it with her trousseau.[1] It measured 70 feet long, 16 feet 3 inches wide, and had 15 pairs of oars. Other vessels discovered in similar conditions have almost the same dimensions.[2] The ships had no deck. Most of them were propelled by both oar and sail, like that found at Gokstad, and which had a mast about 42 feet high with a single sail. It has been estimated that the Viking ship could reach a speed of approximately 10 knots and carry a crew of 40 to 100 men. The fine workmanship of the boat, with its skilfully constructed hull, was equalled by the dexterity of the navigators, who were remarkably gifted observers, and who, steering westward, must have established a direct route from Bergen to Southern Greenland.[3]

The technical qualities of these ships have to be stressed in order to explain not only the extent of the invasion of the Northmen, but even more the discoveries which marked the Viking Age. The achievements of each of the Scandinavian peoples are fairly well known and have often been defined,[4] but the distinctions between them have perhaps been overdone, so that what a learned contemporary calls Viking internationalism[5] is in danger of being completely overlooked and overshadowed. Nevertheless the fact remains that the Danes, whose territory had adjoined the Frankish Empire since the conquest of Saxony, took the initiative in the expeditions which ravaged first Gaul then Great Britain. It was they who conceived the idea of sailing up rivers and systematically pillaging territories far inland. The Norwegians on the other hand, facing the coast of Scotland, began by taking their ships into those parts as well as to Ireland; they then turned their bold gaze still further to the north, to the Faroe Islands, to Iceland and even to Greenland, and it is within the bounds of possibility that they discovered America in the tenth century. The Swedish thrust opened a route towards the

---

[1] The Exhibition: *Art norvégien. Mille ans de tradition Viking*, Paris, 1954. See also a commentary on this exhibition by Michel Eude, *Ann. de Normandie*, Oct.–Nov. 1954, pp. 219 et seq.

[2] L. Musset, op. cit., p. 46; Marc Bloch, *La société féodale*, pp. 30–31; W. Vogel, *Geschichte der deutschen Seeschiffahrt*, p. 90 et seq.

[3] They used the compass at an early date. The author of the *Landnámabók* refers to the 'compass', but adds that the first Icelandic settlers were not acquainted with it.   [4] See for example L. Halphen, *Les Barbares*, 1st ed., pp. 290–309.

[5] The phrase is L. Musset's, op. cit., p. 65.

east, through the Baltic countries, where under the name of
Varangians or, as has been ingeniously suggested, wandering
merchants,[1] they settled in Russia, sailing down the Volkhov
from the point where it entered Lake Ladoga, then up the
Dnieper towards the Black Sea, establishing military posts which
were also trading centres at Novgorod, Smolensk and Kiev.[2]
Little was known about these journeys until the Swedes came
into contact with the Greeks. Several of them who had just
completed a long and dangerous journey accompanied ambassadors from the Eastern Emperor Theophilus (839) to the
Court of Louis the Pious, and asked his permission to make their
return journey to Sweden through the Frankish Empire. They
asserted that the route they had taken on the way to Constantinople had obliged them to pass through the midst of
weird and barbaric peoples, and that on the return journey they
did not wish to be exposed to the same dangers. These strange
men, half merchants, half diplomats, declared that they were
Russians (Rhos); they aroused the suspicion of the Emperor
Louis the Pious who regarded them as spies. His fears were not
allayed until, having made enquiries about their identity, he
learnt that they were of Swedish nationality.[3] The truth is that
the Swedes were not content to be merely pioneers and merchants. They took advantage of the disappearance of the Avars
to create in the Ukraine a state around Kiev; this was actually
the first Russian state. Moreover the name of Russians which
they assumed was none other than the primitive name given
by the Finns to the Swedes.[4]

This great Scandinavian epic was enacted on a vast stage
stretching from America to the Black Sea. The historian is bewildered by the multiplicity and variety of its aspects, whilst
the economist is hard put to it to form a balanced judgement

---

[1] L. Musset, op. cit., p. 53.
[2] L. Halphen, op. cit., p. 306. Amongst these itinerant merchants there were
some Norwegians. The author of the *Landnámabók* (translated into German under
the title *Islands Besiedlung* in the coll. *Thule*, XXIII, p. 104) mentions a Norwegian
nobleman who was known as Bjorn of the Furs because he had made the journey
to Novgorod. Weary of these expeditions, but a wealthy man, he set sail for Iceland.
[3] *Annales Bertiniani*, 839 (ed. Waitz, pp. 19–20).
[4] L. Musset, op. cit., p. 69, n. 1.

on such many-sided activities, some of which were destructive
whilst others were rich in promise for the future. Must we, however, in our efforts to clarify a situation of unusual complexity,
necessarily accept a solution which, as even its author admits, is
over-simplified? It consists in considering the Scandinavians
who came to the West as pirates (Vikings) and those who made
their way to the East as merchants (Varangians).[1] This alternative has the serious disadvantage of excluding the Norwegians who explored and colonized virgin lands, but it may
usefully be borne in mind as an expression of what the continental peoples felt about the Scandinavians in the ninth
century. The Danes, who invaded Gaul and Great Britain, and
to whom the name Vikings was applied exclusively, undoubtedly
had a detestable reputation in the West. At the end of the tenth
century, and consequently almost one hundred years after they
had settled in the Duchy of Normandy, they were still regarded
as pirates by the historian Richer.[2]

Many attempts have been made to explain the name Viking.
The radical *vik* has no connexion whatever with the Latin *vicus*,
meaning the village. It is a geographical term frequently found
in Scandinavian place-names and meaning a bay. An examination of the map of Iceland, which more than any other Scandinavian country has preserved its integrity, its ancient tongue,
and where old place-names have generally been retained in
their primitive form, will reveal a considerable number of such
names ending with the suffix *vik* and always situated by the sea
or at the extreme end of a bay.[3] The word *vik*, then, used as a
component of Viking, had best be taken to have its original
meaning of bay.[4] The *vik* frequented by the Viking was not a
trading post, nor even a repository for merchandise, it was quite
simply a little bay in which he anchored. When later the word
was taken over and diverted from its primitive meaning, to be

[1] See L. Musset, op. cit., pp. 52–53.
[2] 'Piratae, pyratae.' *Hist. de France*, I, pp. 12, 16, 22, 96; II, pp. 272, 292.
[3] The places where the immigrants chose to found their rustic settlements often,
in the *Landnámabók*, bear names ending in *vik*. They preferred to settle near the spot
where they had landed.
[4] See W. Vogel, *Wik-orte und Wikinger* (*Hansische Geschichtsblätter*), LX, 1936, pp.
5–48. The article is interesting, though its conclusions seem open to question.

used on the Continent and in Great Britain as a name for a trading post, it had long formed part of the Scandinavian hero's name with its original meaning.

It is not within the scope of this work to retrace the history of the Norse invasions of the West, which may possibly have been foreseen by Charlemagne. The conquest of Saxony and of North Albingia, and the subjugation of the Abodrites, brought the Danes into contact with the Franks, and the Emperor had already had a foretaste of the offensive spirit of this seafaring people.[1] Nor was he unaware of the weak spot in his own empire, the inadequacy of his fleet and of his sea defences, as may be seen from the series of measures taken from 800 onwards for the protection of his northern seaboards: the organization of flotillas, the grouping of ships on the Scheldt, the repairing of a lighthouse at Boulogne and the setting up of a system of watches and guards along the North Sea.[2] Unfortunately the Danes too knew, and better than anyone else, the chinks in the Frankish armour, and the knowledge encouraged them in their offensives. Their incursions, which began as early as 814, consisted first of all of systematic attempts at plunder in the Frankish Empire. In their attacks, which were always effective, they made full use of their undoubted naval superiority, the speed of their ships which favoured surprise attacks, and their shallow draught which enabled them to sail up rivers as easily as on the open sea. For nearly half a century their surprise raids paralysed the economic activity of Gaul, and were all the more effective since rivers, great and small, were then the busiest lines of communication, and towns and monasteries were to be found in great numbers along their banks. They were the cause of many hurried flights, some of which have been related in detail.

One of the most famous accounts we owe to Ermentarius, the author of the *Histoire des Miracles et des translations de saint Philibert*.[3] He has told how the monks of Noirmoutier, fleeing

---

[1] L. Halphen, *Charlemagne et l'Empire Carolingien*, p. 94.

[2] At the first call, free men were to hasten to defend the shore on pain of a fine of 20 *solidi*. Ch. de la Roncière, *Hist. de la marine française*, I, 1899, p. 72.

[3] Published by R. Poupardin under the title: *Monuments de l'histoire des abbayes de Saint-Philibert*, Paris, 1905. (Collection de textes pour servir à l'étude et à l'enseignement de l'histoire.)

before the threat of the invading Northmen, travelled through Gaul with their relics, stopping at Saint-Philibert de Grandlieu, Cunault in Anjou, Messai in Poitou, and finally ending up at Tournus in Burgundy, where they settled for good. This chronicler, who began writing before the death of Louis the Pious (840) and finished his work shortly after 862, had an outlook far beyond the confines of his monastery, and we owe to him perhaps the most moving and sincere account ever written of the invasions of the Northmen. In sober language he succeeded in evoking the general terror they caused, the flight of people seized with panic and at the same time the collective paralysis which on several occasions inhibited all resistance[1] and, as we shall see, incited the invaders to exact enormous tributes from the local inhabitants as the price of their departure.[2]

The number of ships grows larger and larger [writes Ermentaire],[3] the great host of Northmen continually increases; on every hand Christians are the victims of massacres, looting, incendiarism, clear proof of which will remain as long as the world itself endures; they capture every city they pass through, and none can withstand them; they take the cities of Bordeaux, Périgueux, Limoges, Angoulême and Toulouse. Angers and Tours, as well as Orleans, are wiped out; the ashes of many a saint are carried away. Thus little by little is coming to pass that threat spoken by the Lord through the mouth of his prophet: 'A scourge out of the North shall spread abroad over the inhabitants of the earth.'

Some years later an incalculable number of Viking ships sails up the River Seine. The situation in those parts grows worse. The city of Rouen is invaded, sacked and set on fire; those of Paris, Beauvais and Meaux are captured; the fortress

---

[1] The truth of this description was confirmed by the German attack of 1940. The irruption of a hostile army provided with unexpected means almost inevitably induces panic in the invaded population.

[2] We should, however, beware of exaggeration. Resignation was not general, as witness one notable example, when thanks to the tenacity of Charles the Bald, the great Viking invasion of 851–862 ended in the liberation of the Seine and Somme basins, a feat which during the year 859 would have appeared quite inconceivable. F. Lot, *Naissance de la France*, p. 451.

[3] The translation is based on the text given in our *Textes d'histoire médiévale*, Paris, 1951, pp. 132–133.

of Melun is laid waste; Chartres is occupied; Evreux is plundered as well as Bayeux, and all the other cities are invaded in turn. There is hardly a single place, hardly a monastery which is respected, all the inhabitants take to flight and few and far between are those who dare to say: 'Stay where you are, stay where you are, fight back, do battle for your country, for your children, for your family!' In their paralysis, in the midst of their mutual rivalries, they buy back at the cost of tributes that which they should have defended, weapons in hand, and allow the Christian kingdom to founder.

The economic consequences of the Viking invasions were serious. The renaissance which had been gaining ground from the late eighth century was brought to a complete halt. They also struck a mortal blow at the great ecclesiastical estates. F. Lot has given a striking example of this, and one all the more significant in that his choice has fallen on one of the greatest religious foundations of the Merovingian period, the Abbey of Saint-Wandrille in the diocese of Rouen. The monastery was burnt by the Northmen in 858, and the monks fled after its destruction. The abbey did not rise again from its ruins until the tenth century. The great historian's comparison between the landed wealth of the monks at the close of the Merovingian era and that of the abbey in the mid-twelfth century proves that the Scandinavian invasion of the ninth century destroyed it completely.[1] The author's observations on the composition of its revenue after the passing of the Northmen are significant. The monks did not regain possession of any of their great domains and their fortune took on a new character. It consisted chiefly of tithes and quit-rents; there were no longer any *villae*.

The transformation was not always so fundamental, but everywhere it went deep. Even in cases where an abbey remained in possession of its domains, the invasions of the Northmen and the anarchy they spread abroad brought about the decomposition of the traditional organization. Secular agents (mayors, *advocati*, etc.) took advantage of the general disorder

---

[1] F. Lot, *Etudes critiques sur l'abbaye de Saint-Wandrille*, p. lxv et seq.

to usurp the property of which they were in charge. Peasants living on *mansi* and liable for forced labour on the demesne fell into the habit of neglecting it. So as to salvage what could still be saved, this forced labour which they no longer carried out was replaced by the payment of dues. The land of the *indominicatum* had to be split up and leased out and the dismemberment of the demesne meant that the land was taken over by a new class of land workers – the settlers (*hospites*). This upheaval took a long time to accomplish, but it is true to say that the Viking invasions hastened the decadence of the traditional régime of large-scale land ownership.

On the other hand it was under cover of anarchy and the resulting chaos that so many rural seigneuries sprang up on the soil of Gaul. The Viking technique of infiltration, of sailing up rivers without encountering any serious obstacles, eventually provoked counter-measures. Means of defence were hastily organized. The walls of the old Gallo-Roman cities which had fallen into ruins and sometimes even been completely demolished, were built up again;[1] above all, castles – fortresses in other words – sprang up almost everywhere, and these numerous *castella*, erected more often than not by royal agents, eventually became a source of anxiety to Charles the Bald himself, and in 864 he ordered the demolition of buildings put up without authorization.[2] His anxiety was well-founded, since on pretext of defending a given area of the city and under cover of some such title as count, viscount or lord of the manor, those who had built these castles and installed themselves therein with a garrison were usurping the sovereign's royal rights, his legal dues, tolls and market-dues;[3] they took possession of lands and demanded from those farming them the dues in kind and the quit-rent owing to their real owners, they levied requisitions and looted Church possessions without the least scruple.

[1] Vercauteren, op. cit., p. 372. See for instance a diploma of Charles the Fat which mentions the restoration of the city wall of Langres '*ipsum civitatis murum*' 15 January 887. *Karoli III Diplomata*, Berlin, 1937, p. 244, no. 152.

[2] Capitul. of Pîtres.

[3] The whole body of usurped rights is often referred to as *vicaria* (in French 'voirie'). The name covers those legal dues and others collected by a subsidiary official known as a 'voyer' (*vicarius*) placed under the authority of a count. Seigneurs often took them over for their own benefit.

We have only to listen, for instance, to the lamentations of
Gontier (*Guntherius*), Bishop of Le Mans who occupied the see
in the late ninth and early tenth centuries (890–913);[1] the
situation there had completely changed since the death of the
great Bishop Aldric, of whom Gontier was the third successor.
The episcopacy of Aldric, one of Louis the Pious's nominees, had
marked the zenith of the bishopric of Le Mans; he had re-
organized the revenues of the Church, rebuilt the cathedral,
and in the middle years of the ninth century the Bishop was the
real master of the town and the province. After his death, however, the city was captured by the Northmen, the cathedral
burnt down (865 or 866), and there was perpetual fear that
these 'pagans' might return to the attack. The day of the churchmen was over; that of the great laymen had begun.[2] Two little-
known personages, Roger and Ralph, who were respectively
first count and first viscount of Maine,[3] invaded the Church
lands and spread terror inside the city. The episcopal censure
on these persons, who had in their service a faithful band of
followers, gives the impression that they were brigands pure
and simple; in fact they founded two dynasties. Their example
was followed in Maine by many other laymen whose destinies
were less exalted but who built castles there and established
seigneuries in the tenth century, often at the expense of the
peasants and churches they claimed to be protecting.

The experience of Le Mans was only one of many. The founding of most of the aristocratic dynasties was equally turbulent
almost everywhere. Following in the steps of the authors of
L'Art de vérifier les dates, numerous scholars have endeavoured to
trace the still obscure origins of these noble houses, and have
expended much valuable time and ingenuity in drawing up
probable genealogies. It is doubtful whether the results are in
every case worthy of the efforts they have called forth, and local

[1] *Actus*, pp. 341–347.

[2] In the chapter on Carolingian France in the *Histoire de France*, libr. Larousse,
I, p. 162, Jean Devisse has admirably illustrated the part played by the 'grands
laïques nécessaires au royaume' in the struggle against the Northmen. Circumstances played into the hands of the aristocracy.

[3] *Hist. du Comté de Maine au Xe et au XIe siècle*, pp. 45–46 and 127. Cf. *Le film de
l'histoire médiévale*, pp. 45–48.

research workers would do better to direct their curiosity to a different field – that of objects and not of men; let them study the formation of the rural seigneuries, those new fortunes which, more intangible than the old,[1] and more widely distributed, often overlapping each other, resulted from the usurpation of royal rights, purchases, gifts and also thefts of land and quit-rents.

The Viking invasions had still further economic repercussions in Gaul. The Atlantic seaboard and the northern and western districts suffered badly, the Northmen in the course of several decades having sailed in turn up every river flowing into the Channel and the Atlantic Ocean, whilst the eastern part of the country enjoyed a comparative respite. They went only a very little way up the Rhône and left its tributaries alone completely. Burgundy was spared and monks congregated there in unusually large numbers.[2] When the monks of Noirmoutier sought a permanent refuge, it was on the banks of the Saône that they eventually found it. Early in the tenth century a duke was to found, near Mâcon, an abbey, Cluny, which was to become one of the most famous in the Christian world and was to exert an unusually wide influence. That of Vézelay too, founded in 860 by Girard de Roussillon and which prided itself on having acquired the remains of St Mary Magdalene,[3] became one of the most famous shrines in the whole realm of France. The rise of Burgundy, which was not confined to the sphere of religion alone, was due to many causes, but the fact that it was a place of refuge during the Viking invasions did much to further its growing importance.

From the last third of the ninth century, these invasions entered on a new phase. Organized looting had been the aim of the early campaigns. Once the up-river raid had been carried out, the band returned to the starting point with their booty and wintered near the estuary of the river up which they had sailed, in a sheltered spot which the invaders may perhaps have

[1] Cf. a shrewd remark of G. Roupnel, *Hist. de la camp. fr.*, p. 341, n. 36: 'Jusqu'au XIIIᵉ siècle on est autorisé à considérer le domaine seigneurial . . . non comme un ensemble d'immeubles, mais comme une collection de droits.'
[2] J. Devisse, *Hist. de France* already quoted, I, p. 163.
[3] J. Bédier, *Les légendes épiques*, II, p. 71.

called the *vik*. Gradually however their strategy underwent a change. Pillage became a means of blackmail. The terror they inspired encouraged them to trade on threats and to impose a heavy tribute on the populations as the price of their departure. These tributes, which were known as Danegeld, almost came to be regarded as ordinary taxes. They weighed heavily upon the monasteries and did much to impoverish them.[1]

The Danes however had loftier ambitions. Gradually they ceased to be pirates and became actual conquerors and permanent settlers. At the close of the ninth century the northeast of Britain became a Danish colony, and the occupation, which by the beginning of the eleventh century had extended over the whole of England, lasted until 1042. On the continent the Scandinavian chieftain Rollo and his Vikings had definitely settled down in the ecclesiastical province of Rouen.[2] In 911 a Danish feudal state was founded in the kingdom of France: Normandy. The economic contribution of these Scandinavians who settled on the banks of the Seine was considerable. For the moment we shall consider only one of their innovations which is of outstanding importance. They gave France a navy – an achievement to which the vocabulary of French bears ample testimony. The whole marine and even seafaring vocabulary of our language is Norse.[3] It has taken from the Scandinavian all the terms used to denote not only the component parts of a ship and its rigging, but also the details of seamanship. The word 'vague' (wave) itself is borrowed from this same language – an additional and decisive proof of Frankish indifference to things of the sea. The French navy was the creation of the Northmen, or more precisely of the Danes.[4]

*

[1] F. Lot, *Les tributs aux Normands et l'Eglise de France au IX° siècle*, Bibl. Ec. Chartes, LXXXV, 1924, pp. 58–78. Many gold objects imported from the Frankish Empire and discovered in Scandinavia came from tributes levied by the Northmen. Holger Arbman, *Schweden und das karolingische Reich*, Stockholm, 1937, p. 171.

[2] They settled there in great numbers. See Adigard des Gautries, *Les noms de personnages scandinaves en Normandie de 911 à 1066*, Lund, 1954.

[3] F. Lot, *Naissance de la France*, p. 512. See also de la Roncière, *Histoire de la Marine*, p. 113.

[4] Rouen was the site of the Royal Naval Arsenal, known as the Clos des Galées.

More spectacular was the Norwegian contribution to the transformation of the European economy. They were explorers and discovered Iceland in the ninth century and Greenland in the tenth and perhaps even the eastern seaboard of the United States. Icelandic historical texts of remarkable interest, the Book of the Icelanders (*Islendingabók*) by the priest Ari the Learned,[1] and the anonymous Book of Colonization (*Landnámabók*), were twelfth-century anthologies embodying recollections of these voyages and of the settling of these seafarers in distant lands. Illustrated by the dramatic accounts given in the sagas, checked against the findings of toponomy and archaeology, they offer the most remarkable information we possess about the maritime activity of the Western Europeans up to the great discoveries of the fifteenth century. Endowed with a keen sense of observation, the Norwegians methodically and persistently sought for a sea route to the west, starting from the coast of Norway. Their repeated attempts, marked out by accurate compass bearings, brought them after a hundred years to Vinland, in other words to North America.

This amazing discovery achieved by Scandinavians about the year A.D. 1000 has long aroused the passionate interest of geographers, ethnologists and historians. 'The riddle of Vinland', Charles de la Roncière[2] called it, and his successors have perpetuated the phrase. We cannot do better than follow their example, since even today the subject is still wrapped in mystery. If it is, in fact, beyond dispute that the Icelanders, after gaining a foothold in Greenland, ventured forth with local people in search of new lands and found a country they named Vinland, it has yet to be ascertained what this country was. The theory put forward by the explorer Nansen, who identified Vinland with the Fortunate Islands and the Canary Archipelago,[3] has been refuted. It conflicts with a statement made by Adam of Bremen who, from information supplied by the King of Denmark Svend Estrithsson, places Vinland in the

[1] It has been translated into French by Félix Wagner, Brussels, 1898, in the Bibliothèque de la Faculté de Philosophie et de Lettres de l'Université de Liège, fasc. IV.
[2] *Annales de géographie*, XXII, 1913, pp. 267–270.
[3] Ibid., XXII, p. 267.

North Atlantic and makes his description tally with that of Greenland and Halogaland;[1] it conflicts also with that of the Icelandic historian Ari the Learned,[2] according to whom Vinland was inhabited by tribes belonging to the same family as the natives of Greenland. The most recent historians approach the problem with profound caution, refusing to place Vinland exactly and committing themselves only to the single assumption that this country was situated to the south-west of Greenland, in the direction of Labrador, Newfoundland or Nova Scotia.[3]

We may, however, in company with a German scholar less hostile to Icelandic traditions,[4] and without believing their stories implicitly, recall what the sagas have to say about the discovery of Greenland and the exploration of Vinland. The coast of Greenland was sighted as early as 900 by a certain Gunnbjörn, but it was not until 981 or 982[5] that it was explored by the Norwegian Eric the Red, who had been compelled to leave Iceland as the result of a murder; he sailed around the southern tip and along the ice-barrier, and settled on the western coast. In 986 another Icelander who was sailing towards Greenland, having been put off his course, discovered the mainland of America but did not land there; he was a son of Eric the Red named Leif, who in 1003 discovered the country which his compatriot had only glimpsed. His wanderings probably led him first to *Helluland*, the modern Labrador, then along Nova Scotia and finally into the region of Vinland where he spent the winter. A second expedition was undertaken by his brother Thorvald in 1005; thirty men went with him. They returned to Greenland three years later after the death of their

---

[1] Adam of Bremen, *Gesta pontificum Hamburgensis ecclesiae*, IV, 38.

[2] *Livre des Islandais*, trans. Wagner, p. 67.

[3] L. Musset, op. cit., p. 226.

[4] E. Zechlin, 'Das Problem des vorkolumbischen Entdeckung Amerikas und die Kolumbusforschung', *Historische Zeitschrift*, CLII, 1935, pp. 12–13.

[5] It has even been asserted that Greenland was explored as early as 835, on the evidence of a Bull of Gregory IV dated that same year, and a diploma of Louis the Pious in which St Ansgar is appointed Bishop of Hamburg and entrusted with the evangelization of Scandinavia, Greenland, Iceland and the Faroe Islands, but these decrees, the originals of which no longer exist, are more than suspect. Henry S. Lucas, 'Medieval Economic Relations between Flanders and Greenland', *Speculum*, 1937, p. 169.

leader who had been murdered by the natives. This setback in no way deterred the explorers, for about 1010 the victim's brother-in-law Thorfinn Karlsefni set out in his turn with 180 men and women to settle in Vinland, but three years later, discouraged by the hostility of the native peoples, they gave up their attempt at colonization. A fourth expedition may have been attempted by one of Erik's daughters – a warlike female – but it met with no greater success.

Vinland remained in memory as a rich country, producing wine and grain, a country where there was no ice or snow and where, since the fields were always green, there was no need to store fodder for the cattle. What core of truth is contained in these fascinating descriptions, and in the account in the sagas designed to magnify the tenacity of a family of adventurers? Between complete scepticism, which the evidence of Adam of Bremen and Ari the Learned does not justify, and excessive credulity which should naturally be resisted, there are grounds for concluding that the Scandinavians were, in fact, in the tenth century and in the early years of the eleventh, the discoverers of America.[1]

This affirmation is strongly supported by the fact that they were undoubtedly superb navigators, and the following extract from the *Landnámabók*[2] gives us admirable proof of the care and accuracy with which detailed observations made by the explorers were collected for the greater benefit of future navigators:

> Men of experience say that from Stad[3] in Norway to Horn on the east coast of Iceland[4] you have to proceed under sail for seven days and that from Snaefells,[5] which is the nearest point, it takes four days sailing to Hvarf[6] in Greenland. But they also say that if you sail direct from Bergen to Hvarf [*Farvel*] in Greenland, you pass within 12 nautical miles of

[1] Such is the conclusion of Charles de la Roncière, who himself took it from the supporter of the America theory Henri Vignaud.

[2] From the German translation already quoted (p. 212, n. 1), p. 62.

[3] Stattlandet, one of the most westerly points on the Norwegian coast.

[4] A small headland enclosing the Bay of Nordfjördur on the east coast of Iceland.

[5] Name given to the north coast of the Gulf of Faxafloi in the west of Iceland.

[6] Cape Farvel, in English Farewell, in southern Greenland.

the south of Iceland. From *Hernar*[1] in Norway to Hvarf [*Farvel*] in Greenland you must continue sailing westward; you then sail to the north of Shetland, the island of which[2] is visible only when the sea is perfectly calm, then to the south of the Faroe Islands, but a considerable distance away from them so that the sea appears to be about half-way up the rocky coast, then to south of Iceland and not very far away from it so that the birds and whales coming from it can draw near to the ship. From Reykjanès in the south of Iceland it takes three days sailing southward to *Jöhlduhlaup* in Ireland[3] and from Langanes[4] in northern Iceland it takes four days sailing northward to reach Svalbard[5] in the *Hafsbotn* and one day to go from Kolbeinsey[6] to the uninhabited coast of Greenland.[7]

This unadorned but accurate description given us by the Icelandic historian is an almost complete map of the North Atlantic world discovered by the Norwegians. The pioneers set out for these unknown lands from the west coast of Norway, and most of their bases are known to us. They were harbours long established by the Norwegians along their ocean seaboard. The most northerly was Halogaland with the Lofoten islands, already a busy export centre during the early Middle Ages. Trade was carried on there in furs and seals which the inhabitants, intrepid hunters, went to Lapland to catch.[8] That country, which at that date was considered to be a large island,[9] held a strange fascination for foreigners in the eleventh century

[1] Unidentified.
[2] It is actually an archipelago.
[3] Unidentified.
[4] A long, narrow headland in the north of Iceland.
[5] Group of islands in the ice-bound Arctic Ocean, the most important of which form the Spitzbergen Archipelago.
[6] Small island to the north of Grimsey Island which is itself to the north of Iceland.
[7] Its eastern seaboard, nearest to Iceland.
[8] See O. A. Johnsen, *Norwegische Wirtschaftsgeschichte*, pp. 16–17, who gives details about this trade taken from an Anglo-Saxon translation of the History of Orosius written in the reign of Alfred the Great.
[9] 'Insula vicinior Normanniae, magnitudine ceteris non impar.' Adam of Brémen, op. cit., IV, 37.

because of the midnight sun and the long winter nights.[1] Further to the south was Trondhjem, the old Nidaros,[2] from which at the end of the ninth century most of the Norwegians who emigrated to Iceland set out, the Sogne fiord, on which a place named Vik calls up memories of a Viking embarkation, then Bergen,[3] and lastly the Oslo fiord on which was a port named Sciringesheall which may have been replaced by that of Tonsberg.[4]

The Norwegians had long been acquainted with Scotland and Ireland; they welcomed any and every opportunity of raiding their coasts and carrying off slaves. Their westward expeditions in search of unknown lands took them first to the islands nearest their own seaboard, the Shetlands, then to the Orkneys and Faroes, but their first major discovery was that of Iceland.[5] First explored in 860 and 865 it was then systematically colonized from 874 onwards by a succession of wealthy and aristocratic Norwegians who followed the example set by one of their number Ingolfur Arnason, the first colonizer to settle in Iceland.

It is difficult to determine the causes of this emigration which during the sixty years it lasted (870–930) transplanted to Iceland between 30,000 and 35,000 people.[6] The despotic rule of

[1] Adam of Bremen, loc. cit., describes with admiration this island which at the time of the summer solstice has fourteen days of continuous sunlight but which in winter has none at all for the same number of days.

[2] In the eleventh century this town became the ecclesiastical capital of Norway (*metropolis civitas Nortmannorum*) and had then a large population. Adam of Bremen, IV, 32.

[3] O. A. Johnsen, op. cit., pp. 99–102, mentions the relatively late beginnings of the port of Bergen. The settlement there came into being because of the need for a regular outlet for the produce of Northern Norway: cod, furs, sealskins, seal and whale oil. It was essential to have a commercial centre through which they could be exported.

[4] Johnsen, op. cit., has shown that Tönsberg was better served by its hinterland than Skiringssal. Both ports were situated in the district known as Vikin in Old Norwegian; it was the area stretching around the Oslo fiord. It faced south, towards Denmark and Germany, whilst the inhabitants of the west coast (Westland) were early attracted by the west. Johnsen, pp. 10–11.

[5] Iceland had long been known to them. The monk Dicuil (825) mentions that monks had stayed in the island. Could it have been explored at an even earlier date? The problem is not an easy one, since doubts are still entertained about the identification of the country known as 'Thule', a word which was already being used at the time of Pytheas. H. S. Lucas, 'Medieval Relations . . .', *Speculum*, 1937, p. 170.

[6] The figure is that suggested by L. Musset, *Les peuples scandinaves*, p. 61.

Harold Fairhair (874–933), King of Norway, who aimed at unifying his kingdom and exacted from his subjects tributes they regarded as intolerable, may have been responsible for some departures, but it can hardly be doubted that the colonization of Iceland was undertaken from economic motives.[1] One thing is certain, that it led to a wave of emigration of such vast proportions as to alarm King Harold, who was compelled to put a stop to it lest he should see his kingdom depopulated. The absorbing interest of this occupation lies in the fact that the emigrants found in Iceland a country which was almost completely uninhabited, and in which only a handful of Irish anchorites had landed in the eighth century,[2] so that thanks to the *Landnámabók* we have accurate information, disregarding certain legendary details which have crept in but which can easily be picked out, as to how colonization was effected in the different sectors of the island, north-west, north-east, south-east and south-west.

There was a succession of departures from Norway and the island exerted a growing attraction. The emigrants, the majority of whom were Norwegians from the west coast, do not seem to have left without the intention of returning, and there was continual close contact with their native land. These departures were individual, each of the emigrants sailing in his own boat. Most of them took with them twenty or thirty men, and these companions were freemen or freed slaves. They also took away with them Celtic slaves captured in Ireland or Scotland by the Vikings,[3] many of whom already had numerous sea voyages and acts of piracy to their credit. The *Landnámabók* is of incomparable value to the historian of economic facts because of the clear and precise details it gives about the method of land occupation. The immigrant's first thought on setting foot on Icelandic soil was to take possession of a piece of land which would provide him with his own domain. Often he found it quite near the bay

[1] Þorkell Johannesson, *Die Stellung der freien Arbeiter in Island bis zur Mitte des 16 Jahrhunderts*, Reykjavik, 1933, p. 13.

[2] Gougaud, *Les Chrétientés celtiques*, Paris, 1911, pp. 136–137, and our *Textes d'histoire médiévale*, p. 268. See above, p. 227, n. 5.

[3] All the above details about the populating of Iceland are taken from the *Landnámabók*.

where he had landed. Sometimes he had to search around and did not definitely settle until a whole year had gone by. The appropriation was always on an individual basis, and frequently gave rise to violent altercations and murderous quarrels.

The boundaries of a plot of land were marked out by lighting a series of fires all around the area it was proposed to occupy. The ritual nature of this method of delimitation is obvious. According to the author of the *Landnámabók*, King Harold, who looked upon himself as ruler of the island, had forbidden new occupants in certain areas which were particularly sought after, to take more land than they could travel round between sunrise and sunset, and they were obliged to light a series of fires and see that they did not go out. An additional condition was imposed on women: they had to make their round accompanied by a two-year-old heifer. It was probably thought that an estate possessed by a woman should not be as extensive as that allotted to a man. This ban, the traditional nature of which is evident, reveals the same prejudice as that which led the Salian Franks to lay down the clause in the Salic Law forbidding a woman to inherit land. Women were not considered suited to farming.

There was never any question of agrarian communism. Individual ownership was the general and absolute rule. When a new occupant wished his companions to enjoy the benefits of his land, he shared it with them.[1] The estate thus created became for these emigrants family property handed down to blood heirs, and often kept the name of the first owner. On it he built his house, which was hollowed out of the ground and roofed with turf, or was built of wood. Only the pasture-lands escaped individual ownership and were left free for use by all. The *Landnámabók* mentions one park which held 2,400 sheep. The rearing of pigs was also developed.

This Book of Icelandic Colonization, an almost unique document in the history of human land settlement, presents the

---

[1] This marked individualism has been stressed by the German historian Karl Wührer, *Beiträge zur ältesten Agrargeschichte des Germanischen Nordens*, p. 84, and he adds 'Das Fehlen jeglicher Art von Markgenossenschaft ist bekannt'.

reader with a succession of several hundred immigrants who became the founders of the chief Icelandic families. These men were by no means poor. The majority of them were already wealthy[1] and took precious metals with them. One possessed an important treasure, gold picked up in Lapland before he set sail for Iceland. Another had acquired wealth by trading in Novgorod. Above all they imported silver, which was apparently not used for coining until A.D. 1000 and which in the early stages of colonization was used as a basic standard.[2] In a new and uninhabited country like Iceland, internal exchange was almost non-existent and this silver was useless, but the circulation of this precious metal soon increased and a study of very ancient scales of fines has enabled one scholar to note the stages of its progress. This evaluation was made possible by the appearance, when colonization had ceased, of a new standard which was no longer based on metal; it consisted of a fixed quantity of woollen cloth. Whilst at the beginning of the tenth century 6 ells of wool represented one silver *eyrir*,[3] towards the end of the same century it took 1 mark, or about 8 *eyrirs* of wool, to procure one single *eyrir* of precious metal. This revaluation of silver is accounted for by its gradual disappearance, the settlers having been compelled to make numerous purchases outside the island, without having in return island products to sell which might enable them to bring back precious metal to Iceland, the equivalent, in other words, of our own currency. It was only after A.D. 1000 that by exporting fish the Icelanders were in a position to improve their trade balance.

This exceptional wealth of documentation enables us to reconstruct the successive phases of colonization of a completely new country, and its integration into the economic life of early medieval Europe; it is a unique piece of good fortune, which the economist should turn to the best possible account. Nevertheless the westward expansion, the leap into the unknown

[1] Johnsen, op. cit, p. 30.
[2] Silver was valued by weight. The units used were the *eyrir* = 27 gr., and the mark (mörk) worth 8 *eyrirs* = 216 gr. Johannesson, op. cit., p. 36, n. 2.
[3] This new standard expressed in wool was known as a *lögeyrir*, that is to say a 'legal *eyrir*' – the word *log* meaning law – because it had been instituted by a legislative decree. Ibid., p. 37.

11. Medieval seafarers (IXth and Xth centuries) (from Venetian mosaics)

Atlantic world, which is the most striking feature of this Scandinavian dynamism, should not overshadow the part played by the Vikings in the economy of the North Sea and the Baltic. Rivals of the Frisians whom they supplanted, they were the forerunners of the German navigators and merchants of the Hansa. In spite of the difficulties of navigation between the numerous islands in the straits, their ships succeeded in finding a passage through them, and the Danish kings had no hesitation in establishing their seat at Roskilde, on the largest of the islands, that of Zealand. The life of a seafaring community was organized at an early date in a country whose inhabitants were sailors born and bred. Each of the Danish ports had its own sector.[1] From Ribe on the western coast of the peninsula, sailing ships set out for Frisia, Saxony and England. The port of Aarhus on the Kattegat ensured sea communications with Fünen, the Isle of Zealand, Scania and even Norway, but the most important trade centre in Denmark in the ninth and tenth centuries was undoubtedly Hedeby, a fortress surrounded by a semi-circular wall.[2] It still enjoyed considerable prestige in the days of Adam of Bremen, though the town had been ruined in 1051.[3] This place commanded the whole of the trade between the West and Sweden, since many merchants preferred to cross the Schleswig isthmus via the Eider and the Sli rather than risk the voyage round Jutland, so that Hedeby may be said to have played in the Carolingian economy a rôle analogous to that of Kiel in our own day. If the historian of the Bishops of Hamburg is a reliable authority, it was the home port of ships sailing to 'Slavonia', that is to Pomerania and Prussia as well as to Sweden. Thus Hedeby helped to open up those relations between the West and the Baltic for which the way had been prepared during the maritime hegemony of the Frisians.

---

[1] Exact details are given us by Adam of Bremen, op. cit., IV, 1, who was always well-informed. On the quality of his documentation, cf. Manitius, *Gesch. der lateinischen Literatur des Mittelalters*, II, p. 398–413.

[2] In German *Haithabu*. Excavations have recently been carried out on the site. See Ed. Ennen, *Frühgesch. d. Europäischen Stadt*, p. 58 et seq.

[3] Adam, however, already calls the town by the name of its successor: 'Apud Sliaswig quae et Heidiba dicitur.' For Schleswig-Hedeby, see Arbmann, *Schweden u. das Karol. Reich*, p. 18 et seq.

Ships leaving Hedeby for Sweden landed at Birka, in one of the Mälar Islands, but the prosperity of this latter port lasted only a century and a half (800–950),[1] and Sigtuna further to the north, at the end of a fiord and in a more sheltered position, displaced it in the eleventh century.[2] Scania also was a busy trading centre. Its capital Lund, which became the seat of an archbishopric and for a short time the capital of Scandinavia, was the pride of the Vikings, and according to a legend, the geographical source of which is obvious, the conqueror of England, King Canute the Great, claimed to have made it the equal of London. The trade carried on there, however, according to Adam of Bremen, savoured more of piracy than honest business. The Vikings had accumulated a great store of gold there, the result of looting carried out with the complicity of the Kings of Denmark, who in return for their goodwill demanded payment of a tribute.[3] Slave trading was carried on there on a considerable scale.[4]

The Baltic islands were also centres of trade. L. Musset has described the original character of the one which, by reason of its central position, dominated the whole of the trade in that sea, the Isle of Gotland.[5] No merchants in the real sense of the word were to be found there; it was the peasants themselves who by maritime trade augmented the modest living they obtained from the sea. The most famous of all the islands, however, was that of Bornholm[6] since its harbour offered exceptionally good shelter. It was a port of call for ships on their way to 'the Barbarians and the Greeks'. Situated halfway between the

---

[1] During that period, Birka was the centre of the fur trade in the south-west Baltic. Its past greatness has been revealed by archaeological discoveries. H. Arbman, op. cit., p. 248.

[2] L. Musset, op. cit., pp. 74–75. At the end of the eleventh century Adam of Bremen still knew Birka 'in media Sueoniae posita'. IV, 20.

[3] Adam of Bremen, IV, 6.

[4] The memory of this trade still lingered on in the *De gestis rerum Anglorum* of William of Malmesbury, who mentions the bands of slaves bought in England (*agmina mancipiorum in Anglia coempta*) and taken to Denmark. Erik Bromberg, 'Wales and the Medieval Slave Trade', *Speculum*, 1942, p. 264.

[5] Op. cit., p. 76. Cf. M. David, 'Gotland l'île aux cent églises'. *Miscellanea G. de Jerphanion*, Rome, 1947, pp. 93–118.

[6] 'Holmus . . . celeberrimus Daniae portus et fida stacio navium, quae ad barbaros et in Graeciam dirigi solent.' Adam of Bremen, IV, 16.

southern coast of Scandinavia and the Pomeranian seaboard, it catered for traders from Sweden sailing towards the Slav countries and who were attempting to reach the Greek Empire across the plains and steppes of Poland and Russia.[1] A rich

Scandinavian Expansion to the North-east (ninth to eleventh centuries)

literature, half historical, half legendary, gives us some idea of these caravans of adventurers, who were both robbers and merchants, and who carried out sensational raids. Beaver and marten skins bought from the Finns and Lapps in exchange for woollen clothing were their chief stock-in-trade. These raids

[1] H. Pirenne, *Hist. de l'Europe*, p. 81 et seq. and p. 150.

belong to the ninth and tenth centuries, but continued to a later date, and in the historical work of Adam of Bremen as well as in several of the sagas can be heard echoes of these obviously fantastic travels which took their heroes from Lapland to Constantinople and even as far as Iran and Turkestan. With great daring Swedes even succeeded in making the entire journey along the only existing land route across Finland and the principality of Russia, but the wildness of the peoples through whose country they had to pass compelled them to abandon this route. The perils of the sea appeared the lesser of the two evils.[1]

This insistence on Scandinavian expansion has been deliberate. During the Dark Ages, and especially in the tenth century which has a bad reputation with historians, these Nordic peoples achieved feats comparable to those of the fifteenth-century navigators and which enabled a cultured man like Adam of Bremen[2] to have in the eleventh century a clear and accurate idea of the North Atlantic, the North Sea and the Baltic. This widening of the bounds of human knowledge was their work. The economist too should not fail to evaluate at their true worth the services rendered to European civilization by these Vikings in spite of the acts of piracy of which they were guilty. These men will have to be borne in mind when we attempt to resolve the difficult problem of the rebirth of the towns. A long-standing prejudice has tended to side-track inquirers and has led them to devote their attention to the Mediterranean basin, the generally accepted source of all urban civilization. If we wield the divining rod with sufficient skill, we may perhaps discover, in those lands which border the North Sea and the Baltic, several springs as yet untapped.

---

[1] Adam of Bremen, IV, 18.
[2] See his geographical sketch, IV, 10.

CHAPTER II

The Resurgence of Town Life
and of Commercial Activity

THE SECOND HALF OF the ninth century saw the opening
of a period marked by a fresh wave of invaders: Northmen on the Atlantic and North Sea coasts, Hungarians
in Central Europe, plundering Slavs on the eastern frontiers of
the Empire, and in the south the Saracens.[1] Yet, although this
period was disturbed by perpetual raids, and in the western
part of the Frankish Empire by the phenomena of political dissolution, it did not end in collapse or even in a serious upheaval
such as that which accompanied the fall of the Roman Empire.
After more than a hundred years of unrest and uncertainties,
there dawned at last the great eleventh century, a century of
economic as well as of religious and intellectual revival. Unfortunately this revival, less miraculous and complete than has
been claimed, was preceded by a century of incubation which
is one of the least well known in the whole medieval past. Nevertheless the temptation is great to pick out the preliminary signs
of a recovery which was to be marked by a renewal of collective
life and the introduction into it of a series of innovations:
merchants settling down in one place, goods warehouses being
built in towns, stalls appearing, then small shops and workshops,
and populations no longer consisting solely of clerics, nobles and
peasants, industries coming into being, capitalism making its
timid appearance under the name of 'commenda', the oldest
form of production loan, and hitherto unknown in the West.

These signs are not easy to discern, since they are few and far
between and often obscure, but we should not be discouraged,

[1] R. Kötzschke, *Allgemeine Wirtschaftsgeschichte des Mittelalters*, p. 300.

235

and research teams in France and elsewhere have already embarked on the study of what German scholarship calls the *Frühgeschichte* of European town life and are endeavouring to detect the first symptoms of a dawning capitalism.

Since the subject raises a whole host of questions, it is as well to pick out the important problems and to state them in the clearest terms. The first essential is to reconstruct the actual setting of urban life. The towns of the Late Empire did not remain shut up within their walls, and we have already seen[1] how, from Merovingian times, they were spreading beyond them, when suburban monasteries became centres of population. Moreover, there were other urban settlements besides the *civitates*. Many fortresses (*castra*) were founded, especially in the Meuse and Rhenish zones, and gradually throughout the whole of Germany. They were garrison sites, but at the same time places of residence for royal officials,[2] and like those at Aix-le-Chapelle and Nijmegen, for the Carolingian sovereigns themselves.[3] The unrecorded factor in Western Europe was the penetration and integration of the merchant and the artisan into urban life.

The desire to explain the revival of trade gave rise to Henri Pirenne's famous theory[4] on the rise of the merchant class, which may have recruited its first members from adventurers who were not tied to the land, men who were out to make money and who in the course of time grew less venturesome and settled permanently in one place. It is an attractive explanation and one which contains a core of truth.[5] We are, however, inclined to think, as will be seen, that the formation of the merchant class was not such a simple matter and did not everywhere proceed on the same lines. The local inhabitants were partly responsible for it, and monastic influence should not be

---

[1] See above, p. 109 et seq.

[2] F. L. Ganshof, *Etude sur le développement des villes entre Loire et Rhin au moyen âge*, Paris, Brussels, 1943, p. 13.

[3] On this question of the stability of residence of the early medieval kings and emperors, see a searching study by M. H. Sproemberg, 'Residenz und Territorium im niederländischen Raum', *Rheinische Vierteljahrsblätter*, VI, pp. 113–139.

[4] A brilliant exposition of it is to be found in his *Histoire de l'Europe*, pp. 153–156.

[5] The history of the Vikings proves this. See above, p. 232.

left out of account. From the problem of the birth of the medieval town, with its commerce and crafts, from the further
problem of the origins of the merchant class, the economist
turns next to that of the beginnings of capitalism. Big business
is not a recent phenomenon; there were businessmen in
Republican Rome, and even more of them under the Empire.
The store of gold amassed by the Vikings at Lund[1] was not
meant to remain unproductive. It was, however, in Venice
that for the first time in the Christian world capitalists, in other
words men who owned personal wealth, increased it by commercial enterprises. Thus we shall arrive at the same conclusions as a contemporary historian[2] who believes that the
Saracen conquest was a stimulus to western economic activity.
His opinions may be accepted on condition that the period at
which this stimulus became effective is set back one, or even
two, centuries.

*

It is an over-statement to claim that town life completely disappeared in the Carolingian period, and we have already
registered a protest against so categorical a statement.[3] Is it even
correct to say that the kings ceased to live in towns? The early
Carolingians began by imitating the example of the Merovingians, who loved country life, but as we follow their travels,
which thanks to the Royal Annals are known to us in detail,
it soon becomes obvious that before long they reacted against
the rustic habits of their predecessors. Pepin the Short, and
Charlemagne during the first ten years of his rule, still remained
devoted to their family estates at Quierzy, Herstall, Attigny;
but from 776 onwards Charlemagne was attracted by the
Rhenish and German towns. We are familiar with the rhythm
of his existence. Seven or eight months of each year were given
up to major military expeditions. Then from just before Christmas until after Easter he stayed with his court in some place

---

[1] See above, p. 232.
[2] M. Lombard in his article already quoted, 'L'or musulman du VIIᵉ au XIᵉ
siècle'.
[3] See above, pp. 172–179.

which pleased him. His favourite residence was at Aix-la-Chapelle, but we also find him spending the winter at Worms, Frankfurt, Würzburg and Regensburg. His example was followed by Louis the Pious, who in 822 had buildings erected at Frankfurt for his court to live in.[1] The King of Western France, Charles the Bald, did not winter in Germany, but this nomad prince liked to celebrate the great festivals of Christmas and Easter in the episcopal towns of his kingdom, at Châlons-sur-Marne, Tours, Rheims, Bourges and Chartres.[2] Without going so far as to say that the Carolingian rulers deserted their royal *villae*, particularly those at Compiègne and Quierzy, and fully admitting that the fascination exercised by the pomp of the religious ceremonies which were celebrated in the cathedrals often decided their choice of a winter residence, this attraction exerted by the 'octopus' towns deserves special emphasis.

The most significant point to bear in mind is that the towns continued to exist. The new and interesting factor as we approach the eleventh century is not so much the revival of town life which, thanks to the Church, never entirely ceased to exist, but the appearance of a new kind of town in which trades and crafts introduced an element unknown in the ancient world, a town which was no longer the city of antiquity. Its originality consisted in the simultaneous existence of a *portus*, a market, a merchant and business quarter alongside churches, clerics' houses and the garrison *burg*. The problems to which this coexistence gave rise, the conflicts and clashes it engendered, were a continually recurring feature of the history of these communities. We shall merely try to note the first tentative expressions, the first fumbling steps of an economy which was attempting to achieve some measure of organization.

The later works of that great historian Henri Pirenne, however, give the impression that there was a complete eclipse of town life and of trade at the close of the Merovingian era, an eclipse brought about by the Saracen invasion, and that it was not until three hundred years later that there were signs of a revival which began to take shape in the late tenth century and

---

[1] *Annales Regni Francorum* (ed. Kurze, Hanover, 1895, p. 159).
[2] F. Lot and L. Halphen, *Le règne de Charles le Chauve*, 1st part (840–851), *passim*.

was an established fact in the eleventh. A powerful 'idea-force' permeates his description of this evolution. The great central idea to which he was passionately devoted was the Mediterranean character of the town and town life. Brutally dislodged from the Mediterranean basin by the rapidity of the Saracen conquest, the Western economy merely vegetated until, partly through the intermediary of Venice and partly because of the amazing détour accomplished by the Swedes, who had established contact with Byzantium through Russia, trade and town life awoke to new vigour. There then came into being a merchant class, drawn from amongst adventurers and outlaws banded together in caravans, which created the capitalist spirit in Western Europe.

It was in his *History of Europe* that the great historian first gave a clear and vivid account of such an evolution. It should be borne in mind that this work, though published after his death,[1] was actually written in 1917, when Pirenne was interned in the barracks at Holzminden in Germany, and that it grew out of a course in economic history given during his captivity to Russian students who were his fellow-prisoners. If a complete lack of books did not prevent the author from producing a vigorous and lively survey, the conditions in which he conceived and wrote it helped to give it a schematic character. Pirenne was not romancing in his chapters on economic and social organization, for he was too much of a realist to lose contact with the land itself, but he over-simplified. Carried away, perhaps, by his conviction that the Mediterranean basin was, and remained, the cradle of European economic life, he attached an exaggerated importance to the trade with the East which, though modest in volume, continued uninterrupted throughout Merovingian times, and rather under-estimated the many transactions which, through the whole of the Carolingian period and right up to the eleventh century, were being carried on within and on the periphery of the Frankish Empire.

There is no cause to return to this first point, since in a previous chapter we endeavoured to reduce to its correct proportions the trade carried on in the West up to the Saracen

[1] See the Preface by M. Jacques Pirenne.

conquest. The time has now come, however, to concentrate on the three following centuries, which might be called the age of the great depression, to which only a fresh stimulus from Byzantium put an end in the mid-eleventh century. Has there not been a tendency to exaggerate the apathy which prevailed during that long period when trade was carried on chiefly in markets? Numerous documents testify to the existence of these markets, they are referred to in many capitularies, and the founding of them is the subject of a large number of diplomas issued by kings and emperors in the ninth and tenth centuries. What exactly were these markets like? This is a question of fundamental importance which it is all the more imperative to answer since most historians have treated them with a scorn which seems to us excessive.

Permission to set up a market (*mercatum concedere*), at the same time making over to the recipient of the concession the dues (*teloneum*) to be levied therein, was a privilege which had been frequently granted by the kings to religious houses from the beginning of the ninth century. These markets were often held weekly, sometimes more frequently. In some cases they were held yearly, thus acquiring the character of a fair. The name 'public market' (*mercatum publicum*) applied to them in many deeds, and the added fact that permission to start them had to be obtained from the sovereign, who could also suppress them,[1] show that they ranked as public institutions. This status was no new thing. Fairs and markets existed in the Roman Empire and the public authorities had a say in their administration, maintaining that it was their business to keep law and order there, and benefiting financially from them, since as owners of the land on which the *nundinae* were held they were entitled to certain dues. For these reasons 'there grew up the idea, which became a principle of public law, that the right to start a market, to authorize its creation, or to sanction a market already in existence, belonged to the state alone'.[2]

The Merovingian kings inherited this tradition but made no

---

[1] Edict of Pîtres. For the official character of certain markets, see Kletler, *Nordwesteuropas Verkehr*, p. 76 et seq.

[2] P. Huvelin, *Essai historique sur le droit des marchés et des foires*, Paris, 1897, p. 102.

attempt to carry it on; almost all the diplomas establishing fairs and markets and attributed to them are faked. The Carolingian rulers took a firmer line and there was a new spirit abroad.[1] Many more markets were created during the ninth century. They became an instrument in the sovereigns' economic policy, but any real evaluation of their effectiveness must, unfortunately, be based on texts which give only one side of the picture, since the information comes chiefly from royal and imperial privileges granted to churches. Lacking more varied sources, we might at the outset be tempted to draw the conclusion that the Church was the main beneficiary of these concessions,[2] which would be an over-statement. The worst disadvantage, however, of this one-way information service is that after studying the ninth- and tenth-century texts relating to markets we are in danger of minimizing their importance and of regarding them on the whole as trading centres of little or no account, used only as an outlet for the agricultural produce of certain ecclesiastical estates. Actually the contrary seems to have been the case, and in Carolingian times and right into the eleventh century, almost all trade was concentrated in the markets and fairs, since there were still no permanent sites where goods of any kind could be sold. The sovereigns were well aware of this, and regarded the establishment of a market as vitally necessary for a region.[3]

It has to be recognized that of the markets of which the foundation deeds have chanced to survive, many served modest villages. It is obvious, for instance, that the markets granted by Pepin I of Aquitaine to the monks of Sainte-Croix de Poitiers in the now vanished localities of *Cajoca* in Poitou and *Fulchrodo*

---

[1] We are in full agreement with a shrewd point of view expressed by P. Huvelin, op. cit., p. 150.

[2] P. Huvelin appears to have thought this was the case. Ibid., p. 151.

[3] This is evident from the preamble of a diploma granted by Louis the Pious giving permission for a market to the Abbey of Corvey, 838: 'Quia locum mercationis ipsa regio indigebat.' P. Huvelin, ibid., p. 163, n. 2. The following evidence taken from a diploma of Otto III, 993, is even more striking. It refers to the creation of the market at Selz, the establishing of which the Emperor justifies by declaring that 'moneta et mercatus necessaria sunt multitudine populorum undique illuc confluentium, simul etiam monachis et populis ibi commanentibus et habitantibus'. Huvelin, ibid., from *Dipl. reg. et imp. Germ.*, II, p. 151.

in Angoumois,[1] as well as that which Charles the Bald authorized the monks of Beaulieu to 'construct' in the small commune
of Sionac in Corrèze,[2] were frequented only by peasants from
the surrounding countryside and by pedlars, yet the fact that
they existed at all is of considerable importance, proving as it
does that even in small villages buying and selling were being
carried on. Are there not, for that matter, in our modern communities, more small shops than large stores? It is therefore
incumbent on any student of those diplomas in which sovereigns
granted privileges to differentiate between the country markets
and those established in the towns. These latter were numerous
and attracted merchants from outside. Thanks to another
diploma of Pepin, king of Aquitaine, we know that in 838
markets were already in existence at Angers.[3] They were to
be found also in many other towns during the ninth century,[4]
though most of our information about early medieval town
markets comes from diplomas of the Germanic kings and
emperors in the tenth century.[5] The one which had been set up
in Worms by the predecessors of Otto the Great and confirmed
by that same prince in 947 was not purely local in character,
since it was frequented by merchants (*negociatores*) and foreign
craftsmen (*artifices*), in particular by Frisians.[6] The market

---

[1] *Recueil des actes de Pépin Ier et Pépin II, rois d'Aquitaine*, Paris, 1926, p. 9, no. iii.
[2] *Cartulaire de Beaulieu*, p. 16, no. v.
[3] *Recueil des actes de Pépin Ier et Pépin II, rois d'Aquitaine*, p. 114, no. xxviii.
[4] The most important of all medieval fairs were those held at Saint-Denis. Their
history has been related by Léon Levillain, *B.E.C.*, XCI, 1930, p. 7 et seq. First
authorized by Dagobert I, it was subsequently confirmed by all his successors up
to Louis the Pious and stoutly defended by the abbots of the monastery. The wars
waged by the sons of Louis the Pious, and the invasions of the Northmen, explain
why the monks did not obtain from Charles the Bald, who became their abbot in
867, a fresh confirmation of their privileges. In the tenth century, however, it
occurred to them to revive this source of income, and they forged a bogus deed of
immunity to which they appended the name of Dagobert. This affords yet another
proof of the rôle which markets and fairs continued to play in France during the
tenth century.
[5] This point has been well brought out by Paul Kletler, *Nordwesteuropas Verkehr*.
See Hans Planitz, 'Frühgeschichte der deutschen Stadt (IX–XI Jahrhundert)' in
Zeitschrift der Savigny-Stiftung für Rechtgeschichte, Germ. Abt., 1943, pp. 1–91.
[6] 'Qualiter antecessores nostri . . . concessissent ut quanticumque negociatores
vel artifices seu et Frisiones apud Uuangionem advenissent . . .' *Dipl. reg. et imp.
Germ.*, I, p. 165, no. 84. In the grant of market dues made by Conrad, King of
Germany, to the Bishop of Würzburg, 918, mention is made 'a cunctis quis cum

which the Abbot of Saint-Gall asked this same prince to set up at Rorschach near his monastery in 947 was intended particularly for people travelling to Italy and Rome.[1] In founding the market at Bergamo in 968, the profits from which were conceded to the local bishop, Otto I planned to attract to the town merchants from the Veneto and the region around Ferrara,[2] but it was in Germany that markets flourished particularly in the tenth century. There is no doubt that the princes of the House of Saxony sought by this means to stimulate, one might even say to awaken, economic activity within their realms.

Several documents – though unfortunately they are few and far between – belonging to the early eleventh century, take us right into these markets and give us some idea of the variety of goods on sale there. The list of dues for the Abbey of Saint-Vaast d'Arras in 1036[3] is the most illuminating. Cloth was the chief merchandise offered for sale.[4] Next came foodstuffs: fish, sturgeon, salmon, herring, shad and whalemeat; butcher's meat, bacon, dripping, salt meat; salt, honey, oil, butter, cheese (English or Flemish),[5] fruit and wine. Raw materials could also be bought, raw or tanned hides, animal skins; iron, steel, wool, thread as well as woad, or dyestuffs. In addition to cloth there were also 'tacons' or soles and footwear made from cowhide,

mercatus sui mercimonio ab universis provinciis et civitatibus illuc conveniunt'. Ibid., p. 32, no. 35.

[1] Ibid., p. 175, no. 90: 'Suggessit quendam locum nomine Rorscacha ad jus ipsius monasterii pertinentem mercatum ibi haberi ad Italiam proficiscentibus vel Roman pergentibus esse commodum.'

[2] 'Stabilire portum et stationem navium scilicet venientium ex Venetiis et Clumaclis Ferariensis partibus sive undecumque venientium.' Ibid., p. 500, no. 364.

[3] This scale of charges, published in the Cartulary of the Abbey of Saint-Vaast, has been re-edited by G. Fagniez in *Documents pour servir à l'histoire de l'industrie et du commerce en France*, I, pp. 56–65, no. 98. The list of dues for Méron, on the banks of the Loire near Montreuil-Bellay (1080–1082), *Cart. de Saint-Aubin*, I, p. 263, no. ccxxi, gives us a list of the provisions sold in a small market. A summary of the text runs as follows: 'No dues shall be paid for that which a man carries on his own back, except for feathers, wax, tallow, foreign articles and those which are costly. The charge will be 1 denier for a bed and bedding, 4 for a wedding trousseau [*de trossello maritali*], 1 denier for an unshod horse or mare and 2 if the animal is shod; for an ox, donkey or pig 1 obole [= ½ denier]; for 3 ewes or 3 goats 1 denier; for a *quadrans* of wool 1 denier.'

[4] 'De pannis et majoribus mercaturis.' Ibid., p. 57.

[5] 'Majus pensum . . . casei anglici . . . Pensum casei flamengi.'

manufactured goods, knives, sickles, spades and spade handles, ropes, wooden vessels, probably implements connected with vine-growing.

Looking back over all the goods mentioned in this price-list,[1] it is clear that most of the needs of a people still in the early stages of development were catered for. In the tenth and early eleventh centuries, the market was the equivalent of certain modern bazaars which offer their customers foodstuffs, clothing and articles in everyday use, but with this difference that the buyers' requirements were infinitely more modest, and since industrialization was still in its early infancy, it was in the domestic workshops on the *villa* or on the family *mansus* that some of the tools were made and clothing woven and made up, a fact which is quite evident from that invaluable document the *Capitulare de villis*.[2]

Industry was still in a rudimentary stage of development. The producer was only rarely an employer of labour. He worked for someone else. In the great abbeys as on the royal domains, workmen were to be found living together in trade guilds and working for the monks. In the Abbey of Saint-Riquier, for example, there was a blacksmiths' quarter, a second for shield-makers, others for saddlers, bakers, cobblers, wool-carders, fullers, furriers, 'makers of wine'.[3] This pattern was almost certainly characteristic of the world of merchants too. The privilege granted by Otto I to the Bishop of Worms[4] mentions the *negociatores* and *artifices* who came to that town; presumably he was referring to workmen whom merchants had taken into their service. The weaver received from the merchant draper the wool for weaving, and when the work was done returned it to his master who paid him a wage. Trade was essentially a service; the Latin word from which the French 'métier' is

---

[1] Certain goods, notably foodstuffs, were displayed on the ox-wagons (*carrus*) or carts (*charetee*) on which they were brought to market, doubtless to avoid undue handling which would be bad for perishable goods. Other things, manufactured articles such as cloth, knives, ropes, were sold on stalls (*stalli*). Cf. Imbart de la Tour, 'Des immunités . . .' in *Etudes d'histoire dédiées à Gabriel Monod*, p. 71.

[2] See above, p. 183, n. 3.

[3] Inventory of quit-rents and dues owing to the Abbey of Saint-Riquier. *Chronique de l'abbaye de Saint-Riquier*, published by F. Lot, Paris, 1894, p. 307.

[4] See above, p. 242, n. 6.

derived, *ministerium*, means a duty performed, and in particular a task carried out by a servant. The artisan is a *ministerialis*, that is to say a man performing a special service in an establishment or under the orders of a master.[1] Henri Pirenne, however, thinks that at a fairly early date certain artisans sold direct to customers the products made from raw materials which were their own, since as early as the eleventh century we find bakers displaying their bread *super fenestras*;[2] but in all probability direct sale in a shop was for a long period limited to that trade alone.

Amongst the problems raised by the history of early medieval industry, one of the most obscure is that of the origins of the Flemish cloth-trade, the most famous industry in Northern Europe. A few scanty texts have been tortured in an attempt to make them yield up the secrets of its source. Various ninth-century documents refer to Frisian cloths (*pallia fresonica*) of excellent quality which, if the monk of Saint-Gall is to be believed,[3] Charlemagne sent as gifts to the Caliph Haroun al Raschid, and which according to Ermoldus Nigellus were remarkable for the brightness of their colours.[4] These fine-quality cloths were brought in by Frisian merchants, to whom their production and manufacture have also been attributed, on the grounds that they reared sheep on their humid grasslands. This supposition is most unlikely, and it is more probable that these cloths, which were known as *fresonica* because Frisians traded in them abroad, were manufactured in Flanders. A curious poem entitled 'The Quarrel of the Sheep and the Flax',[5] the author of which was a contemporary of Pope Gregory VII, shows that in the latter half of the eleventh century Flanders was already making magnificent fabrics superior to anything which England or Gaul could produce. Gaul buys them, Flanders makes and exports them, declares the poet quite explicitly. Whilst admitting

---

[1] The editors of the Polyptyque of Irminon have given precise definitions of the *ministerium* and the *ministerialis*. (Ed. Aug. Longnon, I, Introduction, p. lvi.)

[2] 'Villes, marchés, et marchands au moyen âge', in *Les villes et les institutions urbaines*, I, pp. 117–118.

[3] Monk of Saint-Gall, *Gesta Karoli Magni*, II, 14.

[4] *Poème sur Louis le Pieux*, ed. and trans. by E. Faral, Paris, 1932, pp. 210–211.

[5] 'Conflictus ovis et lini . . .' For this poem see an excellent article by Van de Vyver and Charles Verlinden, 'L'auteur et la portée du *Conflictus ovis et lini*', in the *Revue belge de philologie et d'histoire*, XII, 1938, pp. 59–81.

that the Frisians produced coarse cloths, several Belgian historians are inclined to think that the Flemish cloth trade, which from the end of the eleventh century experienced an undoubted expansion, had been in existence for a very long time, and that the cloth known as Frisian was in reality Flemish.[1] Pirenne, always on the look-out for Roman survivals in the civilization and economy of the Early Middle Ages, believes that this cloth trade, which was already engaged in export at the time of Charlemagne and Louis the Pious, was itself a continuation of the industry carried on under the Roman Empire by the Morini and the Atrebates and known to us from several allusions by fourth- and fifth-century writers, the author of the *Historia Augusta* and Paul Orosius. It had, he maintained, inherited the superior technique of the Romans, whilst the Frisian coarse cloth trade retained the primitive methods of barbarian manufacture.[2]

*

The royal and imperial diplomas, so valuable for the study of Carolingian markets, provide significant information about their importance. In fact, the establishments which received permission to found them very soon obtained also the privilege of minting money. *Mercatus* and *moneta* appear side by side in numerous deeds as if the two concessions went hand in hand; they were, in fact, complementary. A fairly large currency was needed for a market, particularly since gold coins were not available. In these markets, forged money was often slipped into circulation.[3] The proper conduct of markets, which was normally the responsibility of the sovereign, was entrusted to the holder of the concession, who was required to exercise control over the coinage. That was doubtless the main reason why the Carolingian kings of the latter half of the ninth century granted to establishments holding market concessions the right

---

[1] This is the conclusion reached in a famous article by Pirenne, 'Draps de Frise ou draps de Flandre', in *Vierteljahrschrift für Sozial- und Wirtschaftsgeschichte*, VII, 1909, pp. 308–315. It was taken up again by Van der Vyver and Ch. Verlinden in the Memoir quoted in the previous note.

[2] See the article quoted above, p. 312.

[3] See above, p. 159. Cf. M. Prou, *Les monnaies carolingiennes*.

to coin deniers in their mints. It is tempting to interpret this relinquishing of privilege as an act of weakness. In actual fact it was a necessity, since Otto the Great, an energetic prince, followed in the footsteps of his predecessors and handed out monetary concessions in large numbers.[1] One fact, however, makes it clear that in granting them he had no intention of renouncing his royal rights. In spite of the wide variety of money in circulation, the unity of the coinage was maintained in Germany, through the strict surveillance exercised by the sovereign, who was able to impose on the seigniorial coins the title and weight of the royal deniers.[2]

Was the sale of coins permitted in the market? We dare not say definitely that it was. We simply know that gold was one of the goods which could be bought, probably in ingots.[3]

It is not enough to show that the public markets represented the normal form of trade from the ninth century onwards. In the growth of medieval towns and the formation of the merchant class, they played a decisive part which has too often been disregarded. In various diplomas authorizing their establishment, notably those of Otto the Great, there recurs one phrase which deserves particular attention. The sovereign grants the licence to construct or build a market,[4] consequently the reference is

---

[1] The following are examples of these concessions:

30 May 946. Grant by Otto I to the Abbey of Corvey of two *villae* 'cum moneta et theloneo'. *Dipl. reg. et imp. Germ.*, I, p. 157, no. 77.

7 October 950. To his vassal: 'mercatum et monetam'. Ibid., p. 210, no. 129.

952. To the Bishop of Osnabrück: 'monetam et mercatum publicum'. Ibid., p. 230, no. 150.

9 June 965. St Maurice of Magdeburg: 'mercatum in Magadaburg et monetam'. Ibid., p. 417, no. 310.

9 April 973. To the convent of Herford: 'de quodam mercato cum omnibus inde exigendi usibus id est moneta et teloneo'. Ibid., p. 583, no. 430.

[2] Ch. Edm. Perrin, 'L'évolution d'une monnaie: le denier de Cologne', *Ann. d'hist. éc. et soc.*, IV, 1932, pp. 194–197. Cf. A. Suhle, *Deutsche Münz- und Geldgeschichte*, Berlin, 1955, p. 42 et seq.

[3] 1036. 'Omnis homo, sive liber sive non, si emerit aut vendiderit aurum . . . theloneum debet.' List of dues for Saint-Vaast d'Arras, in Fagniez, *Documents*, p. 62. The fact will seem less surprising if we remember that the list was an eleventh-century one and dealt with a region, Flanders, which developed economically at an unusually early date.

[4] 10 August 965. 'Quare omnibus constet nos . . . venerabilis Adaldagi Hammaburgensis (Hamburg) ecclesie archiepiscopi flagitationibus annuentes, *construendi mercatum* in loco Bremum [Bremen] nuncupato illi concessisse licentiam.'

to a material structure, an installation of a permanent nature. Once again a close scrutiny of the texts yields the required information. Foreign merchants visiting the markets generally brought their wares by water, and when unloading had to find some place in which to store them. Thus here and there in the ninth century, and more frequently and more explicitly in the tenth, the word *portus* appears in conjunction with that of *mercatus* to indicate the place where the unloaded merchandise was deposited.[1] Yet it was not enough merely to store the merchandise; lodging had also to be found for the merchants. The seigniorial *burg* or the old episcopal city sometimes took them in, but from an early date they preferred to live in a new settlement which was exclusively their own, and Bruges is a curious example of this phase of evolution. Although the account by Jean Long, the Chronicler of Saint-Bertin who has retraced its history, dates only from the fourteenth century, it deserves to be quoted because it conjures up a lifelike and fascinating picture of the birth and growth of a merchant town:[2]

> In order to satisfy the needs of the castle folk, there began to throng before his gate near the castle bridge traders and merchants selling costly goods, then inn-keepers to feed and house those doing business with the prince, who was often to be seen there; they built houses and set up inns where those who could not be put up at the castle were accommodated. The phrase they used was: 'Let's go to the Bridge.' The houses increased to such an extent that there soon grew up a large town which in the common speech of the lower classes is still called 'Bridge', for Bruges means 'bridge' in their patois.

[1] H. Pirenne has shown that the word *portus* occurs often in Flanders from the ninth and tenth centuries, and has quoted with supporting texts the examples of Bruges, Ghent, Valenciennes, Tournai. 'Villes, marchés et marchands', in *Les villes et les institutions urbaines*, p. 114. The word is also found in many other regions, however; it is used for example to denote the little ports attached to the monastery of Beaulieu on the Dordogne: 'Fluvium Dordoniae . . . cunctos portus.' *Cartul. de Beaulieu*, p. 92, no. 4. Thus the distinction drawn by M. Rolland, 'Le problème de la continuité à Tournai et dans la Gaule du Nord', in *Ann. hist. éc. et soc.*, 7, 1935, p. 258, between the *mercatus* and the *portus* seems to us artificial. There were large and small markets just as there were large and small ports. When Otto the Great instituted markets in all his towns, they were not peasant markets.

[2] The Latin text has been reproduced by Fagniez, *Documents*, I, p. 54, no. 95.

Two elements went to the making of these merchant settlements: a floating population, made up of itinerant merchants, real commercial travellers, who went from place to place with their packs, visiting fairs and markets,[1] and a stable population, the 'residents', who made a living by exploiting the market. The poverty of our information does not permit us to 'film' one of the most vital moments in urban evolution, the moment when the periodic market became a permanent one. Many historians have refused to attribute the honour of founding the merchant towns to the markets, which they regarded as artificial attempts at colonization.[2] Whilst admitting the validity of certain objections and the insignificance of some of the markets, it is nevertheless difficult to deny the part played by the market in founding the medieval town. The truth is that with the complexity characteristic of all human phenomena, there was a certain ebb and flow. The market founded with the assent of the sovereign, and often at his express wish, exerted a definite attraction for those engaged in trade, since when they frequented it they were sure of finding customers, metal currency, safety for their persons, since the local seigneur, whether layman or cleric, was obliged to maintain law and order there, anchorage for their boats and a warehouse for their goods. Would a seigneur, on the other hand, have gone to the expense of founding a market if he had not known beforehand that he was setting it up on a known and busy highway, on the banks of a river much used by ships carrying merchandise?[3]

One word, *wik*, became very popular in the Germanic-speaking countries to denote the new merchant towns, those provisional and temporary groupings which were well on the way to becoming settlements with permanent dwellings. We have already made its acquaintance.[4] In Iceland, still an empty

---

[1] 'Itinerantes undique confluentes a Reno usque ad Albian et Sale, transeuntes ad ipsum locum negocii, properantes, euntes et redeuntes.' Planitz, *Frühgeschichte der deutschen Stadt*, p. 41.

[2] H. Pirenne, 'L'origine des constitutions urbaines au moyen âge', in *Les villes et les institutions urbaines*, I, pp. 44–45.

[3] The author of the *Gesta abbatum Fontanellensium*, writing in the ninth century, describes the Seine as a great commercial highway: 'Sequana commerciis navium gloriosus [sic].' Imbart de la Tour, *Des immunités . . .* p. 75.

[4] See above, p. 215, in the form *vik*.

wilderness when it was explored by intrepid seamen, the word was used to denote the bays in which the early explorers landed, but contaminated by the Latin *vicus*, it changed its meaning, and an expert on medieval town life has brought to light in an old Saxon glossary[1] a definition which reads: *wik*, that is the place where merchants live (*wik, vicus ubi mercatores morantur*). We shall not join him in recapitulating every place on the Continent ending in *wik*, and of which the most important are Quentowik, Bardowik, Schleswig, Osterwik, Brunswick. We shall mention only the one significant example of Duurstede; this North Sea port, situated on the Lek, was called *villa Dorsteti* until the tenth century, and then took the single name of Wik, which described its function more accurately.[2]

The *wik*, a merchant settlement, generally grew up in the vicinity, but outside, the area known to contemporary scholars as the 'pre-urban core' of the seigniorial burg or the walls of the *civitas*. One medievalist has put forward a shrewd explanation of the deep, psychological reasons for this choice.[3] The human climate inside the walls, he says, was not very congenial even if there had been room for them to live there. Division into specialized districts is an unchanging law of town life, and one which holds good for every age. In our modern towns the business quarter is quite distinct from that of the clerical or the military set. Each Paris *arrondissement* has its own special population. An inhabitant of the VIII[e] would not dream of going to live in the III[e] or the XX[e], just as a resident in the two latter would feel like a fish out of water if he moved to the Marbeuf quarter. The position – making all due allowances – was exactly the same in the early stages of medieval town life. The historian Richer mentions one oft-quoted example when,

[1] Planitz, *Die deutsche Stadt im Mittelalter*, pp. 54–55.

[2] 'In villa quodam Dorsteti nunc autem Wik nominata.' Diploma of Otto I, 1 April 968, confirming the Church of Utrecht in various privileges. *Dipl.*, I, p. 181, no. 98. By an opposite process the port of Quentowic which had been destroyed by the Northmen, became Etaples when it was rebuilt on the opposite bank of the Canche. The earlier name may have been rejected because the word *wik* was meaningless to the inhabitants of a romance-speaking region. The name Etaples (= storehouse; in Latin *stabulum*; in German *Stapel*) was a translation of it. It continued to suggest the traditional name of the place.

[3] Ganshof, *Développement des villes*, pp. 27–28.

describing one of the sieges experienced by the city of Verdun
at the close of the tenth century, he shows how the merchant
quarter was surrounded by a wall like a fortress and set apart
from the city – that is to say the episcopal city – by the Meuse
itself, but connected with it by two bridges.[1] The case of
Cologne is no less significant. Its first walls date back to the
early centuries of the Christian era.[2] This ancient city might
well prove to be an example of historical continuity, but the
author of a scholarly work on the history of the origins of the
European town[3] warns us against any such tempting and
ready-made conclusion. The continuity is only apparent. There
was one vital difference between the Roman town and its
medieval counterpart. The most lively quarter in the medieval
town was the Rhine suburb with its vast market, but this was
outside the Roman walls. It may be objected that already under
the Late Empire there were a large number of artisan workshops on the periphery, but they were in the *suburbium*, and so
outside the town proper. The situation was reversed in the
Carolingian era: the Rhenish suburb on the banks of the Rhine
became the living heart of the town and the real centre of
gravity. Its evolution did not stop there. It went steadily on in
most of the towns where an active merchant settlement came
into being alongside the ancient *civitas*. Each quarter kept its
special character, but eventually the two towns merged into
a single whole, enclosed and joined together by a new wall. It
is known, for instance, that about A.D. 1000 the Bishop of Worms
rebuilt his city walls and took inside them the market, the mint
and the Jewish quarter.[4]

*

The oldest merchant settlements came into being in the
Austrasian part of the Frankish Empire.[5] The vast area which

---

[1] 'Negociatorum claustrum, muro instar oppidi extructum, ab urbe quidem
Mosa interfluente sejectum, sed pontibus duobus interstratis ei annexum.' *Histoire
de France*, ed. R. Latouche, II, p. 132.   [2] Ganshof, op. cit., p, 11. n. 1.
[3] Edith Ennen, *Frühgeschichte der Europäischen Stadt*, pp. 88–89.
[4] Planitz, *Die deutsche Stadt im Mittelalter*, p. 41; Ganshof, op. cit., *passim*.
[5] 'Über 20 neue Orte ausser des Römerstädten entstanden in dem austrasischen
Teil des Frankenreiches in denen Burg und *vicus* sich in der Karolingerzeit zu-
sammenfanden.' Planitz, *Die deutsche Stadt*, p. 46.

included Flanders, Brabant, the Meuse region and the Rhine valley has remained ever since the fourth century the nerve centre of the West. It was the cradle of the medieval merchant town. If Henri Pirenne's conclusions on the economic eclipse brought about by the Saracen invasion in the Western Empire are not wholly acceptable, his theory that this entire region in Carolingian times displayed a vigorous commercial life which was quite unique is thoroughly sound.[1] The causes of this astonishing vitality were many and varied: a powerful tradition dating back to the Late Empire and perhaps even earlier;[2] the seafaring activity of the Frisians in Merovingian times;[3] the continuous close relations between the Continent and Great Britain, which made the Rhine valley a busy highway up to its very mouth;[4] the many navigable rivers with which the country was intersected; lastly the prestige of the early Carolingians which made the Rhineland and Austrasia the political centre of the West. Belgian and German historians have brought to light a considerable number of texts, though unfortunately not very detailed ones, which show us merchant settlements springing up from the ninth century onwards. In order to supplement them, they have made full use of the valuable information afforded by coins, as well as by archaeological excavations.

M. Ganshof has located two *portus* on the Meuse, at Maastricht and Namur, and three on the Scheldt, one in the vicinity of the royal *palatium* at Valenciennes, a second at Tournai, and a third near the Abbey of Saint-Bavon at Ghent.[5] The researches of contemporary German scholars and in particular

---

[1] 'Les villes du moyen âge', in *Les villes et institutions urbaines*, I, p. 354.

[2] The excavations at Bavai confirm this.

[3] See above, p. 135.

[4] The importance of the relations of the Frisian land with Great Britain from the sixth to the ninth century has been emphasized and illustrated with a wealth of detail by Paul Kletler, *Nordwesteuropas Verkehr*, p. 9 et seq. The author has discovered the routes followed by pilgrims and other travellers making for Rome, and in particular that taken by Alcuin in 781; his ship took him as far as the mouth of the Rhine; he stopped at Utrecht and Duurstede, sailed down the Rhine past the 'castella' as far as the mouth of the Moselle, referring to Mainz in passing.

[5] *Développement des villes*, p. 22, n. 9. Cf. Ganshof, *La Belgique Carolingienne*, Brussels, 1958, p. 120 et seq.

those of M. Planitz and Fräulein Ennen, have thrown much light on the economic activity which flourished on the banks of the Rhine in Carolingian times. We know, for example, that there was a Frisian colony in Mainz from the end of the eighth century.[1] Though the town was sacked by the Northmen in 886, the movement of trade continued during the tenth century. Strange and exotic coins were in circulation there, as one Arab traveller noted with amazement.[2] Activity was not confined to the old Roman cities. Traces of it have been found in other places such as Bonn.[3] The picture which emerges from a number of careful and detailed studies is one of trade settlements crowding along the great river and its tributaries, as well as along those which, like the Rhine, flow into the North Sea. They were merchant colonies, the density of which cannot easily be estimated, but which paved the way for those of the twelfth century.

Further east, commercial life flourished exceedingly in the tenth century, a truly great century for the kingdom of Germany. Trade routes based on those followed by armies greatly increased in number under the Emperor Otto;[4] towns sprang up which were at once religious centres and merchant settlements. Whilst in the West the religious city existed long

[1] Planitz, *Die deutsche Stadt*, p. 43.

[2] Ibrahim Ibn Ahmed at-Tartûschi. The same person observed that spices imported from the East were to be found there also. Ganshof, *Développ. des villes*, p. 24, n. 19. Strasburg also was a busy economic centre; its inhabitants travelled by river and by land (navigio aut terreno id est cum carris et saumariis) for purposes of trade (negociandi causa). Privilege of Otto I to the bishop, 13 February 953. *Dipl.*, p. 243, no. 162.

[3] Edith Ennen, 'Einige Bemerkungen zur frühmittelalterlichen Geschichte Bonns', in *Rheinische Vierteljahrsblätter*, XV–XVI, 1950–1951, p. 187, thinks that in the ninth century merchants were already living in the *vicus Bonnensis*, mentioned for the first time in charters of 795 and 804. Her theory is based on a reference to a wine-trade contained in a deed of 821, and an allusion by the Abbot of Prüm (845) to a rich merchant of Bonn. This example gives an indication of the line being followed by contemporary scholars in their endeavours to detect the beginning of medieval trade with the help of seemingly trivial texts.

[4] Paul Kletler has described this eastward trade expansion, of which the moving spirit in the tenth century was the Emperor Otto the Great. He ends with these words: 'So war schliesslich doch ein Verkehrsgebiet entstanden das sich von Niederrhein, ja von England bis nach Böhmen erstreckte'. Op. cit., p. 174. For trade routes and river system in the time of the Ottos, see also Planitz, *Die deutsche Stadt*, pp. 60–63.

before the merchant settlements, cities such as Regensburg,[1] Magdeburg and Hamburg[2] are examples of a simultaneous growth in both directions. The first kings of Germany,[3] beginning with Conrad I, made it their aim to transform them into complete towns. The most striking example is that of Magdeburg, which Otto the Great made his favourite place of residence. He increased its religious prestige by founding there, with patient persistence, first a great monastery dedicated to St Maurice, then a cathedral and finally a metropolitan church;[4] but at the same time he ensured its economic prosperity by setting up a new market on high ground in the town, and building a common protecting wall around the *wik* and the *burg*.[5] The privileges which gave bishops and abbots rights of jurisdiction over markets stipulated that the merchants frequenting them should enjoy, on arrival and departure and during their stay, the most complete safety.[6] Although the sovereign conceded his rights, these merchants whether residents or visitors, still remained under his protection and

---

[1] The bishopric of Regensburg was created about 739. During the ninth century a merchant settlement was founded (*pagus mercatorum*) which stretched from the Danube to the vicinity of the church of Saint-Emmeran and which was joined on to the old town in 917. Planitz, op. cit, p. 69 and plan, p. 38.

[2] In the pre-Carolingian era, Hamburg was little more than a fortress used as a place of refuge (*Fluchtburg*). It became a bishopric in 831 and a metropolitan see in 834. Side by side with the episcopal burg a merchant settlement developed, but both Burg and Wik were destroyed by the Scandinavians in 845 (Planitz, op. cit., p. 50) and struggled back to life only slowly.

[3] The example had been set a century earlier by Charlemagne himself. Imbart de la Tour, *Des Immunités* . . . , p. 71, has shown that Aix-la-Chapelle had become a trade centre from which caravans set out for Brittany, Rhaetia, Italy. Others travelled down the Rhine and the Danube towards the Slav countries and Byzantium.

[4] Robert Holtzmann, *Kaiser Otto der Grosse*, Berlin, 1936, pp. 79–84. See also A. Brackmann, *Magdeburg als Hauptstadt des deutschen Ostens im frühen Mittelalter*, Leipzig, 1937 and G. Piltz, *Magdeburg, Stadt am Strom*, Dresden, 1955.

[5] Planitz, *Die deutsche Stadt*, pp. 6–7. For the prestige of Magdeburg in the tenth century, see P. Kletler, op. cit., p. 167 et seq. This period of prosperity was followed by one of trial and tribulation at the end of the tenth century and the beginning of the eleventh.

[6] In 946 Otto the Great granted to the monastery of Corvey two *villae*, and added: 'Mercatum vero constituant publicum in illis ubicumque abbati placuerit locis pacemque firmissimam teneant aggredientes et regredientes et ibi manentes eodem modo sicuti ab antecessoribus regibus jampridem aliis publicis mercatorum locis concessum erat.' *Dipl.*, I, p. 157, no. 77.

continued to be his men.[1] The town remained a royal town and the king's suzerainty was gradually extended to all the inhabitants. This solicitude resulted in a rapid development of town life. According to statistics worked out by the Viennese scholar Kletler,[2] it is possible to list twenty-nine new markets created by privileges granted by the Ottos during the sixty-six years from the accession of Otto the Great to the death of Otto III (936–1002), and they themselves were only continuing a work already initiated by their predecessors, notably by Conrad I (911–918).[3] Many of these markets created in the tenth century were situated in places which later became cities or fairly important towns, Würzburg, Nordhausen, Magdeburg, Bremen, Verden, Minden, Halberstadt, Quedlinburg, Erfurt, Dortmund, Lüneburg, Merseburg. The example of Germany is clear proof that the tenth-century market represented a decisive step in the urbanization of medieval Europe. Founded as a deliberate instrument of policy by far-sighted rulers, these markets, on well-chosen sites and advantageous both to those who frequented them and to those settled permanently in these privileged towns, contributed substantially towards the economic transformation of a country to which civilization came late.

Nothing comparable is to be seen in Western France, which may explain why Romance historians, unlike their German colleagues, have often evinced a certain scepticism as to the

[1] See for example one of Otto the Great's diplomas authorizing the Bishop of Hamburg to found a market in Bremen. After enumerating the privileges granted to the Metropolitan, the Emperor goes on: 'Quin etiam negociatores ejusdem incolas loci nostrae tuitionis patrocinio condonavimus, precipientes . . . quod in omnibus tali patrocinentur tutela et potiantur jure quali ceterarum regalium institores urbium.' *Dipl.*, p. 422, no. 307. When a town was granted a royal privilege, it became a royal town and each of its merchants a *mercator regis*, a *homo imperatoris*. A diploma of Otto II dated 975, confirming a concession granted by his father Otto I to the merchants of Magdeburg, shows that they enjoyed this status. Planitz, *Frühgeschichte der deutschen Stadt.*

[2] Op. cit., pp. 136–137.

[3] In 918 Conrad gave to the Bishop of Würzburg 'thelonei debitum quod ad eundem locum Uuirciburg dictum debet persolvi a cunctis qui cum mercatus sui mercimonio ab universis provinciis et civitatibus illuc conveniunt'. *Dipl.*, p. 32, no. 35, and to the Bishop of Eichstädt 'licentiam publice negociationis mercatum constituere'. Ibid., p. 33, no. 36. Henry I did little to help the churches; it does not necessarily follow that he did not found markets.

effectiveness of the rôle played by the markets in the ninth and tenth centuries.[1]

In Germany on the other hand results came swiftly. A most efficient network of communications was opened up for the transport of the raw materials and merchandise found within the kingdom itself; silver, copper, lead from Goslar and the Alps, wool from most districts, mineral salts from various places, wine from the West, from the banks of the Rhine, the Moselle and the Danube, corn, wax, honey from almost everywhere. The pacification of Central Europe, the creation of urban centres and the improvement in communications had also a further result, which a pious chronicler of the mid-eleventh century, the monk Raoul Glaber, noted with satisfaction: 'Almost all who at that time wished to go to Jerusalem to visit our Lord's tomb began to forsake the customary sea-route and to cross the country of King Stephen of Hungary; he contrived to make this a safer route for them all.'[2] In spite of the tribute paid by the chronicler to the sovereign who had just been converted to the Christian faith, this deviation from the normal route was mainly due to the kings and emperors of Germany.[3]

The picture in the West was quite different. For *Francia occidentalis* the tenth century was a period of stagnation. There were in Gaul a large number of cities going back to the days of Ancient Rome, and even of *castra* which, like Dijon, had a long history. Monastic foundations had already in Merovingian times created centres of population outside city walls. On the other hand many towns which under Charlemagne and Louis the Pious had enjoyed half a century of tranquillity and even prosperity experienced, with the invasions of the Northmen, a

---

[1] See for instance the conclusion reached about these markets by Ch. Pfister in *Les destinées de l'Empire en Occident de 395 à 888*, Paris, 1st ed., 1928, p. 600. The majority, he states, were merely small local markets to which peasants came week by week to sell foodstuffs.

[2] Raoul Glaber, *Les cinq livres de son histoire*, III, I (ed. Maurice Prou, Paris, 1886, p. 52).

[3] In 918 safety and security still left much to be desired. In the diploma in which King Conrad granted the Bishop of Eichstadt permission to institute a public market, he gave him authority also to build fortresses and castles for defence against the incursions of the 'pagans', in other words Hungarians (aliquas munitiones et firmitates contra paganorum incursus moliri).

period of poverty and decay. Town life received a check, and feudal anarchy delayed the revival of the towns. It has been observed[1] that the basin of the Oise awoke to commercial activity later than Flanders. We have only to compare Laon, the capital of the later Carolingians, with Magdeburg, which at the same period was the favourite residence of Otto the Great, King of Germany. The contrast is obvious. Laon was not a Roman city, but it already had a bishopric in the middle of the sixth century; it had become essentially and almost solely a fortress defended by a strong garrison. In spite of an assertion made by the historian Dopsch, it is not until 1071[2] that we find the first mention of a market where fish and meat were sold, clearly a small country market. No attempt was made by the French kings in the tenth century to create a merchant quarter in that town. At the same period the town of Magdeburg, though of much later origin, was already an important commercial centre. Even Paris, which purported to be the capital under Charles the Fat, did not undergo any change until a century and a half later. Only then did the first trade guilds make their appearance. An annalist may have recorded the presence of merchants on the Seine in 861, but that does not affect the general picture.[3]

In addition to its late commercial expansion, the urban development of Gaul was marked by a second characteristic feature. There may have been no merchant settlements (*vici mercatorum*), but there was something else. In the *suburbium* of most of the cities, a settled population crystallized in the tenth century around abbeys which had been there since Merovingian times. The settlement so formed was known as the *burgus*. The old Germanic word *Burg* took on a new meaning.[4] It was no longer a fortified place, 'ein befestigter Platz', as it is

---

[1] F. Vercauteren, *Etude sur les 'civitates' de la Belgique Seconde*, p. 462.

[2] Vercauteren, op. cit., p. 344. The reference in question occurs in a diploma of Philip I confirming the gift made by his predecessors to the Church at Laon of the dues levied in the city markets on butchers' and fishmongers' stalls (pro stationibus carnis ac piscium). *Recueil des actes de Philippe I*, by M. Prou, Paris, 1908, p. 160, no. lxi.

[3] M. Poète, *Paris*, I, p. 83 et seq.

[4] How was the transition effected? The oldest burgs were apparently surrounded by a palisade or by a ditch which turned them into fortified enclosures. At the end

still defined in German lexicons.[1] In the Romance countries, the word gradually came to mean a market.[2] The monastic burgs which in the eleventh century sprang up in such numbers around the towns as well as in the country districts always had their markets, in which law and order were the responsibility of the monks who received in return income in the form of dues. We shall return to the subject of the rural burgs when considering the agricultural revival; here we shall deal only with those which grew up on the periphery of cities.[3] Their creation, which came later than that of the *vici mercatorum* in Germany, also contributed, though in a lesser degree, to a renaissance of urban life. These monastic and episcopal burgs, situated outside the confines of the old Roman, clerical and military city, became the home of a half-agricultural, half-artisan population which may be compared to the 'suburbanites' of our own day. The burg of Saint-Vincent, for example, at the gates of Le Mans, was made up of a population of humble folk belonging for the most part to the *familia* of that great monastery, and also to those of the bishop and perhaps of the count, working men engaged in the most widely varying trades, and many of them rejoicing in picturesque surnames.[4] It was they who in 1070 were to foment the revolt known as the Commune of Le Mans. Its very failure is significant, proving as it does that in the western towns, predominantly agricultural, no powerful merchant settlements had come into being, and that consequently no upper middle class strong enough to defend the rights of the community effectively had been able to emerge. The small shopkeepers and craftsmen whose names and trades[5]

of the eleventh century a seigneur in Maine was still requiring the monks of Saint-Vincent du Mans to surround their burg by a well-made ditch, as he had surrounded his own. 'L'établissement des bourgs', extr. from *Le Moyen âge*, 1937, no. 1–2, p. 3.

[1] The definition is taken from *Brockhaus Konversations-Lexikon*, v. Burg.

[2] See W. Vogel, 'Wik-orte und Wikinger', *Hansische Geschichtsblätter*, LX, p. 10.

[3] Helpful information will be found in *Le Bourg de Saint-Germain-des-Prés*, by Françoise Lehoux, Paris, 1951, Introduction, pp. xi–xviii.

[4] 'La Commune du Mans, 1070', in *Mélanges Louis Halphen*, pp. 377–382. The popular, even vulgar, nature of some of these names is significant: Witless (*Pauper sensu*), Play-the-Fool (*Faciens-stultitiam*), Bear (*Ursus*), Punchbottom (*Verberat nates*), Three-Testicle (*Qui dicitur habere Tres testiculos*).

[5] A list of these trades is given in the article already quoted.

have come down to us in the Saint-Vincent Cartulary were incapable of resisting William the Conqueror and his powerful army.

Paris too at an early date was ringed with settlements inhabited by merchants, but which were not called burgs until the twelfth century: Saint-Germain-des Prés, Sainte-Geneviève, Saint-Médard, Saint-Germain-l'Auxerrois.[1] Likewise at Rheims, *suburbia* which had grown up around abbeys took the name of *burgi* when they acquired a certain importance, but that was not before the end of the eleventh century. The burg of Saint-Remi is mentioned for the first time in 1090.[2] It would be a simple matter to trace in the ecclesiastical provinces of Gaul all the burgs which were formed on the outskirts of cities. It is most unlikely that a single one of them could produce a birth certificate earlier than the eleventh century.[3]

In the merchant settlements, and also, though later and in smaller numbers, in certain monastic burgs, there grew up a class of specialist merchants. (*negociatores*) who were to be at one and the same time a class of producers and of bankers, which was to become the leaven of medieval secular society. What was its origin? Pirenne's answer, as we know, was that it probably emerged from 'a mass of vagabonds scattered all over the world' in the eleventh century. He quoted the example of St Godric of Finchale who, born of poor peasant stock in Lincolnshire, joined a troupe of wandering merchants when he had saved up a few pence. He followed them from fair to fair, and after becoming a merchant by profession, eventually made enormous profits.[4] His example is typical of many, and the Viking world could provide a host of others. Yet was the

[1] The term Bourg Saint-Germain-des-Prés makes its appearance only in 1159 (Fr. Lehoux, op. cit., p. 1), those of Saint-Marcel, Saint-Médard and Sainte-Geneviève between 1158 and 1163. Ibid., p. xviii.

[2] F. Vercauteren, op. cit., p. 93.

[3] The semantic evolution of the word *burgensis*, which originally meant the inhabitant of the burg, would also be worth following up. This inhabitant of the *Burg* was destined to become the bourgeois, and consequently a person as far removed from military matters as possible, the citizen of a commune, enjoying the privileges granted to it, and assuming its obligations. Petit-Dutaillis, *Les communes françaises*, p. 254. Halfway between came the inhabitant of the monastic burg who enjoyed the special protection of the abbey.

[4] *Les villes et les institutions urbaines*, I, p. 366.

260 *The Laborious Birth of a Western Civilization*

merchant class drawn solely from the ranks of these outsiders? Modern scholars dispute this.[1] Not all who engaged in trade in the tenth century were, like the future St Godric, *negociatores vagantes*. We have seen that the Carolingian sovereigns had in their employ palace merchants[2] who were really official commercial travellers whose task it was to buy for the court, whereas our modern commercial representatives are the accredited salesmen of a firm. There is nothing to prove that these merchants disappeared after the reign of Louis the Pious, who willingly entrusted these duties to Jews. The protégés of Otto I, those merchants who in this prince's diplomas figure as *homines imperatoris*, were their successors. Many of them were still Jews.[3] They even increased in number, for instead of handing out individual concessions to such and such a merchant, the prince eventually extended his generosity to all the *mercatores* of a town like Magdeburg, each being liable to be called on to do him service. The abbey merchants did not go out of existence either. The inventory of dues for Saint-Riquier mentions at the head of the list of the various *vici* inhabited by the monastery's specialist craftsmen, a *vicus negociantium*,[4] in other words a quarter or street[5] in which the abbey

---

[1] Ed. Perroy, 'Les origines urbaines en Flandre d'après un ouvrage récent', *Revue du Nord*, 1947, pp. 49–63, and J. Lestocquoy, *Les villes de Flandre et d'Italie sous le gouvernment des patriciens, XIᵉ–XVᵉ siècle*, Paris, 1952. Perroy considers that many middle-class fortunes must have originated in lucky speculation by local people caught up by force of circumstances in the commercial round (p. 57). Lestocquoy has concentrated on the beginnings of the urban upper-class in the Flemish towns. Several historical texts such as the *Gestes* of the Bishops of Cambrai recall the first patricians to be active in the towns of Flanders. They are local people and not wandering merchants. We get the impression, says the author (p. 36), that we are dealing with business in the modern sense of the word, with the handling of capital and perhaps the monopoly of foodstuffs. The best known of them all, a certain Werimbold of Cambrai, came of a Cambrai family and never left his native town. He had no need to go far afield in search of wealth and fortune.

[2] See above, p. 167.

[3] Magdeburg had a great number of them. In the concession of the right of *ban* to Saint-Maurice of Magdeburg (9 July 965) the Emperor Otto I refers to the 'Judei vel ceteri ibi manentes negociatores'. *Urkundenbuch des Erzstifts Magdeburg*, I, Magdeburg, 1937, pp. 54–55, no. 38. This diploma gives the impression that the majority of merchants living in Magdeburg were Jews.

[4] *Chron. de Saint-Riquier*, ed. F. Lot, p. 307. Imbart de la Tour, *Des Immunités . . .*, p. 80, emphasizes that these *negociantes* formed a class apart from the ordinary tenant population.

[5] This inventory shows us the word *vicus* in process of changing its meaning. It

merchants lived. These merchants were agents (*ministeriales*) of the monastery, their real function being to buy things for the abbey and perhaps also to sell its surplus agricultural produce.[1]

It seems probable that all these *negociatores*, the officials of temporal princes and of monasteries, did a great deal to swell the numbers of the merchant class. They gave it some measure of stability, though no doubt it opened its doors also to certain landowners and wealthy farmers who, attracted by the rise to fortune of the professional merchants, determined to imitate them.[2] We agree with a contemporary Belgian historian that this new class of men which took root in the towns of the West was made up of varied elements. M. Sabbe[3] has distinguished several types of merchant: the Jewish merchant, the local merchant in business in only a small way, the rich merchant engaged in trade in distant parts. Their origins were no less varied than their way of life and conduct.

In spite of this diversity, those merchants engaged in a common profession and leading a life beset by innumerable hazards probably sought to group themselves together at an early date. In the North their associations took the form of the gild. This word, Germanic in origin, first appears in the eighth century. One of Charlemagne's Capitularies of 779 refers to *ghildonia*, societies for mutual aid, and forbids their members to be bound by oaths.[4] The gilds or confraternities (*geldonias vel confratrias*) to which Hincmar, Archbishop of Rheims, alludes three-quarters of a century later[5] when prohibiting the feasts (*pastos et commessationes*) to which they gave rise and controlling their activities, had the same charitable and religious character.

no longer denotes a small isolated township, but a quarter in a settlement, and as the houses were built along a communal street, the word was beginning to assume the meaning of 'street' which it took on in the twelfth and thirteenth centuries.

[1] Imbart de la Tour, ibid., p. 79, believes that the abbeys were like great modern landowners who send their peasants to sell their corn and wine in the market or at the fair.

[2] This theory has been advanced by Perroy, see above, p. 260, n. 1.

[3] 'Quelques types de marchands des IXe et Xe siècles', *Revue belge de Philologie et d'Histoire*, 1934, p. 176 et seq.

[4] Capitulare Haristallense, clause 16: 'De sacramentis per gildonia invicem conjurantibus ut nemo facere praesumat.' *Capitularia*, ed. Boretius, I, p. 51.

[5] Statutes of Hincmar, Archbishop of Rheims, suppressing abuses to which the confraternities gave rise, 852, in Fagniez, *Documents*, I, p. 52, no. 93.

They were not yet associations of merchants or craftsmen, or
at any rate this aspect of them is not discernible in the prelate's
instructions. It is not until the beginning of the eleventh century
that we find an association of this nature, that of the merchants
of Tiel[1] (*mercatores Tielenses*), who carried on a brisk trade
with Great Britain. An ecclesiastical chronicler, Alpert,
historian of the Bishops of Metz,[2] was severely critical of these
merchants and bitterly poured out his hatred of them.[3] He
accused them of untrustworthiness, dishonesty, adultery. He
also reproached them – and this complaint is more unusual and
more deserving of note – with acting not justly and lawfully but
in accordance with their own wishes, and taking advantage of
an imperial charter which had been granted to them and confirmed.[4] These merchants and inhabitants of Tiel were therefore
grouped together in an association which had its own privileges
and jurisdiction. It is tempting to compare them with the merchants of Magdeburg and other imperial towns which in the
tenth century profited from the favours conferred on them by
the Ottos. Once again we have the opportunity of observing
one of those phenomena of action and reaction so characteristic
of social life. The business profession was developing a community spirit, and the merchant gilds, like the syndicates of our
own day, must have been powerful and influential bodies, but
the concessions granted them by Germanic kings and emperors
out of generosity and self-interest had the effect of transforming
these private confraternities into official corporations, endowed

[1] Tiel, a town in the Low Countries, in the province of Guelders, on the Waal,
a branch of the Rhine.

[2] This chronicler, who was a monk of Saint-Symphorien of Metz and lived at
the beginning of the eleventh century, wrote a work entitled *De diversitate temporum*,
which had no very definite plan and was more in the nature of memoirs. The author
was particularly interested in the events taking place in the Low Countries. Cf.
Manitius, *Gesch. der lateinischen Literatur des Mittelalters*, II, pp. 278–283.

[3] 'Set licet pauca, non detrahendo, set ex intimo corde condolendo, hic inserere
quibus moribus et institutis isti Tielenses ab aliis viris differant. Homines sunt duri.'
De diversitate temporum, II, 19, in *P.L.* 140, col. 481.

[4] 'Judicia non secundum legem, set secundum voluntatem decernentes, et hoc ab
imperatore karta traditum et confirmatum dicunt.' Loc. cit. Note particularly this
reference to an imperial privilege granted expressly to these merchants. It is invaluable, since archives usually contain only documents relating to ecclesiastical
foundations, since they were the only establishments to care for their archives.

with powers of jurisdiction and their own code of laws (*jus mercatorum*). The process was slow but steady, and was helped on by medieval man's liking for regulation and privilege.

A historian of these corporations has shown[1] that the Tiel merchants headed the long line of merchant gilds. Their constitution has not been preserved; the oldest known to us are those of the *Caritet* of Valenciennes probably dating back to about 1050,[2] and the regulations of the merchant gild (*gilda mercatoria*) of St Omer,[3] the original edition of which appears to date from the late eleventh century. In the matter of gilds, as of merchant settlements, Flanders and the Rhineland were far in advance of the rest.

The long-debated question as to whether there was any link between these gilds and the old Roman *collegia* of merchants and craftsmen can be answered firmly in the negative. The problem has arisen chiefly in connexion with the Parisian 'hanse' of water-vendors; it has been said that their corporation was derived from that of the Parisian boatmen, 'nautes', whose existence is attested by an inscription of the time of Tiberius. In actual fact there was no connexion whatever between these two bodies separated by a thousand years of history,[4] just as all relationship has been disowned between the municipalities of the Late Empire and the medieval communes. The water-vendors appear on the stage of history only in the twelfth century. If ancestors have to be found for the merchant gilds, they should be sought not in the Gallo-Roman corporations, but in the Christian confraternities, which increased in number from the early days of Christianity 'for the needs of body and soul'.[5] We have, moreover, just seen that the early gilds were themselves well-meaning confraternities. Had the provost of

---

[1] E. Coornaert, *Les corporations en France avant 1789*, Paris, 1941, p. 56 et seq.

[2] E. Coornaert, 'Des confréries carolingiennes aux gildes marchandes', *Mélanges d'hist. sociale*, II, 1942, pp. 5–21.

[3] Published by Pirenne and Espinas, 'Les coutumes de la Gilde marchande de Saint-Omer', in *Le Moyen âge*, 1901, pp. 189–196.

[4] Emile Picarda has proved this quite definitely in a work entitled *Les marchands de l'eau, hanse parisienne et compagnie de l'eau*, Paris, 1901, Bibl. de l'Ec. des Hautes Etudes, Sc. philolog. et hist., fasc. 134. Cf. Pirenne, 'A propos de la hanse parisienne des marchands de l'eau', *Les villes et institutions urbaines*, pp. 193–197.

[5] The Church was born into a medley of confraternities which were taking the

the merchants of Paris, a vitally important section of the Paris municipality, been the direct successor of the provost of the water-vendors, the city would have been only too proud to link his origins with the boatmen who were contemporaries of Tiberius. This legendary claim to distinction must, however, be abandoned.

We have laid particular stress on markets, which, during the tenth century, increased in number in the Frankish Empire and most of all in Germany, because their creation had profound repercussions on town life and was an important factor in its transformation, but no illusions should be maintained about the volume of business transacted in them. The very insignificance of the coin chiefly used in trading, the silver denier, invites caution. There was as yet no question of capitalism. Gold was almost entirely absent from the transactions, at least from those carried out openly. The lending of capital was still unknown. For the dawn of medieval capitalism we have to turn to Venice. Several documents, though they are still few in number, throw light on its early stages.

It first appeared in the form of a contract of 'commenda', in which a man of means, with liquid capital at his disposal, and a number of gold *solidi* which he had saved up, lent his reserves to a merchant sailor. He unhesitatingly accepted his share of the risks inseparable from seagoing trade, then divided with him the profits of the undertaking if it succeeded.[1] Such loans were already being negotiated in Venice in the early ninth century, as may be seen from a bequest in the will of a wealthy Venetian, Giustiniano Partecipazio, in the year 829. His fortune consisted chiefly of land, but there is mention of a bequest of

place of the family and the disintegrating State. Le Bras, 'Les confréries chrétiennes. Problèmes et propositions', *Rev. hist. de Droit*, 1940–1941, p. 313. He goes on: 'Rien ne pouvait comprimer le besoin qu'ont les âmes de solidarités consenties. . . . Le principe fondamental des confréries chrétiennes qui est la solidarité spirituelle s'établissait fortement. Afin de préserver ou de délivrer du Purgatoire, Boniface créa, propagea des "familiarités" qui unissent les fidèles à une abbaye.' His disciple Lull continued the tradition which Benedict of Aniane generalized. The whole of the West was covered with monastic colonies of suppliants. In them may be found the origin of the gilds and the leagues (hanses). In the twelfth century the two words were identical in meaning.

[1] Yves Renouard, *Les hommes d'affaires italiens du moyen-âge*, Paris, 1949, pp. 14-15.

1,200 *livres* to come from *solidi* which he had increased by speculation. According to a clause in the will the legacy was to be paid out only if the merchandise was brought safely into harbour and was not shipwrecked.[1] Transactions of this kind increased in Venice during the ninth century; they were already common practice in 840, for the treaty concluded by the Emperor Lothar with the Doge of Venice for the maintenance of peace between that city and its neighbours refers to contracts of this kind;[2] it shows that the operation of lending money to a merchant for his business was not unknown in Venice at that date.[3]

In the *commenda* the capitalist alone provided money; the merchant sailor contributed only his labour. Other methods of lending also made their appearance in Venice in the following century. In 975 the widow of the Doge Pietro Candiano renounced the profits from contracts which had been entered into by her husband.[4] Besides the *accomentatio*, that is to say the *commenda*, the deed of renunciation mentions two others: the *rogadia*[5] and the *collegantia*. This latter contract, which was widely practised in Venice, was no longer a simple money loan but a specifically bilateral transaction (*societas*).[6] The capitalist provided the greater part of the money, but the merchant also contributed his quota, to which he added his labour. In the oldest known deed of *collegantia*, dated 1073, the capitalist lays down two-thirds of the capital and the merchant the other

[1] 'De laboratoriis solidis si salva de navigatione reversa fuerint.' Quoted by Gino Luzzatto, 'Les activités économiques du patriciat vénitien', *Ann. d'hist. éc. et soc.*, IX, 1937, p. 26. There is an English translation in R. Lopez and I. Raymond, *Medieval Trade in the Mediterranean World*, pp. 39–41.

[2] 'Et hoc stetit de cautionibus sive de quibuslibet commendationibus . . .' Pactum inter Lhotharium imperatorem et dominum Petrum ducem Venecie, art. 23, *Capitul.*, ed. Boretius, II, 1, p. 134.

[3] 'Si quis aliquid dederit ad negociandum.' Ibid.

[4] Y. Renouard, loc. cit.

[5] The *rogadia* is defined by the single word *precatio* in the Glossary of Du Cange, who refers back to the *Statuta Venetorum* of 1242. It was probably a request for a loan.

[6] According to A. Sayous, 'Méthodes commerciales en Italie', *Ann. d'hist. éc. et soc.*, I, 1929, p. 166, the two contracts, *accomentatio* and *collegantia*, were identical in origin. In both a capitalist entrusted to a merchant about to set out on a voyage goods to sell or capital for the purchase of goods which in turn were to be sold. In accordance with accepted practice, three-quarters of the profits went to capital and one-quarter to labour. For economic life in Venice during the tenth century, see Kretschmayr, *Geschichte von Venedig*, I, Gotha, p. 185 et seq.

third. As for the nature of the commercial transactions in which the Venetians engaged, it has been specified by the author of a valuable work on *Les hommes d'affaires italiens au moyen âge*.[1] They sought, he said, to dominate the stream of trade which linked Europe with the Near and Middle East. In Alexandria they sold slaves, wood and weapons from the West and brought back spices, woollen materials and also a little gold. This gold enabled them to buy in Constantinople silks, purple dye and luxury articles. All these goods were then re-exported to the urban centres of Lombardy.

If Venice was the first centre of genuine capitalist activity, it was because in the tenth century *aurea Venetia* was the only city in the Christian world with an upper class which possessed gold, acquired through its contacts with Byzantium and the Moslem world. Its example was followed, but at a later date, by Pisa and Genoa.[2]

These were still only the first signs of a nascent capitalism. Its spirit was slow to permeate Northern Europe, where fortunes consisted exclusively of land. Nevertheless towards the close of the eleventh century, with the growing practice of pilgrimages to distant parts[3] and the First Crusade, a more pressing need for ready money began to make itself felt, and trading in money made its appearance in a disguised form. Crusaders and pilgrims who were without deniers had to resort to credit to cover the expenses of their equipment and of their long journey. By a strange paradox it was the rich monasteries which became their bankers. They lent them the deniers required for their immediate needs, and the transaction allowed

---

[1] Y. Renouard, p. 16 et. seq.

[2] Ibid., p. 22. On the Genoese economy see Roberto Lopez, 'Aux origines du capitalisme génois', *Ann. d'hist. éc. et soc.*, IX, 1937, pp. 429–454.

[3] This statement appears to contradict Alphandéry's views on the spirit in which pious people in the tenth and eleventh centuries undertook these pilgrimages, and in particular that to the Holy Places. The spirit of poverty was an essential prerequisite, and no one, he states, set out without previously getting rid of his worldly possessions. *La Chrétienté et l'idée de croisade*, 1st part, Paris, 1954, coll. *L'évolution de l'humanité*, no. 38, p. 12. This was an ideal set before the pilgrims, and one which found its poetic expression in the Legend of St Alexis. The reality, however, was different. The strictest and most enthusiastic of pilgrims, even those who regarded the departure for Jerusalem as the final journey from which there was no return, could not dispense with certain material necessities.

these abbeys to lay out to good advantage the capital accruing from collection of their quit-rents.[1] The contract was a mortgage; the borrower left the monks a piece of his land from which they drew the income, and the resulting sum was not deducted from the total amount of their credit. In addition, if the money lent was not paid back on the agreed date of foreclosure, the abbey retained the property involved, so that mortgage was one of the methods by which monasteries acquired land,[2] until such time as a scrupulous Pope, Alexander III, forbade it in a Council held at Tours in the mid-twelfth century, on the grounds that it savoured of usury.

Unfamiliar with the idea of capitalism because they had not a sufficiently large currency and were still ignorant of the financial procedures by which the deficiency could be made good, *Francia occidentalis* and Germany, where trade was just gaining a foothold, made no attempt until the twelfth century to stimulate it by contributions of capital. Merchants and markets, as we have tried to prove, existed there at an early date, but there was still nothing in the nature of a banking organization, nor were there businessmen like those who appear to have been found in Venice as early as the ninth century.

[1] R. Genestal, *Rôle des monastères comme établissements de crédit étudié en Normandie du XIe à la fin du XIIIe siècle*, Paris, 1901, pp. 1–20. Later the author wonders how the mortgage benefited the borrower, and concludes that in addition to cases of financial distress, it was chiefly those setting out on long journeys, and above all for Jerusalem, who were most naturally led to mortgage their property. Cf. R. N. Sauvage, *L'abbaye de Saint-Martin de Troarn*, Caen, 1911, pp. 218–226. See also a 'gift' of 160 melgorian *sous* made by the monks of Saint-Victor de Marseille to two brothers setting out for Jerusalem, 'ad extinguendam paganorum sceleratam effusamque rabiem'. In return the crusaders gave, sold and delivered up (donamus, immo vendimus, tradimusque) a *mansus*. *Cartul. de Saint-Victor*, no. 143. This was a disguised loan against security. Many more examples could be quoted.

[2] Genestal, op. cit., p. 77, believes that this was the habitual aim of monks, the purchase of land being at that time the only lasting investment, and one which monks sought in preference to all others.

CHAPTER III

The Expansion and Development of Agriculture in the Eleventh Century

O UR ATTEMPT TO TRACE the revival of town life – reasonable though such a project may have seemed – has shown that the reality was far too complex to be accurately described by so simple a phrase. Town life did not disappear at the time of the Great Invasions, any more than after the Saracen conquest. It continued to exist, thanks to the Church, and even experienced a renaissance, as we have seen, under the early Carolingians. The *razzias* of the Northmen checked it in the second half of the ninth century, and it was only later and by slow stages that a new form of town life, that which was to be predominant in the Middle Ages, came into being. It was not until the end of the eleventh century and the appearance of the communes that it grew and developed in the kingdom of France.[1] In Germany, on the other hand, the tenth century was the decisive period. The town, unknown to the ancient Germans, originated there under the Ottos.

Rural life, however, presents a very different picture. There the transformation was fundamental, and the eleventh century was a decisive one. The documents themselves offer striking proof of this. Several regions have no charters at all until the end of the tenth century; the majority have only a few,[2] with

---

[1] 'Les concessions des communes en France commencent à la fin du XIe siècle'. Petit-Dutaillis, *Les communes françaises*, p. 18.

[2] Those dated the tenth century and earlier, that is from a time when abbeys still had no chancellery and no efficiently organized archives, should be treated with suspicion. Many were forged after the event. The detection of these forgeries is an art in which certain scholars such as Julien Havet have excelled and have shown remarkable critical skill.

the exception of Burgundy which, spared by the Northmen, welcomed in a stream of monks and large numbers of wandering laymen from the late ninth century, and which enjoyed an unusually early tranquillity.[1] From the early eleventh century onwards, however, documents are to be found everywhere in considerable numbers. There was a rebirth of the written word symbolic of that taking place in economic life.

Medievalists have sought a reason for this miraculous leap forward. Demography has suggested one: 'From the middle of the tenth century', wrote Pirenne,[2] 'the population of Western Europe, delivered at long last from the pillaging of Saracens, Northmen and Hungarians, took an upward trend which cannot be assessed accurately, but the results of which can be observed in the following century. It is quite clear that the domanial organization was now no longer adequate to cope with the excess of births over deaths. A growing number of individuals, obliged to leave their family farms, had to look about them for new resources.' In order to satisfy the needs of an increasing population, more cultivable land was required,[3] which explains why the eleventh century has been called the great age of land clearance.

Other and less spectacular causes contributed towards this transformation. The Viking invasions in Western Europe, those of the Saracens on the shores of the Mediterranean, and to a lesser degree the incursions of the Hungarians in the east, brought in their wake devastation and upheaval comparable to, sometimes even more serious than, those caused by the Great

---

[1] See above, p. 221.

[2] *La civilisation occidentale au moyen âge du XIe au milieu du XVe siècle*, p. 62. M. Genicot also, *Les lignes de faîte du moyen âge*, p. 206, is quite certain that from the close of the tenth century, or in any case from the middle of the eleventh, the population of the West increased quickly and steadily.

[3] G. Duby, *La société aux XIe et XIIe siècles dans la région mâconnaise*, p. 8, has made a special study of the possibilities of expansion necessitated by a high coefficient of family increase in this region. He shows that they were reduced by restrictions on marriage, large numbers of children entering religion or growing old, unmarried, in the family home. Moreover it is difficult to trace the genealogy of families at this period, especially peasant families. Duby notes that out of 48 heads of families living about the year A.D. 1000, and whose family trees are known, 6 had more than three sons, 12 had three sons, 15 had two and 15 had only one. Daughters are not mentioned.

Invasions. Many monasteries were ruined, and when the invaders had departed were compelled to reorganize their landed property on new bases. It is a known fact that large-scale farming stands up to political and economic crises less effectively than cultivation based on family farms. As often happens in troubled times, the conditions of life underwent a change. Strange though it may seem, there were still slaves in the ninth century. In almost every deed of sale or of gift connected with a domain, there is a reference to: *mancipia utriusque sexus*.[1] They were the accessories of the *villa*. They were handed over to the new owner along with the streams and the mills. They were an integral part of the estate. The condition of the serfs or fellow-freedmen who had been given a *mansus* was different. They were liable for forced labour which was often hard and sometimes arbitrary, and to harsh restrictions, such as that which forbade them to marry serfs belonging to a different lord, but they were peasants (*rustici*) who were compelled to do only definite and specified farmwork on their master's reserve. They were not, like the slave in the ancient world, or like the *mancipium* of the Early Middle Ages, until he ceased to exist, 'human horse-power',[2] available for any and every purpose. The gradual extinction of slavery[3] which still lingered on in the Carolingian era with the survival of numerous *mancipia*, resulted in a marked falling off in the supply of

---

[1] This is no empty formula. For example a deed of gift to the Abbey of Beaulieu in April 916, *Cartul. Beaulieu*, no. lx, contains the names of the *mancipia* of both sexes to be found on the estate (*caput mansionile*). The history of the disappearance of slavery in the kingdom of France could be written only after a systematic scrutiny of tenth-century charters. The last mention of *mancipia utriusque sexus* occurs in a royal diploma of 962. *Recueil des actes de Lothaire*, p. 37, no. xcii.

[2] This vivid phrase is borrowed from Ct. Lefebvre des Noëttes, *L'attelage, le cheval de selle à travers les âges*, p. 183, to whom we are indebted for many shrewd observations on the subject of slavery. Ibid., pp. 174–183. Marc Bloch has rightly stressed that serfs, who inherited the old name for a slave (*servi*), were not really human horse-power. 'Les inventions médiévales', *Ann. d'hist. éc. et soc.*, VII, 1935, pp. 634–643.

[3] It seems likely that this extinction was a slow rather than a rapid process. Future historians, in just the same way, will note the decline of domestic service in the twentieth century without being able to fix any definite date for its disappearance. As Marc Bloch says (ibid.), the abolition of slavery was not complete and was confined to Christian society. Elsewhere war and the slave-trade continued to provide owners with 'human cattle', Greeks, Slavs, Negroes and Moors.

12. A plough and a harrow, Medieval wagons XIIth century (from Bib. Nat. MS Latin, 14267)

'horse-power'. In order to counteract this, some modification had to be made in the organization of work.

Failure to keep roads in repair may have been one of the consequences of the decrease in slave labour, but bread-making and the grinding of flour had to go on. The water-mill took the place of the stone roller and the grindstone which needed men to work them.[1] Its use became general in Carolingian times. Thus a new driving power, that of water, replaced what man could no longer provide, which explains why this particular invention, already known in the first century B.C., only came into general use at a comparatively late date. Its widespread adoption was delayed as long as slaves were available to work the grindstones.[2]

The more efficient use of animal power was the chief discovery of the Early Middle Ages. Three inventions greatly increased the haulage power of the horse and the ox: the shoulder collar, shoeing, and the harnessing of draught animals one behind the other.[3] Harness of the modern type first appeared in the tenth century, and shoeing in the time of Charlemagne.[4] Whether or not the decline of slavery preceded the change in harnessing, as Marc Bloch has stated,[5] is of little importance. The fact that it came first does not rule out any connexion between the two. In fact it illustrates an awareness of the need to increase the power of those animals which were called on to make up for the lack of slaves. A glance through eleventh-century charters reveals a large number of purchases of horses and at a relatively high price.[6]

---

[1] Marc Bloch, 'Avènement et conquêtes du moulin à eau', *Ann. d'hist. éc. et soc.*, VII, 1935, pp. 538–563.　　[2] Roger Grand, *L'agriculture au moyen âge*, p. 619.

[3] Lefebvre des Noëttes, *L'attelage, passim*.

[4] The scale of dues for Meron (Anjou) from 1080 to 1082, *Cartul. de Saint-Aubin*, I, p. 263, makes a distinction between the shod and the unshod animal. The former had to pay two deniers, the latter only one, an indication of the importance shoeing had assumed in the eleventh century.

[5] 'Les inventions médiévales', *Ann. d'hist. éc. et soc.*, VII, 1935, p. 634 et seq.

[6] The following examples are taken from the second half of the eleventh century: 'Dedimus ei quendam equum quatuor libras valentem.' *Cartul. de Saint-Aubin d'Angers*, I, p. 308. – 'Quendam caballum quinquaginta solidorum.' Ibid., p. 311. – 'Quendam caballum quatuor libras valentem.' Ibid., p. 316. – 'Caballum emptum LX sol.' *Cartul. de Saint-Vincent du Mans*, no. 459. It will be seen that a horse was then worth 2½ to 4 *livres* in country districts.

The decline of slavery, followed by the total disappearance of the *mancipia* during the troubled period of the late ninth and the tenth centuries, had its repercussions on the management and organization of the domain. The *mancipia* worked in gangs or individually on the reserves of the great domains. In order to achieve the same results without them, it would have been necessary to exact far more forced labour from the tenants of *mansi* and to compel them to undertake even more intensive work on the *indominicatum*. It would have been a waste of time even to ask them! Those liable to forced labour were already neglecting the tasks which lay so heavily upon them, and the agents supervising their efforts (*avoués*, mayors, *villici*), who were far from conscientious and greedy for gain, diverted most of the profits to themselves.[1] In face of the dissatisfaction caused by a traditional, but obsolete method of farming, many ecclesiastical landowners, and probably laymen too, dropped the system of direct exploitation which had become not only unproductive and costly, but often impossible; they abandoned the system of forced labour, and no longer exacted from their tenants anything beyond rent in money and dues in kind.[2] They shared out the greater part of the reserve amongst various tenants, keeping for themselves just enough to satisfy the needs of their families. In Gaston Roupnel's[3] apt phrase, they replaced the system of direct exploitation by one of regular income. They began to regard themselves as landlords.[4]

This evolution was to end in the triumph of the small farm

[1] A. Luchaire, *Manuel des institutions françaises*, p. 286, and particularly Ch. E. Perrin, *Rech. sur la seign. rur.*, p. 671 et seq.

[2] We find a heartfelt and even naïve example of the discontent caused by direct exploitation in the preamble of a notice taken from the Cartulary of the nuns of La Charité d'Angers: 'De terra tradita ad vineas aedificandas. Inter alia bona que multa et maxima tempore Teburgis abbatisse fuerunt facta . . . hoc maximum bonum fuit factum: scilicet terra Elemosinarie . . . ad vineas edificandas fuit tradita. Videns vero congregatio sancta magnam laboriositatem terre et omnia necessaria, videlicet boves, bubulcos, et cetera, *invenerunt lucrum satis parvissimum propter nimium dispendium*. . . . Itaque terra ad vineas edificandas hominibus est tradita.' Marchegay, *Archives d'Anjou*, III, p. 20. The admission is significant, and the only available remedy lay in handing over to expert farmers a ruinous concern which did not bring in enough profit to cover expenses.

[3] *Hist. de la campagne française*, p. 270.

[4] 'De grand propriétaire à rentier du sol', is the title of one of Marc Bloch's sub-chapters in *Les caractères originaux de l'histoire rurale française*.

already in existence during the Late Empire, and in the simultaneous decline of the domanial system, but it was given momentum and spread over a wider area because of the increase in population which marked the eleventh century. It was not only large estates which were divided; small ones too were being split up. The *mansus* had already become too big for the requirements of a single household.[1] It was being replaced by new smallholdings, which were given different names in different parts of the country. Several of these such as the 'bordage' in the West appeared only in the eleventh century. Other new features of rural life began to emerge at this same period, which was decisive in the history of the western countryside: a uniform redistribution of cultivated land within the farm itself, the creation of burgs, the organization of the village which replaced the *villa* within the framework of the rural seigneurie.

*

The late tenth and the eleventh centuries witnessed a profound change in the appearance of the countryside, due first and foremost to the increased area of cultivated land. In the north an extensive drainage programme was initiated by the Counts of Flanders. Areas of land to be cleared of forest and intersected with dykes were granted to incoming settlers, and workmen receiving land lost no time in forming those associations later to be known as 'wateringues'.[2] As this work of land clearance went doggedly forward, the area became thickly populated. Numerous villages came into being, recognizable today by their names ending in *capelle*, the Latin origin of which betrays their more recent creation. The example set by the draining of the polders in Holland and Flanders was followed in the gulf of St Omer, where new lands (*terre nove*), reclaimed from the sea, were brought into cultivation,[3] and along the Atlantic seaboard, in Poitou and along the coast of Saintonge.[4]

One factor went almost unrecorded, and that was a more concentrated, less casual use of the land. 'About 1050', writes

[1] See above, p. 195.
[2] H. Pirenne, *Histoire de Belgique*, I, p. 149 et seq.
[3] H. Sée, *Les classes rurales*, p. 226.
[4] R. Grand, *L'agriculture*, p. 255.

Marc Bloch,[1] 'the great age of forest clearance began, the greatest increase in cultivable area ever witnessed by our land since prehistoric times.' This laborious task was chiefly a battle against the tree. The land clearances coincided with a rise in population, for which the settlers were chiefly responsible. As so often happens when various factors appear to emerge simultaneously, the historian finds it difficult to establish a correct relationship between them and to distinguish between cause and effect. It seems likely that a general peace, following on a hundred years of invasion and anarchy led, as after so many wars, to an increased birth-rate and also brought about a revival of agriculture which at that time was the principal form of economic activity. An ever-increasing body of documentation has made it possible to trace the various forms taken by this agrarian renaissance in different parts of the western world.

The area around Paris, which from the end of the tenth century had become the Ile-de-France and the centre of the realm, had been the scene of an unusually early agricultural development, of which the Polyptyque of Irminon offers the most convincing proof, but land clearance went steadily on. The early Capetians appear to have been animated by a concern for the public safety when they intensified the work of forest clearance along the road from Orleans to Paris which joined their customary place of residence during the eleventh century to their new capital. Various place-names are significant: *Les Essarts* is one which recalls the memory of those distant events.[2] These same kings, however, left untouched in the wide belt around Paris numerous forests, in particular that of Orleans, which were hunting reserves. French scholarship has not yet produced an exhaustive study of La Beauce, yet it would be interesting to know how this region, 'with its subsoil of bone-dry chalk',[3] became a magnificent corn-growing district. We

---

[1] *Les caractères originaux*, p. 5.

[2] R. Grand, op. cit., p. 248. The word comes from the Latin *exarare* = to plough up. This place-name was beginning to be fairly common in the eleventh century: 1071–1080. 'Terrae noviter ibi exertae quae nova exarta vulgo dicuntur.' *Cartul. Dunois de Marmoutier*, p. 34.

[3] The description applied to it in René Musset's *Géographie de l'histoire. Hist. de France*, libr. Larousse, I, p. 48.

know only that in the early twelfth century the monks of Saint-Père de Chartres made every effort to install settlers on their lands – a move obviously intended to intensify cultivation. The monks of Saint-Denis also were anxious to get a better return from their lands, and in the account he wrote of his administration Suger, describing the areas cleared at Vaucresson, goes on to say that he had leased them out in order to ensure for his abbey a fixed income which direct cultivation would not have brought in.[1]

The eleventh century was a turning point in the agricultural life of Western France. It is true that neither Maine nor Anjou were waste land, and we have seen[2] that in Merovingian times there were already many settlements (*vici*) in the diocese of Le Mans, but the régime of large-scale landownership did not take root in that region as it did in Eastern Gaul and in the Ile-de-France. The greater part of the land remained uncultivated. At the beginning of the Middle Ages, it was an area covered with moorland and forest, with here and there small farms in temporary cultivation.[3] Many hermits sought refuge there in order to lead lives of asceticism, and they were still there in the twelfth century, in remote corners untouched by the agricultural revival.[4] The end of the tenth century, however, saw the dawn of a real resurrection, and a mass of documents from the Cartularies of various abbeys, Saint-Vincent du Mans, Marmoutier, Saint-Aubin d'Angers, La Trinité de Vendôme, and many others enable us to follow step by step the progress of land clearance and the repopulating of the countryside. This improvement was effected in a uniform manner almost everywhere. Land was given to farmers known as *ruricolae, rustici, hospites*. It was generally uncultivated, and at times the person drawing up the deed went out of his way to stress how desolate it was.[5]

---

[1] R. Grand, op. cit., p. 105.   [2] See p. 65.

[3] 'L'économie agraire et le peuplement des pays bocagers', *Revue de Synthèse*, XVII, no. 1, 1939, p. 46.

[4] Gabriel Le Bras, 'Part privilégiée du Maine dans l'histoire religieuse', *La Province du Maine*, 2nd series, XXXIII, 1953, pp. 179–180. See also René Musset, *Le Bas Maine*, Paris, 1917, p. 231.

[5] 'Predicta tellus, receptaculum ferarum, consita arboribus inutilibus scilicet vepribus, dumis et sentibus, horribilis, sterilis, et vacua ab omni habitatore humano erat.' *Cartul. de Saint-Vincent du Mans*, no. 242.

The area was assessed and measured and the annual dues to be paid by the new owner were fixed in proportion to the cultivable surface.[1] The plots were surrounded by a ditch, and these invaluable documents provide the answer to a question which puzzled Marc Bloch when, in a study of these enclosed lands, he wrote:[2] 'The most serious query at the moment is the actual antiquity of the hedges.' The answer is now quite clear: 'These hedges began to appear in the eleventh century.' The means of enclosure consisted of a ditch, a bank and a hedge. The ditch was the most frequently mentioned in deeds, and it has been suggested that it was dug to ensure the draining away of water in districts where the soil was non-porous. This is not a very likely explanation.[3] The most essential requirement was a protective barrier to keep out the cattle grazing in the meadows and still more to prohibit communal grazing on fields brought into cultivation by the strenuous toil of the first settlers. The hedge became the symbol of those numerous small family farmsteads which rarely have foundation deeds going back earlier than the eleventh century.

The wooded districts of Maine and Anjou and the adjacent areas owe their basic originality to the fact that they were brought into cultivation comparatively late. The traditions of the domanial régime lay less heavily than elsewhere on those who cleared the land. They did not come up against the compulsory servitudes of the *villa*, being bound only by those of the rural seigneurie, and in those districts which had no domanial past such services were merely those resulting from the usurpation of royal rights, the right of 'ban' (*bannum*) and

---

[1] Ex: 'Que priusquam exculta fuerit mensurabitur et juxta mensuram reddet et censum.' Same *Cartul.*, no. 226. See 'L'établissement des bourgs', *Le Moyen âge*, 1937, pp. 14–15.

[2] 'Les paysages agraires, essai de mise au point', *Ann. d'hist. éc. et soc.*, VIII, 1936, p. 271.

[3] The explanation has been suggested by G. Roupnel, *Hist. de la campagne fr.*, p. 229, but with his deep feeling for everything connected with the land, he has not pressed the point unduly, and has shown (p. 230) that by far the most important part of the enclosure was the hedge, and that the farmer was obliged to enclose his property and fence off his field. Proof of this is to be found in the charters themselves, as in the following example, dating from the early twelfth century, *Cartul. de Saint-Aubin d'Angers*, I, p. 148: 'Concessit etiam de silva que juxta est quantum opus erit ad claudenda ipsa prata.'

the right of 'voirie' (*vicarium*).[1] The word generally used in Maine to denote the small farm granted to a newcomer was 'bordage' (*bordagium*).[2] Its structure was almost always the same.[3] The nucleus was a house (*domus* or *borda*)[4] already built or still to be erected. Beside it was a garden in which the settler grew vegetables (peas and beans) and textile plants (flax and hemp).[5] In almost every case, quite near his house and adjoining the garden, there were one or more plots of good land known as 'ouches' (*osca*), an old Celtic word which Gregory of Tours was the first to bring to notice.[6] It was sown with wheat. The 'ouche' provided the farmer with bread, but other plots were given him as well as meadows. The 'bordage' was usually worked with the help of draught animals and it was even customary to assess its area by the number of oxen used in cultivating it.[7] Yet the forest remained always close at hand and a description of the 'bordage' is rounded off by an indication of the rights of forestage and pannage. According to a tradition copied perhaps from Germany, the peasant had permission to send his pigs to feed in the nearby forest and also to gather enough wood for the building of his wooden house,[8] for his fences, his barrel hoops and also his domestic fuel.[9]

[1] The *vicaria* was the sum total of the dues collected by a subordinate official on the orders of the count, who was known as the *vicarius*. Cf. *L'établ. des bourgs*, p. 7 et seq.

[2] See *Agrarzustände im westlichen Frankreich während des Hochmittelalters*, VSWG, XXIX, 1936, pp. 105–113.

[3] The following charter from the *Cartulaire de la Trinité de Vendôme*, II, p. 40, no. 327, is typical and shows the type of concession given to those responsible for clearing the land: 1086 'Ad rusticorum insuper ruricolarum mansionem construendam dedit, *ut est consuetudo*, terram videlicet ad edificandam domum curtimque cum orto et unicuique rustico dimidium arpentum terrae ad ruricolandum.' See our commentary in 'Défrichement et peuplement rural', *Le Moyen âge*, 1948, pp. 84–85.

[4] *Cartul. de la Trinité*, II, p. 23, no. 318.

[5] 1067. *Cartul. de S. Vincent*, no. 483, 'fabos et pisicum, cannabum et linum'.

[6] *Défrichement et peuplement rural*, p. 86.

[7] 1060: 'Terra duorum boum.' *Cartul. de la Trinité*, I, p. 242, no. 138. – Eleventh century: 'Terram . . . que quatuor booum arature sufficere possit.' *Cartul. Quimperlé*, no. 23.

[8] Many buildings, even churches, were still made of wood. The church at Sceaux (Sarthe) was not rebuilt in stone until the latter half of the eleventh century: 'Tempore quo eadem ecclesia edificari de lapideo opere cepta est, que tunc adhuc de vilibus constructa erat lignis', we read in an entry in the *Cartul. de Saint-Vincent*, no. 143, somewhere between 1050 and 1100.

[9] This was the right of pannage and estovers. The eleventh- and twelfth-century

As land clearance progressed, the countryside became a chequered pattern of woods and farmland, of contrasting light and shade. The language of eleventh-century man conveyed this contrast by two words which continually recur in charters: *boscum et planum*.[1] It found its expression in literature too when the Norman poet Wace wrote of 'cil del bocage, et cil del plain'.[2] Place-names also have perpetuated it, as in Saint-Remy-du-Plain and Saint-Rigomer-des-Bois, two neighbouring communes in the Department of Sarthe. This contrast reminds us of the unremitting work of clearance which was transforming the 'wood' into the 'plain',[3] whilst preserving as much of the forest as was needed for the requirements of the population and the sport of the huntsmen.

Clearance proceeded at such an increasing pace that it almost took on the character of a vast collective enterprise. It might almost be compared to the modern housing estates springing up around our cities, and as in their case too, one may well ask whether the work proceeded haphazardly or according to a preconceived plan. In many cases it was the latter. A series of charters, uniform in character and almost always dating from the second half of the eleventh and the first third of the twelfth century, show us burgs actually being founded by ecclesiastical and secular overlords. To make a burg, to erect a burg, to institute a burg,[4] are the phrases generally used by those drawing up deeds. Burgs grew in number in the country as well as on the outskirts of towns, and seigneurs vied with each other in founding them. Thus in 1055

charters frequently mention these concessions, both the grazing of pigs (*pasnagium porcorum*) and the permission to gather wood 'ad ardendum et ad domos construendas et ad circulos faciendos'. It may be added that the exercising of them was a frequent cause of litigation. See *L'établissement des bourgs*, p. 16, n. 58.

[1] *Cartul. Dunois de Marmoutier*, no. 132. Cf. 1070: 'Miles Simon . . . dedit terram nomine Campus planus in bosco et plano.' *Cartul. Trinité*, I, p. 360, no. 227.

[2] Marc Bloch, *Les caractères originaux*, p. 58.

[3] The following deed gives us some idea of the actual process of clearance in the eleventh century. The men began by felling trees in one sector of the forest and building houses on the site; they cleared a further area only if the need arose: 'Do quoque eis de Plessiaco ad habitationem tali tenore ut *prius constituant domos* in plano et, cum opus fuerit, in prefata sylva.' *Cartul. de la Couture du Mans*, no. 13.

[4] *L'établissement des bourgs*, p. 3.

the seigneur of Bouère[1] and the monks of Marmoutier founded burgs close together, and each forbade the other to lure away his neighbour's settlers into the rival and adjacent burg. This keen competition was symptomatic. The seigneurs who were founding burgs were anxious to create centres of agricultural activity as well as of trade, since rural burgs, like those being founded on the periphery of cities, had their own markets. There was, in fact, no essential difference between them. It would therefore be pointless to enumerate the privileges enjoyed by the settlers in these burgs, since they were the same as the concessions granted to those in the suburban burgs. One point alone needs to be remembered – that they were often built on the sites of cemeteries,[2] and it has been discovered that the reason for this strange choice was the desire of the monastic founders that their settlers should enjoy the security afforded by consecrated ground.

The eleventh-century burgs did much to bring new life and vigour to the countryside. Side by side with the old *vici*, they introduced into Western France, which had neither those large villages of Germanic origin to be found in the east, nor the settlements formed by Gallo-Roman *villae* in other parts of

---

[1] Mayenne, ibid., p. 6, n. 30. At about the same time (1060) the same monks of Marmoutier received from Gui, seigneur of Laval, a piece of land on which to found a burg near his castle, that is near Laval, 'quandam terram ad burgum faciendum juxta castrum suum id est juxta Vallem'. *Cartul. manceau de Marmoutier*, p. 331. This was the beginning of the town of Laval. There is no point in drawing what would be a purely artificial distinction between an urban and a rural burg, except in cases where, as with Saint-Vincent du Mans, a burg was created within the suburb of a city. Otherwise all burgs had a similar origin. Certain of them, however, favoured by a variety of circumstances, became towns in the course of centuries, as did Laval. Others such as Bouère and the majority of the rest, remained rural settlements.

[2] See for instance the Abbot of La Couture's reference to his men in the cemetery at Tennie: 'hominibus nostris de cimiterio de Teneia', *Cartul. Couture*, no. 152. Cf. also in the same Cartulary, no. 49: '1135. Preceptum capelle de Vado Seclart.' The matter concerned a chapel, a cemetery and a burg which the Abbot of La Couture wanted to build at Guécelard, a dependency of the parish of Parigné-le-Pôlin, of which the monks of Saint-Mesmin d'Orléans were patrons. The monks of the two monasteries reached the following agreement: 'Cimiterium de quo agitur in spacio duorum arpennorum extendetur et sacrabitur et quicquid de cimiterio et de hominibus *in eo manentibus* ecclesie pertinens exierit monachorum Culture erit.' Consequently the settlers attached to the new burg were accommodated in the cemetery, which had just been built and consecrated.

Gaul, fair-sized enclaves of population living together in groups. On the whole, however, the scattered dwelling was the normal pattern of population in wooded country. This is evident from the names of the 30,000 inhabited places listed in the Topographical Dictionary of Sarthe. Many of them consist of patronymics with the suffix *-erie* or *-ière* tacked on. Careful search would in some cases bring to light the names of the first men who settled on the 'bordages'.[1]

Brittany was no more familiar with the classic domanial régime of the Carolingian period than were the forest regions. The *villae* there were small in size, and the framework of rural life was the parish (*plebs*) itsclf divided into 'trèves' (*tribus*).[2] Yet the age of great forest clearances left its mark in the province, and in the eleventh century we find new farms coming into existence and known as 'borderies' and 'hébergements'.[3] Monastic burgs were created in the eleventh century and as in Maine it was sometimes into cemeteries that the monks attracted outside settlers, so as to put them beyond the reach of any authority other than their own.[4]

Burgs were established in Normandy also. Nowhere had the Scandinavian invasions wrought such havoc as in this province, but though no one disputes the magnitude of the devastation, scholars are not agreed about the nature of the economic changes which took place in Normandy during the eleventh century. Basing their theories on a variety of arguments, linguistic, toponymic, textual, the 'Scandinavists', as they have

[1] We shall quote only one example. The place known as La Grafardière (commune of Courdemanche, Sarthe) owes its name to Robert Grafard who owned it at the end of the eleventh century. *Cartul. S. Vincent*, no. 244.

[2] See above, p. 198. See J. Loth, *L'émigration bretonne en Armorique*, and René Largillière, *Les Saints et l'organisation chrétienne primitive dans l'Armorique bretonne*, Rennes, 1925.

[3] *Cartul. de Redon*, no. 312. Cf. H. Sée, *Etude sur les classes rurales en Bretagne*, p. 30.

[4] The Abbot of Redon and, the monk Josselin agreed to the request of a widow who had come with her two children to ask the latter for a piece of land in the cemetery of La Primaudière, so that she could build a house there and live permanently 'sub dominatione ac tuicione abbatis et monachorum'. *Cartul Redon*, p. 335, no. 379. The following deed, taken from the same cartulary, is even more significant: 'Praeterea concessit ut supradicti monachi habeant in perpetuum sub sua dominatione homines quos de extraneis partibus adduxerint et in predicto cimiterio secum habitare fecerint ita quod nulli mortalium in aliquo nec in parvo nec in magno sint obnoxii nisi S. Salvatori suisque monachis.'

been called,[1] have endeavoured to prove that the Normans and
their dukes introduced a new régime when they took possession
of the country. A famous text by the historian of the early
dukes, Dudo de Saint-Quentin,[2] has been invoked as evidence
of this agricultural revolution. The land of Normandy was waste
and desolate, writes the chronicler, it was without knights and
was no longer under the plough, it was also devoid of cattle and
uninhabited by men. It no longer offered any means of livelihood. It was then, Dudo goes on, that Rollo began to measure
out the land for his companions and to divide it up with a cord
for his followers. This partition of the deserted Norman land
by means of a cord is a legend, thought up by a clerk with a
lively imagination, who having himself seen land being divided
into plots, invented a wholesale carving up of the neglected
Norman countryside, and gave the credit to the first of the
Norman dukes. Whilst not denying the Norse contribution, we
cannot subscribe to the theory that the newcomers brought
about a systematic revolution. Agricultural development in
Normandy followed the same lines as in neighbouring provinces; yet we should beware of going to the opposite extreme
and purporting to discover astonishing evidence of permanence
in a region from which others have declared that the Vikings
swept away all traces of a previous domanial civilization.[3] It is
in fact striking to find so many settlers (*hôtes*) mentioned in
Norman charters of the eleventh century; in Normandy, as in
Maine and Brittany, there were 'bordages' as well as 'char-
ruées', or small plots of land cultivated with a single plough.[4]
These are proof of the fragmentation of former great domains

[1] Lucien Musset, *Les domaines de l'époque franque et les destinées du régime domanial du
IXe au XIe siècle* (Notes pour servir d'introduction à l'histoire foncière de la Normandie), Caen, 1945, p. 10.

[2] *De moribus et actis primorum Normanniae ducum* (ed. Lair, p. 147). Dudo, who was
a Canon of Saint-Quentin and whom the Comte de Vermandois had sent on a
mission to Richard I, Duke of Normandy, began to write this work about the year
1000 at the latter's request, and finished it about 1017. Manitius, *Gesch. der latein.
Liter.*, II, pp. 257–265, is severely critical of this chronicler, and accuses him
of a total lack of critical ability. Dudo wrote down everything that was told him
without making any attempt to ascertain the truth. His statements must be accepted
with caution.

[3] L. Musset, op. cit., p. 77.

[4] Ibid. p. 65.

and of the spread of small farms. The fact that in certain deeds the *clausula* relating to water-courses may still occur just as in deeds of gift for *villae* in Merovingian times, need occasion no surprise and should not lead to exaggerated conclusions; formulae are notoriously conservative. On the other hand it is worth noting the disappearance of *mancipia* from the wording of the deeds,[1] evidence that Normandy was drawn into the movement which ended in the suppression of slavery. If gifts of *villae* still figure in some diplomas, it should be remembered that the temporal establishments of dispossessed abbeys had to be built up again,[2] and a Duke of Normandy could hardly compensate these great foundations by the mere paltry offer of a few plots of land. On the whole the agricultural revival of Normandy in the eleventh century presents the same features as that in the forest regions.

Yet another remote province presents this same picture of a devastated countryside which for several centuries had dragged out a mute, poverty-stricken existence and which, freed of its invaders, rose again from its ruins during the eleventh century – that was Provence. The wretchedness of its condition in Carolingian times can only be guessed at through a few sparse documents such as the fragment of the polyptyque of Saint-Victor de Marseille[3] discovered in 1854. It is a description, written about 802, of thirteen *villae* belonging to the abbey. Most of the holdings of which these domains consisted were referred to as *absae*, meaning empty and deserted; only a few sheep grazed on the others. Conditions everywhere were lamentable. Yet the very silence of the texts, almost unbroken for several hundred years, is even more eloquent. The cartulary of this extremely ancient abbey contains hardly a single document previous to the early eleventh century. In that of Lérins, the famous monastery which up to the sixth century was one of the centres of religious and intellectual life in the Christian world, the oldest genuine deed belongs to the year

---

[1] L. Musset, op. cit., pp. 58–59.

[2] See for example F. Lot, *Etudes sur l'abbaye de Saint-Wandrille, passim.*

[3] *Dict. d'archéologie chrétienne*, X, 2nd part, art. Marseille, coll. 2232. The text is published in the *Cartul. de Saint-Victor*, ed. B. Guérard, pp. 633–654.

990, a date which coincides with the expulsion of the Saracens from La Garde-Freinet which was their stronghold. The full-scale campaign conducted by the Count of Provence, William the Liberator (973 or 983), set the country free. It marked the beginning of an economic revival in Provence and the Alpine region of South-eastern Gaul, as well as in Catalonia.[1]

The revival of agricultural activity assumed an unusual form which may be accounted for by the anarchy which had pre-vailed in those regions up to that time. Great *villae* may have existed there during the Late Empire, but in the tenth century they were no more than a vague memory; not the slightest trace of them remained. As for the people, they had sought refuge in villages perched on hilltops, where the inhabitants lived crowded together, a type of settlement characteristic of the Mediterranean regions and going back to a very remote past. This high, fortified village has remained typical of Provençal settlements. The word which most accurately defined them was *castrum*, but the general term *villa* was also used for settlements of this type, which were often owned jointly by several masters[2] and rounded off by a cluster of lands grouped around them and at the foot of the hill. This is yet another instance of the fluidity of meaning characteristic of the vocabulary of medieval charters, and which makes them difficult to interpret with any degree of accuracy.

With this revival, which brought a new awakening to a region which had long been sunk in apathy and inertia, the word *mansus* reappeared in Provençal charters just at the time when the abbeys were rebuilding their estates. They scarcely ventured now to lay claim to whole *villae*, but contented them-selves with small domanial units which are often known as *mansi*. The Provençal *mansus* is freehold property; it must not be thought of as the appendage of a *villa*.[3] It was essentially a

---

[1] Proof of this is to be found in the diplomas granted by King Lothar to the monasteries of Ripoll, Rosas, San Cugat del Valles between 982 and 984, as well as to Gui, Duke of Roussillon, to whom were given empty lands situated along the sea-coast from Collioure to Banyuls (9 July 981). *Recueil des actes de Lothaire*, nos. 45, 49, 50, 51.

[2] See '*Quelques aperçus sur le manse en Provence au X⁰ et au XI⁰ siècles*', in *Mélanges Clovis Brunel.*   [3] Ibid.

dwelling, a farmer's smallholding. The farmer himself gave it its individuality and its name, as may be seen from the fact that the *mansus* was renamed when it passed into other hands.[1] Whilst in other provinces the *mansus* eventually came to mean nothing more than a unit of land measurement before going completely out of use, in Provence it was gradually moving towards the meaning attached by Mistral to the word *mas* in his *Trésor dou Felibrige*: 'A country house, a property, a farm.'

In actual fact the farmer of the Provençal *mansus*, the *cultor*, closely resembled the *hospes* met with elsewhere. In most cases he was only the tenant, and owed the freeholder, its real owner, a yearly payment, either quit-rent or a due called the *tasca*.[2] This consisted of a portion of the harvest and was a kind of field-rent. The rights of the former occupants do not always appear to have been respected, and long after the expulsion of the 'pagans' the recollection lingered on of the violence with which many had hurled themselves upon the lands newly restored to cultivation, and had trampled down the old boundaries.[3] The geographical nature of the region and its settlement pattern did not give rise to the construction of burgs similar to those in the wooded areas. The *castrum*, the hill village, several centuries old, took their place. These hill villages, however, also had their markets, and the cramped quarters in which their inhabitants lived fostered early in their history a strong communal spirit, with the result that sooner

---

[1] 1080: 'Sciebant scriptum hominem qui excoluerat mansum nomine Benedet Pela a quo homine accepit nomen Mansum Benedet Pela. Longo tempore post obitum Benedet Pela venerunt duo successores ejus qui inter se diviserunt mansum in duas partes. Unus vocabatur Salamus et alter Fereng. Posthec mutatum est nomen: una pars vocata est Salamuns et altera Fereng.' *Cartul. de Saint-Victor*, no. 1089. This account also gives us an example of the splitting up of a *mansus*.

[2] See ibid., and the same *Cartul.*, no. 207. The *tasca*, which is also found in Burgundy and Dauphiné, was the standard payment in areas which had recently been cleared. It was convenient for the lessee, who was sure of having nothing to pay so long as his land was producing nothing, and it guaranteed him against the fluctuating hazards of production, but it was less satisfactory for the seigneur whom it obliged to exercise a strict supervision.

[3] See the preamble of the Bref de Cadière (*breve de Cathedra*) of the late tenth century, ibid., no. 77: 'Cum gens fuisset e finibus suis videlicet de Fraxeneto expulsa et terra Tolonensis [the Toulon region] cepisset vestiri et a cultoribus coli, unusquisque secundum propriam virtutem rapiebat terram, transgrediens terminos ad suam possessionem.'

than elsewhere peasant assemblies met to settle questions which concerned the population as a whole. As early as 1092 we find the majority of the inhabitants of the *castrum* of Saorge, 206 persons in all, men and women, meeting in front of the Church of the Virgin to ask the monks of Lérins to organize parish worship there.[1]

The anarchy prevailing on the coast, and which the 'pagan' Moors created without any serious attempt being made to stop them until the end of the tenth century, was not confined to the coastal areas alone; it spread throughout the whole of the south-eastern Alpine region. For three centuries the economic life of this vast area was paralysed. The almost total lack of contemporary documents meant that the history of Dauphiné was for long a blank page. One famous text, though a relatively late one, Charter XVI of the *Cartulaire de la Cathédrale de Grenoble*,[2] which we owe to Bishop St Hugues who occupied the see in the early twelfth century contains a very brief description of that dreadful time, and also of the restoration, brought about by the Bishops of Grenoble, which followed it. 'After the destruction of the pagans', we read, 'Isarn the Bishop built the church at Grenoble. As he had found but few inhabitants in this diocese, he brought in noblemen, middle-class and poor people from distant parts to restore Graisivaudan [*terra Gratianopolitana*]; he gave these men *castra* to live in and lands to cultivate, and over these lands the Bishop retained his seigniorial rights and remained entitled to the services which were his due in accordance with a decision agreed upon by both parties.' The tendentious nature of this document is obvious,[3] the Bishop's purpose being to foil the claims of the secular counts and establish the prior claim of the episcopal authorities. The only point worthy of note in this preamble is the fact that the Saracen invasion had left a lasting mark. The economic consequences of the anarchy it brought in its train were the same as in Provence: the destruction of an old domanial system, then

---

[1] *Cartul. de Lérins*, I, p. 164, no. 169.

[2] *Cartulaires de l'église cathédrale de Grenoble*, p. 93.

[3] N. Didier, 'Etude sur le patrimoine de l'église cathédrale de Grenoble de la fin du Xe siècle au milieu du XIIe', extr. from *Ann. de l'Univ. de Grenoble*, XIII, 1936.

after the liberation an agrarian revival for which small farmers were in the main responsible. Their usual type of holding was not the *mansus*, but a much smaller unit the 'chabannerie' (*chabanaria*), with an area only half that of the *mansus*. The installation of the farmer on the land to be cleared was often accompanied by a 'half and half' agreement (*ad medium plantum*).[1] The first five years were devoted to clearing the whole area. Once the land had been brought into cultivation, whether it was field or vineyard, it was then divided into two halves, one of which became the property of the clearer.

This contract, which is none other than the 'complant', had long been practised in the Vienne region,[2] which remained unaffected by the ravages of the Saracens. The Rhône valley was not an invasion route; like that of the Rhine, it was strongly defended. Vienne, the capital of the kings of Burgundy-Provence, retained its common port.[3] The same was true of Avignon[4] and of Arles,[5] whose ports on the Rhône were still being frequented by ships when the Moorish *razzias* were bringing the economy of the Alpine regions to a standstill. It would moreover be a mistake to exaggerate and over-dramatize their atrocities.[6] The blame for these rests on several shoulders. During the early centuries of feudalism and the anarchy which characterized it, the public authorities were powerless, so that the defence of the coasts and of a vast mountainous zone like

[1] *Cartul. Cath. Grenoble*, p. 17, no. ix (A); p. 26, no. xvi (A).

[2] There is already one example for 966 in the *Cartul. de Saint-André le Bas de Vienne*, p. 80, no. 113, which also contains many others.

[3] In a gift to the metropolitan church at Vienne there is some question of a vineyard which 'jacet contra portum publicum contra civitatem'. *Cartul. de Saint-André le Bas*, p. 313. Vienne's wealth of early medieval buildings proves that it suffered little at the hands of the invaders.

[4] In 907 the Emperor Louis the Blind confirmed the handing over to the Bishop of Avignon of one third of the dues collected in the port there, *Recueil des actes des rois de Provence*, p. 91, no. 49, and in the following year he gave him one half of those collected down the length of the Rhône (*de desscensu Rodanis*). Ibid., p. 93, no. 50.

[5] In 921 the same Emperor confirmed the church at Arles in possession of the dues collected in the port there from Greeks and other travellers landing, as well as granting them tolls, authority to coin money and rights over Jews. Ibid., p. 106, no. 59. All this is evidence of a certain activity centring round the port and connected with trade.

[6] These atrocities actually consisted of frequent raids for purposes of plunder. Cf. Paul Veyret, *Les pays de la moyenne Durance*, Grenoble, 1944, p. 312.

the Alpine region was in fact an impossibility. Yet agricultural life went on in the more easily protected Rhône valley; great numbers of vineyards were even being planted there, and these plantations owed their existence less to the initiative of religious houses than to that of individuals.[1] Division of land began comparatively early in that part of the country. Soon the former *villa* was no more than a geographical unit. The individuality of the southern system[2] was further asserted by the creation of small farms, and the strong dislike which its inhabitants have always felt for communal restraint broke up the framework which perpetuated the memory of it.

The population's interest in wine-production also showed itself at an early date. The 'half and half' lease was exactly suited to its requirements. The grower drew up with the owner of the waste land an agreement which obliged him to bring it into cultivation and usually to plant it with vines. After five, six or seven years, when the vineyard was beginning to produce results, there was a partition on a fifty-fifty basis, and the grower had the satisfaction of becoming sole owner of a small property which he could then put to any use he pleased.[3] Thus what Gaston Roupnel calls 'la sage indiscipline' of the southern countryside[4] was already in evidence in the mid-tenth century, just at the very moment when its salient features were beginning to emerge. It could probably be discerned even earlier if we could delve further back into its history. In that region, in fact, there was not, as in the woodland West, a radical change in the agrarian landscape during the tenth century. Provence and the Rhône valley are areas with a long history of cultivation, and when in the first available charters we meet the *mansi* being worked by their farmers, we discover traditions which are already firmly established.

The legendary terrors of the year 1000 had no effect whatever on the economic life of the region, any more than the expulsion of the Saracens modified the way of life of the peasants in the

[1] *Cartul. de Saint-André le Bas, passim.*

[2] G. Roupnel, op. cit., p. 215.

[3] 'Queque volueritis de vestra medietate facere facite.' *Cartul de Saint-André le Bas,* p. 81, no. 113.

[4] Ibid., p. 223.

Rhône valley. This is a legend which must be discarded once
and for all. Like many others it arises from the erroneous interpretation of documents imperfectly understood.[1] Burgundy,
the native province of the monk Raoul Glaber who is partly
responsible for spreading the legend,[2] should in itself be enough
to refute it. Unlike many other regions, Burgundy is well
documented for the tenth century because of the founding of
Cluny which took place in 911, for to that great abbey we owe
the preservation of numerous Burgundian charters going back
to the date of its foundation. The establishment of so powerful a
monastery, coupled with the fact that ever since the ninth
century large numbers of monks had flocked there for refuge,
caused its fortunes to evolve differently from those of others
elsewhere. In the province of Rouen, for example, the abbeys,
which had been rich and numerous from Merovingian times,
were ruined by the invading Northmen; they were obliged to
rebuild their temporal power in the eleventh century, and were
unable to regain their former wealth. In Burgundy, on the other
hand, ecclesiastical estates experienced a remarkable prosperity
in the tenth century; Cluny in particular made tremendous
strides. This acquisition of wealth, however, was made at the
expense of the laity, who grew correspondingly poorer, and the
question has been asked as to whether this impoverishment did
not contribute even more than the eleventh-century rise in
population towards the formation of the merchant class, armed
vagrancy and even forest clearance.[3] Historians and geographers in this province, where economic history is much in
favour, have vied with each other in defining the various stages
of land clearance in Burgundy. The Cîteaux area has provided

---

[1] Particular reference is made to certain stock formulae which still recur in
charters considerably later than A.D. 1000, as for instance 'appropinquante fine
mundi'.

[2] It is in fact this monk who after describing a famine and a terrible plague,
continues his account with the following reflexion: 'Estimabatur enim ordo temporum et elementorum in chaos decidisse perpetuum atque humani generis in-
teritum', *Histoires*, IV, 4 (ed. M. Prou, p. 99), but it should be added that this pro-
phecy concerns the year 1033 which was regarded as the millenary of the Passion,
and not the year 1000. Cf. Amann and Dumas, *L'Eglise au pouvoir des laïques*, pp.
457–459.

[3] G. Duby, op. cit., p. 64.

one of the latter[1] with useful chronological data. He has shown that the edges of the plateau were populated in the Gallo-Roman era; the areas in between were occupied during Merovingian and Carolingian times, then from A.D. 1000 land clearance affected the inner heart of the region. The historian[2] confirms the findings of the geographer, and describes the gradual and methodical way in which land was cleared in Mâconnais, which had barely been touched by invasion. The peasant first tackled the light soil of the chalklands, and from the mid-tenth century the work was being pushed on into the forest and lowland areas. It was, however, the very poorest people, men utterly without means, who were associated with this backbreaking toil. Working under the orders of the seigneur, the owner of the great 'condamine', the men who cleared these 'conquered lands' were far worse off than the freeholders on the old estates, who for generations had been living on *mansi* consisting of a small field generally protected by a fence, and other farm buildings.

Once again, ranging over the countryside, we come across differences in structure which prevent too uniform an interpretation of the process by which evolution occurred. Nevertheless, beneath such a variety of methods, it is possible to distinguish a common ideal. All these country folk were animated by one and the self-same ambition, the eternal longing of every western peasant – to create solidly established, permanent farms for their families. As we move eastwards, the feeling for family property in no way diminishes, though it came up against a more formidable obstacle in the domanial system. Yet in the end it wore it down. There too we see the gradual deterioration and decay of that régime which had appeared to be so firm and compact an organization, perhaps the most valuable lesson we can learn from the history of the rural seigneurie in Lorraine. The *villa* there was breaking up in the tenth century.

The cause of the disintegration has been sought in the

---

[1] L. Champier, *Cîteaux, ultime étape dans l'aménagement agraire de l'Occident*. Extr. from the 26th Congress of the Soc. Sav. de Bourgogne, Dijon, 1953, pp. 255–256.

[2] G. Duby, pp. 9–14.

tendency shown by both lay and ecclesiastical seigneurs to split up their estates in order to increase the number of fiefs at their disposal.[1] This fragmentation had the effect of upsetting the original domanial régime which depended partly on the collaboration of the peasants on the *indominicatum*, but the consequences were so serious that it is tempting to assume that the demesnial organization was already in decline when the seigneurs were apparently bent on destroying its unity. The evolution which was eventually to substitute a system of leased farms for direct farming, with its uncertain and fluctuating profits, may possibly have begun as early as the ninth century. The defects of a régime which has been dubbed archaic[2] were further accentuated at an early date by another break-up no less disturbing, that of the *mansus*,[3] which split into sections and which during the eleventh century was continually yielding ground to the 'quarter'. The name of this new smallholding was significant; it indicated the quarter of a *mansus*. The fragmentation resulting from an increase in the peasant population did much to undermine the traditional domanial régime. A new organization came into being; it called for a detailed registration of farmers, listing the amount of dues and duties expected from each tenant. The keeping of these *censiers* became increasingly important as the ties binding tenants to the domain were gradually loosened. But in Lorraine, as in many other provinces, the new method of farming, tenure by quit-rent, turned out in practice to be disappointing for the seigneurs, and in the words of the historian most qualified to speak on the rural seigneurie in Lorraine,[4] they appear to have stood by, helpless spectators of the far-reaching changes which were taking place before their very eyes. Yet they were not always to remain passive, and in the following centuries they reacted in unexpected ways, notably in the drawing up of the 'rapport de droits' which was akin to the institution in Germany of *Weistümer*.

---

[1] Ch. E. Perrin, *Recherches* . . . , p. 636.
[2] Ibid., p. 652.
[3] p. 638 et seq.
[4] Perrin, ibid., p. 659.

Agriculture underwent a similar evolution in Germany, but at a later date. The formation and extension of great domains spread over the tenth and eleventh centuries, during which there took place the organization of what German historians call the system of *villicatio*.[1] In Bavaria particularly[2] this type of cultivation continued without appreciable change until the beginning of the twelfth century. Up to that time the seigneur kept for himself a large part of his estate, a huge demesne which was farmed directly. The splitting up of the *mansus* also came later than in Lorraine though the quarter-*mansus* did not make its appearance until the twelfth century. The causes of the dissolution of the *villicatio* system were almost the same as those observed further west. The ties binding the tenant to the demesne were gradually loosened.[3] German scholars, however, have laid stress on the part played in this process of disintegration by 'officialdom', that host of subordinate officials to whom the administration of the domain was entrusted in secular and particularly in ecclesiastical seigneuries. The *ministeriales*, who hitherto had been peasant-tenants, announced their intention of changing their holdings into fiefs and annexing to themselves the income which they had previously collected on behalf of their seigneurs. This claim helped to shake the solidity of the seigniorial régime in Germany. Such usurpations were no novelty.[4] In Lorraine, from the mid-eleventh century, the abbeys had to struggle against the usurpations of their agents who were interfering in the running of the seigneurie. They had to lay down rules concerning the functions of agents in order to ensure that their own rights should be respected.[5]

In Germany too, where the great domain had established itself only in the early Carolingian age, its decline set in later than in Gaul. Georg von Below[6] puts it in the twelfth and

[1] G. von Below, *Gesch. d. deutschen Landwirtschaft*, p. 60 et seq.
[2] Ph. Dollinger, *L'évolution des classes rurales en Bavière*, p. III.
[3] G. von Below, op. cit., pp. 70–71.
[4] They were widespread. In the late eleventh century one of the Comte de Maine's huntsmen asked that his work of feeding the count's dogs should be transformed into a fief: 'Odo, venator comitis, clamabat pastum canibus ejusdem comiti *fevo* habere.' *Cartul de Saint-Vincent*, no. 230.
[5] Perrin, ibid., p. 675.
[6] Op. cit., p. 66.

thirteenth centuries. The author of a recent monograph on the rural classes in Bavaria attributes to the twelfth century that revolution which transformed the organization of the seigneurie and believes that its effects became apparent by degrees. In the thirteenth century the payment of dues in money became general almost everywhere.[1]

*

Before concluding this survey of the rural areas of Western Europe,[2] and as the present work draws to its close, one important question remains to be asked. Did the long span of time from the Great Invasions to the middle of the eleventh century see any substantial changes in agriculture? The land itself gives a reassuring answer, bearing witness as it does to a patient and unceasing effort to clear it for cultivation. In those districts where invasion and anarchy had laid the land waste, farming came back into its own at the end of the tenth century. In regions which, like Burgundy, had remained unaffected, the area sown with cereal crops increased for a variety of reasons, the most compelling of which seems to have been pressure of population, and an attack was made on less fertile land which had previously been neglected. In the west, where there was often little attempt at anything more than temporary cultivation, the 'bocage' was beginning to establish itself, and it may fairly be claimed that innovations were made.

This many-sided activity went steadily on, and at the heart of it all, human, uniform and unchanging, was the small family farm; in other words the method of cultivation was not collective, but individual. The owner of this smallholding was called *ruricola* or *rusticus*, in more specialized cases *hospes*, when he was a newcomer settling on land which he offered to clear. The area allotted to him was not very big, often hardly more than a

---

[1] Dollinger, op. cit., pp. 124–125. These remarks apply only to the old Germany of the West (Altdeutschland), and not to Eastern Germany which von Below (op. cit., p. 65) calls 'das koloniale Deutschland'.

[2] It would have been interesting to review the south-west also, but the region has very few early medieval documents. The domanial régime did not strike deep roots there; the small estate gained the ascendancy at an early date and met with less opposition from the seigneurs than elsewhere.

quarter of the *mansus* which had previously been the portion of
an entire family group. The outstanding feature of agrarian life
in the eleventh century was the spread of this small family farm.
The diffusion of a type of holding known by different names
in different parts of the country – *bordage, borderie, bachellerie,
quartier,* or *censive* – symbolizes the disintegration of the *villa,*
the abandonment of that domanial régime described in such
detail by Fustel de Coulanges. He held that this system covered
the entire territory of the Frankish Empire, an exclusive claim
which we have felt bound to dispute.[1] The small landed property, which dates back to a very remote past, and which was
familiar to Celts, Gallo-Romans and Germans, never ceased
to exist and continued side by side with the great domain. The
dissolution of this great domain is a still unwritten story; the
tenant farms which were an essential element of it gradually
ceased to be an integral part of a vast organism; the method of
cultivation changed; the tenant did less and less work on the
lord's reserve; he fulfilled his obligations by the payment of
dues and quit-rents. As far as the seigneur was concerned,
this new method of working the land was an admission of
incompetence. The great domain had, one might say, gone
bankrupt.

The transformation was no sudden revolution, but rather the
result of a slow evolution which in Germany was not completed
until the thirteenth century. Do the documents give us any
glimpse of these small peasant farms, scattered over the land
in their thousands, comparable to that description of the
Carolingian *villa* provided by the *Capitulare de villis* and the
monastic polyptyques? The comparison is not a true one. There
actually existed an 'ideal' *villa,* that of which the administration
is described for us by Charlemagne, and model *villae,* those of
which Abbot Irminon left us the inventory, but no eleventh-
century peasant has left us a complete picture of his *censive* or
his freehold. There is of course no lack of references to them
in documents, and a search through the innumerable contemporary charters contained in the cartularies would go far
towards satisfying our curiosity. One example will suffice; it is

[1] See above, p. 64.

the very brief description of a Limousin *mansus*, larger than the general run of peasant holdings and containing all the essential features of a farm.

'I give up the *mansus*[1] on which Maifroi has been living with two gardens, three meadows and cultivated and uncultivated land as well as everything belonging to the aforesaid *mansus* and I give up also my wood which adjoins it at a place called Marsac.' [2]

What gave the *mansus* its real value, wrote Roupnel,[3] was less its size than its structure. The peasant must have a garden near his house and often also a small enclosure of very fertile land for special crops; in the west this enclosure is called the 'ouche'. Fields take up the greater part of the holding and are ploughed with oxen. The phrase used by the author of the charter to describe them,[4] and which is the customary one, does not necessarily mean that some of the lands were lying waste. It sometimes refers to the rotation of crops. The south remained faithful to a two-year rotation, the simplest of all. It consisted in cultivating one half of the fields each year, and leaving the other half fallow.[5] Unfortunately very few texts make any reference to the system adopted, or tell us whether in any given district two- or three-year rotation – the only two methods known at the time – was practised.[6] Here, chosen at random from one of the few existing documents, is a purchase of land by Michel Peytavin (*emptio Michaelis Pictavini*), 2 May 1091, taken from the *Cartulaire de Lérins*,[7] in which the buyer promises to give the seller, over and above the price, one denier for the cost of labour in the year in which it bears fruit (*illo anno que [sic] terra fructum portaverit*). In view of the scarcity of docu-

[1] 984–985. *Cartul. de Beaulieu*, p. 130, no. 85. The term *mansus* was retained in Limousin for peasant farms of some importance. In this province too, however, holdings were split up, and *bachelleries* and *borderies* existed side by side with *mansi*. René Fage, op. cit., pp. 65–67.

[2] Commune of Saint-Bazile-de-Meyssac (Corrèze).

[3] Op. cit., p. 262.

[4] 'Cum terris cultis et incultis.'

[5] Roupnel, op. cit., pp. 216–217. This type of rotation had already been recommended by Vergil, *Georgics*, I, lines 71–72.

[6] R. Grand, *L'agriculture au moyen âge*, p. 270.

[7] I, p. 105, no. 115. L'Olivette (Olivet), at Le Cannet (Alpes-Maritimes).

ments, it is useless to attempt to fix geographically the zones in which these two types of rotation were practised; they may possibly have overlapped.[1]

Meadows figure on almost every farmstead, since oxen and cattle had to be fed,[2] but they always occupied a much smaller area than the ploughed fields. Since the early medieval farmer was chiefly concerned with the growing of corn, stock-breeding played only a subsidiary rôle in agriculture. Milk was hardly ever mentioned, and there was only an occasional reference to cheese and butter. Vine-growing, on the contrary, as with the ancient Romans, was vitally important. Christianity itself gave it a fresh impetus by instituting the consecration of the wine in the celebration of the Mass. The importance of the forest increased under Germanic influences; it became, at least in the north of Western Europe, an essential feature of the rural landscape. Whether it was considered as feeding-ground for pigs, or as a source of wood, the villager found resources there which were necessary to him, and which neither his fields nor his meadows could provide.

Possession of the various elements which went to make up a *mansus* was not enough to ensure the smooth working or the prosperity of a domain. A glimpse of Charlemagne's *villae* showed at what cost and with what effort they were run by a large staff, and made to yield the income and produce which the sovereign expected from them. The 'hôtes' and all the small farmers cultivating land on their own account almost certainly came up against equally serious difficulties, and the creation of burgs, endowed by the seigneurs with mills, communal woods and markets, was intended as a partial solution of their problems. The obstacles confronting them were indeed formidable. They cannot all be enumerated, but a patient search through

---

[1] According to certain texts brought to light by M. Bloch, *Caractères originaux* . . . , p. 33, both cycles were practised in Anjou and Maine.

[2] It is exceptional to find any mention of cows. The *Cartul. de Saint-Aubin d'Angers*, I, p. 13, no. 5, mentions a herd of 30 cows belonging to the Count of Anjou, Geoffroi Martel. The latter's provost, having attempted to make the *famuli* of the abbey look after them and having sent them to graze in the monks' meadows, these gentlemen got their own back by shutting up the 'ruminants' for three days and nights without giving them anything to eat or drink.

documents from the ninth to the eleventh centuries would perhaps bring many of them to light. Thus for instance when in a certain charter we find a landowner relinquishing a forest path and enlarging it to the width of a cart, we can assume that he was yielding to a request from farmers because his track led to a mill.[1] Frequent references to boundaries reveal the existence of a large number of country roads; there were also highways known as public ways,[2] from which it might be inferred that they were kept in repair by the public authorities. We know, however, that for hundreds of years these bodies had been incapable of doing so, and their incompetence explains the marked preference of travellers and merchants for river transport. Yet we should not be too hard on the men of the Middle Ages for neglecting what has generally been regarded as the magnificent Roman road system. Its merits have been exaggerated. Modern archaeologists, in fact, severely criticize the Roman paved ways, which they say were too thick and had far too hard a surface.[3] Repair work was neither easy to carry out, nor lasting when completed, which explains why these roads were neglected and abandoned during the early Middle Ages. Nevertheless though the Roman roads were not adequately maintained, the great strides made in harnessing animals for riding or pack-carrying brought a return to travel on horseback. Since the animals were capable of more concentrated and sustained exertion, long journeys were not necessarily avoided at the end of the tenth century.

The historian Richer, who was a monk of Saint-Remi of Rheims, has left an account of a journey he made to Chartres,[4] which he had been invited to visit in order to read a manuscript of Hippocrates. He procured a beast of burden and a servant from his abbot and set out in company with a knight from Chartres. The first stage took him as far as the Abbey of Orbais and covered 28 miles. Next day the travellers lost their way in forests with winding paths and having made an unnecessary

---

[1] *Cartul. Trinité de Vendôme*, II, p. 369, no. 529.

[2] Ex. 'Viam publicam'. *Cartul. Beaulieu*, no. 85.

[3] Lefebvre des Noettes, op. cit. For the structure of Roman roads, see A. Grenier, *Manuel d'arch. gallo-rom.*, 2nd part, I, *Les routes*, p. 317 et seq.

[4] *Hist. de France*, IV, 50 (II, pp. 224–231).

détour via Château-Thierry they arrived tired out at Meaux after a journey of 47 miles. It was more than any horse could stand and the chronicler tells us that his 'Bucephalus' died of exhaustion 6 miles from the town of Meaux. From this fascinating story it is obvious that the roads along which travellers had to make their way at that time were little more than tracks, and that it was very easy for them to lose their way. It will be noted too that fine old buildings were falling into ruins, for Richer thought it his duty to set down in detail the emotions aroused in his breast by the crossing of the Marne at the approaches to Meaux. There were cracks in the bridge, and his resourceful companion had to place first his shield, then wooden planks, beneath his horse's hoofs. The bad state of the roads had its effects on the economy. Good, well-kept roads tend to attract and monopolize traffic, but in parts of the country where there were only tracks, it was more widely dispersed. Only the monasteries which offered hospitality attracted travellers; they were strung out all along the main routes used by wayfarers to whom they offered a night's lodging. The road map of the early Middle Ages is closely connected with these godly posthouses.

*

Is it possible to get any closer to the realities of rural life? For a more intimate picture we have to turn to the graphic arts. Beginning with the Chronographer of 354,[1] first the miniature, then sculpture, delighted in depicting the work of the farmer. The 'calendar of the months' became one of the favourite themes of medieval iconography. Unfortunately, in imitation of the Roman agriculturists, certain of whom like Palladius described the farmer's tasks for each succeeding month, they soon became stylized. Yet the historian cannot afford to ignore those scenes pictured in the miniatures of illuminated manuscripts, or carved in stone medallions on the façades of churches. Their rhythm is monotonous, but painters and sculptors have often succeeded in adding a touch of realism in the shape of accurate details of costume and

[1] Stein, *Le calendrier de 354*, Paris, 1953.

representations of farming implements and rustic equipment. The tenth and eleventh centuries have left several examples which show us country life in action.

Economic history is not concerned with production alone. The flow and distribution of agricultural products are equally vital problems. The rural burgs which proliferated in the latter half of the eleventh century still had their markets for selling the produce of peasants who, we may be sure, had insisted on their being started in the first place. They were to reach their fullest development only in the twelfth century with the appearance of towns incorporated by charter, like Lorris, which were to be the heirs and successors of those burgs, and their charters devote much space to the running and organization of agricultural markets.

An economy as rudimentary as that of the tenth and eleventh centuries could not function without strains and crises. No hint of them is to be found in the diplomatic documents; agreements are concluded with a view to improving conditions. In reading through them we are in danger of missing the tragic reality, but here and there the chroniclers have lifted a corner of the veil. Raoul Glaber has described with an insistence verging on sadism the appalling famine which preceded the year 1033. He notes for instance that at the fair at Tournus in Burgundy, a man was offering human flesh for sale, ready cooked on a butcher's stall.[1]

One further aspect of social life at the same period should not be neglected, because of its repercussions in the sphere of economics. That was the anarchy caused by the weakness of the royal authority and the excesses of the feudal lords, who were often no better than robbers. Some improvement was noticeable at the end of the tenth century, owing to the initiative of churchmen.[2] The peace moves met with a welcome response. The lay population joined with the ministers of religion in taking action against the disturbers of the peace. Raoul Glaber,

---

[1] *Hist.*, IV, 10 (ed. Prou, p. 101). Glaber also mentions the rise in prices. In some places, he says, a hogshead (68 litres) of corn was being sold for 60 sous; the setier (3 litres 27) even went up to 15 sous. Ibid., p. 100.

[2] See Amman and Dumas, *L'Eglise au pouvoir des laïques*, p. 488 et seq.

who was a millenarianist, connected this social defence movement, which originated in Aquitaine, with the era of plenty
which, favoured by beneficial rains, followed the famine of the
preceding year. In these two phenomena, one social the other
natural, he believed he saw a twofold sign of a return to normal
life after a tragic year which had come near to heralding the
end of the world.

Conclusion

THE SEVEN HUNDRED YEARS over which we have ranged
have long been regarded as a period of regression inter-
polated between the economy of the ancient world and
that of medieval Europe,[1] which began with the great eleventh
century. Sociologists and economists have often described them
in harsh and unflattering terms as a period of depression and
atrophy during which a man counted himself lucky if he
managed to remain alive at all[2] and eked out a wretched
existence on the meagre produce of his domain. This characteristic pattern of living came to be called the domanial régime.
Henri Pirenne, however, upset this over-simplified conception
by dating the onset of this period of regression from the mid-
seventh century, the time of the Saracen conquest. This re-
adjustment put the Merovingian era, traditionally included
within the domanial economy because this was regarded as
beginning with the Great Invasions, back into the economy of
the ancient world, which thus enjoyed a prolonged old age,
since it was not difficult to detect in sixth- and seventh-century
documents lingering traces of the old civilization.[3]

Such theorizing, however fascinating it may be, is in fact
more than a little academic. What useful purpose is served by
splitting up the human past into such artificial, water-tight
compartments? A convenient division into periods, useful for
teaching purposes, has had a deplorable effect on the outlook of
historians, and the economic history of the Early Middle Ages
has been one of its victims. The aim of the preceding pages has
been to show that what appeared simple was actually complex,

---

[1] The phrase is that of M. Maillet, *Histoire des faits économiques*, Paris, 1953, p. 109.
[2] Ibid., p. 95.
[3] Pirenne attempted this most ingeniously in *Mahomet et Charlemagne*.

and that this long period was in fact much less empty and more eventful than has generally been supposed. It even witnessed a transient attempt at original organization, in the form of an economy based on Christian principles, for which the driving will-power of Charlemagne was partly responsible. Its outstanding achievement, however, was a fundamental change in the outlook of the West. Marc Bloch has described it in terms of geography: 'Where', he said,[1] 'at different periods of history, did a citizen of Arles or Lyons begin to feel a stranger in a strange land? In the fourth century he felt at home in Carthage and in Greece; on the other side of the Rhine he was amongst barbarians. In the twelfth century he was at home in Lübeck; in Tunis he was amongst infidels, in the Grecian East amongst schismatics.' The northward trend which eventually created the idea of Western Europe, still a reality today, was a slow process, and we have endeavoured to describe its various stages, stressing perhaps unduly the contribution of the Vikings, but it seemed to us that if the assimilation of Germany was a fact of primary importance, the integration of the Scandinavian world into European civilization and a succession of maritime discoveries which took the men of the tenth century as far afield as America, must also be taken seriously into account.

This slow change which we have traced step by step in its many and varied aspects gradually transformed the old Western Roman Empire. We have sought to throw some light on this process, which was no less than an entire human evolution, illuminating in particular its economic features, but there are still dark patches here and there. During these centuries, as indeed in every age, the forward march of mankind was hesitant and stumbling – two steps forward and one backward – and it is the historian's business to record these uncertainties along the way. Nevertheless, having reached his predetermined goal, he may be allowed to look back over that stage of the journey he has just completed – preferring to regard it as a stage in a journey rather than as a historical period since

---

[1] 'Problèmes d'Europe', *Ann. d'hist. éc. et soc.*, VII, 1935, p. 478 et seq.

the phrase indicates more effectively the dynamic nature of human evolution.

*

From the fourth century onward Christianity definitely took root in Western Europe in the form of Roman Catholicism. The authority of the Church was no longer in question. There were still heresiarchs, but no longer any heretical nations comparable to those which had adopted Arianism. The influence exerted on the economy by this henceforth stable form of Christianity cannot be denied, but it is difficult to assess it with any accuracy, since the Gospel did not offer a definite programme of social reform. The Kingdom of Heaven, the coming of which it proclaimed, was not to be enacted on earth, and neither the founder of the new religion nor his disciples intended to reform the economic system of a world they regarded as wicked, and which in any case would soon be vanishing away. Thus the attitude of the early Christians to worldly possessions was one of indifference, even of contempt, as for things which might lure them away from their spiritual calling. However, as the prospect of the Second Coming seemed to recede a little, this heroic but negative attitude had gradually to be modified, and the Church, compelled to submit to the requirements of life on earth, which continued exactly as before, had perforce to adopt a social doctrine which was more positive and less detached from the realities of life here below. Yet this doctrine, imposed as it was by necessity, presented a certain ambiguity since it was inspired by two principles which, without exactly contradicting each other, were not completely in harmony.

On the one hand the Church did in fact set out along the new social path indicated by Christ, the way of charity, and to quote an apt remark of Alfred Loisy[1] it may be said that the Gospel is socialist inasmuch as it wishes to establish among men a community as broad as human life itself and as deep as its wretchedness. On the other hand the doctrine of original sin and its logical consequences for humanity prevented the Church from considering as a possibility the organization of happiness

[1] *L'Evangile et l'Eglise*, 4th ed., 1908, p. 59.

here on earth. This basic pessimism induced a morale of
resignation, so that whilst imposing on the rich the duty of
benevolence towards the poor, it taught the poverty-stricken to
accept their lowly condition as a trial willed by God. These two
fundamental aspects, these two opposite poles of the Church's
social doctrine, must be borne in mind if we are to understand
certain peculiarities in the economic life of a profoundly
Christian society. The ban on lending at interest, for example,
was not only an inheritance from the Hebraic law. It was
justified by the danger to the soul's salvation inherent in the
pursuit of money for its own sake, and also by the duty of
charity laid down by Christ. It was this same duty which
inspired bishops and monks in Merovingian times to increase
the number of hospitals, hospices and charitable institutions,
and to preach almsgiving in and out of season. The teaching of
the Gospels, and particularly the exhortation to fair dealing in
money matters, was the inspiration behind one part of Charlemagne's legislation. On the other hand it was because resignation was preached by Christian morality that slavery continued
to be practised, that the dominance of the great and powerful,
with all its attendant abuses, grew and spread, arousing only a
few protests such as that of Salvian, and that ministers of the
Church, and even the monks themselves, vowed though they
were to poverty, amassed great wealth without giving rise to
any scandal. On the contrary, for in giving to the Church the
believer felt that he was making a sound investment, since he
was exchanging transitory and useless riches, in the shape of
the land he was giving away to the monks, for an everlasting
good which was the reward of his generosity. It must be added
that if for several centuries material progress was at a standstill
and if the spirit of scientific inquiry was slow to awaken, belief
in the millennium was in some measure responsible for this
immobility. By continuing to prophesy that the end of the
world was approaching, it created an atmosphere of indifference
to the natural and physical sciences which promoted worldly
well-being and happiness, and which in the tenth century were
still suspected of being inspired by the devil.[1]

[1] Witness the legends to which the scientific work of Gerbert gave rise.

Neither conservative, since it believed this base world to be too full of injustice and wickedness honestly to wish for its continuance, nor yet progressive since this 'vale of tears' seemed irretrievably damned, the Church certainly acted as the leaven of social change, though to an extent which is difficult to determine, for human events being irrevocable, it is impossible to imagine what would have happened to the western world if it had not been permeated by Catholicism.

If he is to be fair to that great institution, the influence of which was immense and often unexpected, the sociologist cannot afford to overlook the fact that in endowing man with a soul, the Church conferred a heightened value on the individual. This contribution to human dignity and stature would, however, have been more obvious and more directly effective if the Church had drawn from its eschatological and moral doctrine the practical conclusion which was its logical consequence, namely the unconditional abolition of slavery, which was based on the anti-Christian, juridical concept of a man as a thing (*res*). It was a strange lapse from which the historian is obliged to draw a distressing conclusion: economic requirements are almost always urgent enough to silence the categorical imperatives of morality and even of elementary logic. The fact remains, nevertheless, and it is to the Church's credit, that after her triumph was assured, many more slaves were freed under pressure of Christian opinion.[1]

There is a further point which Marc Bloch has also made. This move towards enfranchisement which ended in the final disappearance of slavery was not universal. It was confined to the Christian world. In the Moslem world beyond, and amongst all those peoples known as pagans, the slave trade was still flourishing. Had the Church then which tolerated this distinction, a narrower conception of humanity than its Founder? The truth is that throughout history there has almost always been an 'iron curtain'. The spread of Christianity and the Saracen conquest resulted in the displacement of that raised by the ancient Greco-Roman world. Beyond the boundaries of the Christian world arose a barrier which kept back

[1] Cf. Piganiol, *L'Empire chrétien*, p. 405.

most of the Mediterranean peoples, together with those of Asia Minor, North Africa and Spain. All who lived on the shores of the Mediterranean and were not Christians, along with the pagan peoples of the east and south, made up a hostile world and were beyond the pale of common humanity. The laws of war alone governed their relations with each other. This sharp cleavage had its repercussions on economic life. In spite of a brilliant modern theory about the injection of Moslem gold into the western world, we believe there was no more than a trickle of the yellow metal. A black market certainly existed between Moslems and Christians; 'mercantis' grew rich in the ninth and tenth centuries, especially by selling slaves in Spain. The diatribes of Agobard, Bishop of Lyons, make it plain that they found influential accomplices in the household of Louis the Pious. Yet that was not enough to change the economic situation. It seems more likely that the wealth of the Moslem world excited the envy of Christians and that side by side with the godly motives which prompted the Crusades, less disinterested motives inspired certain of their promoters. In this respect Moslem gold was a stimulus, but a delayed-action stimulus.

It would, however, be wrong to assume that the Christian world had contracted by comparison with the ancient world. Interest has been centred so exclusively on the Mediterranean character of the classical civilization that it is not sufficiently realized to what extent this was offset by the incorporation of Germany, Hungary and later, in the North, that of Scandinavia, into the Christian West. Antioch, Alexandria, Carthage, Tlemcem, Cordova and their *Hinterland*, were no doubt for the time being outside the main field of the European economy, but as a counterpoise to this, the Rhine frontier had been crossed. By a curious reversal of the geographical situation, the Germanic Empire even became in the tenth century the nerve centre of the Christian world, and around it new Christian states, Hungary, Poland, Denmark, Sweden, and Norway, were drawn into the western orbit. New trade routes came into being, each with its chain of markets. In the eleventh century the safest way of getting to Constantinople was through

Central Europe. The Baltic Sea was opened up to navigators, and the chronicler Adam of Bremen described the Norwegian coast as far as the North Cape. In the early twelfth century the Icelander Ari the Learned took his readers as far as Greenland and even to the shores of North America.

These were not merely the feats of a number of explorers, but represented a gradual process of colonization. The alleged eclipse of the early medieval towns was a relative phenomenon, and many factors, the founding of German towns, Hamburg, Merseburg and Magdeburg, for instance, by the tenth-century Germanic kings, could be used to refute any such hard-and-fast conception. It would perhaps be more appropriate to say that town life evolved rather than that it awoke from sleep. The ancient city, which was a political organism (πόλις), was doomed to disappear along with other institutions of the past, but the Church, by adopting the administrative framework of the Roman Empire, ensured the continuance of the traditional *civitates* in which it established its bishops. These cities owed not only their preservation, but also their new expansion to the Church, the 'Regular' church, to the monasteries which were founded on their outskirts and which became new centres of population. In this roundabout way a secular life came back to the towns. Burgs were established, markets too, periodical at first, then permanent; ports, in other words goods depôts, came into existence, followed by commercial and artisan activity which found its outlet at the close of the eleventh century in the first communes, those of Cambrai and Le Mans. It will long be argued as to whether the merchants who formed the basic element of the medieval town were originally recruited from amongst the wandering vagrant *negociatores* who in course of time became respectable and settled down in one place, or from local gentry who had made money out of farming or in the service of the seigneurs. Yet it is most unlikely that any uniform solution will ever be found of this social problem which, because of the dearth of documents, is both complex and obscure. It should be added that at the dawn of this still indeterminate renaissance of economic activity, there emerged signs of a resumption of large-scale Mediterranean trade, in the shape of the bold, shrewd projects initiated in Venice during the late ninth century.

Nevertheless it cannot be denied that the economy of the Early Middle Ages was essentially an economy based on agriculture, which has been dealt with at some length in this book largely in order to dispel certain fixed ideas. The obsession with great domains, which admittedly were important, and the existence of which kept thousands from starving to death in troubled times, has blinded many historians to the fact that in diplomatic documents the general word *villa* was used as an all-embracing title. It was necessary to uncover the reality behind it, and which appears to have taken the form of a steady growth of the small family farm, the first stage in a persistent development which, many hundred years later, was to end, in many parts of the country, in the small self-contained estate. This conclusion may, perhaps, seem paradoxical. The truth underlying it was at first concealed beneath the mask of the *villa*, which itself acted as temporary shelter for a host of small-holdings known as *mansi* or *colonges*. It has also been obscured by the claims of the rural seigneurie, though it has not been difficult to show that this originated in the disintegration of the domanial régime as well as in the growth of feudal anarchy, those concerned taking advantage of their owners' rights and of the usurpation of the ban, the symbol of sovereignty, to impose on the tenant farmers a variety of dues which were often a source of irritation, and to subject them to numerous exactions. Notwithstanding these obstacles, the small farm took deep and permanent root in the soil of Western Europe. It found expression in the *mansus* and its namesakes, farms which represented a happy combination of features revealing their joint Gallo-Roman and Germanic origin: ploughed fields, meadows, a vineyard and common rights in the nearby forest. At the end of the period with which this book deals, there were the first stirrings of an agrarian revival which is generally attributed to a rise in population. New bands of incoming farmers, the settlers (*hospes*), were looking for a place in the sun. Their arrival gave a fresh impetus to forest clearance, and in certain areas like Western Gaul led to a more sensible organization of crops.

Studied in this spirit of realism, the phase of human history stretching from the fourth to the eleventh century turns out to be unusually rich in promise and even in actual achievement. It brought into being a new Europe, unknown to the ancient world, facing outward to the Atlantic and the North Sea, and from this new Europe the western economy took its pattern. Whilst not scorning gold, which continued to be treasured and used for the creation of works of art, particularly those connected with religion, the rulers of the great Frankish Empire created for internal use within their vast Estates a silver coinage which was adequate for the limited needs of their subjects; Charlemagne's denier lasted until the revival of international trade called for the resumption of gold coining in the West. It was, however, in the realm of agriculture that the Early Middle Ages achieved its most far-reaching innovations. During those centuries which are still obstinately known as the 'dark ages', a peasant class settled itself firmly on the soil of Western Europe. All who are familiar with the part played by the farmer in western life will realize that the centuries which witnessed this process of settlement and which saw the origins of the small peasant farm were decisive in the history of western civilization.

If the outstanding characteristic of this period could be summed up in a single phrase we should say – though the modern expression may sound a little strange – that Western Europe was 'desouthernized'. Under the action of Nordic peoples, in a mistier and less sun-drenched setting, a new and predominantly agrarian economy came into existence, an economy in which town life at first played only a subsidiary rôle, in contrast to that of the ancient world, where life had been centred on the city; the surrounding countryside (*pagus*) had been a mere accessory to it, and its inhabitants scornfully known as peasants (*pagani*). The change which took place after the barbarian invasions was not simply an eclipse lasting several centuries, a slow decadence. It was a profound and irrevocable transformation. It is true that when at the end of the eleventh century the Mediterranean was again opened up to the western economy, when the iron curtain was lifted, the horizons of this predominantly rural world were enlarged, and the men of the North re-established contact with those of the South, attracted by Byzantine and Moslem gold, but the agrarian and Atlantic economy was too firmly established for a Mediterranean renaissance to be conceivable; the axis of the European world had definitely shifted. The future of the West lay with those men and women who for more than five hundred years had been settled in Gaul, Great Britain, Frisia, Germany and the Scandinavian countries as well as in Lombardy and Catalonia. Their patient efforts to clear the land, to bring vast tracts of the countryside into cultivation, and settle farmers and their families upon it, to organize trade and barter and infuse new life into urban centres, created in the long run an Atlantic civilization as cultured and refined as that of the ancient world. To record and re-create the early centuries of this slow, upward progress, during which humanity was stumbling and groping towards a new way of life, has been the whole purpose of this book.

Maps

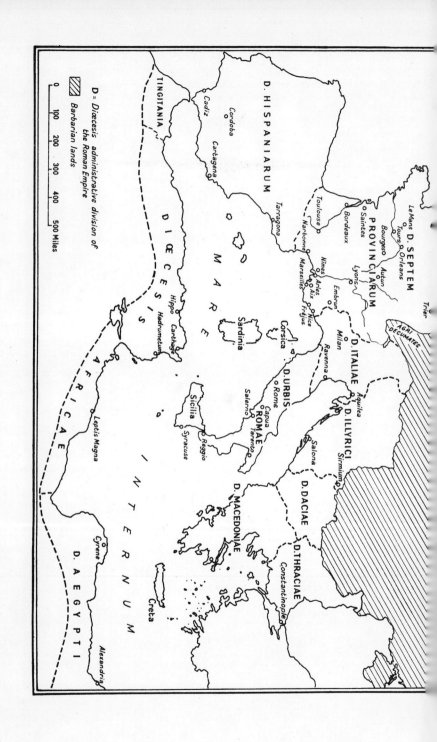

D = *Dioecesis* administrative division of the Roman Empire

Barbarian lands

0 100 200 300 400 500 Miles

TINGITANIA

D. HISPANIARUM

Cadiz

Cordoba

Cartagena

Tarragona

Toulouse

Narbonne

Bordeaux

Saintes

Tours

Bourges

Autun

Orleans

Le Mans

D. SEPTEM PROVINCIARUM

Trier

AGRI DECUMATES

Nimes

Arles

Aix

Marseilles

Frejus

Nice

Embrun

Lyons

Milan

Ravenna

Aquilea

D. ITALIAE

D. ILLYRICI

Sirmium

Salona

DIOECESIS

Hippo

Carthage

Hadrumetum

AFRICAE

Leptis Magna

Cyrene

MARE

Sardinia

Corsica

D. URBIS

Rome

Capua

ROMAE

Salerno

Tarento

Sicilia

Syracuse

Reggio

INTERNUM

Creta

D. MACEDONIAE

D. DACIAE

D. THRACIAE

Constantinople

D. AEGYPTI

Alexandria

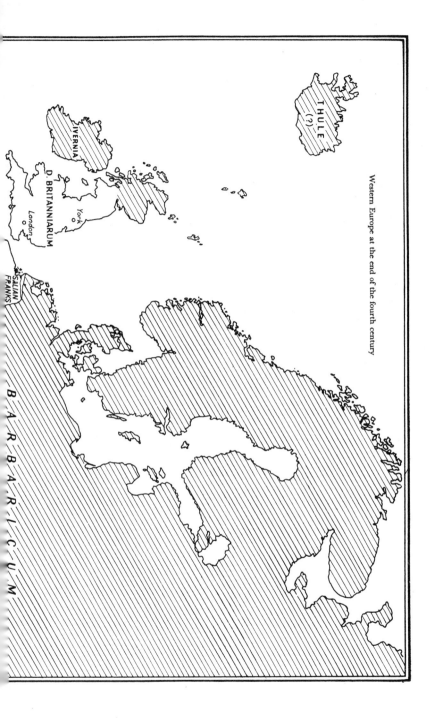

Western Europe at the end of the fourth century

THULE (?)

IVERNIA

D. BRITANNIARUM

York

London

SALIAN FRANKS

B A R B A R I C U M

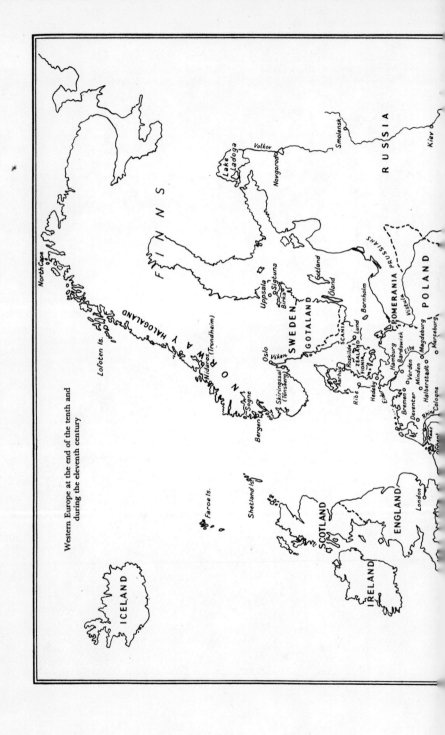

Western Europe at the end of the tenth and during the eleventh century

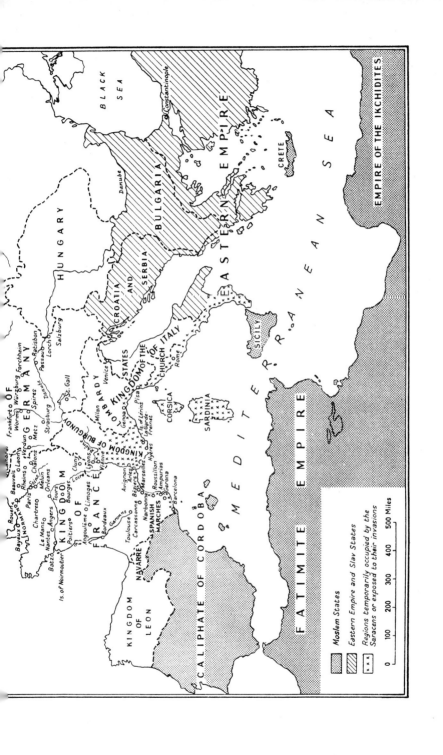

EMPIRE OF THE IKHIDITES

BLACK SEA

Constantinople

EASTERN EMPIRE

CRETE

MEDITERRANEAN SEA

FATIMITE EMPIRE

BULGARIA

SERBIA AND CROATIA

HUNGARY

Danube

Salzburg
Ratisbon
Würzburg Forchheim
Worms
Frankfurt
GERMANY
Verdun
Metz
Passau Lorch
Spires
Strasburg Danube
St. Gall
OF

Cambrai
Rouen Beauvais
Bayeux Laon
NORMANDY
Reims
Paris Châlons
Chartres
Le Mans Orleans
Nantes
Angers
Is. of Normoutier
Batzo
Tours
Poitiers
KINGDOM
OF
FRANCE
Angoulême Limoges
Bordeaux

Garonne

Milan
LOMBARDY
Venice
Pisa
Cluny
Lyons
Vienne
KINGDOM OF BURGUNDY
Avignon
Arles
Béziers
Marseilles
Roussillon
Narbonne
Carcassonne
Toulouse
SPANISH MARCHES
Ampurias
Barcelona
Gerona

Genoa
St. Denis
La Garde Freinet

STATES
OF THE
CHURCH
Rome
ITALY

CORSICA

SARDINIA

SICILY

KINGDOM
OF
LEON

NAVARRE

CALIPHATE OF CORDOBA

Moslem States

Eastern Empire and Slav States

Regions temporarily occupied by the Saracens or exposed to their invasions

0   100   200   300   400   500 Miles

Bibliography

THE SCOPE OF THIS work was too vast for the author to compile an exhaustive bibliography of the kind which would accompany an academic thesis on a more restricted subject.

He has confined himself to an alphabetical list of those authors and works which seemed to him essential, and particularly those of which he himself has made use. He is fully aware that the list is incomplete, and asks the reader to regard it as a general guide to the subject.

Anonymous works and collective publications are placed at the end of the Bibliography.

Articles from periodicals have been quoted when they are sufficiently important to be regarded as independent memoirs, but no special reference has been made to certain notes, helpful though they often are, such as those excellent ones contributed by Marc Bloch to almost every number of the *Annales d'histoire économique et sociale*. Others have been culled from *Speculum* and the *Vierteljahrschrift für Sozial-und Wirtschaftsgeschichte* (= *VSWG*), but these have been indicated in the footnotes.

ALTHEIM, F. *Le déclin du Monde antique. Examen des causes de la décadence*, trans. A. Cœuroy. Paris, Payot, 1953

ARBMANN, E. H. *Schweden und das Karolingische Reich. Studien zu den Handelverbindungen des IXten Jahrhunderts*. Stockholm, 1937

ARBMANN, E. H. *The Vikings*, trans. A. L. Binns. London, 1961

AUBIN, H. 'Die Frage nach der Scheide zwischen Altertum und Mittelalter'. *Historische Zeitschrift* **172**, 1951, 245–63

AUBIN, H. 'Vom Absterben antiken Lebens im Frühmittelalter'. *Antike und Abendland* **3**, 1948, 88–119

BADER, K. S. *Das mittelalterliche Dorf als Friedens- und Rechtsbereich*. Weimar, 1957

BAIST, G. 'Zur Interpretation der *Brevium exempla* und des *Capitulare de villis*'. *VSWG* **12,** 1914, 22–70

BARBAGALLO, C. *Il Medioevo.* Turin, 1935

BARK, W. C. *Origins of the Medieval World.* Stanford, California, 1958 (Stanford Studies in History, Economics and Political Science, XIV)

BEAUDOIN, E. 'Les grands domaines dans l'Empire romain'. *Nouv. revue hist. de Droit* 1897 and 1898

BECHTEL, H. *Wirtschaftsgeschichte Deutschlands von der Vorzeit bis zum Ende des Mittelalters.* 2nd ed. Munich [1951]

BELOW, G. VON, *Geschichte der deutschen Landwirtschaft des Mittelalters in ihren Grundzügen,* ed. Lütge. Jena, 1937

BERGENGRUEN, A. *Adel und Grundherrschaft im Merowing-erreich.* Wiesbaden, 1958

BILLIARD, R. *L'agriculture dans l'antiquité d'après les Géorgiques de Virgile.* Paris, 1928

BLANCHET, A. *Les enceintes romaines de la Gaule.* Paris, 1907

BLANCHET, A. *Les trésors de monnaies romaines et les invasions germaniques.* Paris, 1910

BLANCHET, A. *Manuel de numismatique française.* Paris, **I,** 1912

BLANCHET, A. 'Les rapports entre les dépôts monétaires et les événements militaires, politiques et économiques'. *Revue numismatique,* 19

BLOCH, M. 'La société du haut moyen âge et ses origines'. *Journal des Savants* 1926, 403–20

BLOCH, M. 'La vie rurale: problèmes de jadis et de naguère'. *Ann. hist. éc. et soc.* **2,** 1930, 96–120

BLOCH, M. 'Le problème de l'or au moyen âge'. *Ann. hist. éc. et soc.* **5,** 1933, 1–34

BLOCH, M. 'Avènement et conquêtes du moulin à eau'. *Ann. hist. éc. et soc.* **7,** 1935, 538–63

BLOCH, M. 'Les inventions médiévales'. *Ann. hist. éc. et soc.* **7,** 1935, 634–43

BLOCH, M. *La société féodale. La formation des liens de dépendance.* Paris, 1939

BLOCH, M. *La société féodale.* 2 vols., Paris, 1939, 1940, trans. L. A. Manyon, *Feudal Society.* London, 1961

BLOCH, M. *Les caractères originaux de l'histoire rurale française.* Paris, 1931, reprinted 1952, trans. J. Sondheimer, *French Rural History*, London ,1966. A supplementary volume of Bloch's additional writings in this field, under the same title, ed. R. Dauvergne, Paris, 1956

BLUMENKRANZ, B. *Juifs et Chrétiens dans le monde occidental* 430–1096. Paris, 1960

BOGNETTI, G. P. *Sulle origini dei Comuni rurali del medio evo.* Paris, 1927

BOISSONNADE, P. *Le travail dans l'Europe chrétienne au moyen âge.* Paris, 1921, trans. E. Power, *Life and Work in Medieval Europe*, London, 1927

BONNASSIE, P. 'Une famille de la campagne barcelonaise et ses activités économiques autour de l'an Mil'. *Annales du Midi*, 1964

BOUSSARD, J. 'La vie en Anjou aux XIe et XIIe siècles'. *Le Moyen âge* 1950, 29–68

BRAAT, W. C. 'Les Vikings au pays de Frise'. *Ann. de Normandie* 1954, 219–27

BRACKMANN, A. *Magdeburg als Hauptstadt des deutschen Ostens im frühen Mittelalter.* Leipzig, 1937

BRATIANU, G. I. *Etudes byzantines d'histoire économique et sociale.* Paris, 1938

BREHIER, L. 'Les colonies d'Orientaux en Occident'. *Byzant. Zeitschrift* **XII**, 1903, 1 ff.

BRØNDSTED, J. *The Vikings.* London, 1960

BRUNNER, H. *Deutsche Rechtsgeschichte.* 2nd ed. Leipzig, 1906–28

BRUNNER, H. *Grundzüge der deutschen Rechtsgeschichte.* Munich and Leipzig, 1934

BRUTAILS, A. *Etude sur la condition des populations rurales du Roussillon au moyen âge.* Paris, 1891

BUCHNER, R. *Die Provence in merowingischer Zeit: Verfassung, Wirtschaft, Kultur.* Stuttgart, 1933

BUGGE, A. 'Die nordeuropäischen Verkehrswege im frühen Mittelalter und die Bedeutung der Wikinger für die Entwicklung des Europäischen Handels'. *VSWG* **4**, 1906, 227–277

CESSI, R. ed. *Storia di Venezia.* Vol. I, Venice, 1957

CHAMPIER, L. 'Recherches sur les origines du terroir et de l'habitat en Mâconnais et en Chalonnais'. *Etudes rhodaniennes* **22,** 1947, 206–38

CHAMPIER, L. 'Qu'est-ce qu'une civilisation agraire?' *Ann. Universitatis Saraviensis, Philo-Lettres* 1952, 321–44

CHARAUD, A. M. 'Bocage et plaine dans l'ouest de la France'. *Ann. de Géographie* 1949, 113–25

CHAUME, M. 'Les anciens domaines gallo-romains de la région bourguignonne'. *Mémoires de la Commission des Antiquités de la Côte-d'Or* **XX,** 1934

CIOLI, L. *Histoire économique depuis l'antiquité jusqu'à nos jours,* trans. Bouthoul. Paris, Payot, 1938

COORNAERT, E. *Les corporations en France avant 1789.* Paris, 1941

COORNAERT, E. 'Des confréries carolingiennes aux gildes marchandes'. *Mélanges hist. soc.* **2,** 1942, 5–21

COVILLE, A. *Recherches sur l'histoire de Lyon du Ve au IXe siècle.* Paris, 1928

DAWSON, C. *The Making of Europe.* London, 1939

DEANESLY, M. *A History of Early Medieval Europe.* London, 1956

DECLAREUIL, J. 'Quelques problèmes d'histoire des institutions municipales au temps de l'Empire romain'. *Nouv. revue hist. de Droit* 1908, 547 ff.

DELEAGE, A. *La vie rurale en Bourgogne jusqu'au début du XIe siècle.* Paris, 1941, 3 vols.

DES MAREZ, G. 'Les problème de la colonisation franque et du régime agraire dans la Basse-Belgique'. Brussels, 1926. Review by F. L. Ganshof, *Journal des Savants,* Mar. 1928

DHONDT, J. 'Quelques considérations sur la fin de la domination romaine et les débuts de la colonisation franque en Belgique'. *L'Antiquité classique* **XVII,** 1948, 133–56

DIDIER, N. 'Etude sur le patrimoine de l'église cathédrale de Grenoble du Xe au milieu du XIIe siècle'. *Ann. de l'Université de Grenoble, section Lettres-Droit* **XII,** 1936, 1–87

DIDIER, N. 'Les Censiers du prieuré clunisien de Domène'. *Cahiers d'histoire.* Lyons, 1957, 5–22; 1958, 221–67

DIEUDONNE, A. 'Les monétaires mérovingiens'. *Bibl. Ec. Chartes* **103,** 1942, 20–50

DION, R. *Essai sur la formation du paysage rural français.* Tours, 1934

DION, R. 'Viticulture ecclésiastique et viticulture princière au moyen âge'. *Revue historique* **212,** 1954, 1–22

DION, R. *Histoire de la vigne et du vin en France des origines au XIXᵉ siècle.* Paris, 1959

DOEHAERD, R. 'Au temps de Charlemagne. Ce qu'on vendait et comment on le vendait dans le Bassin parisien'. *Ann. ESC* 1947, 268–80

DOEHAERD, R. 'Le monnayage des Carolingiens'. *Ann. ESC* 1952, 13–20

DOLLINGER, Ph. *L'Evolution des classes rurales en Bavière, jusqu'au milieu du XIIIe siècle.* Paris, 1949

DOLLINGER, Ph. 'Les transformations du régime domanial en Bavière au XIIIe siècle, d'après deux censiers de l'abbaye de Baumburg'. *Le Moyen âge* 1950, 279–306

DOPSCH, A. 'Das *Capitulare de villis,* die *Brevium exempla* und der Bauplan von St. Gallen'. *VSWG* **13,** 1915–16, 41–70

DOPSCH, A. *Die Wirtschaftsentwicklung der Karolingerzeit.* 2nd ed. Vienna, 1920–1

DOPSCH, A. *Wirtschaftliche und soziale Grundlagen der Europäischen Kulturgeschichte.* 2nd ed. Vienna, 1923–4

DUBLED, H. 'Encore la question du manse'. *Revue du moyen âge latin* 1949, 203–10

DUBLED, H. 'Quelques observations sur le sens du mot *"villa"* '. *Le Moyen âge* 1953, 1–9

DUBY, G. 'La société aux XIe et XIIe siècles dans la région mâconnaise.' Paris, 1953, *Bibl. générale de l'Ec. pratique des Hautes-Et., section VI*

DUBY, G. *L'Economie rurale et la vie des campagnes dans l'Occident médiéval.* 2 vols. Paris, 1962

DUMAS, A. 'Quelques observations sur la grande et petite propriété à l'époque carolingienne'. *Revue hist. de Droit* 1926, 213–79 and 613–72

DUPONT, A. *Les villes de la Narbonnaise Première depuis les invasions Germaniques jusqu' a l'apparition du Consulat.* Nîmes, 1942

DUPONT, A. *Les relations commerciales entre les cités maritimes du Languedoc et les cités méditerranéennes d'Espagne et d'Italie du Xe au XIIe siècle.* Nimes, 1942

DUPRAT, E. 'La Provence dans le haut moyen âge (406–1113)'. From *Bouches-du-Rhône, Encyclopédie départementale* **2,** 1924

ENNEN, E. *Frühgeschichte der Europaischen Stadt.* Bonn, 1953

ENNEN, E. 'Zur Stadtwerdung im fränkischer Raum'. *Rheinische Vierteljahrsblatter* **18,** 1953, 5–16

ESPINAS, G. *La draperie dans la Flandre française au moyen âge.* Paris, 1924

FAGE, R. *La propriété rurale en Bas-Limousin pendant le moyen age.* Paris, 1917

FAIDER-FEYTMANS, G. *La Belgique à l'époque mérovingienne.* Brussels, 1964

FASOLI, G. 'Points de vue sur les incursions hongroises en Europe au X*ᵉ* siecle'. *Cahiers de Civilisation médiévale,* 2, 1959, 17–35

FEBVRE, L. 'Deux œuvres récentes d'Henri Pirenne'. *Revue de synthèse historique* 1928, 95–109

FENGLER, O. 'Quentowic, seine maritime Bedeutung unter Merowingern und Karolingern'. *Hansische Geschichtsblätter* **13,** 1907

FOURNIER, G. 'La propriété foncière en Basse Auvergne aux époques mérovingienne et carolingienne'. *Bull. hist. et scient. de l'Auvergne* **LXXVII,** 25–37

FRANZ, F. ed. *Deutsche Agrargeschichte.* Vol. II, by W. Abel, *Geschichte der deutschen Landwirtschaft von frühen Mittelalter bis zum 19 Jahrhundert,* Stuttgart, 1962
Vol. III, by F. Lütge, *Geschichte der deutschen Agrarverfassung vom frühen Mittelalter bis zum 19 Jahrhundert,* Stuttgart, 1963

FRIEDENSBURG, F. 'Münzkunde und Geldgeschichte der Einzelstaaten'. Munich and Berlin, 1926. *Handbuch der mittelalterlichen und neueren Geschichte.* G. von Below and Meinecke.

FUSTEL DE COULANGES, N. D. *Recherches sur quelques problèmes d'histoire.* Paris, 1885

FUSTEL DE COULANGES, N. D. *Histoire des institutions politiques de l'ancienne France.* Paris, 1888–92, and particularly 'L'Invasion germanique' and 'L'Alleu et le domaine rural'

GABOTTO, F. 'L'Agricoltura nella regione Saluzzese dal secolo XI al XV'. *Bibl. Società storica Subalpina* **15,** 1902

GANSHOF, F. L. 'Une étape de la décomposition de l'organisation domaniale classique a l'abbaye de Saint-Trond'. *Fédération arch. et hist. de Belgique,* Congress of Liège, 1932

GANSHOF, F. L. 'Note sur un passage de la vie de saint Géraud d'Aurillac'. *Mélanges Jorga,* Paris, 1932

GANSHOF, F. L. 'Note sur les ports de Provence du VIIIe au Xe siècle'. *Revue historique* **183,** 1938, 28–37

GANSHOF, F. L. *Etude sur le développement des villes entre Loire et Rhin au moyen âge.* Paris and Brussels, 1943

GANSHOF, F. L. *Feudalism,* trans. Grierson. London, 1952

GANSHOF, F. L. *La Belgique carolingienne.* Brussels, 1958

GANSHOF, F. L. 'Note sur le "*praeceptum negociatorum*" de Louis le Pieux'. Milan. From *Studi in onore di A. Sapori,* 103–12

GARSONNET, E. *Histoire des locations perpétuelles et des baux à longue durée.* Paris, 1879

GAUDENZI, A. *Sulla proprietà in Italia nella prima metà del medio evo.* Bologna, 1884

GAUTIER, E. F. 'L'or du Soudan'. *Ann. hist. éc. et soc.* **7,** 1935, 113–23

GENESTAL, R. *Le rôle des monastères comme établissements de crédit étudié en Normandie du XIe à la fin du XIIIe siècle.* Paris, 1901

GENICOT, L. *Les lignes de faîte du moyen âge.* Tournai and Paris, 1951

GERLACH, W. 'Alte und neue Wege in der Stadtplanforschung'. *Hansische Geschichtsblätter* 1935, 208–21

GILLE, B. 'Recherches sur les instruments du labour au Moyen Age'. *Bibl. de l'Ecole des Chartes,* 120, 1962

GIRY, A. 'Histoire de la ville de Saint-Omer et de ses institutions jusqu'au XIVe siècle'. *BEHE Sc. philol. et hist.,* fasc. 31. Paris, 1877

GIRY, A. 'Les établissements de Rouen'. *BEHE Sc. philol. et hist.,* fasc. 55 and 59. Paris, 1883–5

GORCE, D. *Les voyages, l'hospitalité et le port des lettres dans le monde chrétien des IVe et Ve siècles.* Paris, 1925

GRAND, R. 'La genèse du mouvement communal en France'. *Revue hist. de Droit* 1942, 149–72

GRAND, R. 'L'agriculture au moyen âge'. Paris, 1950. *L'agriculture à travers les âges* **III**

GRENIER, A. *Manuel d'archéologie gallo-romaine.* Part II, Paris, 1931–4, Part III, 1958

GRIERSON, P. 'Commerce in the Dark Ages: a critique of the evidence'. *Transactions of the Royal Historical Society,* 5th Series, vol. 9, 1959, pp. 123–40

GUERARD, B. 'Explication du Capitulaire *de villis*'. *BEC* 1853; reprinted in *Mémoires Ac. I. et B.-L.* **31,** Pt I, 1857, 165–309

HAFF, K. 'Geschlechtshöfe und freie Marken in Skandinavien und Deutschland'. *VSWG* **28,** 1935, 126–39

HAFF, K. 'Zu den Problemen der Agrargeschichte des Germanischen Nordens'. *Historische Zeitschrift* **155,** 1936, 98–106

HALPHEN, L. *Etudes critiques sur l'histoire de Charlemagne.* Paris, 1921

HALPHEN, L. *Charlemagne et l'Empire carolingien.* Paris, 1947

HARTMANN, L. M. *Geschichte Italiens im Mittelalter,* especially vol. VI. Gotha, 1892–1911

HARTMANN, L. M. *Zur Wirtschaftsgeschichte Italiens im frühen Mittelalter.* Gotha, 1904

HAUDRICOURT, A. G. 'De l'origine de l'attelage moderne'. *Ann. hist. éc. et soc.* **8,** 1936, 515–22

HEGEL, K. *Städte und Gilden der germanischen Völker im Mittelalter.* Leipzig, 1891

HELIOT, P. 'La question de Quentovic'. *Revue du Nord* **23,** 1937, 250–65

HERLIHY, D. 'The Carolingian Manus'. *Economic History Review,* 2nd. series, 13, 1960–1, 79–89

HIGOUNET, C. 'Observations sur la seigneurie rurale en Rouergue du IXe au XIVe siècle'. *Ann. du Midi* 1950, 121–34

HIGOUNET, C. 'L'occupation du sol du pays entre Tarn et Garonne au moyen âge'. *Ann. du Midi* 1953, 301–30

HOFBAUER, S. *Die Ausbildung der grossen Grundherrschaften im Reiche der Merowinger.* Leipzig, 1927

HOLTZMANN, R. 'Französische Verfassungsgeschichte'. Munich and Berlin, 1916. *Handbuch der mittelalterlichen und neueren Geschichte*

HUBERT, H. *Les anciens Germains.* Paris, 1952

IMBART DE LA TOUR, P. 'Des immunités commerciales accordées à l'Eglise du VIIe au IXe siècle'. *Etudes d'histoire dédiées à Gabriel Monod.* Paris, 1896

INAMA-STERNEGG, K. T. VON. *Deutsche Wirtschaftsgeschichte.* 2nd ed. Leipzig, 1909

JANKUHN, H. 'Der fränkisch-friesische Handel zur Ostsee im frühen Mittelalter'. *VSWG* **40,** 1953, 193–243

JANKUHN, H. *Haithabu: Ein Handelsplatz der Wikingerzeit.* Neumünster, 1956

JANSSEN, E. *Histoire ancienne de la mer du Nord.* Brussels, 1943

JOHANNESSON, T. *Die Stellung der freien Arbeiter in Island.* Reykjavik, 1933

JOHNSEN, O. A. *Norwegische Wirtschaftsgeschichte.* Jena, 1939

JOLLIFFE, J. E. A. 'A Survey of Fiscal Tenements'. *Economic History Review* 1936. 157–71

JONES, A. H. M. *The Later Roman Empire 284–602* 3 vols. + maps, Oxford, 1964

JONES, G. *The Norse Atlantic Saga.* Oxford, 1964

JONES, P. 'Per la storia agraria Italiana nel medio evo: lineamenti e problemi'. *Rivista Storica Italiana,* 76, 1964, 287–348

JULLIAN, C. *Histoire de la Gaule,* especially vol. **VIII,** 2: 'Les empereurs de Trèves: la terre et les hommes'. Paris, 1926

JULLIAN, C. 'Notes gallo-romaines. L'analyse des terroirs ruraux'. *Revue études anc.* 1926, 139–51

KAPHAHN, F. *Zwischen Antike und Mittelalter: das Donau-Alpenland im Zeitalter St. Severins.* Munich, 1948

KARSTEN, T. E. 'Die Germanen, eine Einfuhrüng in die Geschichte ihrer Sprache und Kultur'. 3rd ed. 1928. *Grundriss der Germ. Philologie* **IX,** Trans. into French under the title *Les anciens Germains.* Paris, 1931

KATZ, S. *The Jews in the Visigothic and Frankish Kingdoms of Spain and Gaul.* Cambridge, Massachusetts, 1937

KLETLER, P. 'Deutsche Kultur zwischen Völkerwanderung und Kreuzzügen'. Potsdam, n.d.

KLETLER, P. *Nordwesteuropas Verkehr. Handel und Gewerbe im frühen Mittelalter.* Vienna, 1924

KLINDT-JENSEN, O. *Denmark before the Vikings.* London, 1957

KOEHNE, C. *Die Streitfragen über den Agrarkommunismus der germanischen Urzeit.* Berlin, 1928

KOTZSCHKE, R. *Allgemeine Wirtschaftsgeschichte des Mittelalters.* Jena, 1924

KOTZSCHKE, R. and EBERT, W. *Geschichte des ostdeutschen Kolonisation.* Leipzig, 1937

KULISCHER, J. *Wirtschaftsgeschichte des Mittelalters und der Neuzeit.* I: Das Mittelalter. Munich and Berlin, 1923

LABANDE, E. R. 'Recherches sur les pélerins dans l'Europe des XIe et XIIe siècles'. Poitiers, 1958. *Cahiers de civilisation médiévale* **I,** 159–69 and 339–47

LABANDE, L. H. *Histoire de Beauvais.* Paris, 1892

LACOUR-GAYET, J. *Histoire du Commerce,* especially vol. II (1950), publ. in collaboration with Maxime Lemosse and Marguerite Boulet

LAMBRECHTS, P. 'Le commerce des "Syriens" en Gaule du Haut empire à l'époque mérovingienne'. *L'Antiquité classique* **6,** 1937, 35–61

LAMPRECHT, K. *Deutsches Wirtschaftsleben im Mittelalter.* Leipzig, 1886, 4 vols.

LAMPRECHT, K. *Etudes sur l'état économique de la France pendant la première moitié du moyen âge,* trans. from German by A. Marignan. Paris, 1889

LANTIER, R. and HUBERT, J. 'Les origines de l'art français'. Paris, 1947. *Nouvelle Encyclopédie de l'art français*

LA RONCIERE, CH. DE,. *Histoire de la marine* **I,** Paris, 1889

LATOUCHE, R. 'Un aspect de la vie rurale dans le Maine au XIe et au XIIe siècles: l'établissement des bourgs'. *Le Moyen âge* 1937, 3–21

LATOUCHE, R. 'Grégoire de Tours et les premiers historiens de la France'. *Lettres d'Humanité.* Paris, **II,** 1943, 81–101

LATOUCHE, R. *Les grandes invasions et la crise de l'Occident au Ve siècle.* Paris, 1946

LATOUCHE, R. 'Défrichement et peuplement rural dans le Maine du IXe au XIIIe siècle'. *Le Moyen âge* 1948, 77–87

LATOUCHE, R. 'L'Abbaye de Landevenec et la Cornouaille aux IXe et Xe siècles'. *Le Moyen âge* 1959, 1–26

LAURENT, H. 'Aspects économiques dans la Gaule franque. Marchands du Palais et marchands d'abbayes'. *Revue historique* **183,** 1938, 281–97

LAVEDAN, P. *Géographie des villes.* Paris, 1936

LECLER, J. 'Propriété et féodalité. Qu'est-ce qu'un propriétaire sous l'ancien régime?' *Les Etudes* 1934, 433–49

LECRIVAIN, CH. *De agris publicis imperatoriisque ab Augusti tempore usque ad finem Imperii romani.* Paris, 1877

LEFEBVRE DES NOETTES, C. *L'attelage, le cheval de selle à travers les âges. Contribution à l'histoire de l'esclavage.* Paris, 1931. 2 vols

LEFEBVRE DES NOETTES, C. 'La nuit du moyen âge et son in-. ventaire'. *Mercure de France* May 1, 1932, 572–99

LEFEBVRE DES NOETTES, C. *De la marine antique à la marine moderne.* Paris, 1935

LEFRANC, A. 'Histoire de la ville de Noyon'. *BEHE Sc. philol. et hist.*, fasc. 75. Paris, 1887

LE GENTILHOMME, P. *Mélanges de numismatique mérovingienne.* Paris, 1940

LEICHER, R. 'Historische Grundlagen der landwirtschaftlichen Besitz-und Betriebsverhaltnisse in Italien. Eine Ubersicht in Landschaftstypen.' *VSWG*, 47, 1960, 145–85

LEPOINTE, G. *Histoire des institutions et des faits sociaux.* Paris, 1956

LESNE, E. *Histoire de la propriété ecclésiastique en France.* Lille and Paris, 1910–43, 6 vols.

LESNE, E. 'L'économie domestique d'un monastère au IXe siècle d'après les statuts d'Adalhard, abbé de Corbie'. *Mélanges Ferdinand Lot* 385–420

LESNE, E. '*L'indominicatum* dans la propriété foncière des églises a l'époque carolingienne'. *Revue d'histoire ecclésiastique* **27,** 1931

LESTOCQUOY, J. *Patriciens du moyen âge. Les dynasties bourgeoises d'Arras du XIe au XVe siècle.* Arras, 1945

LESTOCQUOY, J. 'Epices, médecine et abbayes'. *Etudes mérovingiennes, Actes des Journées de Poitiers.* Paris, 1953, 179–86

LEVASSEUR, E. *Histoire des classes ouvrières en France avant 1789* 2nd ed. Paris, 1901

LEVILLAIN, L. 'Essai sur les origines du Lendit'. *Revue historique* **155,** 1927, 241–76

LEVILLAIN, L. 'L'immunité'. *Revue hist. de Droit* 1927, 35–67

LEVILLAIN, L. 'Etudes sur l'abbaye de Saint-Denis à l'époque mérovingienne'. *Bibl. Ec. Chartes* **91,** 1930 *passim*

LEVISON, W. *Aus rheinischer und frankischer Frühzeit.* Dusseldorf, 1948

LEWIS, A. A. 'Le commerce et la navigation sur les côtes atlantiques de la Gaule du Ve au VIIIe siècle'. *Le Moyen âge* 1953, 249–398

LIZERAND, G. *Le régime rural de l'ancienne France.* Paris, 1942

LOESCH, H. VON. 'Zur Grösse der deutschen Königshufen'. *VSWG* **22,** 1929

LOMBARD, M. 'L'or musulman du VIIe au XIe siècle'. *Ann. ESC* **2,** 1947, 143–60

LOMBARD, M. 'L'evolution urbaine pendant le haut moyen age' *Ann. ESC,* 12, 1957, 7–28

328 *The Birth of Western Economy*

LOMBARD, M. 'Un problème cartographié: le bois dans la Mediterranée musulmane VIIe–XIe siècle.' *Ann. ESC.*, 1959, 234–254

LONGNON, A. *Géographie de la Gaule au VIe siècle.* Paris, 1878

LONGNON, A. *Les noms de lieu de la France,* ed. P. Marichal and L. Mirot. Paris, 1922, 5 fasc.

LOPEZ, R. S. *Studi sull'economia genovese nel medioevo.* Turin, 1936

LOPEZ, R. 'Mohammed and Charlemagne; a revision'. *Speculum* 1943, 14–38

LOPEZ, R. 'Le problème des relations anglo-byzantines du VIIe au Xe siècle'. *Byzantion* **18**, 1948, 145–55

LOPEZ, R. 'An aristocracy of money in the early Middle Ages'. *Speculum* **28**, 1953, 1–43

LOPEZ, R. S. and RAYMOND, I. W. *Medieval Trade in the Mediterranean World. Illustrative documents with Introduction and Notes.* Oxford, 1955

LOT, F. 'Etudes critiques sur l'abbaye de Saint-Wandrille'. *BEHE Sc. philol. et hist.*, fasc. 240. Paris, 1913

LOT, F. 'Le *jugum,* le manse et les exploitations agricoles de la France moderne'. *Mélanges H. Pirenne* 1926, 131–8

LOT, F. 'L'impôt foncier et la capitation sous le Bas empire et à l'époque franque'. *BEHE Sc. philol. et hist.*, fasc. 253. Paris, 1928

LOT, F. *La fin du monde antique et le début du moyen âge.* Paris, 1928. 2nd ed., revised and enlarged, 1951

LOT, F. 'De l'origine et de la signification des noms de lieu en *ville* et en *court*'. *Romania* **19**, 1933, 199–246

LOT, F. 'L'histoire urbaine du nord de la France de la fin du IIIe à la fin du XIe siècle'. *Journal des Savants* 1935, 5–10 and 63–80

LOT, F. *L'art militaire et les armées au moyen âge en Europe et dans le proche Orient.* Paris, 1946. 2 vol.s

LOT, F. *La Gaule.* 11th ed. Paris, 1948

LOT, F. *La naissance de la France.* 9th ed. Paris, 1948

LOT, F. 'Recherches sur la population et la superfice des cités remontant à la période gallo-romaine'. *BEHE Sc. philol. et hist.*, fasc. 287, 296 and 301. Paris, 1953

LOT, F. 'Nouvelles recherches sur l'impôt foncier et la capitation personnelle sous le Bas empire'. *BEHE Sc. philol. et hist.*, fasc. 304. Paris, 1955

LUCHAIRE, A. *Les communes françaises.* New ed. by L. Halphen. Paris, 1911

LUSCHIN VON EBENGREUTH, A. *Allgemeine Münzkunde und Geldgeschichte des Mittelalters und der neueren Zeit.* 2nd ed. 1926

LUTGE, F. *Die Agraverfassung des frühen Mittelalters im Mitteldeutschen Raum, vornehmlich in der Karolingerzeit.* Jena, 1937

LUTGE, F. 'Hufe und *Mansus* in den mitteldeutschen Quellen der Karolingerzeit, im besonderen in dem *Breviarium Sti Lulli'. VSWG* **30,** 1937, 105–28

LUZZATTO, G. 'Periodi e caratteri dell'economia medioevale'. *Questioni di storia medioevale,* Milan, 1951, 661–90

LUZZATTO, G. *An Economic History of Italy from the Fall of Rome to the beginning of the Sixteenth Century.* trans. P. Jones, London, 1961

MAILLET, J. *Histoire des faits économiques des origines au XXe siècle.* Paris, Payot, 1952

MARTROYE, F. 'Les patronages d'agriculteurs ou des *vici* aux IVe et Ve siècles'. *Revue hist. de Droit* 1928, 201–48

MASSON, P. *De Massiliensium negociatoribus.* Paris, 1896

MAYER, T. 'Zur Entstehung des *Capitulare de villis'. VSWG* **17,** 1924, 112–27

MAYER, T. *Deutsche Wirtschaftsgeschichte des Mittelalters.* Leipzig, 1928

MEITZEN, A. *Siedelung und Agrarwesen der Westgermanen und Ostgermanen.* Berlin, 1895. 3 vols.

MENGOZZI, G. *La città italiana nell' alto medio evo.* 2nd ed. Florence, 1931

METZ, W. *Das Karolingische Reichsgut. Eine verfassungs-und verwaltings-geschichtliche Untersuchung.* Berlin, 1960

MEYNIER, A. 'Quelques énigmes d'histoire rurale en Bretagne'. *Ann. ESC* 1949, 259–67

MICKWITZ, G. 'Geld und Wirtschaft im römischen Reich des vierten Jahrhunderts. n. Chr.' Helsingfors, 1932. *Societas Scientiarum Fennica, Commentationes humanarum litterarum* **IV,** 2

MICKWITZ, G. 'Le problème de l'or dans le monde antique'. *Ann. hist. éc. et soc.* **6,** 1934, 235–47

MICKWITZ, G. 'Byzance et l'économie de l'Occident médiéval'. *Ann. hist. éc. et soc.* **8,** 1936, 21–8

MONTELIUS, O. *Kulturgeschichte Schwedens.* Leipzig, 1906

MORRISON, K. F. 'Numismatics and Carolingian trade: a critique of the evidence'. *Speculum*, 38, 1963, 403–483

MOSS, H. S. 'The Economic Consequences of the Barbarian Invasions. *Economic History Review* 7, 1936

MUSSET, L. *Les peoples scandinaves au moyen âge.* Paris, 1951

MUSSET, L. *Les invasions. Les vagues germaniques.* Paris, 1965

MUSSET, R. *Le Bas-Maine, étude géographique.* Paris, 1917

NECKEL, G. 'Kultur der alten Germanen'. Potsdam, 1934

NIELSEN, A. *Danische Wirtschaftsgeschichte.* Jena, 1933

NORDEN, E. *Altgermanien.* Leipzig and Berlin, 1934

NORLUND, P. *Viking Settlers in Greenland and their Descendants during Five Hundred years.* Camb. Univ. Press, 1936

PARADISI, B. ' *"Massaricum jus"*: studio sulle terre *"contribu-tariae"* e *"conservae"* nel medio evo'. Bologna, 1937

PATZELT, E. *Die frankische Kultur und der Islam.* Baden and Vienna, 1932. Veröffentlichungen des Seminars für Wirtschafts- und Kulturgeschichte an der Universitat Wien **4**

PERNOUD, R. *Essai sur l'histoire du port de Marseille des origines à la fin du XIIIe siècle.* Marseilles, 1935

PERRIN, DH. E. 'Une étape de la seigneurie: l'exploitation de la réserve à Prüm au IXe siècle'. *Ann. hist. éc. et soc.* **6**, 1934, 450–66

PERRIN, CH. E. *Recherches sur la seigneurie rurale en Lorraine.* Paris, 1935

PERRIN, CH. E. 'Esquisse d'une histoire de la tenure rurale en Lorraine au moyen âge'. *Recueils de la Société Jean Bodin* **III**, 1938

PERRIN, CH. E. 'Observations sur le manse dans la région parisienne au début du IXe siècle'. *Ann. hist. soc.* **2**, 1945, 39–52

PERRIN, CH. E. *Les classes paysannes et le régime seigneurial au moyen âge.* Roneo text, 'Les Cours de Sorbonne'. Centre de documentation univ. Paris, n.d.

PERRIN, CH. E. 'Le servage en France et en Allemagne'. From *Relazioni del X. Congresso Internazionale di Scienze Storiche.* Rome, 1955, **III**, 213–45

PERROY, E. 'Encore Mahomet et Charlemagne'. *Revue historique* **212**, 1954, 232–8

PERROY, E. 'Le monde carolingien'. Fasc. I: *L'Economie carolingienne*. Roneo text, 'Les Cours de Sorbonne'. Centre de documentation univ. Paris, n.d.

PETIT-DUTAILLIS, CH. 'De la signification du mot "forêt", à l'époque franque. Examen critique d'une théorie allemande sur la transition de la propriété collective a la propriété privée'. *Bibl. Ec. Chartes* **86**, 1915, 97–152

PETIT-DUTAILLIS, CH. *Les Communes françaises. Caractère et évolution des origines au XVIIIe siècle.* Paris, 1947

PICARDA, E. 'Les marchands de l'eau. Hanse parisienne et compagnie française'. *BEHE Sc. philol. et hist.*, fasc. 134. Paris, 1901

PIGANIOL, A. 'Le problème de l'or au IVe siècle'. *Ann. hist. soc.* **1**, 1945, 47–53

PIGANIOL, A. 'L'Empire chrétien'. Paris, 1947. *Histoire générale, Hist. rom.* **IV**, 2nd pt.

PIGANIOL, A. 'La Gaule au temps d'Attila'. *Saint Germain d'Auxerre et son temps.* Auxerre, 1950, 119–33

PIRENNE, H. *Histoire de Belgique* **I**, Brussels, 1900

PIRENNE, H. 'Un contraste économique: Mérovingiens et Carolingiens'. *Revue belge de philol. et d'hist.* 1923, 223–35

PIRENNE, H. 'Le mouvement économique et social'. Paris, 1933. *Histoire générale. Histoire du moyen âge.* VIII La civilisation occidentale au moyen âge du XIe au XVe siècle, 1–189

PIRENNE, H. *Mahomet and Charlemagne*, trans. Miall. London, 1939

PIRENNE, H. *Les villes et les institutions urbaines.* Paris-Brussels, 1939. 2 vols. Most of this author's notes and memoirs relating to the history of medieval towns and trade have been reissued in this posthumous work

PLANITZ, H. 'Frühgeschichte der deutschen Stadt'. *Zeitschrift der Savigny-Stiftung*, Germ. Abt. **63**, 1943, 1–91

PLANITZ, H. *Die deutsche Stadt im Mittelalter.* Graz-Cologne, 1954

POETE, M. *Une vie de cité: Paris.* I: La jeunesse. Paris, 1924

POSE, A. *La monnaie et ses institutions: histoire, théorie et technique.* Paris, 1942

POWER, E. *The Wool Trade in English Medieval History.* Oxford, 1940

PRENTOUT, H. 'Litus Saxonicum, Saxones Bajocassini, Otlinga Saxonia'. *Revue historique* **107**, 1911, 385–99

PROU, M. 'Les coutumes de Lorris'. *Nouv. revue d'hist. du Droit française* 1884

PROU, M. 'De la nature du service militaire dü par les roturiers aux XIe et XIIe siècles'. *Revue historique* **44**, 1890, 313–28

PROU, M. *Catalogue des monnaies mérovingiennes de la Bibliothèque Nationale.* Paris, 1892

PROU, M. *Catalogue des monnaies carolingiennes de la Bibliothèque Nationale.* Paris, 1896

PROU, M. *La Gaule mérovingienne.* Paris, n.d.

RENOUARD, Y. *Les hommes d'affaires italiens du moyen âge.* Paris, 1949

RICHE, P. *Les invasions barbares.* Paris, 1953.

ROLLAND, P. 'De l'économie antique au grand commerce médiéval: problème de la continuité à Tournai et dans la Gaule du Nord'. *Ann. hist. éc. et soc.* **6**, 1936, 245–84

RORIG, F. 'Die Europäische Stadt'. *Propylaen-Weltgeschichte* **IV**, 277–392

RORIG, F. 'Magdeburgs Entstehung und die ältere Handelsgeschichte'. Berlin, 1952. *Vorträge und Schriften der Deutschen Akademie der Wissenschaften in Berlin* **49**

ROSTOVTZEF, M. *The Social and Economic History of the Roman Empire.* Oxford, 1926

ROUPNEL, G. *Histoire de la campagne française.* 24th ed. Paris, 1955

ROUSSEAU, E, *La Meuse et le pays mosan; leur importance historique avant le XIIIe siècle.* Namur, 1930

RUGGINI, L. CRACCO 'Vicende rurali dell'Italia antica dall' età tetrarchica ai Longobardi' *Rivista Storica Italiana,* 76, 1964, 262–286

SABBE, E. 'L'importation des tissus orientaux en Europe occidentale au haut moyen âge (IXe et Xe siècles)'. *Revue belge de philol. et d'hist.* 1935, 811–48 and 1261–88

SABBE, E. 'Papyrus et parchemin au haut moyen âge'. 1947. From *Miscellanea, L. Van der Essen,* 95–103

SABBE, E. 'Angleterre et Continent au haut moyen âge'. *Le Moyen âge* 1950, 169–93

SAINT-JACOB, P. DE. 'Etudes sur l'ancienne communaté rurale en Bourgogne'. *Ann. de Bourgogne* **13**, 1941, 1–34; **15**, 1943, 173–84; **18**, 1946, 1–14

SALIN, E. *La civilisation mérovingienne d'après les sépultures, les textes et le laboratoire.* 4 Parts, Paris, 1948–1958

SAPORI, A. *Studi di storia economica medioevale.* Florence, 1940

SAUMAGNE, CH. 'Ouvriers agricoles ou rôdeurs de celliers. Les circoncellions d'Afrique'. *Ann. hist. éc. et soc.* **6,** 1936, 351–64

SAYOUS, A. 'Un manuel arabe de parfait commerçant (XIe siècle environ de notre ère)'. *Ann. hist. éc. et soc.* **3,** 1931, 577–80

SCHAUBE, A. 'Handelsgeschichte der romanischen Völker des Mittelmeergebietes bis zum Ende der Kreuzzüge'. Munich, 1906

SCHILL-KRAMER, E. 'Organisation und Grössenverhältnisse des ländlichen Grundbesitzes in der Karolingerzeit'. *VSWG* **17,** 1924, 247–93

SCHMIDT, L. *Allgemeine Geschichte der germanischen Völker bis zur Mitte des sechsten Jahrhunderts.* Munich and Berlin, 1909

SCHMIDT, L. *Geschichte der deutschen Stämme bis zum Ausgang der Völkerwanderung.* Berlin, 1910–18. 2 vols.

SCHMIEDER, E. 'Hufe und *Mansus*. Eine quellenkritische Untersuchung'. *VSWG* **31,** 1938, 348–56

SCHONFELD, W. 'Die Xenodochien in Italien und Frankreich im frühen Mittelalter'. *Zeitschrift der Savigny-Stiftung,* Kan. Abt. **43,** 1922

SCHWARZ, E. 'Die Urheimat der Goten und ihre Wanderungen ins Weichsland und nach Sudrussland'. *Saeculum, Jahrbuch für Universalgeschichte* **4,** 1953, 13–26

SCLAFERT, T. *Le Haut-Dauphiné au moyen âge.* Paris, 1925

SEE, H. *Etude sur les classes rurales en Bretagne au moyen âge.* Paris-Rennes, 1896

SEE, H. *Les classes rurales et le régime domanial en France au moyen âge.* Paris, 1901

SEE, H. *Histoire économique de la France.* I: Le moyen âge et l'ancien régime. In collaboration with R. Schnerb. Paris, 1939

SEELIGER, R. 'Forschungen zur Geschichte der Grundherrschaft im früheren Mittelalter'. *Historische Vierteljahrschrift* **8,** 1905, 305–61 and **10,** 1907, 305–54

SEGRE, A. 'La circolazione monetaria del regno dei Franchi'. *Rivista storica italiana* 1931

SEIGNOBOS, CH. *Le régime féodal en Bourgogne jusqu'en 1360.* Paris, 1882

SESTON, W. *Dioclétien et la Tétrarchie.* Paris, 1946

SPRANDEL, R. 'Struktur und Geschichte des Merovingischen Adels'. *Historisches Zeitscrift,* 193, 1961, 33–71

SPROEMBERG, H. 'Residenz und Territorium im Niederländischen Raum'. *Rheinische Vierteljahrsblätter* of 1936, 113–40

STEIN, E. *Geschichte des spatrömischen Reiches Vol. I.* Stuttgart, 1928, enlarged French edition, *Histoire du Bas-Empire,* Vol. I, *De l'Etat Roman a l'Etat Byzantin (284–476),* Paris, 1959

STEINBACH, F. *Gewanndorf und Einzelhof.* Düsseldorf, 1927. Historische Aufsätze Aloys Schulte zum 70 Geburtstag

STRIEDER, J. 'Werden und Wachsen des europäischen Frühkapitalismus'. Berlin, n.d. *Propylaen-Weltgeschichte* **IV,** 1–26

THEVENIN, M. *Textes relatifs aux institutions privées aux époques mérovingienne et carolingienne.* Paris, 1887

THIBAULT, F. 'Les *patrocinia vicorum*'. *VSWG* **2,** 1904, 413–20

THIBAULT, F. 'La condition des personnes en France du IXe siècle au mouvement communal'. *Revue hist. de Droit* 1933, 424–77

THOMPSON, J. W. *The Dissolution of the Carolingian Fisc in the Ninth Century.* University of California Press, 1935, Publications in History Vol. 23

TOURNEUR, V. 'Le sou de douze deniers de la Loi des Francs Ripuaires'. *Revue belge de philol. et d'hist.* 1923, 215–22

TOUTAIN, J. *L'économie antique.* Paris. 1927

TULIPPE, O. 'Le manse à l'époque carolingienne'. *Ann. de la Société scientifique de Bruxelles, series D, Sc. écon.* **56,** 1936

VACCARI, P. *Studi sull'Europa Precarolingia e Carolingia.* Verona. 1956

VALOUS, G. DE. *Le monachisme clunisen des origines au XVe siècle.* 3: *Le temporel.* Ligugé and Paris, 1935

VAN WERVEKE, H. 'Note sur le commerce du plomb au moyen âge'. *Mélanges H. Pirenne* 1926, 653–62

VAN WERVEKE, H. 'Economie-nature et économie-argent'. *Ann. hist. éc. et soc.* **3,** 1931, 428–35

VAN WERVEKE, H. 'Monnaies, lingots ou marchandises. Les instruments d'échange aux XIe et XIIe siècles'. *Ann. hist. éc. et soc.* **4,** 1932, 452–68

VERCAUTEREN, F. *Les* civitates *de la Belgique Seconde.* Brussels, 1934

VERHULST, A. E. *La fortune foncière de l'abbaye Saint-Bavon de Gand du VIIIe au XIVe siècle.* French summary of a work published in Flemish. Brussels, 1958

VERLINDEN, CH. 'Problèmes d'histoire économique franque'. *Revue belge de philol. et d'hist.* 1933, 1090–5

VERLINDEN, C. *L'esclavage dans l'Europe médiévale.* Vol. I. Bruges, 1955

VOGEL, W. *Die Normannen und das fränkische Reich.* Heidelberg, 1906

VOGEL, W. *Geschichte der deutschen Seeschiffahrt.* I: Von der Urzeit bis zum Ende des XV Jahrhunderts. Berlin, 1915

VOGEL, W. 'Wik-Orte und Wikinger. Eine Studie zu den Anfängen des germanischen Stadtwesens'. Weimar, 1936. *Hansische Geschichtsblätter* **60** Jahrgang

WEBER, M. *Wirtschaftsgeschichte.* Munich, 1927

WHITE, L. *Medieval Technology and Social Change.* Oxford, 1962

WIART, R. *Le régime des terres du fisc au Bas empire.* Paris, 1894

WUHRER, K. *Beiräge zur altesten Agrargeschichte des germanischen Nordens.* Jena, 1935

ZIMMER, H. 'Über direkte Handelsverbindungen Westgalliens nach Irland im Altertum und frühen Mittelalter'. Berlin, 1909. *Sitzungsberichte der Preussischen Akademie der Wissenschaften*

THULE. *Altnordische Dichtung und Prosa.* XXIII: Islands Besiedlung und älteste Geschichte. Jena, 1928

The Cambridge Economic History of Europe from the Decline of the Roman Empire ed. by J. H. Clapham and Eileen Power
    I. The Agrarian Life of the Middle Ages. Cambridge, 1942, revised ed. edited M. Postan, 1966
    II. Trade and industry in the Middle Ages. 1952

L'art mosan. Journées d'études. Paris, 1953. *Bibl. générale de l'Ec. des Hautes Et. Section 6*

I Goti in Occidente. Problemi. Spoleto, 1955. *Settimane di studio del Centro Italiano di stidu sull'alto medioevo* **III**

KONSTANZ, INSTITUT FÜR GESCHICHTLICHE LANDESFORSCHUNG DES BODENSEE GEBIETES 'Studien zu den Anfängen des Europäischen Städtewesens'. *Vorträge und Forschungen,* 4, 1960

Index